The Other Side of Western Civilization:

Readings in Everyday Life

Volume I

under the general editorship of John Morton Blum

Yale University

The Other Side of Western Civilization

Readings in Everyday Life

Volume I: The Ancient World to the Reformation

Edited by Stanley Chodorow

University of California, San Diego

HARCOURT BRACE JOVANOVICH, INC.

New York   Chicago   San Francisco   Atlanta

ISBN: 0-15-567646-6

Library of Congress Catalog Card Number: 72-94549

Printed in the United States of America

PICTURE CREDITS

Cover: Crusades. A sailing ship crossing the Mediterranean Sea with knights on board and a cleric at the rudder. Miniature painting. Late thirteenth century. THE BETTMANN ARCHIVE, INC.

Page 4: (Top) Tax payment by settler of Roman-occupied provinces. Relief in Neumagen near Trier, Germany. Third century A.D. THE BETTMANN ARCHIVE, INC. (Bottom) Second-style wall painting from the cubiculum of the Villa Boscoreale near Pompeii. First century B.C. THE METROPOLITAN MUSEUM OF ART.

Page 48: (Top left) A peasant doing compulsory work for his lord. Woodcut. THE BETT-MANN ARCHIVE, INC. (Top right) Medieval village. Overall plan showing distribution of arable land, common pasture, and the lord's domain. THE BETTMANN ARCHIVE, INC. (Bottom) Fourth-century Germanic chieftain. Bas relief. CULVER PICTURES.

Page 100: (Top) A monastery school in the Middle Ages. The abbot at the left gives instructions to the monk. At the right, classroom scene demonstrating a monastic spanking. Fifteenth-century miniature. Woodcut. THE BETTMANN ARCHIVE, INC. (Center right) Rouens de Grand Portal. Cathedral de Rouens, France. NEW YORK PUBLIC LIBRARY. (Bottom) Attack and defense of a castle. Late thirteenth century NEW YORK PUBLIC LIBRARY.

Page 172: (Top left) Tailor during medieval times. BROWN BROTHERS. (Top right) Burning of Jews. CULVER PICTURES. (Bottom) Effects of Good Government (detail), Siena, by Ambrogio Lorenzetti. SCALA NEW YORK/FLORENCE.

Page 226: (Top) Family of Country People by Louis Le Nain. Ca. 1642. MUSÉE DE LOUVRE. (Bottom left) Martin Luther by Lucas Cranach, the Elder. THE GRANGER COLLECTION. (Bottom right) Some of the members of New College, Oxford (all students were clerics): English manuscript illumination. Ca. 1453. THE GRANGER COLLECTION.

For Peggy

Preface

The Other Side of Western Civilization, Volume I, introduces some key problems in the history of the common people of Europe before the Reformation by focusing on class structure, the nature of the economy, and patterns and aspects of everyday life. For historical action and ideology to be relevant, they must be viewed in their human context. This volume attempts to present such a view by including readings that evoke the texture of life in premodern times through impressionistic vignettes based on the solid work of social historians. Some of the pieces are taken from the work of the period, but more often—because the ancients rarely described what they considered commonplace—they are historians' re-creations. They deal with such basic questions as: How did people travel? What were the educational institutions like? What were the aims of warfare, and how was war waged?

The parts are arranged chronologically, and in the first section, A. H. M. Jones' "Sanitation and Safety in the Greek City" gives an idea of the quality of everyday life in ancient Greece. An article by M. I. Finley describes some aspects of life in Rome at the peak of the Empire. The nature of early Christianity and the reasons for its widespread acceptance are discussed in three articles.

The early Middle Ages is dealt with in terms of the evolution of the basic social communities and the role of the peasants in feudal society after the time of the barbarian invasions. The practice of knighthood and the crusades are also discussed. Lynn White, Jr., in "The Life of the Silent Majority," and Norman Cohn, in "The Poor in the First Crusade," convey an idea of what life was like for the common man in Europe of the Middle Ages.

Part Three, "The Peak of Medieval Civilization," deals with the major institutions that formed the basis for the twelfth-century renaissance. It treats the rise of the universities along with the monastic orders, focusing on the problem of heretics and intellectual dissenters, including Peter Abelard. Two rather unusual articles deal with aspects of this period that have not generally received sufficient attention. In "Traveling the Roads of the Twelfth Century," Urban T. Holmes, Jr., gives a graphic description of travel in the Middle Ages; and Margaret Labarge, in "The Role of a Baron's Wife," attempts to dispel the stereotyped images of medieval women by studying the actual role aristocratic women played in their society.

Part Four emphasizes the nature of urban life in the fourteenth century, a period torn by war and plague. Included in these readings are a discussion of the development of police power in Siena by William Bowsky; "Hygiene in Fourteenth Century London" by Philip Ziegler, which offers an explanation for the plague's rapid spread through that city; and "Family Life in the Cities" by Lewis Mumford, which provides a concrete view of social life in the medieval towns. H. J. Hewitt's "Feudal War in Practice" reevaluates the nature of medieval warfare, pointing out that it did not conform to the traditional code of chivalry in either theory or practice.

The last section deals with the period leading up to the Reformation, a period marked by increasing urbanization, which led inevitably to changes in the social structure of premodern Europe. Some of these changes are discussed in John Gage's article on the aristocracy in Renaissance Florence, which illustrates the transformation of the medieval aristocracy into an urban class. Progressive urbanization also affected the universities, and J. M. Fletcher's "Rich and Poor in the Late Medieval Universities" details some of the changes that took place and turned a medieval institution into a prototype of the modern university. The last two articles deal with special problems in the Renaissance-Reformation period. In Erik H. Erikson's article on Martin Luther, the psychoanalytic approach to the study of great men in history is encountered. And Philippe Ariès uses an innovative approach to the art of the late Middle Ages and the Renaissance to illuminate "The Emergence of a Concept of the Family" in European society.

A number of people provided important assistance in the preparation of this book. I am grateful to those who commented on the original plan for this work: Jeremy du Q. Adams, Yale University; William Hitchcock, University of California, Santa Cruz; David Herlihy, University of Wisconsin; and Charles T. Wood, Dartmouth College. These critics, as teachers and scholars, read various drafts and played an important role in shaping the book. I am indebted to Thomas A. Williamson and William J. Wisneski of Harcourt Brace Jovanovich who encouraged me throughout. I want also to thank my editor, Ronne Peltzman, and my copyeditor, Susan Wladawsky, for their help. And lest this thanksgiving be too grave, I am pleased to thank my two young sons, who proved that relevance is relative by launching portions of the manuscript as paper airplanes. In dedicating the book to my wife, I acknowledge her role as critic and peacekeeper.

Stanley Chodorow

Contents

* For paired selections, the first page number refers to the headnote, the second to
the selection proper.

Topical Table of Contents

The Other Side of Western Civilization:

Readings in Everyday Life

Volume I

Introduction

The aim of this book is to provide insight into the character of pre-modern society. The selections focus on the social life of western Europe from the ancient world through the Renaissance. They present a composite picture of urban and rural life and of the activities of the social classes and professions.

Social history was first written by the Enlightenment *philosophes*, who reacted strongly against the ancient historiographical tradition that equated history with the history of politics and government. Inspired by critics like Voltaire, who called for a history of men to replace the history of kings, ministers, and courts, writers like Montesquieu sought to describe and explain the social personalities of national groups. Others, in Germany as well as in France, began to focus on the cultural history of Europe—the history of art and literature as well as of society. But the *philosophes* were really uninterested in history even when they were ostensibly writing history. Their conviction that man was progressing toward the realization of his rational capacity underlay their historical work, so that for them, history was only a source of evidence that proved the truth of their conviction.

In the late eighteenth and early nineteenth centuries, men like Goethe, Herder, and Hegel reacted against this attitude. The end product of man's progress in the eighteenth century had been the terror of the French Revolution. Man had not escaped from his history; he had only continued in its ancient course. These writers, the romanticists, thought that society is as much a product of its past as an adult is a product of his childhood and adolescence. For them, historical studies provided the key to under-standing the present. The historical work of the romanticists therefore focused attention on the whole past: social and economic history, cultural history, linguistics, and religious history became an integral part of the study of the past.

Yet the historical field that gained most from the new valuation of historical study was the old mainstay of the genre, political history. The majority of extant documents and narrative sources derived from political action and concerned political organization. It took much longer to develop methods for dealing with the cryptic sources on which social history could be founded than it took to develop methods for dealing with the literate products of the governing elite. Real progress in social history was not made until the 1920s, when Marc Bloch and Lucien Febvre founded the so-called *Annales* school—named for the journal in which they published studies of social and economic history. Inspired by Bloch and Febvre, social historians have produced studies of the social structures that provided the context in which politics, artistic creation, and other human endeavors took place.

Development of the various historical fields has paralleled growing interest in certain periods of history. Nineteenth-century historiography, founded on the romanticists' reaction to the Enlightenment, took a striking interest in the medieval period. This interest contrasts sharply with the attitude of the Renaissance humanists and Enlightenment *philosophes* toward that period. The humanists had coined the phrase "Middle Ages" as a pejorative description of the long period of European history that separated them from the ancient world. The *philosophes* shared humanist attitudes toward the barbarism and superstition associated with medieval society. But nineteenth-century historians increasingly discovered that the origins of modern Europe were to be found in the medieval communities that succeeded to the power of Rome in the sixth century. In fact, chairs of modern history in English universities, founded in the mid-nineteenth century, are often held by medievalists, and today there are over fifty major centers of medieval studies in the United States. The structure of this book reflects this attitude by focusing attention on the life of the Middle Ages. Something more should be said about this emphasis.

While most Western civilization courses begin with ancient Israel or Mycenaean Greece, the social life of these ancient peoples is not, strictly speaking, relevant to the development of European society. The ancient Greeks lived in a different world—geographically, economically, and politically—from that of the European peoples whose social and economic institutions formed the basis for modern society. The societies of Greece and the ancient Near East were antecedents of Europan society, not part of the edifice itself. Although the impact of Roman social life on the development of European society was, of course, much greater than that of Greece, nonetheless, before Europe became a distinct civilization, its social and economic foundations were profoundly transformed by the Germanic invasions. The urban life of the Roman Empire virtually disappeared in the fifth and sixth centuries, and while most modern Italian cities were founded on the Roman *urbs*, the same cannot be said about those of other parts of Europe. In the rural areas also, the influx of Germans changed the nature of Roman society. The provincial nobility was replaced by Germans who occupied their position but lived very differently. The peasantry changed through intermarriage and cultural amalgamation.

My approach has led to a division of the book into five broad chronological periods. The first deals with the ancient world, the next three with the medieval world, and the last with the Renaissance–Reformation period.

Bibliography

For a history of the historian's discipline and the way its focus has changed see Herbert Butterfield, *Man on His Past: The Study of the History of Historical Scholarship* (Cambridge, Eng., 1940). Butterfield has critically evaluated the work of one major school of nineteenth-century historians in his *The Whig Interpretation of History* (London, 1931). His critique is reconsidered in E. H. Carr, *What Is History?* (New York, 1962). The great social historian Marc Bloch wrote an appraisal of his craft which was found among his papers and published as *The Historian's Craft* (New York, 1953). Recently, two numbers of the periodical *Daedalus* were devoted to an assessment of the discipline and fields of history. See *Daedalus*, Vol. 100 (1971), Nos. 1–2.

The Ancient World, 5th Century B.C.– 5th Century A.D.

The five selections in this part focus on ancient Greece and Rome. At the beginning of the fifth century B.C., Greece was the center of Western civilization, extending its influence over the whole Mediterranean world. In the course of the century, Athens became the hub of a far-flung empire held together by its navy, but also possessing a cultural, economic, and political homogeneity. It was an empire of city-states whose cultural and political life was determined by its urban character. Aligned against this empire was the Peloponnesian League, a league of Greek cities led by Sparta. These cities were more autonomous than those in the Athenian orb, but they were held together by similar cultural and political ties. The cities continued to dominate Greek life even after the Macedonians had destroyed the independence of the city-states and built their own empire. It is therefore important to understand the quality of life in the Greek cities, and the first selection, by A. H. M. Jones, brings this life into focus.

During the fifth and fourth centuries B.C., the Romans were just breaking away from the effects of long subjugation by Etruscan kings. As it developed, the Roman state paralleled the Greek city-state pattern, but it retained a distinctive quality of its own. The Romans remained more conscious and prouder of their agricultural origins, and their conception of civic virtue preserved the ideals of life in a community of independent farmers. The social and economic changes of the first century B.C.—which brought thousands of Romans into the city—were therefore extremely important in Roman history. They altered the nature of politics and life in the state.

In ancient biographies of the Roman emperors, their relations with women hold an important place. It is clear that some women exercised extraordinary behind-the-scenes power, but the sources tell us little about the normal conditions of women's life. In the article by M. I. Finley, there is an attempt to use this scanty material as the basis for an evaluation of the place of women in Roman society. The selection not only adds much to our knowledge of this aspect of Roman life, but also reveals the problems historians have in trying to use ancient sources.

Histories of the late Roman Empire focus on the evidence of decline and disintegration of institutions and economic life. But decline was not the only pattern of change in the later empire. There were also profound religious changes that can only be characterized in terms of growth and expansion. Around the time of Christ, there was a great influx of new religions to Rome and the western provinces from the East. In Samuel Angus' "The Appeal and Practice of the Mystery Religions" and A. H. M. Jones' "The Spread of Christianity," these new religions are brought into focus, and their appeal to the population of the empire is discussed. The piece by Jones tries to answer the old question: Why did Christianity win out over the other religions?

Even before it was clear that Christianity was the dominant religion of the empire, Christian missionaries took their new teachings beyond the empire's borders to the Germans. Christians faced almost as much difficulty among the German tribesmen as they had among the Romans, and the process of Christianization of the tribes was slow. E. A. Thompson's essay examines this process and provides a description of early Germanic society.

Bibliography

A good study of the Greek *polis* is A. Zimmern, *The Greek Commonwealth* (Oxford, 1911). See also H. Michell, *Sparta* (Cambridge, Eng., 1964), which studies the character of Athens' great rival. For a picture of Greek life, see Robert Flacelière, *Daily Life in Greece in the Time of Pericles* (London, 1965), and the novel by Mary Renault, *The Last of the Wine* (New York, 1956). For further studies of the cities, see R. E. Wycherley, *How the Greeks Built Cities* (London, 1949).

Two works that will fill in the details of the mob's participation in late republican political life are A. W. Lintott, *Violence in Republican Rome* (Oxford, 1968), and Z. Yavetz, *Plebs and Princeps* (Oxford, 1969), which carries the subject into the imperial period. See also Ronald Syme, *The Roman Revolution* (Oxford, 1939), which is a detailed study of the transition from republic to principate.

For the social context of the life of women in ancient Rome, see W. W. Fowler, *Social Life at Rome in the Age of Cicero* (New York, 1909), and Jerome Carcopino, *Daily Life in Ancient Rome* (New Haven, Conn., 1940). A complete treatment of women will be found in J. P. V. D. Balsdon, *Roman Women* (London, 1962). For a good brief introduction to Roman law, see Barry Nicholas, *An Introduction to Roman Law* (Oxford, 1962), and J. A. Crook, *Law and Life in Rome* (Ithaca, N.Y., 1967).

For background on the mystery religions, see W. W. Fowler, *The Religious Experience of the Roman People* (London, 1911), and M. P. Nilsson, *A History of Greek Religion*, 2nd ed. (Oxford, 1949). Samuel Angus' *The Mystery Religions and Christianity* (London, 1925) is the best work on the mysteries themselves. On the origins of Christianity, see Morton Scott Enslin, *Christian Beginnings* (New York, 1938). On the Christian movement in the Roman Empire, see the classic treatment by Edward Gibbon, *The Decline and Fall of the Roman Empire*, ed. by J. B. Bury, Vol. 1 (New York, 1946), Chap. 15. See also G. E. M. de Ste. Croix, "Why Were the Early Christians Persecuted?" *Past and Present*, Vol. 26 (1963), pp. 6–38; Erwin R. Goodenough, *The Church in the Roman Empire* (New York, 1931); and T. R. Glover, *The Conflict of Religions in the Early Roman Empire* (London, 1909).

For works on the early Germanic peoples, see the first paragraph of the bibliography given for Part 2 (page 56). For the history of the saints who lived among the Roman provincials and the Germans during the period of migration, see *St. Martin of Tours*, trans. by M. C. Watt (London, 1928), which contains the life of St. Martin (d. 397) and selections from the chronicle by Sulpicius Severus, the saint's younger contemporary. The establishment of the Germanic kingdoms in Europe during the sixth century coincided with the missionary activities of monks who were largely responsible for converting the new Europeans and for bringing them into the orb of Roman religion and culture; see Eleanor Shipley Duckett, *The Wandering Saints of the Early Middle Ages* (New York, 1959). The introduction of Christianity to Scandinavia followed a pattern established much earlier among the Germans of St. Sabas' time; see Sigrid Undset, *The Saga of Saints* (London, 1934). See also the description of Iceland's conversion by Thangbrand the Saxon (c. 1000 A.D.) in *Njál's Saga* (from which "Conflict and Settlement in Early Germanic Society," in Part 2 of this volume, is taken), Chaps. 100–05.

Sanitation and Safety
in the Greek City

A. H. M. JONES

Cities were the focal points of Greek civilization, and volumes have been written about them. The Greeks themselves analyzed the different forms of government found among the cities, and the economic life of the cities, their culture, and their populations have also been studied. This selection examines an aspect of Greek city life rarely treated and hard to get information about—the public services. A. H. M. Jones provides us with a glimpse of the ways the Greeks dealt with the familiar and mundane problems of urban life.

Before the selection is read, something should be said about the cities Jones is writing about. His focus is not so much on the ancient Greek city-states and their colonies in the classical period as on the cities founded by Alexander the Great during the fourth century B.C. The Greeks had always extended their control over new territories by founding cities, and this practice was continued under Alexander in the lands he conquered. But whereas the urban colonies of the eighth and seventh centuries B.C. had been set up primarily for commercial purposes, Alexander seems to have had a different aim. He attempted to ensure a mixture of Greeks and natives in the populations of his cities, and many think that he hoped to effect an assimilation of the newly conquered peoples into Greek culture. His cities continued to be Greek—propagators of Greek culture—throughout the Roman and Byzantine periods. Jones draws his material from these communities, in which he found a great continuity.

The public services which the cities provided for their inhabitants naturally varied both in scope and in scale according to their size and wealth. Ephesus and Smyrna, Nicomedia and Nicaea, Tarsus, Antioch, and Alexandria could offer to their citizens amenities and luxuries which the average large town, the capital of a province or of a judicial circuit, could not afford. These again lived on a grander scale than ordinary provincial cities, and among these last there were many gradations, from substantial towns, which took a pride in their games and public buildings, to humble rural communes,

From A. H. M. Jones, *The Greek City* (Oxford: The Clarendon Press, 1940), pp. 211–19. Reprinted by permission of The Clarendon Press, Oxford.

which, though officially dignified with the name of city, lacked the barest essentials of civic life—municipal offices, a gymnasium, a theatre, a market-place, and a public water-supply, to quote Pausanias' list. But despite these wide contrasts in achievement, the ideal to which all cities aspired was montonously uniform. The spread of Hellenism through the near East was to a large extent the product of imitation, and the place of any city in the scale of civilization was gauged by its success in reproducing the culture of the universally acknowledged archetype, the cities of the Aegean basin. Architecture, athletics, music, drama, and education were cosmopolitan; and from Macedonia and Thrace through Asia Minor and Syria to Egypt the cities, one and all accordingly to their varying resources, erected the same type of buildings, celebrated musical and gymnastic games with identical programmes, and provided for their citizens the same opportunities for physical and intellectual culture.

What is to-day considered the most elementary duty of any government, the maintenance of law and order, seems, from the absence of reference to it, to have been almost ignored by the Hellenistic cities. There was indeed in Ptolemaic Alexandria a commander of the night watch ($\nu\upsilon\kappa\tau\epsilon\rho\iota\nu\grave{o}s$ $\sigma\tau\rho\alpha\tau\eta\gamma\acute{o}s$), but he was probably a royal officer; and in general police functions in cities governed by kings seem to have been fulfilled by their commandants. The only civic police on record in the Hellenistic age are the frontier guards of Miletus and Heraclea, one of whose duties it was to arrest runaway slaves. Under the principate many more civic police officers are recorded. These were of several types. Commanders of the night watch ($\nu\upsilon\kappa\tau\omicron\sigma\tau\rho\acute{\alpha}\tau\eta\gamma\omicron\iota$), perhaps based on the Alexandrian model, are found in the second century in several cities of Asia, and regularly in the Egyptian metropoleis of the third century. They commanded a corps of night watchmen ($\nu\upsilon\kappa\tau\omicron\phi\acute{\upsilon}\lambda\alpha\kappa\epsilon s$), who in Oxyrhynchus, a modest town, numbered fifty or sixty: we possess a list of the posts to which they were assigned, seven to the principal temple, the Thoereum, six to the Serapeum, three to the theatre, two to the gymnasium, one to the Iseum, and the remainder one to each street. The watchmen were humble citizens, cobblers, potters, fullers, and the like, and were conscripted for the service, but apparently paid for their trouble.

Frontier guards are in the Roman period commonly found in Asia Minor. The magistrates in charge of this force were styled $\pi\alpha\rho\alpha\phi\acute{\upsilon}\lambda\alpha\kappa\epsilon s$, and their men, the $\acute{o}\rho\omicron\phi\acute{\upsilon}\lambda\alpha\kappa\epsilon s$, who were naturally mounted, were drawn from the sons of the gentry; at Apollonia of Caria a party of ten, with their cadet officer ($\nu\epsilon\alpha\nu\iota\sigma\kappa\acute{\alpha}\rho\chi\eta s$) and the $\pi\alpha\rho\alpha\phi\acute{\upsilon}\lambda\alpha\xi$ himself, were attended by six slaves, who served as grooms. The service was perhaps modelled on the Athenian ephebate, in which cadets in their second year of training garrisoned the frontier forts. It was their duty to tour the outlying villages of the city territory; a decree of the Phrygian Hierapolis forbids them to demand hospitality from the villagers over and above lodging, wood, and chaff, and reproves them for extorting "crowns" from the village headmen. Another inscription, probably also of Hierapolis, bears more directly on their duties: they are instructed to deal with shepherds who graze their flocks in other people's vineyards.

Neither of these forces was capable of dealing with serious crime; to suppress this was the duty of the wardens of the peace (εἰρηνάρχαι). This magistracy is found from the beginning of the second century throughout the Roman East, and was probably created on the order of the Roman government, which controlled appointments to it; irenarchs were not directly elected, but nominated by the provincial governor from a list submitted by the city. They commanded a force of mounted constables (διωγμῖται), and their principal activity seems to have been to hunt down brigands: they acted as examining magistrates, but had no authority to inflict punishment, sending up the delinquents whom they captured to the governor, with a *dossier* of the evidence against them. Their sphere of operations was the country-side. At Smyrna the irenarch pursued Polycarp, when he fled from justice into the country, whereas in a later persecution Pionius, who stayed in town, was arrested by another officer, the commander of the cavalry (ἵππαρχος). This office, originally military, survived under the principate in a number of Asiatic cities, where no doubt, as at Smyrna, it sank to be the captaincy of the city police: the hipparch was also supported by mounted constables (διωγμῖται). Every city had its jail, where prisoners were confined pending their trial: the warders were normally public slaves.

What are to-day regarded as the municipal services *par excellence* are not very frequently mentioned in antiquity. They were in the larger cities at any rate entrusted to a special board, the controllers of the town (ἀστυνόμοι), and what we know of them is largely derived from the Pergamene law defining the duties of this office: as this law, framed by one of the Attalid kings, was inscribed under the principate, it may be inferred that Hellenistic and Roman practice was uniform in this field. The first duty of the *astynomi* was the care of roads and bridges, both in the city itself and in its territory. They had to prevent encroachments on the public highway; the Pergamene law lays down minimum widths for country roads, thirty feet for a main road, twelve feet for a by-road. They had to remove obstructions; shopkeepers were allowed to display their wares outside their shops, but not in such a manner as to block the traffic. They had to prevent rubbish being tipped into the streets, and were themselves responsible for having them scavenged. They had finally to see to the maintenance of the surface. According to the legal authorities, landowners and householders were responsible in both country and town for the paving of the roads on which their property fronted, and the *astynomi* had to enforce this obligation and only as a last resort to give out the work to contract, claiming the expense, plus a fine, from the delinquents. It is difficult to believe, however, that the magnificent and uniform paving which we see to-day in the principal streets of excavated cities was maintained by this system, and it seems likely that householders regularly commuted their obligations for a cash payment, and that the city undertook the work; we know that cities maintained gangs of public slaves for street paving.

The cities were very proud of their streets and spent enormous sums on them. The regular chequer-board system of town planning invented by Hippodamus of Miletus was universally admired in the Hellenistic and Roman periods, and not only were new cities laid out according to this scheme, but many old towns were gradually remodelled to conform to it. The principal streets were very generally flanked by colonnades which sheltered pedestrians from the rain in winter and from the sun in summer. Street lighting seems to have been something of a rarity; the brilliant illumination of Antioch by night was a source of great pride to its citizens, as two of them, Ammianus and Libanius, testify. Some few lights outside public buildings, like the brilliant festoon of hanging lamps outside the *praetorium*, were no doubt maintained by the city, but the ordinary street lamps by the occupants of the shops outside which they hung.

Another care of the *astynomi* was drainage. Progressive cities had a regular system of drains, running under the streets, which carried off both surface-water and sewage. Strabo remarks with surprise that Lysimachus' architects in building New Smyrna failed to provide any, so that the sewage had to flow along open gutters; Josephus praises the up-to-date system installed by Herod in Caesarea; and a century later Pliny, as governor of Bithynia, covered in a malodorous canal which served as the main drain of Amastris. It was the duty of the *astynomi* to see that the drains were maintained in good condition and cleaned; a gang of public slaves did this work. They had also to keep clean the public conveniences, which Pergamum and probably most large cities provided.

For their water-supply all ancient cities relied to some extent on wells and rain-water cisterns, and it was the duty of the *astynomi* to see that the owners of these kept them in good order. As late as the reign of Hadrian so flourishing a place as Alexandria Troas had no other source of supply, but in the Roman period an increasing number of cities built themselves aqueducts which tapped springs often many miles away. These great arched structures, of which many impressive ruins still survive, were enormously expensive, but they brought the advantages of pure, copious, and regular supply, which could moreover be distributed under pressure to all parts of the city; the last advantage was so much appreciated that at Arsinoe of Egypt, where there was no possible source of supply save the canal on which the city lay, a costly pumping-system was maintained. The public water-supply was devoted mainly to public buildings, such as baths, and to street fountains. These were often architectural features of great magnificence—the "nymphaea" of Syria were particularly splendid—and it was one of the duties of the *astynomi* to see that they were kept clean and in repair, and to prevent the citizens from washing clothes or watering animals in them. At Arsinoe only a few private institutions, such as a brewery and a Jewish synagogue, had a private supply. At Antioch many private houses indulged in this luxury, but Libanius suggests that the citizens were lucky in not having to queue up round the public fountains. Aelius Aristides implies that Smyrna was as well off in this respect as Antioch. At Alexandria many private houses had cisterns, fed by a system of underground channels from the Nile, but the common people had to draw their water direct from the river, there being no public fountains. Private users naturally paid a water rate, but this by no means covered the cost of the service.

Precautions against fire were as a rule most inadequate. Nicomedia in Trajan's reign had no apparatus and no brigade; and, though Pliny saw to it that in future hoses and hooks (for pulling down adjacent buildings and thus isolating the outbreak) should be available, he was unable to persuade the emperor to allow him to establish a volunteer fire brigade, such as existed in many Italian cities. The reasons which Trajan gave for his refusal were based on local circumstances; Bithynia, and Nicomedia in particular, was a hotbed of faction, and any association would inevitably be turned to political ends. But a story in the life of Polycarp reveals that in Smyrna also at this date, though apparatus was provided, the general public were expected to turn out to extinguish fires. This suggests that the imperial government, at this time at any rate, uniformly forbade the formation of fire brigades in eastern cities; there is no evidence that it later changed its policy.

Astynomi are not very frequently mentioned, and it is probable that in many smaller cities their functions devolved on the controllers of the market (ἀγορανόμοι). The market was normally a paved square, surrounded by colonnades, on to which opened shops. The city drew a considerable revenue from the rents of these shops, and from leasing sites for stalls, which were regularly placed between the columns of the colonnades; and it was the duty of the *agoranomi* to keep the fabric in repair and to collect the rents. They fixed the hours at which the market opened and closed, and proclaimed them by ringing a bell. They had further to inspect the quality of the goods exposed for sale, and to see that correct weights and measures were used. For this purpose standard weights and measures were kept in their office and those used by traders were tested and stamped by them. The *agoranomi* also enforced currency laws, controlling the rate of exchange, a complicated matter when almost every city issued its own copper coins for local use and these bore no fixed relation to the gold and silver currencies of various standards minted by kings and important cities, or later by the imperial government.

But these were the least onerous duties of the board. It was also required to regulate the hiring of casual labour, enforcing the payment of wages and performance of work as stipulated, but not apparently interfering with the rate of wages or labour conditions. Finally, it was the duty of the *agoranomi* to see that an adequate supply of provisions was put on the market at a fair price: vivid evidence of what was expected of them is afforded by a series of inscriptions in the market of Ephesus, recording the names of agoranomi "under whom there was plenty and fair dealing," and appending the prices which prevailed in their year of office. The means adopted to secure this happy state of affairs varied according to circumstances. Agoranomi were authorized to fix prices by decree and in some cases did so. At Cyzicus, for instance, when Antonia Tryphaena was financing great public works and there was an influx of labour, the agoranomi were instructed by the city to punish any tradesman who raised his prices by disfranchising or deporting him and boarding up his shop and placarding his offence upon it. This was a special measure to meet an emergency, but other inscriptions prove that the agoranomi of Messene in the first century B.C. and of Pergamum in the second century A.D. regularly fixed the prices of certain wares.

Such measures, however, could for obvious reasons be applied only to home-grown produce, and in dealing with importers less drastic methods were used. Delos in the third century B.C. ruled that importers of firewood must declare their prices on arrival to the agoranomi, who could compel them to fulfil their undertaking by banning sale at a higher price and meanwhile charging them for the stall which they occupied. The same law forbade sale by importers to middlemen: Hadrian similarly at Athens endeavoured to keep down prices by eliminating unnecessary middlemen—importers were allowed to sell to local dealers but no further resale was permitted. In times of scarcity, however, no mere regulations were of avail to prevent prices from rising, and in these circumstances not a few public-spirited agoranomi, especially in the Roman period, are recorded to have taken the heroic course of entering the market themselves and underselling the dealers, bearing the loss out of their own pockets.

The most critical question was the supply of corn, which was at once the staple foodstuff, especially for the poorer classes, and was subject to the most violent fluctuations of price. Some larger cities, whose territories were not suited to the production of corn, regularly depended on supplies imported from overseas, and their position was peculiarly insecure: owing to the very high cost of transport imported corn was always dear, and any disturbing factor, a crop failure in one of the producing areas, storms at sea, or political troubles, might raise the price above the purchasing power of the humbler classes. As early as the fourth century B.C. many cities of the Aegean adopted special measures to secure a regular supply. The system was to establish a capital fund (σιτικὴ παράθεσις) which was lent each year to merchants on condition that they used it to import corn to the city. This system ensured a regular supply in normal times, but it did not cope with times of serious shortage. Even cities which were normally supplied from their own territory or the immediate neighbourhood not infrequently got into difficulties: if the local harvest failed, merchants who imported corn to supply the deficiency charged much higher prices than the local population was used to paying.

In such emergencies a persuasive agoranomus might occasionally induce

a merchant to sell below the inflated market price: not a few Hellenistic decrees are preserved which heap honours and privileges on such generous merchants. Local landowners also often came forward and either sold at a cheap
rate or distributed free the corn from their estates. But often the city took
action: a fund was raised by public subscription or by an extraordinary levy,
and corn-buyers (σιτῶναι) were appointed to purchase corn with this sum and
retail it below cost.

The *sitonae*, originally extraordinary officers, had already in some cities,
such as Delos, which depended entirely on imported corn, become a permanent institution in the second century B.C. In the Roman period they were
almost universal; by the second century A.D. they were established, under the
name of directors of the corn supply (εὐθηνιάρχαι), even in the metropoleis
of Egypt. The cities thus undertook as a normal part of the administration
not merely the supervision of the corn market but the actual supply of corn.
They did not always have to rely exclusively on purchase; for some had the
right of levying corn from all landowners in their territory, and most drew
some rent in corn from public lands. Usually, however, they had to buy in
the open market, and many are recorded to have possessed standing funds
for the purchase of corn (τὰ σιτωνικὰ χρήματα), administered by special
treasurers. It would seem that these funds were capital sums, which the
sitonae spent each year on buying corn, and repaid as the corn was sold, and
that the corn supply did not ordinarily involve the government in a loss.
When there was a shortage, however, the richer citizens were expected either
to give corn to the city or subscribe additional sums for its purchase, and
public-spirited *sitonae* often sold corn at below cost price; thus at Magnesia
on the Maeander a *sitones* boasts that he lost 5,000 denarii, and at Aphro-
disias a father and two sons call themselves "*sitonae* of the 10,000 denarii
which they themselves gave."

It is unlikely that the *sitonae* went very far afield for their corn save in
exceptional cases. For an inland city import of corn from any distance was
quite impracticable owing to the prohibitive cost of transport. The most that
the *sitonae* could try to do in a famine was to buy up local stocks and put
them on the market at a moderate price, and in this they were often embarrassed by the avarice of the landowners, who withheld their corn from the
market, hoping for a rise. In Domitian's reign Antioch of Pisidia had to appeal to the provincial governor, who ordered all landowners in the territory
to sell their entire surplus stock to the *emptores coloniae* at one denarius the
bushel (the normal price was about half this sum), and at Aspendus Apollon-
ius of Tyana is alleged to have achieved the same result by the sheer force of
his personality: the anecdote is interesting as showing how much even mari-
time cities relied on local production. Import from Egypt was, it must be
remembered, subject to imperial licence, which was very sparingly granted to
the cities. It is recorded among Hadrian's great benefactions to Ephesus that
he allowed shipments of corn from Egypt, and a *sitones* of Tralles relates

with very great pride that he "bought the sixty thousand bushels of corn from Egypt which was conceded to his native city by our lord Trajanus Hadrianus Augustus and advanced out of his own pocket the price of the corn and all the expenses incurred up to its arrival."

Having supplied the corn, the cities naturally maintained a very strict control on the millers and bakers, lest they should turn the cheap supply to their own profit. At Ephesus the city council was so exacting that it provoked a strike among the bakers, who were however soon brought to heel by the proconsul. At Oxyrhynchus the directors of the corn supply themselves leased mills and had the corn ground, and it would seem that the city also bought the monopoly of baking from the Roman government and operated its own bakeries.

The most direct contribution of the cities to the department of public health was the maintenance of salaried public doctors. Some Greek cities had employed doctors from a very early age, and in the Hellenistic period the practice became general. Under the principate almost every city had a number of official doctors ($\dot{\alpha}\rho\chi\dot{\iota}\alpha\tau\rho\sigma\iota$); Antoninus Pius limited their number to ten for metropoleis of provinces, seven for capitals of assize districts, five for ordinary cities. The principal business of these doctors was to give medical attention to the citizens; they were apparently allowed to take fees but were not expected to confine their attentions to those who could pay. They also served as police doctors, certifying the authorities of the causes of deaths, when suspicious, and of the injuries sustained by plaintiffs in alleged cases of assault. They often also gave instruction in medicine: at Perge a public doctor is praised for the excellent lectures that he gave in the gymnasium, and at Ephesus under the principate they were members of the medical faculty of the local "museum" or university, and took a prominent part in the annual competitions which were held in surgery, instruments, and, it would appear, a prepared thesis and an unprepared problem set by the examiners.

Under the heading of public health may also be reckoned the public baths, of which most cities maintained several, besides those attached to the gymnasium. A charge was made for admission, but it was very small and by no means covered the cost of upkeep: fuel for the heating of the public baths was a large item in the city budget, and there were also the salaries of the bath attendants and stokers, usually public slaves, and the cost of the water. Oxyrhynchus ingeniously made a little money by leasing out the post of cloakroom attendant: stealing the clothes of bathers was a very popular form of petty larceny, and the attendant no doubt made a good thing out of tips. Oil was not normally provided for bathers, but public-spirited citizens often supplied it gratis to all comers on festal occasions.

The Silent Women of Rome

M. I. FINLEY

When historians study the place of women in ancient history, or in any period up to modern times, they are almost always interested in the men. In the case of Roman women, this approach has been determined by the ancient sources themselves. Plutarch and Suetonius used the character of imperial women to expose the character of imperial men. Roman legal sources also permit a glimpse at the position of women in Roman society, and they show that the woman's position improved during the imperial period. The classical Roman law of the late Republic and early Principate strictly limited the independence of women, requiring that their property be administered by men—either their husbands or a guardian—and keeping them in a position of legal subjugation to their fathers or their husbands. By the time of Justinian, however, a woman's dowry was protected from her husband's mismanagement or appropriation, and her power to act on her own behalf had increased. If a man alienated or diminished his wife's property, she could take action against him for damages. Thus, in late imperial times, women possessed significant legal rights, though their status would not meet the standards of equality being established today.

Historians have followed the ancient writers in their attitudes toward women in Roman society. In the following article, M. I. Finley attempts to look behind the façade in order to evaluate the position, or the condition, of Roman women. His sources are no different from those used by others, but he asks different questions of the material. Finley wants to know how women felt about their restricted lives, and he seeks evidence that might reveal their reaction. It is in an article like this one that we can see the importance of question-framing for the historian's enterprise. Often sources that were considered squeezed dry by historical study and interpretation come alive again when new questions are asked of them.

The most famous woman in Roman history was not even a Roman—Cleopatra was queen of Egypt, the last ruler of a Macedonian dynasty that had been established on the Nile three centuries earlier by Ptolemy, one of the generals of Alexander the Great. Otherwise what names come to mind? A few flamboyant, ruthless and vicious women of the imperial family, such as Messalina, great-grandniece of Augustus and wife of her cousin once re-

From pp. 129–42 of *Aspects of Antiquity* by M. I. Finley. Copyright © 1965 by M. I. Finley. Reprinted by permission of the Viking Press, Inc., and Chatto and Windus Ltd.

moved, the emperor Claudius; or the latter's next wife, his niece Agrippina, who was Nero's mother and, contemporary tradition insists, also for a time his mistress. One or two names in love poetry, like the Lesbia of Catullus. And some legendary women from Rome's earliest days, such as Lucretia, who gained immortality by being raped. Even in legend the greatest of them was likewise not a Roman but Dido, queen of Carthage, who loved and failed to hold Aeneas.

Such a short and one-sided list can be very misleading. The Roman world was not the only one in history in which women remained in the background in politics and business, or in which catching the eye and the pen of the scandalmonger was the most likely way to achieve notice and perhaps lasting fame. However, it is not easy to think of another great civilized state without a single really important woman writer or poet, with no truly regal queen, no Deborah, no Joan of Arc, no Florence Nightingale, no patron of the arts. The women of mid-Victorian England were equally rightless, equally victims of a double standard of sexual morality, equally exposed to risk and ruin when they stepped outside the home and the church. Yet the profound difference is obvious.

More correctly, it would be obvious if we could be sure what we may legitimately believe about women in Rome. Legend apart, they speak to us in five ways: through the erotic and satirical poetry of the late Republic and early Empire, all written by men; through the historians and biographers, all men and most of them unable to resist the salacious and the scandalous; through the letter writers and philosophers, all men; through painting and sculpture, chiefly portrait statutes, inscribed tombstones, and religious monuments of all kinds; and through innumerable legal texts. These different voices naturally talk at cross-purposes. (One would hardly expect to find quotations from Ovid's *Art of Love* or the pornographic frescoes from the brothel in Pompeii on funeral monuments.) Each tells its portion of a complicated, ambiguous story. One ought to be able to add the pieces together, but unfortunately there will always be one vital piece missing—what the women would have said had they been allowed to speak for themselves.

> Friend, I have not much to say; stop and read it. This tomb, which is not fair, is for a fair woman. Her parents gave her the name Claudia. She loved her husband in her heart. She bore two sons, one of whom she left on earth, the other beneath it. She was pleasant to talk with, and she walked with grace. She kept the house and worked in wool. That is all. You may go.

Of course it wasn't Claudia who selected and set up this verse epitaph (the translation is Richmond Lattimore's) in the city of Rome in the second century B.C., but her husband or some other kinsman. And it is easy to make cynical remarks not only in this particular instance but in the hundreds of others recording domestic devotion, commonly including the phrase in one variation or another that husband and wife lived together X number of years *sine ulla querella,* "without a single quarrel." Yet there is much to be learned from the very monotony with which such sentiments are repeated century after century, at least about the ideal woman—an ideal formulated and imposed by middle- and upper-class Roman males.

To begin with, until fairly late in Roman history, women lacked individual names in the proper sense. Claudia, Julia, Cornelia, Lucretia, are merely family names with a feminine ending. Sisters had the same name and could be distinguished only by the addition of "the elder" or "the younger," "the first" or "the second," and so on. In the not uncommon case of marriage between paternal cousins, mother and daughter would have the same name, too. No doubt this was very confusing: a welcome confusion, one is tempted to suggest, since nothing could have been easier to eliminate. No great genius was needed to think up the idea of giving every girl a personal name, as was done with boys. It is as if the Romans wished to suggest very pointedly that women were not, or ought not to be, genuine individuals but only fractions of a family. Anonymous and passive fractions at that, for the virtues which were stressed were decorum, chastity, gracefulness, even temper and childbearing. They loved their husbands, to be sure—though we need not believe everything that husbands said when their wives were dead—but as one loves an overlord who is free to seek his pleasures elsewhere and to put an end to the relationship altogether when and if he so chooses.

"Family" comes from the Latin, but the Romans actually had no word for "family" in our commonest sense, as in the sentence, "I am taking my family to the seashore for the summer." In different contexts *familia* meant all persons under the authority of the head of a household, or all the descendants from a common ancestor, or all one's property, or merely all one's servants—never our intimate family. This does not mean that the latter did not exist in Rome, but that the stress was on a power structure rather than on biology or intimacy. A Roman *paterfamilias* need not even be a father: the term was a legal one and applied to any head of a household. His illegitimate children were often excluded, even when his paternity was openly acknowledged, and at the same time his son and heir could be an outsider whom he had adopted by the correct legal formalities. Theoretically his power—over his wife, over his sons and daughters and his sons' wives and children, over his slaves and his property—was absolute and uncontrolled, ending only with his death or by his voluntary act of "emancipating" his sons beforehand. As late as the fourth century A.D. an edict of Constantine, the first Christian emperor, still defined that power as the "right of life and death." He was exaggerating, but around a hard core of reality.

Save for relatively minor exceptions, a woman was always in the power of some man—of her *paterfamilias* or of her husband or of a guardian. In early times every marriage involved a formal ceremony in which the bride was surrendered to her husband by the *paterfamilias:* he "gave her away" in the literal sense. Then, when so-called "free" marriages became increasingly common—free from the ancient formalities, that is, not free in the sense that the wife or her husband had made a free choice of partner—she remained legally in the power of her *paterfamilias*. Divorce and widowhood and remarriage introduced more complications and required more rules. Where did property right in dowry and inheritance rest? In the next generation, too, if there were children? The Roman legislators and lawbooks gave much space to these matters. From the state's point of view it was essential to get the power and property relations right, since the *familia* was the basic social unit. But there was more to it than that: marriage meant children, and children were the citizens of the next generation. Not all children by any means, for as Rome extended her empire to the Atlantic and the Middle East, the bulk of the population within her borders were either slaves or free noncitizens. Obviously the political rights and status of the children were the state's concern and could not be left to uncontrolled private decision. So the state laid down strict rules prohibiting certain kinds of marriage: for example, between a Roman citizen and a noncitizen, regardless of rank or wealth; or between a member of the senatorial class and a citizen who had risen from the class of freedmen (ex-slaves). Within the permitted limits, then, the right to choose and decide rested with the heads of families. They negotiated marriages for their children. And they were allowed to proceed, and to have the marriage consummated, as soon as a girl reached the age of twelve.

The story is told that at a male dinner-party early in the second century B.C., the general Scipio Africanus agreed to marry his daughter Cornelia to his friend Tiberius Gracchus, and that his wife was very angry that he should have done so without having consulted her. The story is probably untrue; at least it is very suspicious because it is repeated about Tiberius's son, the famous agrarian reformer of the same name, and the daughter of Appius Claudius. But true or not, the stories are right in essence, for though the mothers may have been angry, they were powerless, and it is noteworthy that the more "liberal" and enlightened wing of the senatorial aristocracy was involved. Presumably the wife of the fiercely traditional Cato the Censor would have kept her anger to herself in a similar situation; she would not have expected to be asked anyway. Surely the first of the Roman emperors, Augustus, consulted neither his wife nor any of the interested parties when he ordered members of his family and various close associates to marry and divorce and remarry whenever he thought (as he did frequently) that reasons of state or dynastic considerations would be furthered by a particular arrangement.

Augustus and his family personify most of the complexities, difficulties, and apparent contradictions inherent in the Roman relations between the sexes. He was first married at the age of twenty-three and divorced his wife two years later, after the birth of their daughter Julia, in order to marry Livia three days after she had given birth to a son. At the second ceremony Livia's ex-husband acted as *paterfamilias* and gave her to Augustus. Fifty-one years later, in A.D. 14, Augustus was said to have addressed his last words to Livia: "As long as you live, remember our marriage. Farewell." Livia had had two sons by her previous husband; gossip inevitably suggested that Augustus was actually the father of the second, and the first son, Tiberius, was in 12 B.C. compelled by Augustus to divorce his wife and marry the recently widowed Julia, daughter of Augustus by his first wife. Tiberius was eventually adopted by Augustus and succeeded him to the throne. Long before that, in 2 B.C., Julia was banished by the emperor for sexual depravity, and ten years later the same punishment was meted out to her daughter, also named Julia. That does not end the story, but it should be enough except for two further details: first, one reason for Augustus's getting rid of his first wife was apparently her peculiar unwillingness to put up with one of his mistresses; second, Augustus was the author of a long series of laws designed to strengthen the family and to put a brake on licentiousness and general moral depravity in the upper classes.

Augustus was no Nero. There is no reason to think that he was not a reasonably moral man by contemporary standards (granted that his position as emperor created abnormal conditions). Ancient and modern moralists have a habit of decrying the decline in Roman moral standards from the old days. Talk of "the good old days" is always suspect, but it may well be that while Rome was still an agricultural community on the Tiber with little power abroad, little luxury, and little urban development, life was simpler and standards stricter. However, the submissive and passive role of women was very ancient, and certainly by the time Rome emerged as a historic and powerful state, say after the defeat of Hannibal late in the third century B.C., all the elements were already there of the social and moral situation which Augustus both represented and tried in some ways to control. Nor is there any justification for speaking of hypocrisy. No one believed or even pretended to believe that monogamous marriage, which was strictly enforced, was incompatible with polygamous sexual activity by the male half of the population. Augustus was concerned with the social consequences of an apparent unwillingness on the part of the aristocracy to produce legitimate children in sufficient numbers, with the social consequences of extravagant and wasteful living, of *public* licentiousness, and in the upper classes, of *female* licentiousness (which may have been on the increase with the breakdown of political morality in the last century of the Roman Republic). It never entered his mind that moral regeneration might include the abolition of concubines, mistresses and brothels, the end of sleeping with one's female slaves, or a redefinition of adultery to extend it to extramarital intercourse by a married man.

There was no puritanism in the Roman concept of morality. Marriage was a central institution but it had nothing sacramental about it. It was central because the whole structure of property rested on it and because both the indispensable family cult and the institution of citizenship required the orderly, regular succession of legitimate children in one generation after another. There were neither spinsters nor confirmed bachelors in this world. It was assumed that if one reached the right age—and many of course did not, given the enormously high rate of infant mortality—one would marry. Society could not pursue its normal course otherwise. But the stress was always on the rightness of the marriage from a social and economic point of view, and on its legitimacy (and therefore also on the legitimacy of the offspring) from the political and legal point of view. If the relationship turned out also to be pleasant and affectionate, so much the better. It was taken for granted, however, that men would find comradeship and sexual satisfaction from others as well, and often only or chiefly from others. They were expected to behave with good taste in this respect, but no more.

Standards, whether of taste or of law, were profoundly influenced by class. Men like Sulla and Cicero openly enjoyed the company of actors and actresses, but by a law of Augustus and before that by custom, no member of the senatorial class could contract a legal marriage with any woman who was, or ever had been, an actress, whereas other Roman citizens were free to do so. Soldiers in the legions, unlike their officers, were not allowed to marry during their period of service, which was twenty years under Augustus and was raised to twenty-five later on. The reasons for this law were rather complicated, the consequences even more so (until the law was finally repealed in A.D. 197). Soldiers, of course, went on marrying and raising families all the time, and their tombstones are as full of references to loving wives and children as those of any other class. Nor, obviously, could they have acted in this way clandestinely. The law and its agents were not so stupid as not to know what was going on. They merely insisted on the formal unlawfulness of the relationship, and then proceeded to make and constantly to revise regulations for the inevitable confusion: confusion about inheritance, about the status of the children, about the rights of all the parties involved following honourable discharge.

Soldiers apart, we know very little about how these matters worked for the lower classes of Roman society. They were all subject to the same set of laws, but law codes are never automatic guides to the actual behaviour of a society, and neither poets nor historians nor philosophers often concerned themselves in a concrete and reliable way with the poorer peasantry or with the tens of thousands crowded together in the urban rabbit warrens which the Romans called *insulae*. Obviously among these people dowries, property settlements, family alliances for political purposes, and the like did not really enter the picture, either in the establishment of a marriage or in its dissolution. Neither could they so lightly dispense with a wife's labour service, whether on the farm or in a market stall, an inn, or a workshop. It was one thing to "work in wool," as did the Claudia whose epitaph I quoted earlier; it was something quite different to work in wool in earnest.

It would probably be a safe guess that women of the lower classes were therefore more "emancipated," more equal *de facto* if not in strict law, more widely accepted as persons in their own right than their richer, more bourgeois, or more aristocratic sisters. This is a common enough phenomenon everywhere. No doubt they were freer in all senses—far less inhibited by legal definitions of marriage or legitimacy, less bound by the double standard of sexual morality. For one thing, the rapid development of large-scale slavery after the wars with Hannibal and the Carthaginians, combined with the frequent practice of manumitting slaves, meant that a large proportion of the free population, even of the citizen class, was increasingly drawn from ex-slaves and the children of slaves. This alone—and specifically their experience, as females, while they were slaves—would have been enough to give them, and their men, a somewhat different attitude towards the accepted, traditional, upper-class values. Add economic necessity, slum conditions, the fact that their work was serious and not a pastime, and the rest follows.

In all classes there was one inescapable condition, and that was the high probability of early death. On a rough calculation, of the population of the Roman Empire which succeeded in reaching the age of fifteen (that is, which survived the heavy mortality of infancy and childhood), more than half of the women were dead before forty, and in some classes and areas, even before thirty-five. Women were very much worse off than men in this respect, partly because of the perils of childbirth, partly, in the lower classes, because of the risk of sheer exhaustion. Thus, in one family tomb in regular use in the second and third centuries, sixty-eight wives were buried by their husbands and only forty-one husbands by their wives. A consequence, intensified by the ease of divorce, was the frequency of second and third marriages for both sexes, especially among men. This in turn complicated both personal and family relationships, economically as well as psychologically, and the prospect, even before the event, must have introduced a considerable element of tension in many women. Many, too, must have been sexually frustrated and unsatisfied.

None of this necessarily implies that women did not passively accept their position, at least on the surface. It would be a bad mistake to read our own notions and values into the picture, or even those of a century or two ago. The women of French provincial society portrayed by Balzac seem to have been more suppressed and beaten down than their Roman counterparts. The latter at least found their men much more open-handed with money and luxuries, and they shared in a fairly active dinner-party kind of social life and in the massive public entertainments. The evidence suggests that Balzac's women somehow made their peace with the world, even if often an unhappy and tragic peace, and presumably so did the women of Rome. We are told by Roman writers of the educated conversation of women in mixed company. Ovid in *The Art of Love* urged even his kind of woman not only to dress and primp properly, to sweeten her breath, to learn to walk gracefully and dance well, but also to cultivate the best Greek and Latin poetry. It is a pity we cannot eavesdrop on some of these conversations, but there is no Roman

Balzac or Stendhal, no Jane Austen or Thackeray or Hardy, to give us the opportunity.

This brings us back to the silence of the women of Rome, which in one way speaks loudly, if curiously. Where were the rebels among the women, real or fictitious—the George Sand or Harriet Beecher Stowe, the Hester Prynne or Tess of the D'Urbervilles? How, in other words, did "respectable" women of breeding, education and leisure find outlets for their repressed energies and talents? The answers seem to lie within a very restricted range of activities. One was religion. It is a commonplace in our own civilization that, at least in Latin countries, women are much more occupied with their religion than are men. But it would be wrong to generalize too quickly: the same has not been true for most of Jewish history nor for most of antiquity. Much depends on the content and orientation of doctrine and ritual. Traditional Roman religion was centered on the household (the hearth and the ancestors) and on the state cults, and the male played the predominant part in both—as *paterfamilias* and as citizen, respectively—notwithstanding that the hearth was protected by a goddess, Vesta, and not by a god. To be sure, the public hearth, with its sacred fire which must never be allowed to go out, was in the charge of six women, the Vestal Virgins. Other rituals were reserved for women, too, such as the cult of *Bona Dea*, the "good goddess," or such exceptional ones as the formal reception at the harbour, towards the end of the war with Hannibal, of the statue of *Mater Idaea* brought from Asia Minor in response to a Sibylline prophecy which guaranteed victory if that were done. However, the procession was led by a man, "the noblest in the state," as required by the same prophecy. And the Vestal Virgins were subject to the authority of a man, the Pontifex Maximus.

For most of Roman history, then, to the end of the Republic in fact, women were not very prominent even in religion. The change came under the Empire and with the great influx into the Roman world of various eastern mystery cults, carrying their new element of personal communion and salvation. Some of these cults—notably that of Mithras, the soldier's god *par excellence*—were closed to women. Others, however, offered them hope, ultimate release, and immediate status unlike anything they had experienced before—above all, the worship of the Hellenized Egyptian goddess Isis. She became (to men as well as women) Isis of the Myriad Names, Lady of All, Queen of the Inhabited World, Star of the Sea, identifiable with nearly every goddess of the known world. "You gave women equal power with men," says one of her hymns. In another she herself speaks: "I am she whom women call goddess. I ordained that women shall be loved by men; I brought wife and husband together, and invented the marriage-contract."

It was no wonder, therefore, that of all the pagan cults Isis-worship was the most tenacious in its resistance when Christianity ascended to a position first of dominance in the Roman world and then of near monopoly. Christianity itself was soon in some difficulty over the question of women. On the one hand, there was the unmistakably elevated, and for the time untypical, position of women in the life of Christ, and in many of the early Christian communities. Women of all classes were drawn to the new creed. There were women martyrs, too. But on the other hand, there was the view expressed in, for example, I Corinthians 14: "Let your women keep silence in the churches: for it is not permitted unto them to speak; but they are commanded to be under obedience as also saith the law." Women were not allowed to forget that Eve was created from Adam's rib, and not the other way round. Neither in this respect nor in any other did the early church seek to bring about a social revolution. Both the ritual of the church and its administration remained firmly in the hands of men, as did the care of souls, and this included the souls of the women.

Where Christianity differed most radically from many (though not all) of the other mystery religions of the time was in its extension of the central idea of purification and purity beyond chastity to celibacy. For many women this attitude offered release through sublimation. That the traditional pagan world failed to understand, or even to believe, this was possible is comprehensible enough. The Roman aristocracy had long been suspicious of the various new cults. A great wave of orgiastic Dionysiac religion had spread in Italy after the wars with Hannibal, soon to be suppressed by the Senate in 186 B.C. Even Isis-worship had a long struggle with the state before achieving official recognition. Anyone who reads the hymns or the detailed accounts of the cult in Apuleius or Plutarch may well find that hard to understand, but the fact is that Isis, though she attracted all classes, was particularly popular in the *demi-monde*.

Sublimation through religion was not the only outlet for pent-up female energies and female rebelliousness. There was another in quite the opposite direction. In the amphitheatres, among the spectators, the women achieved equality with the men: they relished the horrible brutality of the gladiatorial shows (and of the martyrdoms) with the same fierce joy. Gladiators became the pin-ups for Roman women, especially in the upper classes. And at the very top, the women became, metaphorically, gladiators themselves. The women of the Roman emperors were not all monsters, but enough of them throughout the first century of our era, and again from the latter part of the second century on, revealed a ferocity and sadism in the backstairs struggles for power that were not often surpassed—though they were perhaps matched in the contemporary court of the Idumaean dynasty founded by Herod the Great in Judaea. They were not struggling for the throne for themselves—that was unthinkable—but for their sons, brothers and lovers. Their energy and, in a curious sense, their ability are beyond argument. The outlets they found and the goals they sought are, equally, beyond all human dignity, decency, or compassion.

Obviously Roman women are not to be judged by their worst representatives. On the other hand, there must be something significant, even though twisted, in that small group of ferocious and licentious royal females. Under the prevailing value-system, women were expected to be content with vicarious satisfactions. It was their role to be happy in the happiness and success of their men, and of the state for which they bore and nurtured the next generation of men. "She loved her husband. . . . She bore two sons. . . . She kept the house and worked in wool." That was the highest praise, not only in Rome but in much of human history. What went on behind the accepted façade, what Claudia thought or said to herself, we can never know. But when the silence breaks, the sounds which come forth—in the royal family at least—are not very pretty. Most of the Claudias no doubt fully accepted and even defended the values fixed by their men; they knew no other world. The revealing point is that the occasional rebellion took the forms it did.

The Appeal and Practice
of the Mystery Religions

SAMUEL ANGUS

The Spread of Christianity

A. H. M. JONES

Native Roman religion was family oriented, and the civic religion, as it developed, continued to rely heavily on the *gentes*, or clans. It was a practical and patriotic religion devoted to appeasing the gods who controlled the harvest, war, and civic affairs. Religious leadership was vested in a college of priests drawn from the best families and headed by the *pontifex maximus*, or high priest. With the expansion of Rome's power, the priesthood gained political influence because of its control over the religious calendar. Public business could not be conducted on holidays, and the constant necessity of adjusting the imperfect Roman calendar gave the priesthood considerable power over the timing of public action. If a crucial vote on public policy was about to be taken, for example, the priests could impose a long cooling-off period by adjusting the calendar.

Notwithstanding this power, the priesthood remained remarkably independent during the difficult years of the late Republic and the period following the assassination of Julius Caesar. Caesar did not appropriate the position of *pontifex maximus* when he became *dictator*, and Augustus, his successor, did not take the title until 13 B.C., when the holder of the office died. After that date, however, the title and power of the *pontifex* was held by the emperor, and this continued to be true even after Constantine embraced Christianity.

As the political power of the old Roman priesthood increased, the hold of the old religion over the Roman populace decreased. As the city became the center of power and commerce in an ever-widening empire, leading Romans began to show contempt for the superstitions of the old cults. After the establishment of Roman hegemony over Greece in 196 B.C., the influence of eastern religions permanently altered Rome's religious culture. Greek slaves and traders carried to Rome cults that had come to Greece from Thrace and Phrygia. These were the mysteries, cults through which men and women were initiated into a communal, mystical religious experience. As the old social associations broke down or atrophied in the altered circumstances of Roman imperial life, the new cults filled the need for community, order, and hope.

The great influx of mystery cults coincided with the early decades of the Principate founded by Augustus. After the civil wars that followed Julius Caesar's assassination and led to the annexation of Egypt and the eastern provinces, the religions of these areas gravitated toward the new center of world power in Rome and thence spread through the empire along the trade routes. Augustus and Tiberius themselves were religiously conservative, bent on restoring the ancient glory and customs of Rome. Yet even they favored the mystery cult of the Great Mother, and their successors increasingly favored or at least condoned the establishment of the other mysteries. Two of Rome's most ancient and famous churches, San Clemente and Santa Maria in Trastevere, were built over the ruins of Roman houses in which there had been Mithraic shrines. There were thousands of such sanctuaries throughout the city and the empire.

This was the religious milieu in which the Apostles and their disciples began to preach Christianity. In fact, early Christianity resembled the mystery cults in its organization. Christian churches were like cells made up of relatively few members each and organized under the Roman laws governing private associations. Though the number of Christians grew, they did not gather together in one large community, but continued to meet in small groups. The persecutions that began in earnest during the third century drove these communities underground and made them seem even more mysterious than before. Hostile outsiders suspected Christians of crude antisocial activities, and the secrecy of the communities only enhanced this image. Similar criticism was leveled at other mystery cults; for many Romans, all of them were subversive and perhaps even savage.

We know very little about early Christian communities and even less about the mystery cults. In fact, most of our information about the mysteries comes from Christian apologists who distorted the character and appeal of the rival cults. What was that appeal? What did the cultists do? Why did the cults, Christianity included, attract so many adherents among the Roman population, and why did Christianity win out over the others? In the first selection in this section, Samuel Angus elaborates on the attractions, demands, and practices of the mysteries. He uses pagan literary references and archeology to counter the effect of the biased accounts left by Christian writers. In the second selection, A. H. M. Jones considers the success of Christianity. The Judaean religion possessed some advantages over the other cults. Jones finds these advantages at the base of Christian success.

THE APPEAL AND PRACTICE OF THE MYSTERY RELIGIONS

A Mystery-Religion was a personal religion to which membership was open not by the accident of birth but by a religious rebirth. The hereditary principle of membership known to the state-religions of Greece and Rome

From Samuel Angus, *The Mystery Religions and Christianity* (London: John Murray, 1925), pp. 65–67, 87–90, 144–48. Reprinted by permission of John Murray (Publishers) Ltd.

and to the church-state of Israel was superseded by that of personal volition which has been the dominating principle in religious history since the days of Alexander the Great. The religion of the *thiasos* had replaced that of the *polis*. Consequently the Mysteries, with their pronounced subjectivity and variety of impression, responded to and augmented the individualism inaugurated in the Mediterranean world by Alexander and consummated by the Roman Empire.

That religion is primarily a personal matter is a commonplace to us; it was an epoch-making discovery to the leading peoples of the Roman Empire. So strong was the racial consciousness of the Jews that they for the most part conceived God's dealings with them as moving within the Covenant. Individualism was at any time but a passing phase in their religious experience. It is true that Jeremiah and Ezekiel rescued the individual, and that Ezekiel carried individualism to such an extent as to overlook the effects of heredity and the constitution of society by which we are members the one of the other. It was in the services of the Synagogue that the personal religion and piety of Israel attained fullest expression. The religions of Greece and Rome were corporate entities—the religious experience of their social and political systems. Men worshipped for the good of all collectively rather than for the good of their own souls. These religions, like every religion that allies itself with temporal power, collapsed with the state systems which they had buttressed. In the ensuing confusion and amid the welter of centuries of strife personal needs became more clamant. These needs were at least partially satisfied by the Mysteries, which contemplated man irrespective of the polity or social conditions under which he lived. "With them," says Cumont, "religion ceases to be bound to the State in order to become universal; it is no longer conceived as a public duty, but as a personal obligation; it no longer subordinates the individual to the city-state, but professes above all to ensure his personal salvation in this world and above all in the next." To Orphism must be attributed in no small measure this shifting of religious emphasis. Athens, too, took a momentous religious step in the abolition before the sixth century B.C. of gentile privileges in the Eleusinian Mysteries in favour of free choice. Unlike the state religions the Mysteries as personal cults produced saints and ascetics, and martyrs. Livy records how "a multitude" of the members of the Dionysiac brotherhoods lost their lives in an attempt by the Government to extirpate them. Many and severe were the persecutions to which the Isiac faith was subjected about the beginning of the Christian era. The presence of skeletons in the Mithraic chapels testifies to this day to the martyrs who, as devoted *milites Mithrae invicti*, suffered at Christian hands. In the personal cults the worshippers were united by the ties of fellowship with the deity of their choice, by the obligation of common vows, by the duty of personal propaganda, and by revivalistic enthusiasm. The pious could in ecstasy feel himself lifted above his ordinary limitations to behold the beatific vision, or in enthusiasm believe himself to be God-inspired or God-filled—phenomena in some respects akin to the experiences of the early Christians on the outpouring of the Spirit.

One reason why the Mysteries were so long anathema to the rulers of the West was that, as personal religions, they concerned themselves little with public life, centring their attention on the individual life. They accentuated that indifference to citizenship in society at large which was charged against the Jews, and not without some justification against the Christians, and which proved one of the chief factors in the disintegration of ancient civilization. . . .

Both in preparation for initiation and in the practice of the Mysteries obligations of painful self-mortification were laid upon those celebrants who would excel in the cult, or become hierophants, or reap the fullest advantages of adherence. The period was past when men offered the fruit of their bodies for the sin of their souls, but was succeeded by another epoch when men, by personal bodily torture and discomfort, would expiate their sins and placate the deity. The naturalistic origin of the Mysteries, with violent and sanguinary survivals, rendered it too easy to retain repulsive self-mutilations against which the moral consciousness of a humaner era struggled with only partial success. The cruel elements were never wholly eliminated, though some Mysteries took on a more humane aspect than others, notably Orphism and the Hermetic Revelation Religion. Those of Phrygia and the related Anatolian cults were among the bloodiest; next came the Syrian cults, but these were gradually refined by the development of a solar monotheism. That of Isis was the most respectable, while that of Mithra was the most sober. But in each and all it was, by a true religious instinct, perceived that man must enter into fellowship of the deity's sufferings if he would participate in the deity's joy. In studying the cruel side of the Mystery-cults we must remember that the religious thought of the world was struggling with the twofold problem of the relation of the material to the spiritual, with but dim rays of that light which Christian idealism has shed upon the enigma, and of the means whereby man can most securely enter into union with God. In an era of religious excitation no price was too high to pay to attain quietude of heart. The worst forms of self-mortification were generally performed by, but by no means restricted to, the priesthood.

The religious self-mutilations were of Oriental provenance. The most familiar are those of the Galli of the Great Mother (contemptuously called *semi viri* by Juvenal and *Gallae* by Catullus), which consisted in the laceration of their flesh with broken pottery, gashing of their limbs with knives during delirious dances and processions, self-flagellations or mutual floggings, and finally the perpetration of the culminating act of self-effacement in imitation of the act of their patron Attis under the pine-tree. The male sevitors of the Ephesian Artemis were eunuchs, as were also the priests of Atargatis, the *dea Syria*. The rites of Bellona, identified with Ma, Isis, and Cybele, were equally bloody with those of the Great Mother. Her black-robed *fanatici* made offerings of their own blood and slashed their bodies while raving ecstatically with a sword in each hand. Blood drawn from the lacerated thighs of the priests and partaken of by the candidates was the seal of initiation.

The probation for entry into the Mithraic communion was more prolonged and the degrees of preparation more numerous and exacting than for other cults, though not so orgiastic as those of Anatolia. The number, however, and nature of the Mithraic grades are somewhat uncertain, perhaps owing to the disturbance of the original economy—whatever it was—by the introduction of the astral theology of the seven planets and the still later solar theology of the twelve signs of the zodiac. Students of Mithraism usually follow Jerome in affirming the existence of seven grades: *Raven*, *Hidden* or *Secret One* (? *Cryphius*), *Soldier*, *Lion*, *Persian*, *Sun-runner* (*Heliodromus*) and *Father*, of which the *Lion* is the most frequently met and that of *Father* the most coveted. Phythian-Adams contends for the number six as being correct and original. On the other hand, Celsus would indicate perhaps eight grades when he states that in the Persian Mysteries there is a ladder with seven gates with an eighth gate at the top. The first three stages, according to Porphyry, preceded initiation, so that the subsequent grades marked degrees of spiritual rank after initiation. Either the communicant himself or the officiating priest or those present, were obliged to wear masks corresponding to the *Raven* and *Lion*, and a garb corresponding to the other characters. By the strictest kind of freemasonry the initiate was tested at each stage, and his spiritual career was marked by ordeals, feigned or real, and by an austere discipline which demonstrated his courage, sincerity, and faith. He submitted to a baptism of total immersion. He was called upon to pass through flame with hands bound and eyes blindfolded, or to swim rivers. In some cases at least the neophyte jumped down a precipice: whether this was done in symbol merely or was an actual leap we cannot tell. If an actual jump it must have taken place outside the Mithraic chapels, which were too small to permit of such a gymnastic feat. A Heddernheim relief represents a neophyte standing in snow. Animal sacrifices, mostly of birds, were made in the chapels. At some stage the neophyte was obliged to witness or even to take part in a "simulated death to produce reverence." A case is recorded in which the emperor Commodus, on initiation, polluted the chapel by perpetrating an actual murder upon a celebrant. What was the nature of this symbolic death we may not be certain, though theologically it was perhaps viewed as vicarious rather than sacrificial, as we may infer from the evidence of the practice of animal sacrifices. Suggestive symbolic ceremonies were enacted at each stage of initation. Tertullian records that the neophyte, on attaining the degree of "Soldier," was offered, at the point of a sword, a crown or garland, which was then put upon his head only to be thrust away with the confession "Mithra is my crown." Such a soldier was "signed" on the forehead with a hot iron. Thenceforth he renounced the social custom of wearing a garland even at a banquet. According to Porphyry, on entry upon the next degree, that of "Lion," the initiate's lips were purified with honey. . . .

At first sight it seems inexplicable that the Oriental mystic and even orgiastic cults, so humble and barbarous in their origin, frowned upon on their first entry by the governments, winning the majority of their followers from the lower, slave and artisan, classes, supported for centuries by private contributions, often exacting austerities and maintaining customs which exposed the votary to the derision of the crowd, and even endangered his health, should have exercised such an increasing sway over the Graeco-Roman world, and, but for Christianity, would have conquered. They did not afford the only religious refuge of the age: why did they afford a refuge to so many? There were intellectual systems like Greek philosophy, and Gnosticism; there were ethical forces like Judaism, while state-religion asserted itself in repeated pagan revivals and most conspicuously in the imperial cult. These entailed practically no outlay on the part of their adherents. But the mystery-cults demanded that self-sacrifice which has always distinguished Free Churches as contrasted with Established Churches or philosophic schools. Reflect on what it cost to be a regular adherent of the Isiac cult. There were the austerities and fasts, which could not be agreeable to the flesh. Festal white robes had to be procured in honour of the deity, and would regularly demand the fuller's services. The well-equipped Isaea had to be erected and the cost of maintenance met by those who used them. An elaborate and expensive priesthood had to be maintained by the offerings of the faithful. On an ostracon in the Berlin Museum, bearing date August 4, A.D. 63, a priest of Isis gives a receipt to a working man thus: "I have received from you four drachmae, one obol, as collection of Isis for the public worship." Devotion to the Egyptian Madonna resulted in costly statues adorned with abundance of precious stones. Even the inventory of the articles in one small shrine of Isis proves amazing liberality. An inscription from Delos of about 200 B.C. tells how Serapis in a dream-oracle objects to the continuance of his cult in hired premises and demands the building of a temple. Although Apuleius was the son of a rich municipal official, from whom he and his brother inherited the large fortune of two million sesterces, he was obliged to sell his scanty wardrobe to procure funds sufficient for initiation into the rites of Osiris after having been admitted to those of Isis. The frescoes of Herculaneum give some idea of the sacerdotal college attached to any regular Isaeum. There were the senior or high priest and assistant priests and acolytes. These *sacerdotes*, unlike the semi-civic priests of Greece and Rome, devoted all their time to their ecclesiastical offices, and did not generally earn their living by practising a craft or speculating in a business. The altar fires had to be supplied and tended, and the morning sacrifices to be provided. In the statutes of the Iobacchoi of Athens are regulations as to the contributions of each member and the penalty for default of payment. The museum of Thebes contains an inscription detailing the offerings to the Kabiri for one season (cir. 332 B.C.). In special cases long pilgrimages were made, which entailed absence from the ordinary means of earning a livelihood, in addition to costly fares paid to greedy ship-masters, and the still more costly land travelling. Moreover, some eager souls in pursuit of salvation sought initiation into several Mysteries, though how the cost was met by any but the rich is difficult for us to conjecture, for men had to earn their bread then as now. The prosperous Syrian merchant, the Jewish banker, the Roman landlord, the successful Greek physician, the speculating freedman could afford to indulge in any expenditure for religion; but these upper classes constituted a smaller minority then than nowadays. Of course there was much voluntary service given by slaves, artisans, and soldiers; but all this was rendered outside the long hours of toil, and is itself a testimony to the deep conviction on the part of candidates that there was something worth while in the Mysteries. It is true that in the religious guilds the rich members laudably realized their brotherhood with their poorer "brethren," and often bore the whole or the chief part of the expenses incurred in the maintenance of the cult and in furnishing the sacred meals. In the regular offerings the poor contributed their mite, and they that were rich brought much. Unselfishness and generosity were by no means unknown virtues among the pagans, and were not invariably conspicuous in Christian guilds, as we may infer from Paul's description of the abuses in connexion with the *Agape* in Corinth.

The *taurobolium* cannot have been other than costly. The officiating priest's stipend had to be paid, the labour supplied, the timber prepared for the trench, the bull, doubtless of exceptional quality, had to be purchased; the sacramental garments, saturated in blood, were either fulled or kept as souvenirs of the baptismal rebirth, and so rendered economically valueless.

Some idea of the demands made upon the generosity of votaries in the construction and upkeep of the Mithraea may be gathered from the fact that the second largest Mithraeum discovered, that of Sarmizegethusa, had accommodation for a maximum of 100 members, while the majority of the chapels could not accommodate a half of this number. Upon this limited *sodalicium* fell the cost of the excavation of the grotto, the arching of the roof, the chiselling of stone benches for the worshippers, the altar with its sacrifices, the carving of the Tauroctony and the Mithraic *agape*, the sacred meals and initiations, the holy lights, and all the other cult apparatus. The "brethren" were generally legionaries whose *stipendium* was small, or oriental slaves whose *peculium* was modest indeed.

Enough has been said to make it clear that votaries in the Mysteries were not—generally speaking—prompted to seek initiation with a view to material gain, or to find a cheap religion, or to escape tithes. Indeed, these ancient initiates had recourse to religions which were costly because those religions which were provided free failed to lay hold of their imagination or satisfy their religious cravings.

As the Mysteries themselves presented a good and a bad side, so there were among their adherents and priests good, bad, and indifferent. Human nature being what it is, some initiates lived in the high latitudes of spiritual exaltation, enjoying religious serenity, while others remained content with the external pomp and symbolism, only vaguely intelligible to them, and never surmounted a superstition which saw in religion a magic or means of compulsion to be applied to the deity for selfish ends. Doubtless entrance into the Mysteries was sought from base motives by some. For the ordinary members initiation entailed financial loss rather than gain, but unscrupulous priests had abundant opportunity of using their holy office for self-aggrandizement. The sordid transaction of the senior priest of Isis, as told by Josephus, though an extreme case, is hardly solitary. The zeal of highly organized priesthoods, like that of Isis, for donations and endowments probably corresponded to a similar zeal on the part of the abbots and friars of the Middle Ages, such as is exposed, e.g. in Scott's *Fair Maid of Perth*. It is quite clear from Apuleius' account of the repeated initiations of Lucius that the Egyptian priests at Cenchreae and Rome took advantage of his credulity to enrich their cult and so benefit themselves. The initiatory fee was fixed by the goddess herself. A list of things required was furnished by the priest, which Lucius provided with even greater liberality than was necessary. At his initiation he was clad in "the cloak of Olympus," very richly embroidered, in which he was presented to his fellow-worshippers, after which followed feasts and banqueting, for which doubtless Lucius himself had paid in hard cash. A year later the goddess's grasping priests advised a further initiation into the rites of Osiris, for which it was necessary to sell his clothes to procure the necessary fees, and shortly thereafter the goddess required a third initiation, in the preparation for which he was "guided by the enthusiasm of my faith rather than the measure of my fortunes," relying on his earnings as a professor of rhetoric at Rome. The priesthood might be sought because of the secured income attached to its functions, because of the powerful influence wielded by it over the initiates, or because of the opportunity for influencing public opinion, or even, in later days, for interfering in politics.

THE SPREAD OF CHRISTIANITY

The third, fourth, fifth and sixth centuries were a profoundly religious age. The lower classes had probably always been religious; now all classes were so without exception—rationalists and free thinkers were practically unknown, and Epicureanism, the materialist school of philosophy, had virtually

From pp. 320–25 of *The Decline of the Ancient World* by A. H. M. Jones. Copyright ©
1966 by A. H. M. Jones. Reprinted by permission of Holt, Rinehart and Winston, Inc.,
and Longmans, Green and Co. Ltd.

died out. Everyone believed that there were supernatural powers, who would be angered by neglect of their worship, by moral offences and, in the case of Christians, by wrong beliefs about their nature, and who on the other hand could be placated by certain rites and would be pleased by good moral behaviour.

The interest of the higher powers extended both to the individual and to the community. It was problematical how far individuals could expect the divine favour in return for due respect to God or the gods, but they hoped that special petitions would be granted, and most if not all anticipated bliss or punishment beyond the grave according to whether they had pleased the heavenly powers or no. It was universally believed that the prosperity of the state depended on a right relation with God or the gods. It was for this reason that pagan emperors persecuted the Christians, who were in their view contumacious atheists, who neglected and insulted the gods, and thereby provoked them to send plagues and famines and barbarian invaders to punish the empire. Diocletian, in a law redolent with religious feeling, imposed heavy penalties on incest, because it gravely offended the immortal gods, who had hitherto always favoured Rome. Constantine expressed the fear that the quarrels of the African church might move the Highest Divinity to wrath against the human race and the emperor himself. The pagans regarded the sack of Rome in 410 as clear evidence that the gods were offended by the imperial ban on their worship twenty years before. Justinian regarded the reconquest of Africa and Italy as God's reward for his suppression of heresy and, on the ground that the purity of life of the clergy "brings great favour and increase to our commonwealth, whereby it is granted to us to subdue the barbarians," forbade clerics to play dice or go to the theatre or the races.

The age was also superstitious. Throughout antiquity there was a general belief in magic, the inducement by incantations, rites or charms of a desired natural event, such as rain, the death of an enemy or, very commonly, the defeat of a chariot in the races. There was also a general belief in various forms of divination and the pseudo-science of astrology was popular. Maleficent magic, private divination and astrology were all crimes, but commonly practised. The lower classes also believed readily in miracles, but the educated do not seem to have shared this belief; there is a remarkable lack of the miraculous element in the literature of the first three centuries of our era, both pagan and Christian. A change begins with the fourth century. The philosophers Plotinus and Porphyry had been sceptical of miracles; the latter's successor Iamblichus defended them and is reported to have performed them. Henceforth the greatest philosophers were famed for their "theurgy" as it was called, and it was his miracles rather than his doctrines that made Maximus the idol of Julian. In Christian circles similarly there was in the mid-fourth century a great outburst of miracles, and they were accepted and indeed welcomed by the major intellectual figures of the church.

When Constantine was converted in 312 Christians were an insignificant minority in the empire; when Phocas died in 610 pagans were an insignificant minority. Beyond this it is difficult to go statistically, but the advance was probably most rapid in the century following Constantine's conversion. The advance was uneven and patchy. In the early fourth century the great majority of Christians belonged to the urban lower classes, though they included some decurions and even some *honorati*; the peasantry, except in Africa and Egypt, were almost entirely pagan.

As Christianity became not only secure but fashionable and a passport to official advancement, it went up in the social scale, and this movement was assisted by the fact that fair numbers of humble persons, who were already Christians, advanced into the official aristocracy. The educated classes, brought up on pagan literature, found the new faith with its uncouth scriptures rather unpalatable, and adopted it more slowly; the academic profession was particularly resistant and many professors remained pagan down to the sixth century. The high Roman aristocracy, in whose minds the pagan gods were closely linked with the traditions of the Roman state, remained pagan until the early fifth century. The peasantry, innately conservative, clung stubbornly to their old cults, unless they were uprooted from their environment and put into the army, in which case they adopted the official religion, whatever it might be at the time: the army was Christian under Constantius II, pagan under Julian, Christian again under Valentinian and Valens. There were still 80,000 rural pagans for John of Ephesus to convert in 542 in the provinces of Asia, Caria, Lydia and Phrygia, one of the first homelands of Christianity, and at the end of the sixth century Pope Gregory found pagans at Tarracina in Italy, and Tyndaris in Sicily, and in large numbers in Sardinia, where they paid an annual douceur to the provincial governor for his connivance at their cult. In Spain the council of Toledo in 589 declared that "the sacrilege of idolatry is rooted in almost the whole of Gaul and Spain," and the allusion is, as the other documents prove, to peasants who still venerated sacred trees and fountains, and kept Thursday, the day of Jupiter, as their weekly holiday.

There were curious local contrasts. In Africa, which had become predominantly Christian by the end of the third century, the cities of Calama, Madaura and Sufes were still pagan more than a century later. In Mesopotamia, Edessa had been converted in the early third century, but its neighbour Carrhae remained faithful to its old gods even after the Arab conquest. Antioch was already under Julian a Christian city; its neighbour Apamea still defended its temples under Theodosius I. Maiuma, the port of Gaza, petitioned Constantine for a city charter and got it because it was Christian. In Gaza itself the Christian community amounted to 280 persons, men, women and children in 396, and the pagan cult was openly celebrated in all the temples despite Theodosius I's penal laws.

The conversion of the neighbouring peoples was very spasmodic. King Tiridates, restored to the Armenian throne in 298, became a Christian and imposed his religion on his subjects, anticipating the Roman empire in the official adoption of Christianity. In Constantine's reign a Roman woman, carried as a slave to the Iberian kingdom, preached the Christian faith there and thus founded the Georgian church; and Frumentius, a young man from Tyre, shipwrecked on the coast of the Axumite kingdom, was made the king's secretary and converted him, thus founding the Abyssinian church. On the other hand the Nobades and Blemmyes of Nubia enjoyed until Justinian's day the right of worshipping in the temple of Isis at Philae, and many of the Saracen and Moorish tribes on the frontiers of Syria and Africa were still pagan in the sixth century. The Goths were converted in the middle of the fourth century, and passed the brand of Christianity which they had learned, which was unfortunately Arian, to the Vandals, Burgundians and other east German tribes; but the Franks in the west remained pagan until Clovis was converted in 496.

There was practically no organized missionary activity; bishops were usually content to demolish pagan temples. Pagan sacrifice was officially banned by Constantine at the end of his reign, but again tolerated from Julian's accession in 361 until 391, when Theodosius forbade all forms of pagan cult. The law was laxly enforced and had to be repeated in 407 and 415 in the west, and in 423, 435, 451 and 472 in the east; even later Anastasius prohibited bequests for the maintenance of pagan cults. Pagans also suffered increasing disabilities. Honorius and Theodosius II excluded them from governmental posts, Leo from the legal profession, Justinian from academic chairs. In 529 he even ordered all pagans to receive instruction and be baptized on pain of confiscation and exile.

Paganism was not so much a religion as an amalgam of cults of very various kinds, united by mutual tolerance and respect and by syncretism, whereby the local gods were equated with those of the Greek and Roman pantheon. The cults were normally local. Carthage worshipped the Heavenly Goddess (Caelestis), identified with Juno, [and] Ephesus [worshipped] her peculiar many-breasted Artemis; the Syrian towns had their several Baals, usually dubbed Zeus, but sometimes like Marnas of Gaza or Elagabal, the black stone of Emisa, retaining their native names; each Egyptian city had its patron, Hermes (Thoth), Aphrodite (Hathor) and the rest. There were also some gods and goddesses, like Mithras or Isis, who had achieved an international reputation, and were worshipped by congregations all over the empire. They generally promised a blissful future life to their devotees, if they kept certain rules and performed certain rites; the cult of Mithras was particularly objectionable to Christians because it so closely resembled their own, and seemed to be a parody of it. Animal sacrifice was fairly general, but there were many peculiar rites, from the *taurobolium* of the Great Mother, in which the initiate was literally bathed in the blood of a bull, to the ritual prostitution practised at Heliopolis and Apheca in Phoenicia.

Educated pagans were mostly monotheists or pantheists, adoring one god, the ineffable Monad of the Neoplatonists or the Unconquered Sun, and regarding the other gods as subordinates or emanations of the One. They combined a lofty philosophy, normally Neoplatonist, with a deep respect for the pagan myths, which they interpreted allegorically, and for pagan cult practices, which they regarded as divinely enacted symbols of esoteric truths.

Paganism had no theology beyond Neoplatonic philosophy and the amalgam of myths belonging to the various cults, which were very imperfectly synthesized. It possessed a fairly generally accepted moral code, which differed only in emphasis from the Christian code. It had no organization, cults being conducted by cities, villages or private societies. This was felt as a weakness by Maximin and Julian, who appointed high priests, analogous to bishops, in each city, and a high priest of superior rank, analogous to the metropolitan, in each province. Except in Egypt there was no professional clergy, priesthoods being in general held by laymen, sometimes annually, sometimes for life; those of the civic cults were usually elected by the city council.

The strength of paganism was that it was all things to all men. It gave to the peasants rites to promote fertility and ward off pests; to serious men and women, anxious about their welfare beyond the grave, the mystery cults; to intellectuals a profound if rather nebulous philosophy. Its temples and ceremonials had a strong aesthetic appeal. Its myths and ritual were inextricably intertwined with the great literary heritage of Greece and Rome, which was dear to all educated men, and with the glorious traditions of the Roman state.

Paganism was not a heroic religion. Some pagans fought for their temples, but there were few pagan martyrs, and most were content to bribe the authorities to connive at their worship or to carry it on secretly. Nevertheless paganism kept up a tenacious rearguard action against Christianity; pagans still hoped that the old gods would come into their own again not only under Julian (361–63), but under Eugenius (392–94) in the west, and even during the rebellion of Illus in Zeno's reign (484) in the east. On all these occasions the Christians were fearful that the dream of the pagans might come true. Relapses from Christianity to paganism were still sufficiently common in 425 to provoke a renewal of the penal laws against apostates.

The austere monotheism of early Christianity did not long survive the great influx of converts which began in the early fourth century. The memory of holy men of the past, and in particular of martyrs, had always been cherished by Christians, their tombs venerated and the anniversaries of their death commemorated by special services. In the fourth century chapels were built over their tombs and anniversaries became popular festivals. It came to be believed that, having intimate access to God, they could press their devotees' petitions on him, and it was soon popularly believed that they could answer petitions themselves. For all practical purposes they came to be worshipped as minor gods. Their bodies were believed to have magical powers and a vast number of miracles were performed at their tombs.

Genuine martyrs' bodies were far too few to satisfy public demand and usually with the aid of visions, many more were found. Pope Damasus (366–84) discovered many at Rome, Ambrose unearthed two saints, Gervasius and Protasius, at Milan, another pair, Vitalis and Agricola at Bologna, and yet a third pair at Milan. In 415 Lucian, the priest at Caphargamala in Palestine, discovered the bodies of Gamaliel, his son Nicodemus and, most precious of all, the protomartyr Stephen; we possess the circular letter in which Lucian described his discoveries to the churches of the empire, and the body of S. Stephen was soon dissected, and portions of it reached Africa and the Balearic Isles. The bodies of contemporary holy men, especially hermits, were also much sought after, and there were sometimes bitter battles for the corpse.

Christianity
in the Germanic Tribes

E. A. THOMPSON

Christianity came to the Germans in two ways. Even before the major migrations began in the late fourth century, preachers had entered the territories controlled by the tribes and made some headway. By the time the Visigoths, Ostrogoths, and Burgundians crossed the borders of the empire, they were Christian, although they did not follow the orthodox doctrine promulgated by Rome and most of the other great sees. For more than a century there were significant differences and animosity between these German Christians and the orthodox native population. Some of the tribes did not receive Christianity before the invasions and were converted only after they had settled in the old Roman territories. For these groups, conversion was rapid and at least nominally complete, since the king led his people into the Church en masse. The Franks followed their King Clovis into the fold, and the English kings did the same for their peoples. In this section, however, we are interested in the Christianization of tribes like the Visigoths, who were converted little by little and among whom Christians were for a long time isolated.

To understand the position of Christians among the early Germans it is necessary to reconstruct the society of those peoples. The bulk of the sources that purport to present a picture of the early Germans were written long after their primitive tribal life had been permanently altered by contact with the Romanized population of the empire. In spite of this, scholars have constructed elaborate theories about the structure of the early communities of Germans. Some of these theories are monuments to the creative imagination.

The earliest theory, published in 1768, pictured the Germans as free farmers living in communities whose institutions were the prototypes of the liberal, democratic institutions developed in the eighteenth and nineteenth centuries. The members of these communities inhabited *Marks*, territorial units encompassing many homesteads and named for their position on the *marches*, or frontiers, of the Roman Empire. In the yearly assemblies of these *Marks*, the free warrior peasants took care of common affairs and elected their chiefs. Here was the noble savage, and in fact the original presentation of this picture was explicitly influenced by Rousseau's speculations. In the nineteenth century, those who elaborated the theory changed it slightly by making property ownership in the *Marks* communistic rather than private. The free warrior peasant and the democratic political organization remained, however.

In the late nineteenth century, the great French historian Fustel de Coulanges attacked the *Mark* theory, pointing out that there was no evidence to support it. He argued that the word *marca* in the ancient Latin texts simply meant "boundaries," and there was no such thing as a *Mark* or the community that was supposed to occupy it. Fustel's criticism was largely ignored, but it did force proponents of the *Mark* theory to change the name of their creation; a nonexistent *Mark* by any other name exists. Further work on the history of the Germanic communities has shown that their society was aristocratic and that the free warrior peasant did not exist. The elective chieftainries and democratic institutions were also figments.

In this selection, E. A. Thompson demonstrates the method used to reconstruct ancient German society while he analyzes the position of Christians within that society. His source is an example of a common medieval literary genre, the biography of a saint. Saints' lives were a popular type of didactic literature during the Middle Ages, and they quickly became stylized and formularized. Many of the lives were written before the saint was canonized and were in fact products of the effort to get him canonized. Once the requirements for becoming a saint were established, the hagiographers made certain that the demands were met by their man or woman. Even if the work was written after canonization, it had to preserve the image of the saint and thus participated in the same formularized tradition. Thus Thompson has to distinguish between glimpses of the real St. Sabas and his society and those elements of the story determined by the hagiographical tradition. Since many of the stories were written an appreciable time after the events occurred, there is the further problem of dealing with anachronisms and misconceptions introduced into the account.

A complete text of the *Passio S. Sabae* and of certain kindred documents was published by Delehaye more than forty years ago. These works give us priceless information about early Visigothic Christianity and especially, of course, about Sabas himself, who was martyred on 12 April 372. They are also invaluable for the study of the society which produced Ulfila and the Gothic Bible. The *Passio* does what the works of Caesar and Tacitus never do—it brings us for the first time into a Germanic village and enables us to see something of how the villagers managed their own affairs. Yet it has received strangely little attention either from students of Roman history or from students of early Germanic society. . . . Here it is proposed to glance at the *Passio* as a source for the social organization of the Visigoths in the days of Ulfila.

We know from our other sources that the Visigoths, whenever they went to war, elected an over-all military leader who is called in Latin *iudex* and in Greek *dikastes*. But the *iudex* seems to have had as little personal authority as Germanic chiefs had had in the days of Tacitus. He could "advise" and "urge" his followers to accept his point of view, but he could not impose his will upon them: he had no powers of coercion. Power, such as it was, rested with the *optimates*, as Ammianus calls them, or the *megistanes*,

From E. A. Thompson, "The *Passio S. Sabae* and Early Visigothic Society," *Historia*, Vol. 4 (1955), pp. 331–38. Reprinted by permission of Franz Steiner Verlag, Wiesbaden.

as they are termed in the *Passio*. These no doubt formed a sort of Council and (though the point is not directly attested) they may have been the chiefs of the φυλαί of whom Eunapius speaks. For Eunapius tells us that the Visigoths were organized in "tribes" under tribal leaders, and the word φυλαί is no doubt equivalent to the Latin *pagi*. At any rate, there were tribal chiefs, as we may call them, below the general military leader of the people as a whole. But the *Passio*, as we have said, deals in the main with humbler people than the chiefs and the optimates: it is primarily concerned with the village in which Sabas lived, though it is by no means silent about the relations between this village and the central authority.

It depicts a time of persecution when the loyalty of the villagers to the pagan gods is to be put to the test: by order of the megistanes the villagers will be required to eat sacrificial meat in public. How this decision was conveyed to the villagers is unknown. But village affairs are discussed in the first instance by a village council; and this council has determined that the villagers among them who are Christian must be spared in spite of the order of the megistanes: the Christians in their midst shall merely be induced to eat unconsecrated meat rather than sacrificial meat so that a true test may be avoided and the persecutors cheated. This is the plan on which the council has decided, but it must be discussed by all the villagers assembled together before it can be put into practice. Sabas like the other villagers has the right to speak, and he comes forward on two separate occasions and uses his right boldly: he will not submit to any such subterfuge as the council had suggested —he will never deny his Christianity. Accordingly, the plan put forward by the council members has to be modified; and when a representative of the megistanes comes round to the village to see how the test is progressing, the village councillors tell him that in fact there is one Christian among them— Sabas himself.

The whole of this scene described in the third chapter of the *Passio* is a vivid representation of a clan society in action. There is no indication that Sabas' procedure in disagreeing with the council's decision was illegitimate or even unusual. He merely expressed freely an opinion which was unpopular. The scene does not quite prove that the decisions of the villagers had to be unanimous before action could be taken, though this may have been the case. At any rate, there was no machinery for suppressing Sabas' opinion or for preventing him from making his views known to the visiting chief; and still less was there any means of compelling him to change his attitude and to fall in with the opinion of the majority. Nor was Sabas an isolated case. We learn from another source that in addition to Sabas other Christians were given an opportunity of coming forward and speaking bravely on behalf of the faith in their respective villages. A further point is also noteworthy. After his first speech refusing to eat the meat the village council compelled Sabas to leave the village for a while, but shortly afterwards permitted him to come back. Now this does not in itself mean that the freedom of the villagers was disappearing and that a man who expressed an unpopular opinion was liable to be penalized. Sabas, as we shall see, had offended against the gods of the community by refusing to share their meal; and an offence against the gods was an offence against the community itself. Sabas' temporary expulsion was due to this offence—his refusal to take part in the sacrificial meal of the villagers—and not to the unpopularity of his opinions as such or to his being a Christian. The fact that he was a Christian was known to the villagers throughout the proceedings and even before the proceedings began, and was not resented by them. Indeed, when the news reached the village that the persecution had been initiated the first thought of the village councillors was how they could save Sabas. The temporary expulsion, then, was not due to Sabas' Christianity but to his unwillingness even to make a show of joining in the sacrificial meal. To that extent the expulsion was unconnected with the persecution as such.

It is a pity that it was not to the author's purpose to tell us more about the sacrifice and the sacrificial meal, which evidently formed an integral part of Visigothic village life. In a clan society the communal eating and drinking were a symbol and a confirmation of mutual social obligations. The man who refused to eat the sacrificial meat with his fellows thereby dissociated himself from their religion and from their social duties and rights: he had made himself an outcast. That is why the public eating of sacrificial meat was regarded by the megistanes as a test for men suspected of having become Christian. On the other hand, it is noteworthy that when he was first expelled from his village Sabas was soon allowed to return. On the second occasion the villagers might not have expelled him at all if pressure had not been put upon them by the visiting chief; and even then the saint might well have been spared if the village councillors could have shown to the persecutor that Sabas was a man of some property (v. infra). But even so Sabas was not lynched: action was not taken on the spur of the moment without a hearing of the merits of the case. On the contrary, the case was heard, and the action was taken by a man who had some measure of recognized authority. True, Sabas was not put to death by his fellow villagers: the men who killed him came from outside the village. Yet the villagers in the end did nothing to help him, but abandoned him to his fate. He had put himself outside their protection by his refusal to join in their sacrificial feast. Now the presbyter Sansalas, who is also mentioned in the *Passio*, does not seem to have been a Visigoth, for he is thought to bear an Asian name; and he was presumably descended from the Asian prisoners who had been carried off by the Visigoths during their great raids on Asia Minor in the mid-third century. Accordingly, it is of great interest to notice that Sansalas was not requested, so far as we know, to partake of the sacrificial meal, and although he was tortured he was not put to death. His crime was less than that of the Visigothic tribesman Sabas. Sansalas' offence was that he was a Christian, and this in a man of Asian descent was an offence during the period of the persecution but it was not a capital offence. Sabas' crime was that he had offended against the gods of his people, and for this as a Visigoth he became an outcast and was put to death.

To return to the village council: we do not know how this was chosen or who composed it. We might perhaps guess that it consisted of elders who were noted for their long experience of affairs and for their wisdom or for their prowess as warriors or hunters. At any rate, the council's two known functions were, first, that it represented the village in meetings with a member of the confederate council, and, secondly, that it discussed the business of the village before bringing it to the general assembly of the villagers. In this last point it resembles the council which pre-considered the business that was to come before the general assembly of the warriors in the first century A.D. The "national" council, as it were, which Tacitus describes in his *Germania* (xi. 1) is reproduced on a smaller scale by the village council referred to in the *Passio*. Finally, it may be observed that there is no mention of a village chief or headman, and if one had been present at these proceedings the author of the *Passio* could not well have avoided making some mention of him. The unnamed, persecuting "leader" (*archon*) of the *Passio* comes to Sabas' village from outside and knows little or nothing about the villagers. He must be the leader of some larger unit than the village, and I have little doubt that he was one of the "tribal" leaders like those referred to by Eunapius.

What light does the *Passio* throw on these tribal chiefs, as we have called them? If the confederate chief possessed few coercive powers in wartime, it is unlikely that the tribal chiefs occupied a stronger position in times of peace. True, it would be easy to conclude from one or two sentences in the *Passio* that the persecution of the Christians in Sabas' village was initiated by "the persecutor" or "the leader," that is, by an unnamed chieftain. But in fact what the *Passio* shows is that the chiefs were merely responsible for seeing that the persecution was actually enforced. A number of phrases in the *Passio* indicate clearly that the persecution was initiated not by any one ruler or chief but by the confederate council. Indeed, in one passage the author explicitly states that Atharid acted "on the order of the impious ones." The plural should be noted. It unquestionably means the confederate council, the megistanes; and that the ultimate responsibility for the persecution lay with the megistanes is shown again and again by the language of the *Passio*. When the confederate council decided to persecute the Christians, the tribal chiefs went round the villages to see how the council's instructions were being carried out; and when a chief, as representative of the council, came to a village the members of the village council would appear before him and would give him the information which he required. This, at any rate, was the procedure in Sabas' village, and there seems to be no reason why we should not generalize from it. But the tribal chiefs were merely the instruments through which the council acted. In times of peace and indeed for the most part in wartime also even the confederate chief is not known to have had any power over the life, liberty, and property of the tribesmen except in so far as he carried out the decisions of the council. What we should greatly like to have is some information on the part which the village or at any rate the village councillors were allowed to play in the election of a tribal chief. But of this we know nothing. We cannot say whether the humble villagers had any rights at this date when it came to the choosing of a tribal leader.

However that may be, it is certain that the old egalitarian system which Tacitus had described long ago was disappearing among the fourth-century Visigoths. Quantities of property had begun to accumulate in private hands c. 370, and political power was also tending to concentrate in private hands. This is strikingly illustrated in a vivid scene depicted in the *Passio*. When the unnamed tribal chief in the course of the persecution heard that Sabas was an unrepentant Christian, he had him summoned to his presence. He then turned to the members of the village council, who were present, and asked them whether Sabas owned any property. He was told that Sabas owned nothing more than the clothes on his back. Thereupon the chief considered the saint to be of no consequence and said, "Such a man can neither help nor harm us," and ordered him to be driven out of the village. The mere fact that the author of the *Passio* turns aside to record this remark of the chief's would seem to suggest that the words were in his opinion significant and disturbing: in connexion with these words he calls the chief *anomos*—he was no respecter of tribal custom. Clearly, at that date not only had private property associated itself in the chief's mind with social power but the poor man unlike the man of property could "neither help nor harm" the execution of the confederate council's resolutions. There were sharp divisions of wealth in Visigothic society in the days of Ulfila.

In fact, the Christians in Gothia in Ulfila's time seem in general to have been drawn from the humbler strata of society. The descendants of the Roman prisoners taken in the raids on Asia Minor in the third century will scarcely have been of much social influence among the Visigoths. The Christian presbyter and his associates who were used by Fritigern as intermediaries during his negotiations with Valens in 378 are explicitly said to have been humble persons. The Audian bishop Silvanus was presumably the descendant of Roman prisoners. True, he may have been a Visigoth who adopted this Roman name on his conversion; but to believe that is merely to multiply hypotheses, and in fact Epiphanius describes him not as a Goth but as being "from Gothia." It can scarcely be doubted that Ulfila himself, like Selenas after him, was also the offspring of a very humble family in Gothia, and not being a pure-blooded Visigoth he would not have been a member of any clan. His foreign descent would have rigorously excluded him from membership, unless he had been willing to undergo the pagan rites of initiation and adoption, which in a man of Ulfila's uncompromising Arianism can scarcely be considered as a possibility. It is true that three arguments have been put forward to show that Ulfila was a well-to-do and perhaps even noble Visigoth; but these arguments cannot stand. They are (i) that he was free to leave Gothia in 348 when the first persecution took place; but then it would follow that all those who were driven out or who fled in the persecutions were well-to-do, which was not the case; (ii) that he acted as ambassador to Constantius; but the Christian who acted as ambassador to Valens, as we have just seen, is known to have been of humble birth—these Christians were doubtless chosen as envoys because they might as Christians carry more weight with the Romans than barbarian pagans could do; (iii) that Eusebius of Nicomedia would not have made him bishop if his position among his people had not been a distinguished one; but Eusebius' action only suggests that Ulfila's position was distinguished not among the Visigoths as a whole but among the Christians in Gothia—and his distinction was due not to his birth but to his learning. Finally, the one Visigothic Christian about whom detailed information has survived, Sabas, is explicitly stated to have owned no property whatever and to have been therefore of no political account. At all events, nothing in our evidence suggests that the tribal nobility had been seriously affected by Christianity in the decades preceding 372; and indeed the *Passio* gives us positive evidence to the contrary, for it was "the megistanes throughout Gothia" who had decided on the persecution in the first place.

Finally, the *Passio* makes it clear that the confederate council, the megistanes, were able to exert stronger pressure on the villages than the latter, we may suspect, would have submitted to in the days of Tacitus. The fact is that to some extent the persecution of the Christians in 369–72 was imposed on the villages from above, and it was the megistanes who specified the test of the public eating of the sacrificial meat without any consultation, so far as we know, with the rank and file of the Visigoths. Indeed, the council in Sabas' village was reduced to a subterfuge in its effort to avoid carrying out the orders of the megistanes: they proposed to allow Christians to eat unconsecrated meat instead of sacrificial meat "so that they might keep their own men unharmed, and deceive the persecutors." In the second wave of persecution the council was actually willing to declare without ado to the prosecutor that there was no Christian in their village. They were even prepared to make this declaration on oath, a fact which suggests that enthusiasm in the village for the decisions of the megistanes was not always unbounded. But once again the obstinacy of Sabas himself foiled their well-intentioned deceit; and they admitted with some reluctance that in fact there was one Christian among them. Thereupon the chief, who had come to the village to see how the persecution was progressing, "ordered" Sabas to be driven out of the village. On the first occasion on which Sabas was expelled it was the village council who had ordered him to go. But on the occasion of the second expulsion the village council appears to have been given no voice in the matter: they simply received instructions from the tribal chief to drive Sabas out. In the final wave of persecution the henchmen of the tribal chief Atharid were able to beat and torture Sabas without any consultation with the rest of the villagers and without bringing any charge against him, though it may be significant that Sabas suffered thus when not actually present in his own village.

Clearly, political power has to some extent become concentrated in the hands of the optimates, and the village council is no longer in a position to assert its rights boldly on every issue that affects it. But individual Visigoths were not afraid to disobey outright the most stringent orders of the tribal chief who represented the megistanes. At one stage in the torturing of Sabas the saint was tied hand and foot to two axles of a cart, and was thrown on his back on the ground to spend the night in this predicament. But when his guards fell asleep an old woman, who had stayed up all night to prepare meat for the members of her household, took pity on him and set him free. Had she not been willing to defy the confederate council the saint might well have finished his career there and then. Again, when his executioners had brought Sabas to the river Musaeus (Buzău) where they were to drown him they at first proposed to set him free: Atharid, they thought, would know nothing of it. And it was only when Sabas himself insisted that they should carry out their orders that they plunged him into the water. Finally, the whole course of events in Sabas' village shows that feelings for one's neighbour—or perhaps we should say kinsman—were stronger than respect for the orders of the optimates.

It is a curious picture. The persecution was enforced by the megistanes, whose reasons for doing so will be examined elsewhere. But the Visigoths at large, it seems, did not care very much whether one of their number ate the sacrificial meat or not—if he were willing to eat any meat, that would suffice. When no persecution was on foot Christian and pagan seem to have lived on friendly terms within the one village; and in times of persecution, if we may generalize from the behaviour of Sabas' fellow villagers, regard for one's neighbour was stronger than differences of religion among the rank and file of the Visigoths. Is it a coincidence that this picture of Visigothic life dates from the very eve of the general conversion of the people to Christianity? At any rate, the brotherly and sisterly intimacy of the Christians in Gothia is reflected in the diminutive names by which they addressed one another. As a German scholar has put it, the names of practically all the martyrs, in so far as they are Germanic, are "Kurznamen, Kosenamen, Beinamen, oder Spitznamen." But no "Kosenamen" are applied to chiefs like Winguric or Atharid or even the Christian Arimerius, who is known from a somewhat later period. The simplicity of these lowly Christians and their earnest truthfulness are reflected in the one document that they have left us, the *Passio*, which is in fact a letter from the Church in Gothia to the Church in Cappadocia. It is not the work of a Goth but of a Roman living in very close contact with the barbarians; and although it was scarcely written by the presbyter Sansalas himself, it may well be based on information supplied by him, for he had friends in the Roman Empire, had fled there when the persecution was at its height, and may well have returned there after Sabas' death to await the end of the storm. The vividness and innocence of the *Passio* reveal a community in which fanaticism was confined to the powerful, and humanity to the humble. Delehaye has justly described it as one of the pearls of ancient hagiography.

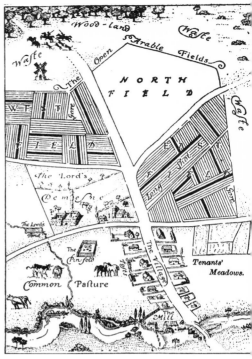

PART 2

The Early Middle Ages, 6th–11th Centuries

In the sixth century, the western Roman Empire fell to the Germans and was replaced by kingdoms based on the peoples making up the major elements of the migrating hordes of barbarians. In Gaul, it was the Franks; in Spain, the Visigoths; in Italy, the Ostrogoths; in North Africa, the Vandals. The migrations profoundly altered the social life both of the Germans and of the old Roman provincial population. Under the pressures of movement and war, the small, autonomous German communities were merged under powerful kings. After the kingdoms were established, these kings consolidated their positions by assuming the mantle of Roman authority. Everywhere in Europe, the German kings sought and received confirmation of their new power from the Roman emperors in Constantinople. For their part, the emperors had nothing to lose by granting the kings Roman titles. It preserved the image of imperial power even though the reality had been gone for decades, and it helped to maintain good relations between East and West.

The first two selections in this section concern the transformation of European society after the invasions. The excerpt from *Njál's Saga* describes the primitive Germanic communities as they existed in Iceland, where the old social patterns persisted long after they had disappeared on the Continent. In the second selection, Lynn White discusses the amalgamation of German and Roman social institutions under the feudal system. Did the growth of this system result from the mixture of the two peoples and a natural amalgamation of their social institutions? Or was the mix catalyzed by unrelated changes, such as the introduction of new technology? The selection focuses on these questions.

The next two selections deal with elements of the European population during the early Middle Ages. Irving Agus concentrates on the Jewish minority—the only minority in medieval Europe that made an impression on the society at large. In Lynn White's "The Life of the Silent Majority," it is the peasantry that holds the attention. In both selections the aim is to right some old misconceptions about the life of these important components of medieval society. The final selection reveals the circumstances in which the majority and the Jewish minority collided, with the resultant slaughter of the Jews. The First Crusade was the impetus for a fervent religious movement among the poor that led to the first major attack on the Jews in European history. Each succeeding crusade created similar movements and kept the Jews of northern Europe under constant pressure. The modern legacy of fear and suspicion among the Jews of Europe can be traced back to the crusading movement of the Middle Ages.

Bibliography

For histories of the barbarian invasions and of the Germanic kingdoms that succeeded to the power of Rome, see J. B. Bury, *The Invasion of Europe by the Barbarians* (London, 1928); J. M. Wallace-Hadrill, *The Barbarian West* (London, 1952); and Eleanor Shipley Duckett, *Gateway to the Middle Ages* (New York, 1938). E. A. Thompson has put his studies of Germanic society into book form in *The Early Germans* (Oxford, 1965). For contrast, see Samuel Dill, *Roman Society in Gaul in the Merovingian Age* (London, 1926). There is an interesting article about the nature of the feud in Max Gluckman, "The Peace in the Feud," *Past and Present*, Vol. 8 (1955), pp. 1–14.

(Note: the bibliographical suggestions in this paragraph also touch on the subject of H. J. Hewitt, "Feudal War in Practice," in Part 4 of this volume.) On the precursors of the medieval feudal army, see G. R. Watson, *The Roman Soldier* (London, 1969), and E. A. Thompson, "Early Germanic Warfare," *Past and Present*, Vol. 14 (1958), pp. 2–29. For surveys of feudalism as a social and economic system—and for discussions of the origins of the system—see Carl Stephenson, *Feudalism* (Ithaca, N.Y., 1940), and F. L. Ganshof, *Feudalism* (New York, 1961). The classic study of the system is Marc Bloch's, *Feudal Society* (Chicago, 1961). Lynn White's thesis has been criticized and discussed in many reviews of his work; see, for example, the critiques of R. H. Hilton and P. H. Sawyer in "Technical Determinism: The Stirrup and the Plow," *Past and Present*, Vol. 24 (1963), pp. 90–100.

Irving Agus' two-volume *Urban Civilization in Pre-Crusade Europe* (New York, 1965), from which "Jews in a Christian Society" is taken, contains a wealth of fascinating material, but see also Guido Kisch, *The Jews in Medieval Germany* (Cambridge, Eng., 1950); Cecil Roth, "The Jews in the Middle Ages," in *Cambridge Medieval History*, Vol. 7 (Cambridge, Eng., 1932); J. W. Parkes, *The Jew in the Medieval Community* (London, 1938); and J. Trachtenberg, *The Devil and the Jews: The Medieval Conception of the Jew and Its Relation to Modern Anti-Semitism* (New Haven, 1944). Norman Cohn's book on millenarianism, *The Pursuit of the Millennium* (Oxford, 1970), from which "The Poor in the First Crusade" is taken, is also relevant.

Most studies of rural life focus on the late thirteenth century and afterward because it is only in that period that adequate historical documentation began to be preserved. For a sociological approach, see George C. Homans, *English Villagers of the Thirteenth Century* (Cambridge, Mass., 1941); J. A. Raftis, *Tenure and Mobility: Studies in the Social History of the Medieval Village* (Toronto, 1964); R. H. Hilton, *A Medieval Society: The West Midlands at the End of the Thirteenth Century* (London, 1966); and Georges Duby, *Rural Economy and Country Life in the Medieval West*, trans. by C. Postan (London, 1968). All these works build on the studies of Homans and of Marc Bloch. For a good general survey of the field, see M. Postan, ed., *Cambridge Economic History*, 2nd ed., Vol. 1: *The Agrarian Life of the Middle Ages* (Cambridge, Eng., 1966). The Cambridge histories are collections of articles by leading scholars, and they have excellent bibliographies.

There are many books on the crusades. A good general history is Steven Runciman, *A History of the Crusades*, 3 vols. (Cambridge, Eng., 1951–54). See also the studies presented in Kenneth Setton and Marshall W. Baldwin, eds., *A History of the Crusades*, Vol. 1: *The First Hundred Years* (Philadelphia, 1955). There is further material on the Tafurs in L. A. M. Sumberg, "The *Tafurs* and the First Crusade," *Mediaeval Studies*, Vol. 21 (1959), pp. 224–46. For a short study of a movement similar to the one described in Cohn's selection, see Dana C. Munro, "The Children's Crusade," *American Historical Review*, Vol. 19 (1914), pp. 516–24. For further studies of millenarianism, see Sylvia L. Thrupp, ed., *Millennial Dreams in Action* (The Hague, 1962), and K. O. L. Burridge, *New Heaven, New Earth: A Study of Millenarian Activities* (Oxford, 1969).

Conflict and Settlement in Early Germanic Society

from NJAL'S SAGA

The sources make it reasonably clear that early Germanic society was status oriented; a man's position depended on his relationship with other members of the group. Any slight or injury could therefore cause an enormous amount of social mischief by altering the status relationships within the community and necessitating retaliation on the part of those whose status had suffered. Furthermore, since every individual was part of a family group, the kinship groups within the community were drawn into the conflict, widening the circle of those affected. The German settlements must have gone through long periods of disquietude after some act touched off a general reshuffling of status relationships. *Njál's Saga* recounts the history of one such period.

The saga comes from Iceland, a community of Norsemen that had been formed during the ninth century when several families left Norway. The impetus for leaving the mother country, according to Icelandic traditions that are considered largely accurate, was the desire to escape the growing power of the king there. The Icelandic families were fiercely independent and established a community in which there was no royal power to challenge their autonomy. This self-conscious beginning engendered among the Icelandic settlers a belief in their own historical importance, and they kept the most complete historical records of any of the early medieval communities. The sagas, a corpus of prose literature produced in the thirteenth century, draw on those records for their stories and characters. *Njál's Saga* is the longest and perhaps the best example of this extraordinary literature.

The society depicted in *Njál's Saga* was probably more stable than the early societies of other Germanic peoples. The isolation of the Icelandic community in the North Atlantic and its antimonarchical sentiments led the Icelanders to preserve the ancient characteristics of their community. On the Continent, the Germans were continually confronting Roman military power and culture, and these challenges permanently altered their society. Throughout the period of migration, the Germans were consolidating their military power under leaders who progressively raised themselves above the communities out of which they rose. Roman ideas of exalted kingship further enhanced the position of these leaders once they had established themselves as conquerors on Roman territory. The Icelandic sagas depict a society that had escaped from such centralization and that had in fact carried the distrust of royal power to an extreme.

Njál's Saga surveys a generation of conflict in Iceland at the time when

Christianity was brought to the island. The conversion of the community, which took place in 1000 A.D., did not cause the conflict, but greatly complicated the communal efforts to resolve it. The Icelanders had set up conflict resolution practices that brought feuding parties together and subjected them to communal pressure to resolve their differences, at the same time providing communal help. The system was founded on the community's desire to maintain peace, and it was therefore aimed at compromising differences in the most equitable manner possible. As a formalized social device for resolving conflicts that might have destroyed the community if they got out of hand, it was the primitive ancestor of the law trial. In *Njál's Saga*, the weaknesses of the system are made tragically evident. Too often one or more parties to the conflict—not the principal parties but auxiliary parties involved because of kinship ties—were not included in the settlement and therefore not bound by it. In the ninth and tenth centuries, this failure of the system led to an almost interminable internecine war. The stabilization of society in the modern era has removed this danger, but modern procedural law still struggles with the problem of who should be a party to its settlement devices.

In this excerpt from *Njál's Saga*, we see the origins and settlement of one conflict in the long series of conflicts recounted in the work. The protagonists are aristocrats within the society. They have retainers, servants, and clients whom they can call on and who therefore become involved in the conflicts. The genealogy of Skapti in Chapter 56 represents an important aspect of the Icelander's view of the community. It is important to know the family and relatives of each person in order to know whom he will support in the complex feuds. It is also a gauge of his character and personality that, in conjunction with the pithy remark of the saga writer ("Thorodd was considered to be deceitful and tricky"), permits the reader to speculate on his future role in the story.

53. Gunnar Is Accidentally Wounded by Otkel
and Insulted by Skamkel

One day in spring Otkel said that they would now ride east to accept Rúnólf's invitation, and all were very glad to hear that. In Otkel's company besides Skamkel there were also his two brothers, Audólf, and three other men. Otkel rode one of the dun-colored horses, and the other ran free at his side. They traveled in an easterly direction to the Markar River, and Otkel galloped ahead of the others. Both horses got out of hand and raced from the path up toward the Fljótshlíd district. Otkel was now riding faster than he cared to.

The same day Gunnar had gone all alone from his home. In one hand he carried a basket with seed and in the other a hand-axe. He went down to

Reprinted by permission of New York University Press from pp. 117–26 of *Njál's Saga* translated by Carl F. Bayerschmidt and Lee M. Hollander, © 1955 by The American-Scandinavian Foundation.

his field and sowed the grain there. He had placed his cloak of fine material and his axe upon the ground as he continued to sow for a while.

Now it must be told that Otkel came riding on faster than he wished. He was wearing spurs and he galloped down over the field, and neither of the two men saw the other. Just as Gunnar looked up, Otkel rode down upon him and grazed Gunnar's ear with one of his spurs. That produced a long gash which immediately began to bleed very much. Then Otkel's companions came up.

Gunnar said: "You can all see that you, Otkel, have inflicted on me a wound which has drawn blood: I consider that a most outrageous offence. First you summon me to the Assembly, and now you trample me under foot and ride over me!"

Skamkel said: "You took that well, but you were no less outraged the time you managed your suit with the halberd in your hand!"

"The next time we meet you will get to see the halberd!" answered Gunnar.

After that they parted. Skamkel shouted: "That's certainly brave riding, fellows!"

Gunnar rode home but told no one about the incident, nor did anyone suspect that the wound had been inflicted by any person.

One day, however, it happened that he told his brother Kolskegg about it.

Kolskegg said: "You must tell this to more people, so that it can never be said that you made any charges against dead men. Your charge will be denied, if you do not secure witnesses who already know what has happened between you two."

Gunnar then told his neighbors about the incident, but there was little comment made at first.

Otkel arrived east in Dale. He and his men received a warm welcome and they stayed there for a week. Otkel told Rúnólf all that had happened between himself and Gunnar. It occurred to one man to ask how Gunnar had behaved.

Skamkel answered: "If he were not among the first families, I would say that he wept!"

"Those are shameful words!" said Rúnólf, "and you will have to acknowledge, when you two meet again, that it isn't in Gunnar's nature to weep. It would be well if better men than yourself do not have to pay for your spite. I think it best that I accompany you when you are ready to ride home, because Gunnar will not harm me."

"I don't want to do that," said Otkel, "because I shall cross the river further down."

Rúnólf gave him good gifts and said it was unlikely that they would see each other again.

Otkel expressed the wish that Rúnólf remember their friendship and look after his son, if the worst should happen.

54. Otkel and Skamkel Are Slain

Now we turn to Hlídarendi again. [One day] Gunnar was outside when he saw his herdsman dashing up. As he rode into the yard Gunnar asked him: "Why such haste?"

"I wished to be a faithful servant to you," said the herdsman. "I saw some men riding down along the Markar River, eight of them altogether, and four of them wore bright-colored clothes."

Gunnar said: "That must be Otkel!"

The herdsman added: "I have often heard Skamkel use much insulting language [about you]; east in Dale he said that you cried when they rode down on you. I have told you this, because I find the abusive talk of such evil men hard to bear."

"Well, we must not be too sensitive about such talk," said Gunnar; "but from now on you shall work only at that which you choose yourself."

"Shall I tell your brother Kolskegg about this?" asked the herdsman.

"No, go in and lie down!" said Gunnar. "I'll tell Kolskegg."

The herdsman went to his bed and fell asleep at once. Gunnar took the herdsman's horse and placed a saddle upon it. He took his shield and girded himself with his sword, Olvir's gift, put his helmet upon his head, and took his halberd. From the weapon there came forth a loud ringing sound. Rannveig, his mother, heard it. She came up to Gunnar and said: "You are wrathful now, my son, and I have never seen you like that before!"

Supporting himself on his halberd Gunnar leaped into the saddle and rode away. Rannveig went back into the room where there was much loud talking.

"You are carrying on loudly," she said, "but louder still was the sound Gunnar's halberd made when he sallied forth!"

Kolskegg overheard this and said: "Great tidings are afoot, no doubt!"

"Excellent," said Hallgerd; "now they are likely to find out whether Gunnar will cry and run away from them!"

Kolskegg took his arms, looked for a horse, and rode after Gunnar as fast as he could.

Gunnar rode across Acre-Tongue and on to Geilastofnar and from there to the Rangá River, and then down to the ford at Hof. There were some women in the milking pen. Gunnar leaped from his horse and hitched it. By this time the others came riding up. The road up from the ford was covered with flagstones.

Gunnar called out to them: "Defend yourselves! Now you can find out whether you can make me shed any tears!"

They all leaped from their horses and attacked Gunnar Hallbjorn foremost.

"Don't you attack!" said Gunnar. "You least of all would I want to work an injury; but I'll not spare anyone, if it comes to saving my life!"

"There is no help for that now," said Hallbjorn, "for you are out to kill my brother, and it would be an [everlasting] shame to me if I merely sat by and looked on."

Thereupon he thrust at Gunnar with a large spear which he held in both hands. Gunnar quickly brought his shield before the blow and the spear pierced the shield. Gunnar then thrust the shield down with such force that it stuck in the ground, and he reached for his sword with such a quick motion that no eye could follow it, and with it struck Hallbjorn on the arm above the wrist so that the hand was cut off. Skamkel ran up behind Gunnar and lunged at him with a large axe. Gunnar turned around quickly, parried the blow with his halberd, and struck the axe near the base of the blade so that it flew out of Skamkel's grasp and into the Rangá River. Then he thrust at Skamkel a second time with his halberd, running him through with it. He then lifted him up on it and threw him down head foremost on the muddy path. Audólf seized a spear and hurled it at Gunnar, but Gunnar caught the spear in flight and hurled it back immediately. It went right through both the shield and the Norwegian and into the ground. Otkel struck at Gunnar with his sword, aiming at the leg below the knee. Gunnar leaped up high and the blow missed him. Thereupon Gunnar thrust at him with his halberd and drove it through him. At that moment Kolskegg came up and rushed at Hallkel at once and dealt him a deathblow with his short-sword. Gunnar and Kolskegg killed all eight in this fight. A woman who had witnessed the fight ran up to the farmhouse and told Mord and begged him to separate them.

"Very likely they are only such fellows," he said, "as may kill each other, so far as I am concerned!"

"No, you can't mean that!" she said; "Gunnar, your kinsman, and Otkel are among them."

"Must you always be jabbering, you old hag!" he said. And he remained lying abed while they fought.

After accomplishing this, Gunnar and Kolskegg rode back. As they were riding swiftly up along the river bank Gunnar was thrown from his horse, but he landed on his feet.

"That's brave riding, brother!" said Kolskegg.

"With those same words Skamkel ridiculed me, when I said that they were riding me down," answered Gunnar.

"But you have avenged that now," said Kolskegg.

Gunnar replied: "I don't know whether I am less brave than other men because I dislike killing men more than they."

55. Njál's Prophetic Counsel

Now these tidings were spread about, and many said that this had not happened any sooner than might have been expected. Gunnar rode to Berg-thórshvál and told Njál about the battle.

Njál said: "You have struck hard, but you were greatly provoked, too!"

"What is likely to happen now?" asked Gunnar.

"Do you wish that I tell you what has not yet taken place?" asked Njál. "You will ride to the Assembly; there you will follow my advice, and from this affair great honor will be afforded you. This will be the beginning of your many slayings."

"Will you give me some helpful advice?" asked Gunnar.

"I will do that," answered Njál; "never slay more than one man in the same family, and never break the agreements which good men make between you and others, least of all in this affair!"

Gunnar said: "I should think that there would be greater likelihood of expecting this of others than of me."

"That may be," answered Njál, "but just remember this in your dealings: if you do what I warned you against, then you will not have long to live; otherwise, however, you will live to be an old man."

Gunnar asked: "Do you know what will bring about your own death?"

"Yes, I do," answered Njál.

"What?" asked Gunnar.

"Something that people would expect least of all," he answered. After that Gunnar rode home.

A messenger was sent to Gizur the White and Geir Godi, for it devolved on them to take over the prosecution in the case of Otkel's slaying. They met and discussed what their procedure should be. They agreed that they should bring suit in all stringency according to the law. The next question was to determine which of the two should take over the prosecution of the suit. However, neither of the two was willing to undertake it.

"It seems to me," said Gizur, "that we have two courses open to us: either, one of us will have to take over the prosecution, and this will have to be determined by lot, or else Otkel will lie unatoned. We can also be very certain that this will be a very difficult suit to institute, for Gunnar has many kinsmen and friends. That one of us who does not draw the lot shall give support to the prosecution of the case and not withdraw from it before the case is ended."

After that they drew lots and it fell to the lot of Geir Godi to take over the prosecution of the suit.

A short time after that they rode east over the rivers and came to that place at the Rangá River where the fight had taken place. They dug up the bodies and named witnesses to the wounds. Then they made known their findings and summoned nine free farmers as witnesses in the suit. They were told that Gunnar was at home with about thirty men. Then Geir Godi asked Gizur whether he wished to ride there with a hundred men.

"No, I do not," he answered, "even though the strength of numbers is on our side." After that they rode back home again.

The news soon spread throughout the entire district that legal proceedings had been instituted in the case, and people said that the meeting of the Assembly was likely to be a stormy one.

56.   The Settlement at the Assembly

There was a man named Skapti. He was the son of Thórodd, whose mother was Thórvor. She was the daughter of Thormód Skapti, the son of Óleif the Broad, the son of Olvir Barnakarl. Skapti and his father were both great chieftains and very well skilled in the law. Thórodd was considered to be deceitful and tricky. Both father and son supported Gizur the White in every suit.

A large company of men from Fljótshlíd and the Rangá River gathered for the Assembly. Gunnar was so well liked that all agreed to stand by him. Now they all came to the Assembly and set up their booths.

In the company of Gizur the White were these chieftains: Skapti Thóroddsson, Ásgrím Ellida-Grímsson, Odd of Kidjaberg and Halldór Ornólfsson.

One day the men went to the Law-Mount. Geir Godi arose and gave notice of a suit of manslaughter against Gunnar for the slaying of Otkel. Another charge of manslaughter he brought against Gunnar for the slaying of Hallbjorn the White, another for the slaying of Audólf, and still another for the slaying of Skamkel. Then he brought a charge of manslaughter against Kolskegg for the slaying of Hallkel. After he had brought all these charges for manslaughter, people remarked that he had spoken very well. After that men went from the Law-Mount.

The Assembly continued in session until the day when the courts were to gather at their appointed places. Then both parties collected all their forces. Geir Godi and Gizur the White stood to the south of the Rangá River court, and Gunnar and Njál stood to the north. Geir Godi enjoined Gunnar to listen to his oath. Thereupon he took the oath. He then brought the charge and had witnesses testify that the listing of wounds had been duly made. Then he had the jury of neighbors seated in their proper places, and he called on Gunnar to examine the members of the jury carefully. Thereupon he called on the jury of neighbors to utter their findings. The neighbors who had been summoned on the inquest then went before the court and named themselves as witnesses, but they made this reservation concerning the suit involving Audólf, that the lawful prosecutor of it was in Norway, and that they would make no findings in his case. As a jury, therefore, they had nothing to do with that suit. After that they uttered their findings in the case of Otkel and declared Gunnar guilty of the charge. Thereupon Geir Godi called on Gunnar for his defense; he had named witnesses in each step of the prosecution as it was presented.

Gunnar now in turn enjoined Geir Godi to listen to his oath and the defense which he was about to urge.

Then Gunnar took the oath and said: "I make this defense that in the presence of witnesses I declared Otkel an outlaw for the bloody wound which he inflicted on me with his spur. Geir Godi, I protest your right to prosecute this suit, and I likewise protest the right of the judges to give judgment, and I hereby declare invalid all the measures taken by you in the preparation of this suit. I make this protest on the basis of my legal right, the inviolable and indisputable right which has been granted me according to the law of the Assembly and the law of the land. Furthermore, I'll tell you something else which I plan to do."

"Is it that you mean to challenge me to the holm, as is your custom, and thus not permit the proceedings to continue in legal manner?" asked Geir.

"Not that," answered Gunnar, "but I shall make accusation here at the Law-Mount that you called on neighbors for an inquest in a case which has no bearing on your suit—I mean the slaying of Audólf; and for that reason I declare you guilty and demand the penalty of lesser outlawry."

Njál said: "Things must not take this turn, for the only result will be that the feud will be carried on with increasing bitterness. Each of you, it seems to me, has a good deal to be said in his behalf. Some of your slayings, as you cannot contradict, Gunnar, are punishable. On the other hand, you have made out a case against Geir Godi in which he will be found guilty. Also, you should know this, Geir Godi, that there is pending against you a suit calling for a verdict of outlawry. This suit has not even been introduced yet, but it will not be dropped if you do not take my words into account."

Thórodd Godi then said: "It seems to me that it would be most conducive to peace if both parties came to an agreement. But why do you say so little, Gizur the White?"

"It seems to me," answered Gizur, "that our case needs some more strong support; one can see that Gunnar's friends are standing by him. The most favorable solution for us would be to have sensible men arbitrate the case, if that is agreeable to Gunnar."

"I have always been ready and willing to make a peaceful settlement," said Gunnar. "It is true that much harm has been done for which you should seek redress; yet I consider that I was hard driven to act as I did."

With the advice of the wisest men it was decided to submit the whole case to arbitration. Six men were to make the award, and it was made right there at the Assembly. It was decided that Skamkel should lie unatoned. One wergild for Otkel's death and the wound which Gunnar had received from the spur were to offset each other. The other slayings were to be paid for according to the worth of each man. Gunnar's kinsmen produced the money, so that all slayings were paid for then and there at the Assembly. Then Geir

Godi and Gizur the White went up to Gunnar and gave pledges that they would keep the peace. Gunnar then rode home from the Assembly. He thanked the men for their support and gave presents to many of them. The whole proceedings redounded greatly to Gunnar's honor. He now remained at home, enjoying the greatest distinction.

The Technology
of Medieval Knighthood

LYNN WHITE, JR.

After the Viking invasions, Europeans waged successful campaigns against their neighbors on all sides. They conquered the Slavs and Wends in the northeast and began to make significant progress against the Moors in Spain. They drove the Saracens and Greeks out of southern Italy and Sicily. They halted the Magyars on their eastern frontier and, in the First Crusade, recaptured the Levant and established a Latin kingdom there. The victories resulted not only from the circumstances of their enemies but also from the superiority of the European armies. The heavily armed knights were formidable warriors against whom other military forces of the period could not stand. So long as the Europeans could meet their enemies in pitched battle, they held a military advantage. How did they develop this proficient military force, so different from both the Roman and old German armies?

The answer to this question is bound up with efforts to explain the origins of the whole feudal system—the social and economic as well as military system of medieval Europe. Debate on this problem has concentrated on the institutional developments that brought Roman and Germanic elements together in the formation of the new society. The debate has been going on for a long time, but one element historians had not considered until the 1930s was the impact of technology as a cause of social change. This selection is taken from a book in which Lynn White has attempted to draw a connection between technological advance and social change in the Middle Ages. The origin of the heavily armed knight is one of the focal points of his studies.

The history of the use of the horse in battle is divided into three periods: first, that of the charioteer; second, that of the mounted warrior who clings to his steed by pressure of the knees; and third, that of the rider

From Lynn White, Jr., *Medieval Technology and Social Change* (Oxford: The Clarendon Press, 1962), pp. 1-5, 11-14, 27-30. Reprinted by permission of The Clarendon Press, Oxford.

equipped with stirrups. The horse has always given its master an advantage over the footman in battle, and each improvement in its military use has been related to far-reaching social and cultural changes.

Before the introduction of the stirrup, the seat of the rider was precarious. Bit and spur might help him to control his mount; the simple saddle might confirm his seat; nevertheless, he was still much restricted in his methods of fighting. He was primarily a rapidly mobile bowman and hurler of javelins. Swordplay was limited because "without stirrups your slashing horseman, taking a good broadhanded swipe at his foe, had only to miss to find himself on the ground." As for the spear, before the invention of the stirrup it was wielded at the end of the arm and the blow was delivered with the strength of shoulder and biceps. The stirrup made possible—although it did not demand—a vastly more effective mode of attack: now the rider could lay his lance at rest, held between the upper arm and the body, and make at his foe, delivering the blow not with his muscles but with the combined weight of himself and his charging stallion.

The stirrup, by giving lateral support in addition to the front and back support offered by pommel and cantle, effectively welded horse and rider into a single fighting unit capable of a violence without precedent. The fighter's hand no longer delivered the blow: it merely guided it. The stirrup thus replaced human energy with animal power, and immensely increased the warrior's ability to damage his enemy. Immediately, without preparatory steps, it made possible mounted shock combat, a revolutionary new way of doing battle.

What was the effect of the introduction of the stirrup in Europe?

The Classic Theory of the Origins of Feudalism, and Its Critics

The historian of Frankish institutions too often recalls to the wearied mind Eliza on the ice: hypothesis clutched to bosom, he leaps from suspect charter to ambiguous capitulary, the critics baying at his heals. So thin and so slippery of interpretation are the written remains from the Germanic kingdoms that one might expect that scholars exploring the sources of feudalism would have made every effort to supplement the extant documents with the archaeological material which, in recent years, has begun so greatly to modify our view of the early Middle Ages. But this is not case: the vast literature of ingenious controversy about feudal origins has been produced chiefly by legal and constitutional historians, and therefore is almost entirely a matter of textual exegesis.

The first stage in the discussion culminated in 1887 with the publication of Heinrich Brunner's "Der Reiterdienst und die Anfänge des Lehnwesens." Brunner codified, synthesized, and extended the findings of his predecessors so brilliantly that his has become the classic theory of the inception of feudal society.

According to Brunner, feudalism was essentially military, a type of social organization designed to produce and support cavalry. The early Germans, including the Franks, had fought to some extent on horseback, but in proportion as agriculture displaced herding as the basis of their economy, the use of cavalry declined. The Franks in particular came to fight almost entirely on foot: indeed, their typical weapon, the *francisca*, was efficient only in the hands of infantry. Brunner believed that as late as 732 Charles Martel's army which met the Saracens near Poitiers was composed primarily of footmen who, in the famous words of the so-called Isidorus Pacensis, "stand rigid as a wall and, like a belt of ice frozen solidly together, slay the Arabs with the sword." Yet in an account of the battle of the Dyle in 891, we are told that "the Franks are unused to fighting on foot." When did this change from infantry to cavalry take place among the Franks?

Brunner worked back through the available evidence and concluded that the armies of Charlemagne and his successors were primarily mounted. In 758 Pipin changed the Saxon tribute from cattle to horses. In 755 the Marchfield, the traditional muster of the Frankish army, was transferred to May, presumably because the number of cavalry had become so large that more forage was needed than was available in March. The military reform must therefore have occurred between the battle of Poitiers, dated by him in 732, and the year 755.

Brunner then turned his attention to the vast and ruthless confiscations of Church lands effected by Charles Martel. There is ample evidence that the great Mayor of the Palace seized these lands and distributed them to retainers in order to strengthen his armed forces. In 743 his son Carloman excused his own retention of these secularized estates "propter imminentia bella et persecutiones ceterarum gentium quae in circuitu nostro sunt . . . in adiutorium exercitus nostri," while Pope Zacharias accepted the deplorable situation "pro eo quod nunc tribulatio accidit Saracinorum, Saxonum vel Fresonum." Martel's diversion of a considerable part of the Church's vast riches to military purposes therefore was contemporary with the shift of the focus of the Frankish army from infantry to cavalry.

No surviving document explicitly connects the two developments, but in view of the great expense of maintaining war-horses, Brunner concluded that they were in fact related. Martel had felt some urgent compulsion suddenly to increase the cavalry at his disposal. In the agricultural economy of eighth-century Gaul, in which soil was the most important form of income-bearing wealth and in which the tax-collecting system was rudimentary, mounted warriors could only be maintained in large numbers by landed endowment. The estates of the Church were available for his purpose; these he seized and handed over to an enlarged body of followers on condition that they serve him on horseback. Failure to fulfil this military duty involved forfeiture of the endowment held under such obligation. The ancient custom of swearing allegiance to a leader (vassalage) was fused with the granting of an estate (benefice), and the result was feudalism. Protofeudal and seigniorial elements had, of course, saturated the very fluid Celtic, Germanic, late Roman, and Merovingian societies; but it was the need for calvary felt by the early Carolingians which precipitated and crystallized these anticipations to form medieval feudalism.

Finally, Brunner tried to discover what military necessity led to such sudden and drastic measures on Charles Martel's part. The northern enemies of the Frankish kingdom did not use cavalry extensively; the campaigns against the Avars were either too early or too late to account for the reform. But the Muslim invasion seemed to fit the evidence. Brunner believed that the Saracenic horde was mounted. While their charges had broken against the glacial line of the shield-wall of the Frankish footmen at Poitiers, Martel had been unable quickly to follow up his victory by means of his slow-moving infantry. Therefore he determined to create an adequate mounted force to be financed by confiscation of ecclesiastical property. Thus, Brunner concluded, the crisis which generated feudalism, the event which explains its almost explosive development towards the middle of the eighth century, was the Arab incursion.

Brunner's synthesis has been the focal point of all subsequent discussion of European feudal origins. It has stood up remarkably well against assaults from all directions. . . .

. . . Why did Charles Martel and his immediate successors brave the wrath of the Church by seizing ecclesiastical properties to endow cavalry? What military circumstance impelled them to disregard the peril of clerical censure, the dictates of conventional morality?

Brunner found his answer in the Saracenic invasion. He claimed that Martel realized that, despite the victory of Poitiers, the Franks would need an adequate cavalry to repel the mounted Muslim armies permanently.

But was the battle of Poitiers in fact so great a crisis? Were the Muslims considered by contemporaries to be the chief danger to the Frankish kingdom? One suspects that our present common judgement has been based less upon the records than upon the rhetoric with which Gibbon proposed to the horrified imagination of eighteenth-century agnostics the spectacle of an Oxford engrossed in perusing the Koran, and of a Europe habituated to circumcision, had Charles's hammer struck less resoundingly. Martel turned his attention to Islam only after he had consolidated his realm. The sole contemporary source connecting his military reforms with the Muslim incursions is Pope Zacharias's letter, already noted, referring to the "tribulatio Saracinorum, Saxonum vel Fresonum." The opinions of immediate posterity as to the relative importance of these three foes is shown by the fact that when, under Louis the Pious, the walls of the palace at Ingelheim were decorated with murals of the deeds of great rulers, Charles Martel was depicted not at Poitiers but rather conquering the Frisians. Indeed, having defeated the Muslims, Martel made little effort for several years to follow up his victory. This would indicate that the Islamic invasion was not an adequate motive for the reorganization of Frankish society to secure cavalry.

Moreover, Brunner believed that the battle of Poitiers was fought in 732: not until 1955 did we learn that the correct date is 733. But the first seizures of Church properties for distribution to vassals occurred in fact in 732 when Charles Martel took lands of the Bishop of Orleans and others so that "honores eorum quosdam propriis usibus annecteret, quosdam vero suis satellitibus cumularet." Poitiers, therefore, cannot have inspired Charles's policy of confiscations for the improvement of his cavalry. His military reforms had begun a year earlier, although doubtless they had not yet greatly modified the structure of the Frankish forces when he met the Muslim invaders.

And finally, was Brunner correct in assuming that the Spanish Saracens at Poitiers were fighting chiefly on horseback? Certainly by the early ninth century the Franks thought of them as "Mauri celeres . . . gens equo fidens." But here again the exhaustive researches of Sánchez-Albornoz into the Arabic sources have clarified the matter. He has shown that even twenty years after Martel's death the Spanish Muslims used cavalry only in small numbers: it was not until the second half of the eighth century that they too shifted the weight of their armies from footmen to mounted fighters. Can it have been the Sons of the Prophet who imitated the Franks rather than the reverse? In any case it is now clear that the Muslim peril did not provoke Charles Martel's military reform and thus establish feudalism in Europe.

Only one alternative explanation of the seizure and distribution of the Church lands has been widely discussed. Roloff suggests that the great *Major palatii*, himself a bastard and usurper, was trying to strengthen his political situation by largesse which would attract to his retinue most of the magnates of the realm. But Mangoldt-Gaudlitz cogently objects, first, that such drastic action, while undoubtedly it would build up Charles's secular following, would likewise risk the dangerous enmity of the Church, the one authority which might consent—and eventually did consent—to legitimatize the rule of his dynasty; second, that Martel, an experienced warrior—Isidorus Pacensis calls him "ab ineunte aetate belligerum et rei militaris expertum"—would more probably be moved by military than by political considerations; and third, that the political situation of Martel's sons Carloman and Pipin was so firm that their immense new confiscations of clerical estates can best be explained on military grounds. But if, unlike Mangoldt-Gaudlitz, we cannot accept Brunner's hypothesis of the Muslim invasion, what military development or crisis in the 730's is adequate to account for such momentous events?

The whole of Brunner's magnificent structure of hypotheses stands, save its keystone. We are faced, in the reigns of Martel, Carloman, and Pipin, with an extraordinary drama which lacks motivation. A sudden and urgent demand for cavalry led the early Carolingians to reorganize their realm along feudal lines to enable it to support mounted fighters in much greater numbers than ever before. Yet the nature of the military exigency which brought about this social revolution has eluded us.

The answer to the puzzle is to be found not in the documents but in archaeology. It was first offered in 1923, at the end of a rambling footnote, by a master of Germanic antiquities. Speaking of the social cleavages which resulted when the new and expensive method of fighting on horseback led to the growth of a specialized aristocracy of mounted warriors, Friedrich Kaufmann remarked, almost as an afterthought: "The new age is heralded in the eighth century by excavations of stirrups." . . .

It is archaeology, then, and not art history, which is decisive for the dating of the arrival of the stirrup in western Europe. And that date may be placed in the first part of the eighth century, that is, in the time of Charles Martel.

However, even if the Benedictine missionaries had worked a bit faster in extinguishing horse-burials, and had thus deprived us of the spade's testimony of the arrival of the stirrup in Germanic lands, we could have discovered by other means that it must have reached the Franks in the early eighth century. At that moment the verbs *insilire* and *desilire*, formerly used for getting on and off horses, began to be replaced by *scandere equos* and *descendere*, showing that leaping was replaced by stepping when one mounted or dismounted. But a more explicit indication of the drastic shift from infantry to the new mode of mounted shock combat is the complete change in Frankish weapons which took place at that time.

The *francisca*, the distinctively Frankish battle-axe, and the *ango*, or barbed javelin, both infantry weapons, disappear in the eighth century, while the old *spatha* lengthens into a longsword for horsemen. Moreover, from the ninth century onward these Germanic longswords were greatly prized by both Byzantines and Saracens. But above all, in the early decades of the eighth century there comes into wide use a spear having a heavy stock and spurs below the blade to prevent too deep penetration of the victim which might result in difficulty in withdrawing the weapon. This quickly developed into the typical Carolingian wing-spear, with a prominent cross-piece. Such lances were used, if we may believe the miniatures, both by infantry and cavalry. But their novel design is intelligible in terms of the new style of mounted shock combat with lance at rest. As we have already noted, a footman or an unstirrupped rider wielding the lance at the end of his arm could seldom have impaled an adversary so deeply that his weapon would get stuck. On the other hand, a stirrupped horseman with lance at rest delivering the stroke with the full momentum of his own body and that of his horse must often have done so, unless his spear were fitted with some baffle behind the blade. The generalization of the wing-spear in itself is evidence that under Charles Martel and his sons the meaning of the stirrup for shock combat was being realized.

The historical record is replete with inventions which have remained dormant in a society until at last—usually for reasons which remain mysterious—they "awaken" and become active elements in the shaping of a culture to which they are not entirely novel. It is conceivable that Charles Martel, or his military advisers, may have realized the potential of the stirrup after it had been known to the Franks for some decades. However, the present state of our information indicates that it was in fact a new arrival when he used it as the technological basis of his military reforms.

As our understanding of the history of technology increases, it becomes clear that a new device merely opens a door; it does not compel one to enter. The acceptance or rejection of an invention, or the extent to which its implications are realized if it is accepted, depends quite as much upon the condition of a society, and upon the imagination of its leaders, as upon the nature of the technological item itself. As we shall see, the Anglo-Saxons used the stirrup, but did not comprehend it; and for this they paid a fearful price. While semi-feudal relationships and institutions had long been scattered thickly over the civilized world, it was the Franks alone—presumably led by Charles Martel's genius—who fully grasped the possibilities inherent in the stirrup and created in terms of it a new type of warfare supported by a novel structure of society which we call feudalism.

Mounted Shock Combat and the Temper of Feudal Life

The feudal class of the European Middle Ages existed to be armed horsemen, cavaliers fighting in a particular manner which was made possible by the stirrup. This *élite* created a secular culture closely related to its style of fighting and vigorously paralleling the ecclesiastical culture of the Church. Feudal institutions, the knightly class, and chivalric culture altered, waxed and waned; but for a thousand years they bore the marks of their birth from the new military technology of the eighth century.

While money had by no means gone out of circulation in the Frankish realm, the West of the eighth century was closer to a barter economy than was either contemporary Byzantium or Islam. Moreover, the bureaucracy of the Carolingian kingdom was so slender that the collection of taxes by the central government was difficult. Land was the fundamental form of riches. When they decided that it was essential to secure calvary to fight in the new and very expensive manner, Charles Martel and his heirs took the only possible action in seizing Church lands and distributing them to vassals on condition of knight's service in the Frankish host.

Fighting in the new manner involved large expenditures. Horses were costly, and armor was growing heavier to meet the new violence of mounted shock combat. In 761 a certain Isanhard sold his ancestral lands and a slave for a horse and a sword. In general, military equipment for one man seems to have cost about twenty oxen, or the plough-teams of at least ten peasant families. But horses get killed: a knight needed remounts to be effective; and his squire should be adequately mounted. And horses eat large quantities of grain, an important matter in an age of more slender agricultural production than ours.

Although in the Frankish realm the right and duty to bear arms rested on all free men regardless of economic condition, naturally the great majority could afford to come to muster only on foot, equipped with relatively inexpensive weapons and armour. As has been mentioned, even from this group Charlemagne tried to raise horsemen by commanding that the less prosperous freemen should band together, according to the size of their lands, to equip one of their number and send him to the wars. Such an arrangement would be hard to administer, and it did not survive the confusion of the later ninth century. But inherent in this device was the recognition that if the new technology of warfare were to be developed consistently, military service must become a matter of class. Those economically unable to fight on horseback suffered from a social infirmity which shortly became a legal inferiority. In 808 the infelicitous wording of a capitulary *De exercitu promovendo* distinguishes "liberi" from "pauperes": the expression is legally inexact, but it points to the time when freedom was to become largely a matter of property. Two capitularies of 825 show how rapidly concepts were moving. One separates "liberi" from "mediocres quippe liberi qui non possunt per se hostem facere"; while the other refers to those latter as "liberi secundi ordinis." With the collapse of the Frankish empire, the feudality which the Carolingians had deliberately created, in terms of the new military method of mounted shock combat, to be the backbone of their army became the governing as well as the fighting *élite*. The old levy of freemen (although not all infantry) vanished, and a gulf appeared between a warrior aristocracy and the mass of peasants. By about the year 1000, *miles* had ceased to mean "soldier" and had become "knight."

Jews in a Christian Society

IRVING AGUS

Histories of European Jews have focused on their role in economic and intellectual life. On the one hand, historians have been concerned with estimating the importance of Jewish merchant and moneylending activities. On the other, they have traced the textual traditions of important philosophical, theological, and medical works that came to Europe through the Jewish communities of Sicily and Spain. Neither of these approaches has revealed much about the nature of the Jewish communities in Europe. In fact, there were two groups of European Jews in the Middle Ages, and they still form distinct communities. In the south, centered in Italy and Spain, Sephardic Jews were an integral part of the society and thus a bridge between the Moslem and Christian communities there. Prior to their expulsion by Ferdinand and Isabella in 1492, the Spanish Jews had participated in one of the most interesting social amalgams in history. Medieval Spain presents a picture of a complex but successful mixture of three religious and national groups that produced a brilliant civilization. This harmony between the Jews and their neighbors was in striking contrast to the relations between Jew and Christian in northern Europe.

The Ashkenazic Jews of northern Europe (*Ashkenazy* is the medieval Hebrew word for "German") were segregated in religious communities that formed the nuclei of the ghettos of the modern era. The Ashkenazy seem to have originated from groups of Jews brought north from Italy in the ninth century by the Carolingian emperors. It was later reported that one of the most famous communities, that of Mainz in Germany, was created when Emperor Charles the Fat brought Rabbi Moses of Lucca north about 887. The Rabbi naturally brought his congregation with him, and the little community expanded rapidly. Irving Agus, the translator and annotator of the selection that follows, suggests that Charles brought the Jews north in order to establish a skilled commercial group in his kingdom. Agus also argues that in the ninth through eleventh centuries, the kings generally protected the Jews because of their virtual monopoly on the arts of business. In order to support this view he has collected a wealth of material from a corpus of literature almost unkown up to now—the Responsa of the great rabbis who functioned as teachers and judges in the Ashkenazic communities. When disputes arose, the questions raised were sent to the great rabbis for decision; their responses touch on every aspect of Jewish life in early medieval Europe.

The Responsa show that in the first three centuries of Ashkenazic life the Jews were borrowers of money, not lenders. The surplus capital produced on the great estates was lent to the Jews for their commercial enterprises at a time when Christians had almost no use for such capital. In one of the Responsa reprinted below, the surplus production of the Archbishopric of Narbonne, managed by Jews, was lent to other Jews for business purposes. It was only in the twelfth century, when Christian merchants became active, that Jews began to lend money to them and to establish the economic pattern that eventually led to the stereotype of the Jewish moneylender.

The Responsa also demonstrate that although the Jews were not popular among Christians, they clung together in the medieval cities not so much because the Christians forced them to as for religious reasons. Adherence to the Talmudic laws demanded a close-knit community that could support and regulate the provisioning of the restricted diet and maintain the religious service. In some parts of Europe, the communities described by the Responsa continued to exist into this century, though the great age of the Responsa came to an end with the First Crusade.

A Responsum of R. Meshullam b. Kalonymous, quoted by R. Asher b. Yehiel.

Q.   A was accustomed to travel for business a distance of a one day's journey from his home, and would stay there a month, three, or five, more or less. One day he went there and did not come back. It was rumored that he was killed there, although no witness appeared to testify directly, or to inform incidentally, that he saw his dead body or that he was one of the murderers. Is his wife permitted to remarry? And is she entitled to her *Ketubah*?

A.   On the strength of the general information thus received, his widow is permitted to remarry and is entitled to collect her *Ketubah*.

a) The murdered merchant was apparently not engaged in selling luxury articles imported from the East, but rather in buying and selling local products. He would roam the countryside a distance of but one day's journey, for several months, and sometimes for almost half a year. The description of A's business habits, however, does pose serious difficulties: Why would he stay away from home for months at a time, when he was but a day's journey from that home? Was travelling so dangerous, or was he so loaded with bulky merchandise, that he could not interrupt his activities even for a few days? There is, of course, the possibility that the text is slightly corrupted. The phrase "a day's journey from his home" may have contained the additional words: "or several days' journey." That would better explain A's long periods of absence from home. The word "month" may be a corruption of the word "week." The latter is unlikely, however, for the main reason for mentioning the fact that A would sometimes stay away for inordinately long periods of time was to point to the possibility that he might still be alive and transacting

From Irving Agus, *Urban Civilization in Pre-Crusade Europe*, Vol. 1 (New York: Yeshiva University Press, 1965), pp. 97–99, 103–04, 122–23, 131–32, 189–95. Reprinted by permission of Irving Agus.

business somewhere. If previously his longest business trip kept him away for but five weeks, it would not be an important factor in the case, and would not be mentioned. This question was probably not sent to R. Meshullam until more than a year had elapsed since A was last seen alive. Therefore, A's business journeys of three and five months' duration are clearly indicated in the text, and attest to the nature of his business activities.

b) Although the evidence for the fact of A's death was very vague, R. Meshullam permitted his wife to remarry. It is true that R. Meshullam relied mainly on talmudic interpretation for his decision, but there is no doubt that he was seriously influenced by the conditions of his day. Thus, R. Asher b. Yehiel, after quoting every relevant talmudic source, and several important precedents including the Responsum of R. Meshullam, adds the statement: "For it is absolutely clear and well known that there were no survivors on the day of the great massacre." Contemporary conditions were therefore taken into consideration. R. Meshullam's opinion was influenced by the fact that murder was a frequent occurrence at the time; a Jew, especially, could not live alone, isolated from the protection of his coreligionists; and thus, if still alive, he would be known to neighboring communities. Apparently, therefore, the Jews of this period knew one another very well, needed the help of local Jews in order to travel from place to place, and could not run away to a distant place without the knowledge of the Jews along the route of his flight.

• • • •

This Responsum was written by R. Eliezer the Great of Mayence, Germany, to his student R. Isaac b. Menahem of France.

Q. L's husband went overseas. Subsequently her cousin (the son of her father's brother) came from overseas and reported that her husband had died there. Is she permitted to remarry? A "scholar" (talmid) was consulted on this matter and he ruled that the testimony of relatives was not acceptable in such cases.

A. The decision of the scholar is correct . . . (only part of the answer is preserved.)

a) Both L's husband and her cousin were overseas in the same place; they may have travelled together. The fact, however, that the legal inquiry had to be sent to Mayence, shows, that it was difficult to obtain additional, and clearly acceptable, testimony from that overseas country. Thus, although we learn here of two Jews who have crossed the sea, and of one who had recrossed it, communication with the country across the sea was not an easy matter. It is possible, of course, that L's husband had died in some obscure place, unbeknown to any other Jew but to her cousin, and that it was for this reason that additional testimony was not obtainable. Ordinarily the cousin would have known that L would have to have clear knowledge of her husband's death. He would have gone to a local court overseas, near the place where the tragedy took place, and tried to establish clearly the fact of the man's death—if it were at all possible. L's husband, therefore, died in an obscure place.

. . . .

A Responsum of R. Isaac son of Judah.

Q.   Non-Jews transported two casks of wine; one was fitted with a bung, while the other was sealed, placed upright, and contained an opening at the tip in which a tube was inserted. (This cask was not quite full, as it had an empty space on top of about half a cubit. The wine contained in this cask was not fermenting.) A Jew accompanied the casks in order to watch them constantly. Late Friday evening the wagon arrived near the outskirts of the town, and when it came near the wall of the town it was already completely dark. The Jew left the wagon in charge of the slave of the nobleman, the owner of the vineyard, who had originally given instructions to that slave to watch the wine as the pupil of his eye, and to make sure no one touched it. The Jew ran to the Jewish section of that town to inquire whether the Jews would take in the wine [at that hour]. They emphatically answered him in the negative and hurried him back to his wine. The casks were exactly as he had left them. He could find no cause for the slightest suspicion that they had been tampered with. Is the wine fit for consumption by Jews, and is there a difference between the wine of one cask and that of the other? Is he guilty of desecrating the Sabbath?
A.   Since the Jew left the casks with the non-Jew, and since the latter knew that he would be away for a definite period of time, the wine in both casks is considered "forbidden wine." If the Jew walked more than two thousand cubits, in open country, after the arrival of the Sabbath, he is guilty of desecrating the Sabbath.

a) The Jew bought grapes from the nobleman, the owner of the vineyard, processed it in the latter's barrels, and then carried it away. Although Jews cultivated vineyards at this time, they often obtained their wine in the above-described manner.
b) The walled town was not the home of the wine-transporting Jew; he merely wanted to stay over for the Sabbath. Note that he runs to the Jews and asks to be taken in together with his merchandise. This is typical: a transient Jew was usually welcomed by the local Jews, who would take him into their homes and extend their protection to him and his merchandise.
c) Again we note that the Jew who transported the wine was not absolutely scrupulous in the observance of Jewish law. The Jews of the town, on the other hand, were properly shocked at his suggestion that they take in

the wine on the Sabbath, even though it would be transported by a non-Jew, thus entailing but a minor infraction of the law.

d) The Jews of the town expected that the transporter of the wine remain at his wagon for twenty-four hours until after the Sabbath. Apparently no serious danger was involved in staying overnight at the gates of the town.

e) Note that the Jews lived in a special section of town.

. . . .

An anonymous Responsum, stemming from the tenth or eleventh century.

Q. One of the home-owners in an alley exclusively inhabited by Jews wanted to sell, or lease, his courtyard to a non-Jew. May the other inhabitants of that alley legally restrain him from settling a non-Jew in their midst?

A. Since the inhabitants of an alley may legally restrain one another from settling a tanner in their midst, because of the objectionable odor of his craft, they may certainly do so in case of a non-Jew. For a non-Jew, a violent man, would clearly inconvenience them, since they would have to be careful against his prying into their affairs, and perhaps even against stealing. Should the Jew nevertheless sell or rent his courtyard to a non-Jew, he would become liable to punishment by ban or stripes.

a) For reasons of security the Jews preferred to live in exclusively Jewish sections of town. There they felt safe, and were free to live in accordance with their religious and social practices without offending the religious sensibilities of the non-Jews.

b) The Jews owned real estate. The use of the term "courtyard" rather than "house" is significant, indicating that the houses were built in closed courtyards that opened into an alley.

c) The offending Jew faced punishment by "ban or stripes." Although we never hear of a case of a person being punished by stripes, responders do refer to this mode of punishment as a possibility. Apparently, the administration of stripes at this period was not meant as actual corporal punishment—was not intended to cause serious physical pain—but rather as a humiliating act intended to cause pain of a psychological nature. In the main it was meant as a religious rather than as a social deterrent.

d) Why did the Jew want to sell, or rent, to a non-Jew? Did he deliberately seek to inconvenience his neighbors because of a grudge he held against them, or could he find no Jewish buyer? The latter was probably the the reason, and indicates that the Jewish population at the time was very small.

. . . .

An anonymous Responsum probably of R. Gershom.

Q. A owed a non-Jew one pound. He asked B to lend him a pound in order to repay his debt to the non-Jew. B took one pound from his pocket-book, which contained twenty-one pounds, and gave it to A. The latter repaid his debt therewith. When he returned home, however, he discovered that non-Jews had plundered his home as well as that of B and of all the Jews of that town. The twenty pounds that remained in B's pocket-book were also plundered. Since B would also have lost the one pound he had lent to A, had he not given it to A, is the latter under obligation to repay it to the former?

A. In view of the fact that A clearly benefitted from B's pound, he must certainly return it to B. But, even if he had not benefitted from it, he would still be obligated to repay it. For as soon as he took the money from B, he became obligated to repay it, regardless of what might happen to that money thereafter.

a) An entire town was plundered. The attack apparently came unexpectedly; otherwise B would have had his money well hidden. If such attacks had come at frequent intervals, no community of merchants could have survived them. People, however, did live in that town, transacted business there, and even carried large sums of money in their pocket-books. Apparently there were strong measures taken to fend off or forestall such attacks. Occasionally these measures were ineffective. It is important for us to know what these measures were, and why they were generally effective.

b) B had in his pocket-book twenty-one pounds. That was a very large sum (equivalent, in buying power, to about five thousand dollars of our money) for a person to carry about. Apparently B often transacted business on a large scale, and needed that much ready cash. Thus merchants at this time transacted business on a large scale.

c) B readily lent a pound to A at no interest and without taking a pledge. Again we note the close cooperation between Jews, their readiness to help one another, and their complete trust in one another. (A pound was a large sum of money; it could buy two vineyards.)

d) A owed money to a non-Jew. He either borrowed that money from the latter, or bought merchandise from him on credit.

·   ·   ·   ·

A Responsum of R. Meshullam b. Kalonymus.

Q. A and C were partners in the management of the affairs of the bishopric of Narbonne. When C died leaving a young orphan, the latter's guardian appointed C's brother, B, to take over the active management of the bishopric on behalf of that orphan. Subsequently A, too, passed away. A's son then sued B, asserting that the latter had earned much profit from the above-mentioned management of the bishopric, while his father was still alive and after his demise, and had failed to give him his share.

A.   If B earned the alleged profit in the normal way (i.e. in a way that involved no special risks), namely: by buying the supplies of the bishopric [and receiving from the suppliers a discount which he kept for himself]; by taking gratuities from the Gentiles with whom he carried on the business of the bishopric; by lending the bishop's money on interest [for the latter's benefit, thus] earning a discount; by selling gold and silver of the bishopric at a higher price than he reported; or by buying gold and silver for the bishopric at a lower price than he charged to its treasury—since these transactions involve no risk, B must share the income from such transactions with A. The latter's son, therefore, may charge B with an oath for the amount of such profit he earned [and is entitled to share in the profit admitted under oath]. A's son, however, may charge B with an oath only for the period since A's demise; he cannot press any claims to profits earned during the period when A was still alive and personally settled his accounts with B. If, however, B earned profit from risky transactions, namely: by using the bishop's money in order to buy merchandise for himself, and then selling this merchandise at a profit; or by selling gold and silver of the bishopric and then investing that money with a partner at half gain—in which case B would be personally responsible for the funds thus used; and were the bishop summarily to demand his money, B would have to exchange or sell his merchandise or his own articles at a low price (and thus suffer a monetary loss) in order quickly to raise the required sum—neither A nor his son would be entitled to share in such profit. A partner is not entitled to share the profits of a transaction when he is not to be held responsible for any losses that may result from that transaction. B, however, must share such profit with C's son, since an orphan is entitled to the profits earned by his money in risky transactions, even though he would not have been charged with the losses had these transactions resulted in losses rather than profits. But as to the profit earned by B from the salt of the bishopric, since he earned such profit through great personal exertion, neither A nor his son is entitled to any share therein.

a) Two Jews were partners in the management of the archbishopric of Narbonne. They bought all supplies, sold its surplus produce, and managed its financial affairs. We are thus confronted with several problems: 1) Why, contrary to church policy, did the archbishop of Narbonne appoint Jews in managerial positions where they could exercise authority over his Christian servants? 2) Why did he have two managers instead of one? Why were these two managers partners? Moreover, it seems that A was not very active in managing the archbishop's financial affairs, leaving most of the responsible and lucrative transactions in B's hands, even though his connection with the affairs of the archbishopric long antedated that of B. Thus A's son alleged that B earned much profit while A was still alive but without the latter's knowledge. This was possible only if B was the active executive while A was merely a silent partner. A's son clearly appears to be a silent partner. For what reason, did the archbishop employ two partners as managers of his affairs, one of them apparently a silent partner? 3) When C died, the guardian of his orphan appointed B as manager of the affairs of the archbishopric. Did the archbishop have nothing to say in the matter? Did he abdicate his right personally to appoint a manager of his affairs, and leave this important function to the guardian of C's orphan? For the latter would naturally appoint a man advantageous to the orphan's interests, rather than to those of archbishop. 4) Both the question and the answer clearly state that all the profit earned by B belongs to the sons of A and C and not to himself. Thus the management of the archbishopric is treated as a private business, the income of which goes to the partnership and not to the person who did the actual work. Why?

There appears to be but a single explanation: The Jews who were intimately acquainted with the business and commercial practices of this period were the only ones eminently qualified to manage successfully the large-scale financial transactions of a rich archbishopric. The archbishop, therefore, had no other choice; he had to appoint a Jew as manager of his affairs. As soon as he appointed one, however, the management of the archbishopric became the private business of that Jew. He thus became the only one legally entitled to its financial benefits. No other Jew would dare supplant him, since such an act would constitute outright robbery. The original appointee, therefore, could sell to another either the whole or part of the benefit to be derived from such management; or bequeath it to his children as an inheritance. We have here an instance of "the law of *Maarifa*" (the law of the exclusive customer), even though the term *Maarufia* is not actually mentioned. A and C either bought or inherited the right to manage the financial affairs of the archbishopric of Narbonne from an earlier manager. C was the active manager and, after his demise, B was appointed to take his place and to carry on his functions for the benefit of C's son. The archbishop had no say in the matter, and had to be satisfied with anyone appointed by the guardian of C's son to take C's place. Had he objected to such an appointment, he would have found himself without a Jewish manager, since no other Jew would trespass on the exclusive property-rights of A and C and of their heirs. If the archbishop wanted a Jewish manager, he had to allow that the benefits of such an office be considered the private property of the original appointee, to be sold or inherited as a personal business establishment.

b) Needless to say that "the law of *Maarifa*" gave the manager security in his position and greatly strengthened his hand in his dealings with his principal. A typical feudal lord of this period was unlettered, brutal, and violent. To deal with such a man, a manager of an estate needed great strength of position. The fact that he was indispensable, since he could not be supplanted by another, gave him that strength, and greatly increased his security of life and property.

c) "Profit in the normal way" and "profit from risky transactions." We have here an accurate description of the functions of a manager of a lord's estate and of the various sources of profit to be derived from such management. It was quite normal, and to be expected, for the superintendent to receive a discount on all supplies he purchased for the estate, to sell the surplus produce of the estate at a higher price than he reported; and to accept gratuities from anyone who transacted business with the estate—these practices were considered legitimate, and thus involved no risk. When, however, the manager invested the idle funds of the estate for his own private gain, he did so at his risk; for whenever such funds were demanded by the lord, the manager would have to produce them immediately. There is no mention here however, of directing the agricultural work of the fields and plantations. Either such work was included in the responder's general phrase "Gentiles with whom he carried on the business of the bishopric," or the Jewish managers were merely engaged in the business phase not in the production phase of the archbishopric. The latter seems more probable.

d) Note that in the tenth century Jews were engaged as superintendents of feudal estates. In Poland they were so engaged in the sixteenth and seventeenth centuries. This fact suggests the possibility that the economic history of the Jews in a feudal country followed a particular pattern (first they were international traders and managers of estates, then local traders and competitors of a rising bourgeoisie, and finally money lenders): In Germany and France this pattern began in the ninth century and the full cycle was completed by the end of the fourteenth century: In Poland it began in the latter century, but was not quite completed at the outbreak of the Second World War.

e) "By lending the bishop's money on interest for the latter's benefit." This is a statement of the responder, and reflects widespread conditions of that period far more accurately than an isolated instance reported in a query. We have here undeniable proof that normally bishops lent their surplus funds at interest. Was this the chief reason for employing a Jewish manager? Apparently not. In the list of the usual practices of a manager that brought in extra profit, the lending of the money of the bishopric at interest does not figure prominently. Moreover, at this time the Jews rarely lent money at interest; more often they were the borrowers rather than the lenders. Managers or superintendents of feudal estates probably lent their surplus funds to Jews at a considerable rate of interest.

f) When C died, his brother B, who was apparently a very capable man, was not appointed as the guardian of the orphan. In all likelihood the appointment of a guardian was made by the community, which considered itself as "the father of orphans." The community leaders, therefore, considered the fact that B would take over his brother's business and run it for the benefit of the orphan, and that another man would thus have to be appointed as the latter's guardian to protect his interests as against B. Thus at this early period the community already recognized its responsibility as the natural guardian of orphans.

g) "Selling gold and silver" and "buying gold and silver" figure prominently among the financial transactions of a lord's estate. The former was probably occasioned by the frequent internecine warfare among the nobility where gold and silver vessels were the main objects of loot; and the latter by the fact that such vessels served as practically the only objects of wealth to be displayed at social functions. In the more sophisticated period of the renaissance, of course, *objects d'art* took the place of gold and silver vessels on the social scene, and thus served as a tremendous spur to the development of art and culture. In our period, however, much cruder tastes prevailed.

h) "Investing that money with a partner at half gain." Here we have the fully developed Jewish *commenda* of sharing equally in the profits, so prevalent in the thirteenth century. Why would B have to find a partner in order to invest that money? For buying merchandise with the archbishop's money he would need no partner, but for "investing" it he would need one. Why? Apparently, selling merchandise on credit, or money-lending at interest, was involved here. This often required the help of the archbishop in enforcing payment, and B could not appear as the active merchant or investor. There is also a possibility that the manager of the archbishopric was expected to devote all his time and attention to the financial affairs of the archbishopric, and would have to be a silent partner in all personal investments.

i) "The salt of the bishopric" was a source of income to which B was personally entitled, since he earned it "through great personal exertion." This neither means, that B worked as a common laborer in order to construct the salt pans nor that he personally supervised workers who gathered the salt. It is possible that B took the initiative in developing salt-producing as a new source of income for the archbishopric, or that he greatly improved the methods used in salt-producing, and thus made it profitable. He may have learned of such improved methods used in foreign countries from co-religionists who travelled to those foreign lands. Thus the Jews not only managed lords' estates, but often introduced new ideas of producing income and new sources of wealth for their employers.

The Life
of the Silent Majority

LYNN WHITE, JR.

Feudal law placed the peasant in formal subjection to his lord, and historians have created a picture of the peasant in accord with his legal status. He is seen as oppressed, subjugated, dismally poor, and tightly restricted by being tied to his land. He lives in a hovel and, in general, his life might be aptly described by Thomas Hobbes' famous description of life in the state of nature: it is nasty, brutish, and short.

What would the peasant have said about this portrait of himself? He might have looked on the progressive strengthening of the bond between himself and his land very differently from the way we moderns look upon it. In the chaotic conditions of the early Middle Ages, it may have been much more important to the peasant that the land was tied to him than that he was tied to it. It was an age when farms needed protection from invaders and marauders and when there were few alternatives to the agricultural life. While a peasant might aspire to the aristocracy, this goal was probably not possible for most, and if he was going to be a farmer, his security on the land was of paramount importance to him. Also, economic and political conditions did affect the lives of peasants, and a peasant, like others involved in economic life, must have had some hope of improving his living standard when peace permitted a limited market economy to function.

Besides the minor fluctuations in the quality of agrarian life, there was a long-term improvement between the tenth and twelfth centuries. This growth in prosperity stemmed both from the advance of agricultural technology, mentioned by White in this selection, and from the expansion of arable land. After the Viking invasions, Europeans took the offensive against their neighbors and settled on the lands of those they conquered. At the same time, lords sought to reclaim lands that had lain fallow during the period of chaos. In order to entice peasants to migrate to areas where prospects and security were uncertain, the lords offered easy terms for holding newly cleared land. Migration to new areas and reclamation work provided the peasantry with a double reward. The productivity of the group as a whole increased, and the peasants were able to improve their status and living conditions.

In this article, Lynn White analyzes the literary evidence for the conditions of peasant life in the eleventh century and relates it to his studies on agricultural technology.

The scholarly literature on peasant life seems to have neglected the earliest detailed description of medieval rustic households. Shortly after 1050, in southern Germany, there was written *Ruodlieb*, a Latin versified novel. Although the author was presumably a cleric, his intention was simply to entertain. Ruodlieb, a young knight, leaves his mother in charge of his inherited lands and fares forth to a variety of adventures. After ten years he hears that his mother is getting old and lonely, so he starts toward home. As he is journeying he is joined by a rascally redhead. The road being muddy, the redhead starts riding through the adjacent fields and is promptly beaten by indignant peasants. As evening comes on, the two travelers approach a village. The redhead calls to a shepherd asking for the names of prosperous persons who might put them up for the night. The shepherd replies that it would be a poor man indeed who could not take in two like them and stable their horses, and that there were many thereabout who would not be embarrassed if a count with a hundred retainers asked hospitality.

Having thus adequately insulted the horsemen, the shepherd goes on to suggest that they stay with a former widow who has a big house near the beginning of the village, and who had recently married the young manager of her properties. This is not to the redhead's liking: "Est vetus hic aliquis," he asks, "cui sit pulcherrima coniunx?"—"Isn't there some old man here with a pretty wife?" There is indeed, and the shepherd expresses no high opinion of the wench's morals.

Ruodlieb, our hero, who has more of the Tennysonian than of the medieval Galahad in his temperament, chooses the shepherd's first recommendation and spends a most comfortable night. The redhead, needless to say, goes to the house of the old man with the flirtatious wife, seduces her, is discovered, and murders the husband. Next morning he is tried in the village church before a judge assisted by what appears to be a jury, and is executed.

The author of the poem has no sociological intent: his description of German peasant life in the middle of the eleventh century is the more valuable because he is simply telling a picaresque story in a context familiar to his audience. Here we view a lively, self-confident, prosperous agrarian society. The village is of considerable size. The houses are built around courts which include stables, barns, storehouses, and latrines. There are many cattle, horses, sheep, goats, hogs, chickens, geese, and bees, not to mention pet dogs and cats, and a large establishment has several hired servants. There is plenty of food, including meat, and for special occasions one drinks wine or mead. Surplus production is sold for money, and there is some participation in commerce:

From White Jr., Lynn. "The Life of the Silent Majority" from pp. 86–100 of *Life and Thought in the Early Middle Ages* edited by Robert S. Hoyt, University of Minnesota Press, Minneapolis. © 1967 University of Minnesota.

spices are twice mentioned, and the hussy has a fur robe. At the house where Ruodlieb stays, a cup magnificently carved of walnut wood, and ornamented with gold, is brought out in his honor. Our author, however, is not romanticizing the peasant: the older men in particular are unkempt, dirty, and rough in their manners.

What are we to think of the fact that this eleventh-century picture of northern peasant life is considerably happier than those found in such well-known poems as *Meir Helmbrecht*, two hundred years later, and *Piers Plowman* in the fourteenth century? The key to the difference is the fact that these works have a moralizing intent: they are denunciations of abuses which undoubtedly existed, but this circumstance should warn us not to consider their descriptions normative. *Ruodlieb* may be trusted as more objective because it has as little purpose of arousing compassion for the peasant as of making us envious of him: the author is merely spinning a good yarn in the setting of the society which he knows.

We have reason to believe that the prosperity of the northern European peasantry which is mirrored in *Ruodlieb* was a relatively recent achievement, and that when the poem was written rural life was in rapid flux. Between 1060 and 1088 a perceptive monk of Saint-Père at Chartres compiled the cartulary of his abbey, which contained no documents earlier than the late ninth century. In his Preface he remarks, "I must warn the reader that the first documents which I shall transcribe will be seen to differ greatly from present usage; for the documents written long ago and now found in our archive show that the rustics of that period did not in any way observe the customs regarding services to which the modern peasants of our own time hold, nor do we today use the words for things which were then part of the common speech."

The problem of measuring the pace of change in Europe's rural life is the more difficult because, so far as I know, we have no glimpse of a rustic establishment earlier than *Ruodlieb* except that in the anonymous *Moretum*, a poem stylistically so charming that from the tenth century onward it was often ascribed to Virgil. Its date has been much disputed, but a *terminus post quem* can be set by archaeology, since it mentions a form of quern which has not been securely established as existing earlier than the four or fifth century. The pattern of peasant life seen in *Moretum* is amazingly primitive—almost neolithic. The evidence is the more valuable because the poet's intention, as in *Ruodlieb*, is descriptive rather than moralistic. But since *Moretum*'s scene is Italy, and the contrast between the Mediterranean and the transalpine climates would normally dictate differences in the styles of agriculture, we cannot judge whether the condition of the northern peasantry was better or worse than that in Italy when *Moretum* was written. One suspects that it was equally stark.

The peasantry which are revealed about 1050 in *Ruodlieb*, then, are a new social phenomenon of great significance for our understanding not only of the later Middle Ages but also of the origins of the modern world. What do we know of their emergence?

Even to tillers of the soil, not all of life is work. Yet, much of it is labor of the hardest sort, and anything which changes the pattern of that labor, or improves the yield from it, alters the entire tone of life. We have begun to see that rural life has never been static, and that in certain periods it has changed with great rapidity. Evidence has been accumulating recently to show that in northern Europe, from the sixth century to the end of the ninth, a series of innovations occurred which consolidated to form a remarkably efficient new way of exploiting the soil. It saved human labor and notably increased the peasant's productivity. By the eleventh century, its full effects were being felt. It is this agricultural revolution which accounts for the prosperity of the peasants in *Ruodlieb*.

What, specifically, were these changes in agricultural methods?

The distinctive implement of medieval agriculture in the North was the *carruca*, a heavy plow, usually with wheels, capable of turning over a furrow rather than merely scratching the soil as the Mediterranean plows did. It was not known in the Rhineland in the first decade of the sixth century when *Lex Salica* was still using *carruca* to mean a two-wheeled cart. There are linguistic indications that some Slavic groups were employing such a plow by 568. By 643 it is found in the Po Valley, and by the 720's *Lex Alemannorum* shows that in southwestern Germany the word *carruca* now meant the new wheeled plow. Presumably it reached Scandinavia about the same time, whence it was taken to Britain by the Norse invasions of the late ninth century.

The first great advantage of the new plow was that it could handle heavy alluvial soils which gave better crops than the lighter soils suited to the older scratch-plow. Second, since its moldboard turned over the furrow, cross-plowing was unnecessary, and this saved human labor. Third, it became possible to plow fields shaped in long strips with the earth gradually mounding toward the center of the strip because the moldboard normally turned the furrow inward toward the center of the strip. This arrangement greatly assisted field drainage, an important matter in the wet northern climate. Obviously, if peasants could manage to adopt the new plow, it was much to their advantage.

There were obstacles, however. Colter, horizontal share, and moldboard offered far more resistance to the soil than the old plow. Whereas a scratch-plow generally could be pulled by a yoke of two oxen, the new plow often required eight oxen. No peasant owned so many. The only solution was a pooling of the oxen of several peasants to form a cooperative plow-team, and a division of plowed strips according to the contribution of each. Such a pooling, however, would be impractical in sparsely settled areas, or in hamlets so small that the plan would collapse if one or two oxen died or were stolen.

Thus, while the increased productivity of the new technique would eventually increase population, a certain density of settlement was required for its introduction.

Yet the existence of an established peasant population was itself an obstacle to the spread of the new plow: the fields cultivated by the old type of plow had to be cross-plowed and therefore tended to be squarish in shape; the laying out of the strips which were the most efficient shape of field for the new plow would require destruction of all existing field-marks and individual property rights. This would be psychologically so difficult that we can safely assume that the new agricultural system spread primarily through reclamation and the settlement of lands hitherto uncultivated.

It would seem, in fact, that after a long period of decline culminating in the fearful plagues of the sixth century, Europe's population began to swing upward again, and with increasing momentum. From the seventh century onward, there is indication of the clearing of forests and the increase of cultivation, presumably much of it in the pattern of the new agricultural system with its higher productivity.

The novel shaping of fields in strips involved unprecedented methods of agricultural cooperation. Squarish fields could be efficiently fenced or hedged to protect growing crops; strip fields could not. The new plow therefore required that all the arable land of a peasant community be divided into two roughly equal parts, one to be planted in the autumn and the other left fallow to regain its fertility for the next year's planting. Each of these two big fields was fenced against animals, but there were no barriers between the strips within each big field, which therefore was called an "open field."

There were unexpected practical advantages of this open-field arrangement. In the earlier period, cattle and sheep of a village seem generally to have been led to forage in the forest or on wild pasture where their manure was lost. Now, under the two-field system, they were habitually put into the fallow field and then onto the stubble of the year's arable after the harvest was gathered. Thus the bringing of new land under cultivation certainly did not reduce the production of meat, dairy products, hides, and wool, but probably increased it. Moreover, droppings of the animals on the open fields notably improved the yield of cultivated crops. Thus the herding economy of the Germans and the cereal agriculture of the Mediterranean were integrated into a new and more rewarding pattern.

In the later eighth century there was another advance, beginning, it would appear, in the region between the Seine and the Rhine. There is some evidence that, in contrast to the autumn planting of southern lands, the earliest agriculture of the Baltic area employed a spring planting. In Charlemagne's reign we find some peasants operating not with two open fields but with three: a fallow, an autumn planting primarily of wheat, barley, or rye, and a spring planting largely of oats and legumes. This three-field rotation of crops put greater demands on the soil than the two-field rotation, but the extensive use, in the spring planting, of legumes with their nitrogen-fixing properties maintained fertility adequately.

For intricate reasons of internal economy, a shift from the two- to three-field system enabled a peasant community to increase its production by 50 per cent, provided that they could clear enough new land. The result was a tremendous spurt in reclamation. Even where adequate new land was not available, or where it was too marginal to sustain the more intensive rotation, the northern peasants generally did what they could to get the benefits of the new system: when they were unable to reclaim a third field from the wild or found it unfeasible to redistribute the arable of their village among three rather than two fields, they nevertheless divided the planted field into two parts, sowing one in the autumn and the other in the spring. The scholarly discussion of field systems has frequently been clouded by failure to recognize that in northern Europe even two-field villages normally planted in the spring as well as in the autumn and thus in some measure enjoyed the benefits of the triennial rotation.

It is fundamental for an understanding of Europe's history that the spring planting was possible only north of the Loire and the Alps, because to the south of that line (except for pockets in northern Spain, Provence, and the Po Valley) summer rains were insufficient. As Henri Pirenne accurately observed, in the eighth century the focus of Europe shifted from the shores of the Mediterranean to the great plains around the Channel and the North Sea where it has remained ever since. The essential reason is to be found in the new productivity of the northern peasantry.

In Charlemagne's last years we find the first evidence of still another innovation which eventually added much to the prosperity of northern agriculture, as distinct from that of the Mediterranean: the modern horse harness. Yokes were well suited to the anatomy of oxen, but were singularly inefficient for horses or mules. The modern horse harness, consisting of a rigid collar attached to the load by lateral traces or shafts, may have come out of central Asia, but it first appears in Europe in a Carolingian illumination of about the year 800. With the new harness, which cost no more than the old, a horse could pull four or five times the load which he could handle with a yoke. For the first time horses were available for plowing, harrowing, and heavy hauling. Moreover, there was great advantage in using them, since they are much swifter than oxen and save human time.

There were, nevertheless, difficulties in the way. Especially in a moist climate, the hooves of a horse are much more vulnerable than those of an ox, and heavy labor quickly breaks them or wears them down. The invention of the nailed horseshoe has long been a matter of ardent controversy, and has been claimed not only for the Romans but even for the pre-Roman Celts. Fortunately archaeologists are coming to realize that the stratification of horseshoes is a matter for great caution. When a horse bogs in mud, the suction caused by its efforts to pull its feet up may well deposit a shoe two or three feet below the surface, and invariably, it would seem, adjacent to a fragment of Aretine pottery. When a horse loses a shoe in a rodent's hole, the small inhabitant of the burrow pulls it downward as often as outward; and there, below, is sure to be a coin of Vespasian. Even earthworms complicate the problem. Where there is a heavy population of worms, they may deposit as much as a quarter of an inch of droppings annually on the surface, with the result that small heavy objects like horseshoes work down into the soil. Since there is no literary or iconographic evidence of horseshoes in antiquity, one is driven for assurance to burials of horses with their masters. The earliest unambiguous archaeological indication of nailed horseshoes comes from rider-graves of the Yenesei basin in Siberia dating from the transition between the ninth and tenth centuries. Simultaneously, they are mentioned in a Byzantine text and in a Latin poem written in Germany. Is it merely a coincidence that at that same moment, from Norway, we have the first word of horses being used routinely for plowing? Surely horseshoes as well as the modern harness were prerequisites.

As more scholars become aware of problems of this sort, more evidence will turn up. It is worth noting that nailed horseshoes were habitual, at least for ridden horses, in *Ruodlieb* (V, 602). Although the British Isles seem to have lagged somewhat, by the end of the eleventh century horses were displacing oxen in agriculture, or had already done so, in regions as separated as northern France and Kievan Russia. Not, however, in the Mediterranean lands which climatically were confined to the autumn planting. In the region of summer rains the spring planting provided an abundance of oats which enabled the northern peasants, save on marginal soils, to use the more costly horse in place of the cheaper ox. The ox, however, was expensive of human time and spirit, and the southern peasants plodded behind him because they could do nothing else. The agricultural revolution of the northern Middle Ages which makes intelligible the peasant life pictured in *Ruodlieb* is relevant not only to Europe's economic life but also to its psychic development.

Agrarian archaeology has begun to inform us that as early as the eleventh century the peasants of the North were beginning to regroup their dwellings. The ox is so slow that plowmen using it had to live fairly close to their fields. When the faster horse came into use for rural labor, one could efficiently live much farther from the fields. The mathematical rule relating the length of a radius to the area of a circle came into play. Many tiny hamlets were abandoned; the peasants agglomerated into the sort of big village which we see in *Ruodlieb*: its economic base is strictly agricultural, but it has tinges of urbanism. In such a village of two or three hundred families one could enjoy not only better defense but also a fine big church, the prompter ministrations of a priest in moments of crisis, more company, better gossip, and more frequent contact with merchants and their wares. In 1939 a German scholar bewailed the "spiritual urbanization" of the peasantry of the thirteenth century. We are coming to see, however, that by the thirteenth century the process was already at least two hundred years old and that its presupposition was the substitution of horse for ox in farm labor.

The availability of horses for heavy hauling likewise much expanded the horizons of the northern peasants. In the early fourteenth century Pegolotti says that wagons of goods drawn by horses travel more than twice as far in a day as those drawn by oxen. The horse therefore greatly increased the range of markets in which a peasant might dispose of his surplus production, provided he had an adequate wagon.

The history of land transport before the railroad has scarcely been investigated. The pivoted front axle for wagons was known to the Romans and continued in use; but horses, with their swift and abrupt motions, could not safely be attached to a heavy load until the whipple-tree was invented. If traces connect a horse directly to the wagon, plow, or harrow, a left turn puts all the strain on the right trace, and vice versa, with danger of breaking the harness. However, if the traces are attached to the ends of a whipple-tree which in turn is linked at its center to the middle of the front of the load, the tug on the traces is equalized, the efficiency of pulling is maintained, and danger to the harness is eliminated. The whipple-tree therefore is essential to the full development of horse traction. I have not been able to find specific evidence of the whipple-tree earlier than the mule-drawn plow and the horse-drawn harrow in the border of the Bayeux Tapestry, now generally dated not later than 1077. Since harrowing a field of heavy clods is such jolting work that a whipple-tree would be particularly useful, it is worth noting that the earliest reference to a horse harrowing is found in *Ruodlieb* (V, 468–469) a quarter century earlier. Moreover, the poet considers horse-harrowing quite customary. I therefore suspect that the whipple-tree, a grubby but important innovation in transportation, was produced by the sort of vigorous eleventh-century peasants whom we find in *Ruodlieb*.

The increased geographical range of habitual contacts made possible by the horse clearly affected the tone and tempo of peasant life. The spread of the watermill was equally significant. Water-powered grain mills, both the simple vertical-axle variety and the more complex geared kind which Vitruvius describes, first appear in the first century before Christ. Nevertheless, for reasons which remain obscure, they did not become common until after the western Roman Empire disintegrated. Thereafter they keep turning up with increasing frequency all over Europe until by the year 1000 they are part of every rural landscape. Domesday Book of 1086 lists 5,624 mills for some 3,000 communities in England, and there are reasons to think that this count of mills is too low. While we have no comparable statistical survey from the

Continent, England was probably not technically in advance of the mainland. Many mills had gearing, and the millwright who built and repaired mills was a common figure among the villagers: together with the blacksmith he familiarized the peasantry with an advancing metallurgical and mechanical technology. In appraising the destiny of the Occident, one cannot exaggerate the importance of the fact that by the eleventh century in Europe—and, it would seem, in Europe alone—every peasant was living daily in the presence of at least one fairly complex, semiautomatic power machine. It is no accident that in the eleventh century water power is first applied to industrial processes other than milling: trip-hammer devices are found both in the forges of smiths and in watermills employed in the fulling of cloth fresh from the loom. Our present labor-saving power technology is rooted in a peasant society which had already learned how to apply new implements, new animal power, and new management systems to the more efficient exploitation of the soil. The agricultural revolution of the early Middle Ages is the backdrop of the eleventh-century beginnings of the modern industrial revolution which has grown exponentially for the past nine hundred years.

Viewed in this perspective, the eleventh century marks a moment of primary mutation in the forms of human life. Is it possible to understand the mental and even emotional changes which enabled the silent masses of Europe's common people to achieve such a breakthrough?

We are beginning to see that the early Middle Ages in Europe witnessed a profound alteration of attitudes toward nature. This shift in the world view was based partly on the agricultural revolution of that era and partly on the revolution in popular religion which was occurring simultaneously.

In the days of the scratch-plow and squarish fields, land was distributed in units which were thought to be sufficient for the support of one family. The peasant paid rent, which was in effect taxes, to the owning-ruling aristocracy, but the assumption was subsistence farming—man was part of nature. The new heavy plow of northern Europe changed this. Since it demanded a cooperative plow-team, the strips which it plowed were distributed in proportion to a peasant's contribution to the team. Thus the standard of land distribution ceased to be the needs of a family and became the ability of a power engine to till the soil. No more fundamental modification in a man's relation to his environment can be imagined: he ceased to be nature's child and became her exploiter. We, who are descended from the peasants who first built such plows, inherit from them that aggressive attitude toward nature which is an essential element in modern culture. We feel so free to use nature for our purposes because we feel abstracted from nature and its processes.

This disinvolvement of man from nature was aided by the slow Christianization of the common people which occurred during the early Middle Ages. Christianity was at first a religion of cities, which embraced only a very small part of the population: as late as the end of the fifth century, at least in the West, there are indications that most peasants were still *pagani*. Even when there was external conformity with the new faith, the essence of popular religion long remained little affected. Merovingian archaeology reveals horrifyingly primitive religious attitudes. Scholars have not yet examined in adequate detail one of the most significant chapters in European history: the gradual spread of the parish system out of the tiny cities into the rude countryside. Not until church towers rose above cultivated fields did the new religion begin to modify the minds and emotions of most men.

Popular religion in antiquity was animistic. Every stream, every tree, every mountain contained a guardian spirit who had to be carefully propitiated before one put a mill in the stream, or cut the tree, or mined the mountain. While one could communicate with these myriad spirits, they were in no sense human: the half-bestial satyrs, centaurs, and mermaids were the symbols of their ambiguity. The Christian saint who displaced the *genius loci* as the most accessible spiritual entity in the new religion was very different. Although he might have favorite shrines, his ear was omnipresent. Moreover, he was completely a man, and could be approached in terms of human interests. The cult of saints ousted spirits from the material objects of nature and liberated mankind psychologically to exploit physical nature freely. The localized *daemon* of antiquity became the medieval demon, a malevolent fallen angel who shared the saint's abstraction from matter and place. One may regard the popular religion of the Middle Ages as gross superstition and still recognize that, as compared with its equivalent in antiquity, it was vastly more sophisticated, and that its new abstraction of spirit from matter fostered a new flexibility in the human utilization of matter.

In the new parish churches of the villages of the early Middle Ages the peasants knelt to talk to the saints. But in those same churches, very privately, they gradually learned to kneel also at the feet of the priest to confess their sins. This was a custom which seems to have been unknown to the Church in antiquity, when public confession and penance were practiced. So far as we can now see, private confession was an Irish innovation spread over Europe by Celtic missionaries in the later Merovingian and Carolingian periods. Under Irish influence, priests in northern Europe particularly came to be equipped with *Penitentials*, manuals for the examination of sin. They trained their illiterate parishioners in moral self-examination, spiritual introspection. In ancient paganism, popular religion had been largely public and corporate, little involved in concepts of personal ethics. The penitential discipline developed by the early medieval Church, and carried by the new network of parishes into the most remote regions of Europe, gradually led to profound changes in the spiritual conformation of peasant culture. It opened the experience of the common people to a new kind of highly personal, interiorized, religion. It confirmed the abstraction of spirit from all externals and thus enabled our European ancestors to cope the more freely with externals. The life of the silent masses during the early Middle Ages therefore marks a major stage in our effort to master both the impulses within us and the forces and resources external to us.

The Poor
in the First Crusade

NORMAN COHN

Popular histories of the crusades focus on the formation of the crusading armies, the trek across Asia Minor to the Levant, and the revival of trade between the East and the West. They also indulge in endless discussions concerning the motives of the crusaders. There is another side to the crusading movement that is not often mentioned or studied but is one of its most significant elements. In Europe, among the common people of the countryside and the towns, the crusades produced a powerful social and religious movement that had profound effects on some sections of the European population. The urban life of the northern European Jews, described in the selection by Irving Agus, was virtually ended by the reaction of the poor to the preaching of the crusades. Among the uneducated classes, the crusades took on eschatological significance, heralding the end of the world and the last judgment. In order for the new world to dawn, all had to be baptized or killed and thus, religious fervor, enhanced by social animosity, resulted in the killing of thousands of Jews and the disruption of the Jewish communities in northern Europe.

Interest in the fate of the Jews runs through Norman Cohn's account of the people's crusade, but the participation of the poor in the Holy Wars produced other social results as well. Towns and villages along the routes traveled by the poor crusaders were devastated by the foraging of the hordes, and stable village communities were upset by the loss of men and women who joined the army. The army also brought the isolated villages into contact with the outside world; this alone must have had a profound effect on the consciousness of the lower classes. But assessing the impact of the poor people's crusades is basically guesswork. Most of those who participated in them died in the process, and those who survived were illiterate, unable to articulate their feelings or ideas.

The half-century that saw the messiahs Tanchelm of Antwerp and Eon of Brittany also saw the first outbreaks of what one may call, without reservation, the messianism of the poor. The context was provided by the first two crusades, in 1096 and 1146.

From pp. 61–70 of *The Pursuit of the Millennium* by Norman Cohn. Copyright © Norman Cohn 1961, 1970. Reprinted by permission of Oxford University Press, Inc.

When Pope Urban II summoned the chivalry of Christendom to the Crusade, he released in the masses hopes and hatreds which were to express themselves in ways quite alien to the aims of the papal policy. The main object of Urban's famous appeal at Clermont, in 1095, was to provide Byzantium with the reinforcements it needed in order to drive the Seldjuk Turks from Asia Minor; for he hoped that in return the Eastern Church would acknowledge the supremacy of Rome, so that the unity of Christendom would be restored. In the second place he was concerned to indicate to the nobility, particularly of his native France, an alternative outlet for martial energies which were still constantly bringing devastation upon the land. The moment was appropriate, for the Council of Clermont had been largely concerned with the Truce of God, that ingenious device by which the Church had for half a century been trying to limit feudal warfare. In addition to clerics a large number of lesser nobles had accordingly come to Clermont; and it was primarily to these that, on the last day of the Council, the Pope addressed himself.

To those who would take part in the Crusade Urban offered impressive rewards. A knight who with pious intent took the Cross would earn a remission from temporal penalties for all his sins; if he died in battle he would earn remission of his sins. And there were to be material as well as spiritual rewards. Overpopulation was not confined to the peasantry; one of the reasons for the perpetual wars between nobles was a real shortage of land. Younger sons had often no patrimony at all and had no choice but to seek their fortune. According to one account Urban himself contrasted the actual indigence of many nobles with the prosperity which they would enjoy when they had conquered fine new fiefs in southern lands. Whether he did so or not, this was certainly a consideration which weighed with many crusaders. And nevertheless it is clear that already amongst the prelates and priests and nobles who heard Urban's appeal at Clermont something was at work which was not simply an expectation of individual gain, whether material or spiritual. As the assembly listened it was swept by emotions of overwhelming power. Thousands cried with one voice: "Deus le volt!"—"It is God's will!" Crowding around the Pope and kneeling before him they begged leave to take part in the holy war. A cardinal fell on his knees and recited the *Confiteor* in the name of the whole multitude and as they echoed it after him many burst into tears and many were seized with convulsive trembling. For a brief moment there reigned in that predominantly aristocratic assembly an atmosphere of collective enthusiasm such as was to become normal in the contingents of common folk which were formed later.

For the appeal at Clermont was only the beginning of an agitation which was at once taken up by many preachers. The Crusade continued to be preached to the nobility by Urban himself, who spent several months travelling through France for the purpose, and by the bishops who had returned from Clermont to their dioceses. It was also preached to the common people by a number of *prophetae,* men who though not equipped with any official authorization had the prestige which always surrounded the miracle-working ascetic. The most celebrated of these was Peter the Hermit. Born near Amiens, he had passed a sternly ascetic life, first as a monk and then as a hermit. He went barefoot and never touched meat or wine. A small thin man with a long grey beard, he possessed a commanding presence and great eloquence; so that, according to one who knew him, his every word and act seemed half-divine. Over the masses he exercised an irresistible fascination. People flocked around him, struggling to pluck from the ass he rode on a single hair to treasure as a relic. Myths proliferated around his life-story. Before ever the Pope had spoken, it was said, Peter had been to Jerusalem. In the Church of the Holy Sepulchre Christ had appeared to him and had given him a letter commissioning him to summon the Crusade. Peter seems to have contributed to the myth by carrying the Heavenly Letter with him wherever he preached. His success as a propagandist was immense. As he passed through northern France an army of crusaders sprang into being. People hastened to sell their belongings to buy weapons and travelling-kit; then, having no longer any means of subsistence, they began to move off. In March, 1096—four months before the official Crusade of the barons was ready—Peter crossed from French into German territory at the head of the horde which he had inspired. And meanwhile other hordes were forming around other leaders in northern France, in Flanders and along the Rhine.

The army which the Pope had envisaged was to have consisted of knights with their retainers, all of them trained in warfare and properly equipped; and most of the nobles who responded to the papal summons did in fact prepare themselves in a sober and realistic manner for the campaign. The hordes conjured up by the preachings of the *prophetae,* on the other hand, consisted of people whose lack of military qualifications was only equalled by their impetuosity. They had indeed no reason to delay and every reason to hurry. Almost all of them were poor; and they came from those overcrowded regions where the lot of the poor was perpetual insecurity. Moreover during the decade 1085–95 life had been much harder even than usual. Precisely in north-eastern France and western Germany there had been an almost unbroken series of floods, droughts and famines. Since 1089 the population had also been living in constant terror of a particularly unpleasant form of plague which would suddenly and without apparent cause strike at town or village, bringing an agonizing death to the majority of the inhabitants. The mass reactions to these calamities had been the usual ones: people had clustered in devotional and penitential groups around hermits and other holy men and had embarked on a collective quest for salvation. The sudden appearance of the *prophetae* preaching the Crusade gave these afflicted masses the chance to form salvationist groups on a much vaster scale and at the same time to escape from lands where life had become intolerable. Men and women alike hastened to join the new movement. Often whole families would move together, with the children and household chattels loaded on to carts. And as the hordes grew they were further swollen by all kinds of nondescript adventurers—by renegade monks, women disguised as men and many robbers and brigands.

To these hordes the Crusade meant something quite different from what it meant to the Pope. The *pauperes*, as the chroniclers call them, were not greatly interested in assisting the Christians of Byzantium, but they were passionately interested in reaching, capturing and occupying Jerusalem. The city which was the holiest city in the world for Christians had been in the hands of Moslems for some four and a half centuries. Although the possibility of recapturing it seems to have played little part in Urban's original plan, it was this prospect that intoxicated the masses of the poor. In their eyes the Crusade was an armed and militant pilgrimage, the greatest and most sublime of pilgrimages. For centuries a pilgrimage to the Holy Sepulchre had been regarded as a singularly efficacious form of penance and during the eleventh century such pilgrimages had been undertaken collectively: penitents tended to travel no longer singly or in small groups but in bands organized hierarchically under a leader. Sometimes—notably in 1033 and 1064—mass pilgrimages had taken place, involving many thousands of people. In 1033 at least, the first to go had been the poor and amongst them there had been some who went with the intention of staying in Jerusalem until their death. In the Crusade too the poor, or many of them, had no thought of ever returning to their homes: they meant to take Jerusalem from the infidel and by settling in it turn it into a Christian city. Everyone who took part in the Crusade wore a cross sewn on to his outer garment—the first badge worn by an army in post-Classical times and the first step towards modern military uniforms; but whereas for the knights this cross was a symbol of Christian victory in a military expedition of limited duration, the poor thought rather of the sentence: "Take up the Cross and follow me!" For them the Crusade was above all a collective *imitato Christi*, a mass sacrifice which was to be rewarded by a mass apotheosis at Jerusalem.

For the Jerusalem which obsessed their imagination was no mere earthly city but rather the symbol of a prodigious hope. It had been so ever since the messianic ideal of the Hebrews had first begun to take shape in the eighth century B.C. Already through the mouth of Isaiah the Lord had bidden the Hebrews:

> Rejoice ye with Jerusalem, and be glad with her. . . . That ye may suck and be satisfied with the breasts of her consolations; that ye may milk out, and be delighted with the abundance of her glory. . . . Behold, I will extend peace to her like a river . . . then shall ye suck, ye shall be borne upon her sides, and be dandled upon her knees. As one whom his mother comforteth, so will I comfort you: and ye shall be comforted in Jerusalem.

In the prophecies of the post-exilic period and in the apocalypses the messianic kingdom is imagined as centred on a future Jerusalem which has been rebuilt in great magnificence. These ancient Jewish phantasies all went to reinforce the great emotional significance which Jerusalem would in any case have possessed for medieval Christians. When, a generation after the event, a monk composed the appeal which he imagined Urban to have made at Clermont, he made the Pope speak of the Holy City not simply as the place made for ever illustrious by the Advent, Passion and Ascension of Christ but also as "the navel of the world, the land fruitful above all others, like another paradise of delights," "the royal city placed in the centre of the world," now held captive, demanding help, yearning for liberation. Moreover even for theologians Jerusalem was also a "figure" or symbol of the heavenly city "like unto a stone most precious" which according to the Book of Revelation was to replace it at the end of time. No wonder that—as contemporaries noted— in the minds of simple folk the idea of the earthly Jerusalem became so confused with and transfused by that of the Heavenly Jerusalem that the Palestinian city seemed itself a miraculous realm, abounding both in spiritual and in material blessings. And no wonder that when the masses of the poor set off on their long pilgrimage the children cried out at every town and castle: "It that Jerusalem?"—while high in the heavens there was seen a mysterious city with vast multitudes hurrying towards it.

While in northern France, Flanders and the Rhine valley the poor formed themselves into autonomous bands, in that other densely populated, highly urbanized area, Provence, they streamed into the army of the Count, Raymond of Toulouse. As a result there developed in that army an exaltation as intense as that which prevailed in the hordes which followed the *prophetae*. Alike in north and south, the poor who went on the Crusade regarded themselves as the elite of the crusaders, a people chosen by God as the barons had not been chosen. When at a critical moment in the siege of Antioch St. Andrew brought the glad tidings that the Holy Lance was buried in one of the churches in the town, it was to a poor Provençal peasant that he appeared. And when the peasant, conscious of his lowly status, hesitated to transmit the news to the noble leaders, the saint reassured him: "God has chosen you (poor folk) from amongst all peoples, as ears of wheat are gathered from amidst a field of oats. For in merit and in grace you surpass all who have been before you and all who shall come after you, as much as gold surpasses silver." Raymond of Aguilers, who tells the story, comes nearest of the chroniclers to sharing the outlook of the poor. It seems to him natural that when some of the poor are killed, miraculous crosses should be found on their shoulderblades; and when he speaks of the *plebs pauperum* it is always with a certain awe, as the Chosen of the Lord.

The self-exaltation of the poor emerges still more clearly from the curious stories, compounded of fact and legend, which were told of the people called "Tafurs." A large part—probably by far the larger part—of the

People's Crusade perished on its journey across Europe; but enough survived to form in Syria and Palestine a corps of vagabonds—which is what the mysterious word "Tafur" seems to have meant. Barefoot, shaggy, clad in ragged sackcloth, covered in sores and filth, living on roots and grass and also at times on the roasted corpses of their enemies, the Tafurs were such a ferocious band that any country they passed through was utterly devastated. Too poor to afford swords and lances, they wielded clubs weighted with lead, pointed sticks, knives, hatchets, shovels, hoes and catapults. When they charged into battle they gnashed their teeth as though they meant to eat their enemies alive as well as dead. The Moslems, though they faced the crusading barons fearlessly, were terrified of the Tafurs, whom they called "no Franks, but living devils." The Christian chroniclers themselves—clerics or knights whose main interest was in the doings of the princes—while admitting the effectiveness of the Tafurs in battle clearly regarded them with misgiving and embarrassment. Yet if one turns to a vernacular epic written from the standpoint of the poor one finds the Tafurs portrayed as a Holy People and "worth far more than the knights."

The Tafurs are shown as having a king, le roi Tafur. He is said to have been a Norman knight who had discarded horse, arms and armour in favour of sackcloth and a scythe. At least in the beginning he was an ascetic for whom poverty had all the mystical value which it was to possess for St. Francis and his disciples. Periodically King Tafur would inspect his men. Any who were found to have money about them were expelled from the company and sent off to buy arms and join the professional army under the barons; while those who had with greatest conviction renounced all property were admitted to membership of the "college" or inner circle of followers. It was precisely because of their poverty that the Tafurs believed themselves destined to take the Holy City: "The poorest shall take it: this is a sign to show clearly that the Lord God does not care for presumptuous and faithless men." Yet though the poor made a merit of their poverty, they were full of cupidity. Booty captured from the infidel was not felt to diminish their claims on divine favour but rather to prove how real that favour was. After a successful skirmish outside Antioch the Provençal poor "gallop on horseback amongst the tents to show their companions how their poverty is at an end; others, dressed in two or three silken garments, praise God as the bestower of victory and of gifts." As King Tafur leads the final assault on Jerusalem he cries: "Where are the poor folk who want property? Let them come with me! . . . For today with God's help I shall win enough to load many a mule!" And later when the Moslems carry their treasures round the walls of the captured city in an effort to lure the Christians out into the open, we are shown the Tafurs unable to hold back. "Are we in prison?" cries the King; "They bring treasure and we dare not take it! . . . What do I care if I die, since I am doing what I want to do?" And calling on "St. Lazarus"—

the Lazarus of the parable, of whom the poor in the Middle Ages made their patron saint—he leads his horde out of the city to catastrophe.

In each captured city the Tafurs looted everything they could lay hands on, raped the Moslem women and carried out indiscriminate massacres. The official leaders of the Crusade had no authority over them at all. When the Emir of Antioch protested about the cannibalism of the Tafurs, the princes could only admit apologetically: "All of us together cannot tame King Tafur." The barons seem in fact to have been somewhat frightened of the Tafurs and to have taken care to be well armed whenever they came near them. That no doubt was the truth of the matter; but in the stories which are told from the standpoint of the poor the great princes regard the Tafur king not so much with anxiety as with humility, even with reverence. We find King Tafur urging on the hesitant barons to attack Jerusalem: "My lords, what are we doing? We are delaying overlong our assault on this city and this evil race. We are behaving like false pilgrims. If it rested with me and with the poor alone, the pagans would find us the worst neighbours they ever had!" The princes are so impressed that they ask him to lead the first attack; and when, covered with wounds, he is carried from the battle-field, they gather anxiously around him. But King Tafur is shown as something more than simply the mightiest of warriors. Often he appears in close association with a *propheta*—in one version it is Peter the Hermit, in another a fictitious bishop who bears that emblem which the poor had made their own, the Holy Lance. And he himself clearly possesses a supernatural quality which sets him above all princes. When—in the story as edited for the poor—Godfrey of Bouillon is to become King of Jerusalem, the barons choose King Tafur as "the highest one" to perform the coronation. He performs it by giving Godfrey a branch of thorns in memory of the Crown of Thorns: and Godfrey does homage and swears to hold Jerusalem as a fief from King Tafur and God alone. And when the barons, feeling that they have endured enough, hasten back to their wives and their domains, King Tafur will not see Jerusalem abandoned but pledges himself to stay, with his army of poor, to defend the new king and his kingdom. In these purely imaginary incidents the beggar-king becomes the symbol of the immense, unreasoning hope which had carried the *plebs pauperum* through unspeakable hardships to the Holy City.

The realization of that hope demanded human sacrifice on a vast scale —not only the self-immolation of the crusaders but also the massacre of the infidel. Although Pope and princes might intend a campaign with limited objectives, in reality the campaign tended constantly to become what the common people wanted it to be: a war to exterminate "the sons of whores," "the race of Cain," as King Tafur called the Moslems. It was not unknown for crusaders to seize all the peasants of a certain area and offer them the choice of being either immediately converted to Christianity or immediately killed—"having achieved which, our Franks returned full of joy." The fall of Jerusalem was followed by a great massacre; except for the governor and his bodyguard, who managed to buy their lives and were escorted from the city, every Moslem—man, woman and child—was killed. In and around the Temple of Solomon "the horses waded in blood up to their knees, nay up to the bridle. It was a just and wonderful judgement of God that the same place should receive the blood of those whose blasphemies it had so long carried up to God." As for the Jews of Jerusalem, when they took refuge in their chief synagogue the building was set on fire and they were all burnt alive. Weeping with joy and singing songs of praise the crusaders marched in procession to the Church of the Holy Sepulchre. "O new day, new day and exultation, new and everlasting gladness. . . . That day, famed through all centuries to come, turned all our sufferings and hardships into joy and exultation; that day, the confirmation of Christianity, the annihilation of paganism, the renewal of our faith!" But a handful of the infidel still survived: they had taken refuge on the roof of the mosque of al-Aqsa. The celebrated crusader Tancred had promised them their lives in exchange for a heavy ransom and had given them his banner as a safe-conduct. But Tancred could only watch with helpless fury while common soldiers scaled the wall of the mosque and beheaded every man and woman save those who threw themselves off the roof to their death.

If one bears these happenings in mind it seems natural enough that the first great massacre of European Jews should also have occurred during the First Crusade. The official crusading army, consisting of the barons and their retainers, had no part in this massacre, which was carried out entirely by the hordes which formed in the wake of the *prophetae*. As the Crusade came into being, observes one chronicler, "peace was established very firmly on all sides and the Jews were at once attacked in the towns where they lived." It is said that already at the very beginning of the crusading agitation Jewish communities in Rouen and other French towns were given the choice between conversion and massacre. But it was in the episcopal cities along the Rhine that the most violent attacks took place. Here, as along all the trade routes of western Europe, Jewish merchants had been settled for centuries; and because of their economic usefulness they had always enjoyed the special favour of the archbishops. But by the close of the eleventh century in all these cities tension between the townsmen and their ecclesiastical lords was already giving rise to a general social turbulence. It was an atmosphere which proved as favourable to the *prophetae* of the Crusade as it was shortly to prove to Tanchelm.

At the beginning of May, 1096, crusaders camping outside Speyer planned to attack the Jews in their synagogue on the Sabbath. In this they were foiled and they were only able to kill a dozen Jews in the streets. The Bishop lodged the rest in his castle and had some of the murderers punished. At Worms the Jews were less fortunate. Here too they turned for help to the Bishop and the well-to-do burghers, but these were unable to protect them when men from the People's Crusade arrived and led the townsfolk in an attack on the Jewish quarter. The synagogue was sacked, houses were looted and all their adult occupants who refused baptism were killed. As for the children, some were killed, others taken away to be baptised and brought up as Christians. Some Jews had taken shelter in the Bishop's castle and when that too was attacked the Bishop offered to baptise them and so save their lives; but the entire community preferred to commit suicide. In all, some eight hundred Jews are said to have perished at Worms.

At Mainz, where there lived the largest Jewish community in Germany, events took much the same course. There too the Jews were at first protected by the Archbishop, the chief lay lord and the richer burghers but in the end were forced by the crusaders, supported by the poorer townsfolk, to choose between baptism and death. The Archbishop and all his staff fled, in fear of their lives. More than a thousand Jews and Jewesses perished, either by suicide or at the hands of the crusaders. From the Rhine cities a band of crusaders moved to Trier. The Archbishop delivered a sermon demanding that the Jews be spared; but as a result he himself had to flee from the church. Here too, although some Jews accepted baptism, the great majority perished. The crusaders moved on to Metz, where they killed some more Jews, and then returned in mid-June to Cologne. The Jewish community had gone into hiding in neighbouring villages; but they were discovered by the crusaders and massacred in hundreds. Meanwhile other bands of crusaders, making their way eastwards, had imposed baptism by force on the communities at Regensburg and Prague. In all the number of Jews who perished in the months of May and June, 1096, is estimated at between four and eight thousand.

It was the beginning of a tradition. While in 1146 the Second Crusade was being prepared by King Louis VII and the French nobility, the populace in Normandy and Picardy killed Jews. Meanwhile a renegade monk called Rudolph made his way from Hainaut to the Rhine, where he summoned the masses to join in a People's Crusade and to make a start by killing the Jews. As at the time of the First Crusade, the common people were being driven to desperation by famine. Like every successful *propheta*, Rudolph was believed to perform miracles and to be favoured with divine revelations; and hungry crowds flocked to him. It was still the episcopal cities with their bitter internal conflicts—Cologne, Mainz, Worms, Speyer and also this time Strasbourg and, when the Crusade passed through it, Würzburg—that proved the most fertile ground for anti-Jewish agitation. From them the movement spread to many other towns in Germany and France. The Jews turned for protection, as they had done half a century earlier, to the bishops and prosperous burghers. These did what they could to help; but the *pauperes* were not to be so easily deterred. In many towns the populace was on the point of open insurrection and it seemed that another overwhelming catastrophe was about to descend on the Jews. At that point St. Bernard intervened and, with the full weight of his prestige, insisted that the massacre must stop.

Even St. Bernard, with all his extraordinary reputation as a holy man and a worker of miracles, was scarcely able to check the popular fury. When he confronted Rudolph at Mainz and, as an abbot, ordered him back to his monastery, the common people almost took up arms to protect their *propheta*. Thereafter, the massacre of Jews was to remain a normal feature of popular, as distinct from knightly, crusades; and it is clear enough why. Although the *pauperes* looted freely from the Jews they killed (as they did from the Moslems), booty was certainly not their main object. It is a Hebrew chronicle that records how during the Second Crusade the crusaders appealed to the Jews: "Come to us, so that we become one single people"; and there seems no doubt that a Jew could always save both life and property by accepting baptism. On the other hand it was said that whoever killed a Jew who refused baptism had all his sins forgiven him; and there were those who felt unworthy to start on a crusade at all until they had killed at least one such. Some of the crusaders' own comments have been preserved: "We have set out to march a long way to fight the enemies of God in the East, and behold, before our very eyes are his worst foes, the Jews. They must be dealt with first." And again: "You are the descendants of those who killed and hanged our God. Moreover (God) himself said: 'The day will yet dawn when my children will come and avenge my blood.' We are his children and it is our task to carry out his vengeance upon you, for you showed yourselves obstinate and blasphemous towards him. . . . (God) has abandoned you and has turned his radiance upon us and has made us his own."

Here, unmistakably, speaks the same conviction which tried to turn the First Crusade into an annihilation of Islam.

PART 3

The Peak
of Medieval Civilization,
12th–13th Centuries

The eleventh century marks a turning point in the history of Europe. For the first time in more than a millennium, Europe was not attacked by outside invaders, and its social and political life was not disrupted by massive migrations. European monarchs now began the long process of consolidating their power, and the Church succeeded in establishing its independence from the secular powers. In the same period, the various elements of early medieval society achieved a maturity marked by stability and increasing institutional consistency throughout Europe. This century of change and development was followed by one of cultural rebirth, the so-called twelfth-century renaissance. Scholastic philosophy, Gothic cathedrals, the revival of jurisprudence and of medical studies, all are products of the twelfth century and were carried over into the thirteenth. Medieval civilization flowered, and the selections that follow deal with the major social institutions that underlay this flowering.

The first two selections introduce the problems created by the reform of the Church and the revival of intellectual life. The spirit of speculation that prevailed in the schools produced an atmosphere in which some failed to observe the boundaries of orthodoxy as they raced from idea to idea. Even in the eleventh century, Church authorities had to face the problem of errant intellectuals, and the problem became more urgent and more difficult in the next century. At the same time, efforts to reform the Church opened the door to heretical attacks; this too became a persistent problem for the ecclesiastical hierarchy during the twelfth century.

The eleventh and twelfth centuries were also the age of the Normans. Norman knights went to the Holy Land, to England, to Spain, and to southern Italy, and they took their feudal system with them. Although feudal institutions varied from area to area, when historians today describe feudalism, they are describing this Norman system. What was it like to grow up within this system, which reached its peak in the twelfth century?

The selection by Sidney Painter recounts the youth of one of the most famous knights of the period.

As commerce and intellectual life grew in the twelfth and thirteenth centuries, they became dependent on the freedom and conditions of travel. The major urban centers became academic and commercial centers, and the network of roads linking them expanded rapidly. Urban T. Holmes' piece describes the conditions of travel along these roads. Charles H. Haskins' selection focuses on one of the products of the increasing commercial as well as intellectual life—the rise of the universities. The international congregations of scholars in Paris and Bologna were created by intellectual ferment, but they depended for their existence on the improving conditions of travel.

The reformed Church achieved a degree of organization and bureaucratic development unequaled in the secular kingdoms of the twelfth and thirteenth centuries. It attracted some of the most talented members of society to its hierarchy and monasteries. It is therefore important to understand the appeal of the religious profession during the period and to try to discover what life as a churchman was like. Two selections in this part, one taken from an episcopal register and one from a monastic chronicle, provide some insight into the alternative careers open to those who entered the Church in the Middle Ages.

The final selection, by Margaret Labarge, returns to a subject taken up earlier, the position of women. The focus here is on aristocratic women who emerged as personalities and powers in the eleventh through thirteenth centuries. Did women hold a better position in medieval society than they had in Roman times? Was there any basis in fact for the new position of women in the literature of courtly love? Labarge's study suggests that neither the glowing picture presented in literature nor the gloomy portrait depicted in traditional historical work is accurate.

Bibliography

For an attempt to understand the nature of heresy, see Jeffrey B. Russell, *Dissent and Reform in the Early Middle Ages* (Berkeley and Los Angeles, 1965), and Gordon Leff, *Heresy in the Later Middle Ages: The Relation of Heterodoxy to Dissent c. 1250–c. 1450*, 2 vols. (Manchester, Eng., 1967). Johan Huizinga's *Waning of the Middle Ages* (Garden City, N.Y., 1954) contains excellent chapters on late medieval popular movements. The standard work on the history of the Inquisition is Henry C. Lea, *A History of the Inquisition of the Middle Ages*, 3 vols. (New York, 1955 [Reprint of 1888 edition]). For studies of ideas and traditions related to heresy, see George Boas, *Essays on Primitivism and Related Ideas in the Middle Ages* (Baltimore, 1948).

For the history of feudalism and the social, economic, and political context of a knight's life, see F. L. Ganshof, *Feudalism* (New York, 1961), and Carl Stephenson, *Feudalism* (Ithaca, N.Y., 1940). Sidney Painter's little book *French Chivalry* (Baltimore, 1940) provides a good survey of the cultural milieu of the knights. See also Georges Duby's excellent article "In Northwestern France: The 'Youth' in Twelfth Century Aristocratic Society," trans. by F. Cheyette, in F. Cheyette, ed., *Lordship and Community in Medieval Europe* (New York, 1968). Duby focuses on knights errant—a class in which William Marshal spent many years—and he tries to assess their place in and impact on twelfth-century society. The classic work on feudal society is Marc Bloch, *Feudal Society*, 2 vols. (Chicago, 1961); see especially Parts IV, VI, and VIII.

The quotation from the tenth-century traveler in the introduction to Urban T. Holmes' "Traveling the Roads in the Twelfth Century" comes from a good article by Robert S. Lopez, "The Evolution of Land Transport in the Middle Ages," *Past and Present*, Vol. 19 (1956), pp. 17–29. See also Margaret N. Boyer, "Roads and Rivers: Their Use and Disuse in Late Medieval France," *Medievalia et Humanistica*, Vol. 13 (1960), pp. 68–80. A short commentary on the same topic is T. W. Parratt's "On Northern Roads in the Middle Ages," *Ryedale History*, Vol. 5 (1970), pp. 3–11. Irving Agus' *Urban Civilization in Pre-Crusade Europe* (New York, 1965) contains a lot of material on Jewish merchant travelers, and later Christian entrepreneurs are the subject of E. M. Carus Wilson, *Medieval Merchant Venturers* (London, 1954).

For the history of education in antiquity and the early Middle Ages, see Henri Marrou, *A History of Education in Antiquity* (New York, 1956), and M. L. W. Laistner, *Thought and Letters in Western Europe A. D. 500 to 900* (Ithaca, N.Y., 1957), Chaps. II, VII, VIII. Laistner's work is a classic on the intellectual life of the Carolingian empire in the ninth century, but he also considers the problem of the relationship between Christianity and classical education in late imperial times. For background material on the schools of the twelfth century, see Charles H. Haskins, *The Renaissance of the Twelfth Century* (Cambridge, Mass., 1927), and Richard W. Southern, *The Making of the Middle Ages* (New Haven, 1953), Chap. IV. On the history of the medieval universities, see Charles H. Haskins, *The Rise of the Universities* (New York, 1923), and H. Rashdall's classic work, *The Universities of Europe in the Middle Ages*, 3 vols., ed. by F. M. Powicke and A. B. Emden (Oxford, 1936). A more recent study, which concentrates on the institutional development of the universities, is Gordon Leff, *Paris and Oxford Universities in the Thirteenth and Fourteenth Centuries* (New York, 1968). For another aspect of the universities, see Astrik Gabriel, *Student Life in Ave Maria College, Medieval Paris* (Notre Dame, Ind., 1955).

On the early history of the ecclesiastical hierarchy, see J. Daniélou and H. Marrou, *History of the Church: The First Six Hundred Years* (London, 1964); Philip Hughes, *A History of the Church*, Vol. 1 (New York, 1952); and Geoffrey Barraclough, *The Medieval Papacy* (New York, 1968). On the origins of monasticism, see D. J. Chitty, *The Desert a City* (Oxford, 1966), and Helen Waddell, *The Desert Fathers* (Ann Arbor, 1957), a translation of early medieval lives of the early monks. On the later history of monasticism, see David Knowles, *Christian Monasticism* (London, 1969). On the culture of monasticism, see Jean Leclercq, *The Love of Learning and the Desire for God* (New York, 1961).

A remarkable amount of literature about women was published in the 1890s, perhaps as a response to the women's suffrage movement. See, for example, A. R. Cleveland, *Woman Under English Law from Anglo-Saxon Times to the Present* (London, 1896); G. Hill, *Women in English Life from Medieval to Modern Times* (London, 1896); and M. A. R. de Maulde La Clavière, *The Women of the Renaissance; a Study of Feminism* (London, 1900). Eileen Power, a highly regarded economic historian, wrote a fine article on women in C. G. Crump and E. F. Jacob, eds., *The Legacy of the Middle Ages* (Oxford, 1926). She also portrayed two women in her book of characterizations, *Medieval People* (London, 1924). See also Wallace Notestein, "The English Women 1580–1650," in J. H. Plumb, ed., *Studies in Social History. A Tribute to G. M. Trevelyan* (London, 1955).

The Problems
of an Aberrant Intellectual

PETER ABELARD

Hunting Subversion
in the Middle Ages

AUSTIN P. EVANS

One of the focal points in the debate between critics and defenders of the medieval Church is its treatment of heretics. The principal ecclesiastical institution set up to deal with dissenters was the Inquisition, which flourished from the thirteenth to the sixteenth centuries. But heresy was not a problem of that period alone. It had been a persistent problem in the early days of the Christian movement and became very serious after the conversion of Constantine. Many of the early heresies arose from theological debates in which the orthodox position became accepted as such only after authoritative decisions had been made by general ecclesiastical councils. Thus, the council of Nicaea rejected Arianism after a lengthy discussion of its tenets, and many other theological positions received the same treatment during the following centuries. The abstruseness of some of these positions should not prevent appreciation of their importance in the history of the ecclesiastical community. Theological differences often split the Church and created alternative authority structures to challenge the orthodox hierarchy.

The decline of intellectual life after the establishment of the Germanic kingdoms in Europe caused a sharp decrease in the number of heretical movements based on the teachings of errant intellectuals. There were few condemnations of such men until the eleventh and twelfth centuries, when the revival of learning, associated with the founding of the first European universities (see Charles H. Haskins' "The Rise of the Universities" in this section), again produced an intellectual atmosphere in which heresy born of sophisticated speculation became a problem for ecclesiastical authorities. Charges made against men like Berengar of Tours and Roscellinus in the eleventh century and Peter Abelard and Gilbert de la Porée in the twelfth repeatedly referred to the danger that their heterodox ideas would mislead the masses and become a threat to the ecclesiastical community.

But the threat that had been real in the third, fourth, and fifth centuries was no longer very serious in the twelfth century. By that time, the ecclesiastical authorities had become so well established and so much a part of the secular as well as religious authority structure in Europe that its attacks on the errant intellectuals appear unjustified, even in a period when the ideal of freedom of thought attracted few adherents.

In the first selection of the pair presented here, Peter Abelard describes the difficulties he found himself in just prior to his first condemnation at the council of Soissons in 1120. The passage comes from his *History of My Calamities* and deals with the period just after he had been castrated by Heloise's uncle in retaliation for his secret marriage to her. Both of the famous lovers retired to cloisters—Peter to the great house of St. Denis, where he quickly attracted attention as a teacher again and where he immediately began having trouble with the authorities.

The concern of the hierarchy with the effect of new and questionable theological positions was not so incomprehensible as it may seem. There was a dramatic increase in the incidence of popular heresy in the eleventh and twelfth centuries that presented considerable difficulties for those in power. The lower-class heretics had little to do with the theological debates in the schools, but for orthodox churchmen, the connection between errant theological ideas and popular heresy appeared real and dangerous. In fact, until the late nineteenth century, most historians treated the popular heresies as religious protests, despite the provocative Marxist interpretation that they were really manifestations of the class struggle. Non-Marxist historians began to take this interpretation seriously only at the end of the last century, when their researches had shown that heretics often attacked the authority of the Church and often had social grievances. It eventually became common to regard heretics as social dissenters. Considering the blurring of the distinction between the medieval Church's religious and worldly functions, it is to be expected that dissent against it would unite social, political, and religious issues.

But it is important to note that while many of the heretical movements had extensive social and political consequences, almost none of them included a specific social or political program. All the sources indicate that the main thrust of the heretics was in the religious sphere, and only one mid–twelfth-century group, led by Arnold of Brescia in Rome, is known to have had a definite political platform. Similarly, there appears to be no decisive correlation between social groups and heresies. Most of the heretics of the early Middle Ages and most of those brought before the Inquisition were peasants or members of the urban lower classes, but this is to be expected since these groups comprised 70 to 80 percent of the population. Heresy was also common among the clergy and the nobility, who were presumably satisfied with the social situation. The validity of the sociological and Marxist theories explaining the nature and origins of heretical dissent, therefore, seems questionable.

Professor Jeffrey Russell has suggested that the dramatic increase in the incidence of heresy during the eleventh and twelfth centuries was connected with the great reform movement often called the Gregorian Reform. The reformers attacked the worldliness of the Church and sought to free it from the power of secular lords. It was natural that the spirit of this movement would spill over the confines of the Church hierarchy and inspire many to attack the ecclesiastical authority and its doctrine without regard to orthodoxy. In the second selection presented here, Austin Evans describes the methods used by the Church to combat popular heresies. These methods, associated with the Inquisition, were developed slowly during the century and a half after the beginning of the papal reform movement.

THE PROBLEMS OF AN ABERRANT INTELLECTUAL

Scarcely had I recovered from my mutilation, when clerics flocked to me, both those of my abbey and others from among my personal followers, and by constant entreaty kept insisting that what I had hitherto done through desire of money and praise I should now do through love of God, devote myself to study. They warned me that the talent the Lord had entrusted to me would be exacted with interest and urged me that, while I had before paid attention especially to the rich, I should henceforth be interested in instructing the poor; they argued that I should realize that the hand of the Lord had touched me especially that, being freed from the allurements of the flesh and the tumult of the world, I might devote myself to the study of letters and become a true philosopher not of the world but of God.

The life in the abbey which I entered was very worldly and disorderly and the abbot surpassed his monks by his base life and bad reputation as much as he did by dignity of office. I frequently and constantly kept speaking out both in public and private against their intolerable irregularities and thereby became offensive and unpopular above measure. They were very glad at the constant pressure of my followers and sought an opportunity of getting me out of the way.

After my supporters had long pressed it and caused embarrassment by their insistence, through the intervention of the abbot and my brother monks, I withdrew to a certain priory to give my time to conducting a school as I had done before. But such a crowd of pupils flocked there that the place became too small to house them and the land too little to sustain them.

While there I devoted myself especially to divinity in keeping with my state but did not give up entirely instruction in the profane arts in which I had more experience and which they especially asked of me. I used it as a kind of hook by which I might draw them, enticed by the flavor of philosophy, to the study of the true philosophy, as it is recorded by Eusebius of Origen, the prince of Christian philosophers. But since the Lord had apparently granted me as much favor in sacred scripture as in profane, my school began to increase in both fields and all the other schools to decline. As a result I aroused the envy and hatred of the heads of the other schools among whom

From Peter Abelard, *The Story of Abelard's Adversities*, translated by J. T. Muckle (Toronto: Pontifical Institute of Mediaeval Studies, 1964), pp. 40–50. Reprinted by permission of the Pontifical Institute of Medieval Studies.

there were two especially who spoke out against me to my back in every way possible and kept objecting that it was quite contrary to the profession of a monk to be engaged in the pursuit of secular literature; they maintained that I had presumed to take a chair in Sacred Science without having studied under a master. Their object was that all teaching in a school be forbidden to me and to effect this they constantly kept pressing bishops, archbishops, abbots and all persons prominent in religion within reach.

As chance would have it I first gave myself to discuss the foundation of our faith by analogies from reason, and composed for my students a theological tractate, *On the Unity and Trinity of God.* They had kept asking of me rational and philosophical expositions and insisting on what could be understood and not mere declarations, saying that a flow of words is useless if reason does not follow them, that nothing is believed unless it first be understood and that it is ridiculous for a man to proclaim to others what neither he nor his pupils can grasp by their intelligence. Such a man, they said, was branded by the Lord as a blind leader of the blind. When most men saw and read this treatise, they were very pleased with it as it appeared to answer all questions alike on the subject. And since these questions seemed especially difficult, the subtlety of their solution appeared the greater.

Then my rivals, especially the two old plotters, Alberic and Lotulf, became greatly aroused and got a council to meet against me; since their masters and mine, William and Anselm, were dead, they sought to reign after them, and, as it were, to be their heirs. Since each of them was at the head of a school in Rheims, by their frequent suggestions, they persuaded their archbishop, Ralph, in association with Conan, bishop of Praeneste and legate in Gaul at the time, to open a meeting at Soissons which they called a Council; I was asked to come and bring with me the treatise on the Trinity which I had written. I agreed.

But before I arrived, the same two rivals had maligned me among the clergy and people with such success that on the day we came the people almost stoned me and a few of my disciples who accompanied me, saying that I had taught and written that there are three Gods, just as they had been brought to believe of me. As soon as I arrived, I went to the legate and gave him the treatise to examine and pass judgment on, offering to correct and to make amends for anything I had written or spoken at variance with Catholic Faith. He straightway told me to take it to the archbishop and those opponents of mine that they who had made the accusation might pass judgment on it. Thereby the saying: *my enemies are my judges* was fulfilled in my case. Time and again they went through and examined the treatise but, finding nothing which they dared to bring against me in the meeting, they put off to near the end of the council the condemnation of the book which they were eager for.

Every day before the council opened, I expounded the Catholic Faith according to my writings to all in public and all who heard me commended with great appreciation both my expression and interpretation. When the people and clergy saw this, they began to say to one another: "*Behold now he speaks openly* and no one utters a word against him. The council is rapidly drawing to a close which as we have heard was convoked especially against him. Do not the judges recognize that they and not he are wrong?" Thereby my opponents became day by day more incensed against me.

One day, with the intention of trapping me, Alberic accompanied by some of his students, came to me and after making some flattering preliminaries, said that he was puzzled at one thing he had noticed in my book, namely, that while God begat God, and there is only one God, yet I denied that God begat Himself. I immediately replied: "If you wish, I shall explain it." Alberic said in turn: "We are not interested in your rational explanation or interpretation but only in the world of your authorities." I answered: "Just turn the pages and you will find my authority." He had a copy of the book with him. I turned to a passage which I knew and which either he had not found or else he was looking only for what would tell against me. And God willed that I quickly found what I wanted. It was a sentence from the first book of St. Augustine, *De Trinitate*. It reads:

> "He who thinks that God is of such power that He begot Himself errs the more as God does not so exist, nor does any spiritual or corporeal creature. For nothing whatever begets itself."

When his disciples who were with him heard this they were dumbfounded and blushed with confusion. But he himself to cover up said: "Yes, but it is to be understood in the right way." I submitted that there was nothing new about his statement but it had no bearing on the present discussion for he asked for only the words, not the interpretation. I added that, if he was willing to listen to the interpretation and reason behind it, I was ready to show that according to its meaning he had fallen into the heresy of saying that He Who is the Father is the Son of Himself. When he heard this, like one in a rage, he resorted to threats and asserted that neither my logic nor my authorities would rescue me in this case. He then departed.

The last day of the council, before they resumed proceedings, the legate and archbishop along with my rivals and some others had a long conference on what was to be decreed regarding me and my book which was the question especially for which they had been convoked. And since they had nothing before them either of my words or writings which they could charge against me, they kept silent for some little time or less openly attacked me. Then Geoffrey, bishop of Chartres, a man outstanding among the bishops both from his reputation for holiness and from the dignity of his see spoke as follows: "You know, my lords present here, that whatever the doctrine of this man be, it along with his talent has gained many supporters and followers among whomsoever he has studied and has greatly lessened the renown of his masters and ours so that, so to speak, his vine extends its branches from sea to sea. If privately and without a trial you deal harshly with this man, which I do not think you will do, you should realize that, even though your decision be justifiable, you will offend many and that there will be numerous persons ready to come to his defense, especially since in the book before us we see nothing which should be publicly branded. And as Jerome says: 'courage when displayed always arouses jealousy and it is the mountain peaks which the lightning strikes.' Be careful not to add to his fame by doing violence to him and thereby bring on ourselves the charge of acting not through justice but envy, as the aforesaid doctor remarks:

'False rumor is soon repressed and the life which follows is the criterion of what has gone on before.'

"But if you are disposed to act canonically against him, have his doctrine and writings brought before us and let him have an opportunity freely to answer when questioned so that, if convicted or if he confesses, he may be utterly silenced. At least such action would be in accordance with the statement of Nicodemus who, wanting to free the Lord Himself, said: 'Does our law judge a man unless it first give him a hearing and know what he does?'."

When they heard Geoffrey, my opponents immediately cried out in a din: "Behold the advice of a wizard! He bids us to meet the verbosity of a man whose arguments and sophisms the whole world could not gainsay." But surely it was much more difficult to argue with Christ Whom Nicodemus urged them to hear according to the prescription of the Law.

When the bishop could not bring them to accept his proposal, he tried by another way to restrain their envy saying that those present were too few for the examination of a question of such importance and that the case demanded more exhaustive enquiry. His further suggestion in this matter, he went on, was simply that my abbot who was present take me back to my abbey, the monastery of St. Denis, and summon there some learned persons who after diligent enquiry would decide what was to be done. Both the legate and all the others assented to his last suggestion. Soon the legate arose to go to celebrate Mass before beginning the session. Through bishop Geoffrey he gave me the permission agreed upon of returning to my monastery, there to await the outcome of the arrangement.

Then my opponents, thinking they had accomplished nothing if the question was to be settled outside of his diocese where they could not use force, since they had little confidence in the justice of their cause, got the archbishop to see that it would be very discreditable to him if the case were transferred to another court and dangerous if I should be thereby acquitted. Straightway hurrying to the legate they got him to change his decision and induced him against his better judgment to condemn my book without any enquiry, to have it burned in the presence of all and to have me confined to perpetual enclosure in a different monastery. They said that it should be enough for the condemnation of my treatise that I had presumed to read it in public and had myself given it to several to copy out although it had not been approved either by the Roman Pontiff or any other ecclesiastical authority. They added that it would redound greatly to the interests of the Christian faith if like presumption on the part of many others were forestalled by their treatment of me. Since the legate was less learned than his office required, he relied very much on the advice of the archbishop and he in turn on that of my opponents.

When the bishop of Chartres saw what was afoot, he straightway brought me news of their scheming and strongly exhorted me not to take it too hard as everybody could see that they were acting too harshly and that I could be sure that their violence proceeding from open envy would be very much to their discredit and to my advantage. He further advised me not to be at all disturbed by being confined within a monastic cloister for he was sure that the legate himself who was ordering this under duress would set me scot-free after a few days when he got away from there. And so mingling his tears with mine, he, as best he could, consoled me.

HUNTING SUBVERSION IN THE MIDDLE AGES

As theme of the present discussion I here set down four quotations, taken from documents of the first half of the thirteenth century and bearing upon the problem of heresy and its suppression:

"The Apostle enjoins upon us the avoidance not alone of evil, but the very appearance thereof."

"Lest the innocent be punished for the guilty, or the stain of heresy be imputed to some through the malice of others, we order that no one shall be punished as a heretic or a believer in heretics unless he has been adjudged such by his bishop or other ecclesiastic who has that authority."

"The question should not be asked whether anyone may be condemned for this crime [i.e., heresy] on the testimony of one witness and common report. The answer obviously is no. . . . For, especially in a criminal action, the proofs should be clearer than light. . . . And for this crime no one should be condemned on presumptive evidence, but should be allowed canonical purgation."

"You should not proceed to the sentencing of anyone except on his own confession or on transparently clear proofs. For it is better to leave a crime unpunished than to convict the innocent."

These precepts, chosen somewhat at random, and others like them, run

From Austin P. Evans, "Hunting Subversion in the Middle Ages," *Speculum*, Vol. 33 (January 1958), pp. 1–15. Reprinted by permission of the Mediaeval Academy of America.

through the official literature dealing with heresy during the thirteenth and early fourteenth centuries. They afford illustration of the best thinking of the time relative to restraints which should be exercised in dealing with "subversion" of that day, despite the fact that, as treason to God, heresy was then considered the most terrible of crimes, by which men's souls were damned for all eternity in the world to come and not merely their bodies in this world. The first excerpt is from a letter of Innocent III to his lieutenants in Languedoc, counseling care and moderation in dealing with Raymond VI of Toulouse; the second and fourth are from decrees of councils called to devise measures to bind up wounds, after two decades of the ravages of the Albigensian Crusade, and to aid in fixing the procedure of the newly established papal Inquisition; the third is from a series of replies, by Guy Foulques, archbishop of Narbonne and soon to be Pope Clement IV, to questions raised by inquisitors after some twenty-five years of experience with the new instrument devised to hunt out and bring to justice the men and women who were unsettling the faith of simple folk. They say, in effect, let us now have done with drumhead courts and impromptu bonfires where people are done to death by the score with only the slightest trace, if any, of legal procedure or the attempt to separate the guilty from the innocent. Let us see to it that, by proper procedure, irrefrangible proofs of guilt are established, or, failing this, let us release the suspect or at least delay sentence until better evidence may be obtained.

This, it must be borne in mind, was the ideal. How far was it possible to hew to the line in the actual conflict with the heretic? How far did procedural expedients, which at the time seemed necessary to cope with an ever present danger, vitiate the ideal? How far did strong and sometimes hard men, thrown into positions of power by the rough and tumble of the fight, succeed in stilling their consciences and in justifying, under the cloak of overwhelming necessity, practices which ill accorded with the principles just expressed? We have been troubled over the past few years, in our preoccupation with subversive elements in our own society, with these and similar questions. It has seemed, therefore, of some interest to devote a few moments to asking how men dealt with them some seven centuries ago. As the subject is obviously too vast for a brief discussion, attention will here be directed primarily to certain questions which occupied the minds of men responsible for the conduct of the inquisitorial courts and which have troubled men over the past few years: the use of anonymous informers or spies; imputation of guilt by association and guilt by kinship; failure to assure adequate counsel to the accused; failure to allow the accused an adequately clear, full, and specific statement of the charges and testimony against him; failure to allow the accused to confront his accusers and those who witnessed against him or even to know who they were. Useful evidence is much more abundant on some of these points than on others, but they will all be included in the discussion which follows; the reader is asked merely to bear in mind that this is intended only as a partial picture of inquisitorial procedure of the thirteenth century and that illustration is drawn almost entirely from the region of southern France.

The use of informers has over the years been such a common practice by judicial or semi-judicial bodies that it may seem hardly worth the time it takes to allude to it here. The extent and quality of such use does, however, hold some interest. We are doubtless all familiar with Trajan's commendation of Pliny, his governor in Bithynia, for refusal to entertain anonymous charges against the Christians. "Such accusations," he said, "ought to have no place in any prosecution. For this is both a dangerous kind of precedent and out of keeping with [the spirit of] our laws." Precedents against the employment of informers are numerous, in both the Jewish and the Christian tradition, for the centuries preceding and following this pronouncement. But in the Middle Ages, as in some later periods, these seem to have been abandoned. The use of informers was common procedure in the hunt for heretics, particularly in connection with the Inquisition, and the informer more often than not was supposed to remain anonymous.

Indeed, many generations before the founding of the papal Inquisition, in connection with the heresy uncovered at Orléans in 1022, our sources tell us an interesting tale of a Norman noble who got wind of a nest of heresy in this town in the Loire valley, reported it to King Robert and, under his direction, insinuated himself into the group, won the confidence of its members, learned their secrets, denounced them, and had the satisfaction of seeing his work crowned with success in their burning. There is no mention of a reward for this activity other than that of having accomplished a good deed, unless his later appearance as one of the canons at St. Peter of Chartres may be interpreted as such. But with the Inquisition rewards, material or other, were not long in coming.

Clauses which illustrate the use of informers and show the length to which Church and State were prepared to go in their efforts to erase heresy, specifically from Languedoc at the close of the Albigensian Crusade, appear in the articles of the Peace of Paris ending the Crusade in 1229 and in the decrees of the Council of Toulouse held later during the same year. By the former all males of fourteen years and above, females of twelve and above, were to take oath to eschew heresy and to report suspects to the authorities, this oath to be renewed biennially; and a bounty was offered for such information if and when it led to actual conviction for heresy. By the latter, in each parish a team composed of a priest and two or three laymen of good repute was to search out heretics, their believers and supporters, and report them to the proper ecclesiastical or lay authorities. This was denunciation on a mass scale and it became a regular element in the procedure of the Inquisition; popes, councils, and inquisitors united in inculcating the duty of the faithful thus to assist in the work of rooting out heresy. But we are still short of the actual employment of informers as a regular element in inquisitorial procedure.

Informers were not long in appearing, however. Guillaume de Puylaurens tells of one Guillaume de Solerio who had been a perfected heretic, had of his own volition withdrawn from the sect, and had been reconciled with the Church. During the Council of Toulouse he had been fully reinstated (*restitutus ad famam*) that he might validly testify against his former associates "concerning whom he knew the truth." The clergy were assembled that they as a body might be briefed by Guillaume.

This incident illustrates one usual form of denunciation, the revelation by a converted heretic of the names of associates with whom he had attended heretical meetings, together with the times and places of those meetings. Councils and inquisitors were constant in their insistence that names of heretics and of their believers should be given to suspects before the Inquisition, and inquisitors spared no pains to secure the co-operation of the converted heretic. Inquisitorial registers surprise the reader by the mass of detail drawn from the witness, covering a period in some instances of twenty-five, thirty, or even forty years, and giving the time and place of heretical gatherings, together with the names of those attending. For example, Saurine Rigaud, who had been a perfected heretic in Languedoc about the middle of the thirteenth century, tells of numerous meetings over a period, in this case of only twelve years, wherein she foregathered with a total of some one hundred suspects whose names she divulged. Witnesses with memories such as hers would gladden the heart of more than one member of some of our hard pressed congressional committees. And there was then no troublesome bill of rights by the terms of which the witness might claim the right to silence.

In addition to the converted heretic, or indeed any suspect who came voluntarily or was cited before the Inquisition and required under oath to testify concerning all those, at the time living or dead, whom he had seen at heretical meetings, there were the regularly employed agents or spies of the inquisitors who were used to uncover heretics and, if they had fled the jurisdiction of the court, to hunt them out and entice them back into territory where they could be apprehended or to arrange for their extradition. Two illustrations of men of this type may be briefly sketched.

The first is that of Arnaud Sicre of Ax, a village in the foothills of the Pyrenees. Arnaud's mother, Sybilla, had been a notorious heretic, whose property had been confiscated, and Arnaud himself was not entirely free from suspicion. Being anxious to regain the family estate, he accepted the counsel of his brother, who felt that the delivery of one or more heretics might net him that boon. Arnaud, thereupon, crossed the Pyrenees and searched throughout Aragon and Catalonia, on the trail of Guillaume Bélibaste, one of the last of the Catharist leaders in the region south of Toulouse, who had in 1312 sought asylum over the Pyrenees and had gathered about him some remnants of the faithful. After a long hunt Arnaud found them, succeeded in winning their confidence, and developed a ruse whereby he hoped to lure them into the territory of Foix. For nearly a year he absented himself on the ground that he was searching out some relatives in Aragon whom he wished to bring into relationship with Bélibaste. The time of his absence he spent not at all in Aragon but in the region of Pamiers, France, arranging with the bishop of that place, Jacques Fournier, the details of his plan for delivering the heretics into the hands of the Inquisition. Receiving the full approval of the bishop, together with a sum of money to aid him in carrying out his plan, he returned to his friends at San Mateo, in the province of Tarragona. To them he told a story of the illness of one relative, who was thus unable to journey to San Mateo but who besought Bélibaste to come to her that she might receive the consolation of his ministrations.

There is no need to recount the rest. The ruse worked. On the journey they had to cross a corner of the county of Foix, where officers of the Inquisition were waiting to arrest them. Taken to Carcassonne, Bélibaste proved obstinate and was relaxed to the secular arm and burned. Arnaud Sicre was warmly congratulated for his fine work by Jacques Fournier and the inquisitors, Bernard Gui and Jean de Beaune, who salved his conscience by the assurance, if that were needed, that such people could be caught only by the aid of one of their number who would betray them or by agents who succeeded in securing their trust.

Arnaud had spent some three years, from 1318 to the spring of 1321, in trapping his heretic. In the fall of the latter year Bishop Fournier, feeling that he might still further aid the Inquisition by recounting what he had learned, invited him to depose before that body. His deposition fills some thirteen folios of the register of Jacques Fournier (MS. Vat. lat. 4030), one of the fullest and most informative of the inquisitorial registers now extant. It is a long and, as may well be imagined, a pretty story. But Sicre did not end there his service to the Inquisition. Throughout the following two or three years he continued the search for heretics, with satisfactory results. The little group of Bélibaste's followers was hounded down to the last man. Unfortunately, however, we are not informed whether Sicre finally regained the family property, the lust for which had started him on his career.

The other illustration concerns the person and activity of Blaise Boyer, a tailor and prominent citizen of Narbonne of about the same period as the preceding. He had been suspected of cultivating the Spiritual Franciscans, had confessed at Carcassonne in 1325 before the inquisitor Jean Duprat, was given a light penance, involving freedom from prison, from confiscation of property, and from the necessity of wearing crosses, and was sent off to Sicily to search out heretics and bring them to justice. He operated, not only in Sicily, but in Provence, Italy, and even as far east as Cyprus, in at least one case returning a suspect from Sicily to southern France at his own expense. So exemplary was his conduct over a period of three years, and so favorable were the letters from inquisitors in Sicily that Henri de Chamay, then inquisitor at Carcassonne, in 1328 gave him final absolution, requiring only that he make a pilgrimage to Nîmes and give twenty livres for the founding of a chapel. Boyer's slight brush with the Inquisition seems not to have lessened the esteem of his fellow citizens, for he appears as a member of the town council of Narbonne in 1331, 1338, and 1346. However, under date of 5 November 1351 Pope Clement VI wrote to the archbishop of Narbonne stating that four citizens of the city had petitioned him to have the case of Boyer before the Inquisition re-opened. It was rumored, they said, that he had escaped judgment from the Inquisition by "prayers, gifts, and favors,"—i.e., by bribes—to the scandal of simple Catholic Christians. The pope urgently requested that the archbishop inquire into the truth of the matter and correct anything that was amiss. It would be interesting to learn how Blaise Boyer fared under this investigation, but on this our sources are silent.

There was some risk involved, however, in reporting heretics. We learn from a letter, written in 1234 by Gregory IX to the bishop of Toulouse, that a priest by the name of Hugh, in the bishopric of Cahors, had appealed to the pope for protection from the relatives of two women whom, in obedience to the injunction of the Council of Toulouse (1229), he had haled before his bishop; by the latter they were adjudged heretical and turned over to the secular arm to be burned. Being now threatened with death, he petitioned for transfer to a safer spot. Gregory asked the bishop to look into the matter and to arrange a suitable transfer if conditions warranted.

This was a simple case, illustrative of what apparently happened frequently, particularly during the early years of the Inquisition. But let us consider one much more involved from 1324–1325, a period almost one hundred years later. In the foothills of the Pyrenees, south of Pamiers, one Guillaume Traverii, priest in Verdun-sur-Ariège, charged before the Inquisition that six people of the region were tainted with heresy, and he secured nine others to join with him in this charge. The six were forthwith apprehended and held in custody, under the ban of excommunication when they refused to confess and seek absolution. Testimony was taken, but was of a nature to arouse the suspicions of the acting inquisitor Jacques Fournier, as noted above bishop of Pamiers and later Pope Benedict XII. Finally, under questioning, one of the witnesses broke down, and the truth then came out. Guillaume Traverii, so the record runs, "seduced by a malign impulse and a hateful spirit" had manufactured the charges against the six and had suborned his confederates. Our knowledge of the whole episode comes only from the record of the deliberations of the commission of *jurisperiti*, called to assist in the case, and from the final sentences imposed upon the false accusers and witnesses. But what we have is sufficient to give a lively impression of the possibilities in the situation. Peter Marenges, one of the group against whom charges had been brought, had been a heretic, had confessed, and had received absolution. Were he convicted again of heretical acts, that conviction would automatically entail relaxation to the secular arm for burning. All of the accused had been under sentence of excommunication for a year and were thus without the consolations of the Church. They were also in danger of being declared heretics, without further proof, under the rule that a suspect who remained excommunicate for a year became by that fact alone a heretic. The question arose in the commission, then, what penalty should be recommended for the false priest, Guillaume. On this there was some difference of opinion. The general feeling was that he should receive the judgment which would have been imposed upon Peter had he really fallen again into heresy, but some thought strict imprisonment enough. The final sentence declared by the inquisitor consigned him to *murus strictus*, in chains and on "the bread of sorrow and the water of tribulation," with no hope of amelioration of sentence at a later time. Of the others all, except Bernard Faber who had confessed and broken the case, were condemned to prison, either mild (*murus largus*) or harsh (*murus strictus*); all without exception were to be exhibited in all the towns and villages of the diocese, with yellow crosses and red tongues sewed to their clothing, as awful examples of the sin of falsely testifying. Those whom they had traduced were to be suitably indemnified from the assets of the guilty.

Were this an isolated case, it would hardly be worth mentioning in the present context. But the records of sufficient incidents of like sort have come down to us to create the impression that such framing of innocent people was by no means rare. The temptation thus to meddle in other people's affairs or to dispose of a rival or an enemy was always present. The very harshness of the judgment meted out to the guilty may be taken as some indication of the seriousness of the problem for the inquisitors. It should, one would think, have operated as a deterrent to one tempted thus to settle an old grudge. It might even have given pause to those officials, lay or ecclesiastical, who opened the gates for this sort of thing by inviting all to spy upon their neighbors.

Among other questions involved in the problem of the suspect and getting him before the court is that of the definition of heresy. Could the charge of heresy be brought against one who habitually associated with heretics, actual or presumed, or was related by family ties to a heretic? In law one was not a heretic until he had been declared such by competent authority, after his error had been pointed out to him and he had refused to recant. But in discovering these the Inquisition found it expedient to spread wide its nets, to bring before it all manner of men, guilty or not, and to ask them sweeping questions in order to secure clues regarding those actually implicated in heresy. Illustration of this is to be found abundantly in a manuscript of Toulouse from about 1250, where are recorded some five thousand auditions, frequently, so far as one can judge, including testimony from practically the whole adult population of villages in the region southeast of that city. In these the witnesses were instructed under oath to tell anything they knew about heretical beliefs or activities, of themselves or anyone else, living or now dead. This was obviously a fishing expedition, the questioning turning at times upon who was present at small gatherings, attended by the witness, at which heretical leaders were present and what was the degree of involvement of each, at other times the center of interest seeming to shift to following the activities of certain families more or less prominent among the lesser nobility of the region. Information thus gathered could serve for more searching questioning of those who appeared to be the more deeply involved in heresy.

That association with heretics, either chance or prolonged, might raise a suspicion of heretical tendencies can hardly be a matter of surprise or comment. Prudent men tried to assure themselves against possible unfavorable future report by appearing during the "time of grace," or the period at which, in the opening of the court in a given region, the inhabitants were invited to appear freely before it, confess any commerce they may have had with heretics, name their associates, and receive light penances. Thus we find that a peasant, who discovered that two men whom he had hired as harvest hands were heretics, appeared before the inquisitor, confessed the fact, and was cleared. Another who had inadvertently accepted heretics as passengers on his river boat between Moissac and Toulouse, when he learned they were heretics reported to the inquisitor and was penanced to a pilgrimage to St. James of Compostella. Or, again, there were the witnesses before the court who thought a suspect was probably a heretic because, among other things, he was friendly with suspects and believers or with those defamed of heresy. Just how much weight was given this sort of testimony in actually assessing the guilt of any individual, it would be difficult to judge; that the court allowed it some weight is attested by the fact that the notary recorded it. But in the questioning of suspects the inquisitor was definite in his inquiries whether the defendant, or those whom he might name, were by specific beliefs or acts implicated in heresy. The suspect was asked if he had "adored" perfected heretics, had accepted their blessing, listened to their teaching or preaching, had eaten of food blessed by them, had given anything to or accepted anything from them, had escorted them anywhere, had protected or hidden them; that is, was he a believer, receiver, defender, or protector of heretics. Any of these acts constituted proof of belief in heresy and made one liable to severe penalties. But it was only upon his own confession—and this accounts for the introduction of torture into the procedure of the Inquisition—or the concordant testimony of at least two witnesses that a man could be adjudged guilty of heresy.

Much the same is true of family connection as ground for considering a man or woman a heretic. There are a good many illustrations of suspicion of heresy being lodged, either popularly or officially, against an individual on nothing more tangible than this. One of the best advertised cases is that of the count of Foix, who was under grave suspicion of heresy quite largely because he harbored his sister Esclarmonde, a notorious heretic. According to the anonymous author of the second part of the *Chanson de la croisade albigeoise*, he defended himself stoutly against the charge before the Fourth Lateran Council, on the ground that in harboring her he was merely honoring his feudal oath. However, though he was never actually convicted of heresy, the suspicion remained. There is another illustration, better authenticated, of a man called before the Inquisition in 1254 on suspicion of heresy. It was charged that his mother had been hereticated a short time before and, since he visited her frequently and occasionally gave her provisions, he seemed to give assent to her evil ways. He was required, under oath, to promise obedience in all things to the inquisitor and to pledge all his property. Six others, including his wife, went surety for him to the amount of 50 livres. There appears to have been no room for filial piety in face of the danger threatened by the spread of heresy. My last illustration of this point concerns one Raymond Amélius, a monk of Saint Polycarp in the diocese of Narbonne. Three of the nine counts alleged against him at his trial for heresy in 1337 concerned the conviction for heresy of his paternal grandfather, of his grandmother, and of his maternal uncle. Such heredity was held to place him under grave suspicion of heresy.

The wife and offspring of a convicted heretic were also liable to serious disability in regard to inheritance and right to hold public office. As in confiscation in other criminal actions, the dower rights of the wife were respected provided she had married prior to her husband's commerce with heretics and was not herself a heretic. On the other hand, the heir of a deceased heretic had no right to the property unless he could show that he had held it for a period of forty years and that he was not himself a heretic. Moreover, wife and heir of one convicted of heresy, who knew and acquiesced in the heresy of husband and father, were deprived of all right to the property, including the dower, and the heirs were rendered incapable of holding any ecclesiastical benefice or public office—to the second generation in the male line, to the first in the female line. Documents containing appeals for restitution of property confiscated in southern France by officials of Alphonse of Poitiers and King Louis IX fully illustrate the financial disabilities suffered by the heirs of heretics.

These few illustrations may suffice to show how tempting was the charge of heresy and how all-pervasive was the action of the court of the Inquisition. Much injustice was probably done as the result of the testimony of ignorant, overzealous, or hostile neighbors or of the action of inquisitors who considered themselves prosecuting attorneys rather than judges. None the less, it would be hazardous to conclude that men and women were in the thirteenth century widely condemned as heretics on the basis of association or kinship with heretics, however much common report may have tarred them with that stick and however much such connection may have drawn unfavorable attention to them on the part of ecclesiastical or lay authority and operated to deprive them of rights in property or office.

Let us now turn to consideration of some of the disabilities suffered by the man who found himself actually before the court of the inquisitor? He stood alone. Apart from the opportunity afforded him to mention the names of persons who might support his allegations of enmity toward him, on the part of some members of the community, and the opportunity to secure, if he could, those who would stand surely for his appearance when called by the inquisitor, there was no one upon whom he normally could rely for assistance. Only rarely do we read of witnesses in his behalf; except under the most limited conditions he could employ no counsel; under the rules he did not know the names of his accusers or of those whom the court called as witnesses, nor could he confront them. He was allowed to see the charges and the testimony against him, but these were generally communicated to him in summary rather than in full text.

Let us examine these points. Little time will be spent upon the question of witnesses in his behalf. For a witness to appear before the court, at the call of a suspect and openly favoring his cause, would lay him open to the charge of defending a heretic. Had the procedure of the court provided for such appearance few would have been found willing to risk the danger involved. As I mentioned above, a man whose case was before the Inquisition could escape imprisonment provided he could find sureties who would pledge a certain sum to guarantee his appearance when called. But he was not always successful in finding such sureties. It might also be his good fortune to find support, partial or complete, on the part of one or more witnesses called by the court. Of this the best illustration which has come to my attention is that of the trial of Bernard Otho, together with his mother and three brothers, held at Carcassonne in 1236–1237. Starting with no less a person than the archbishop of Narbonne, one hundred and eleven witnesses were examined on four specific points. There was much variation in the answers. The archbishop, as Bernard's "diocesan," had no hesitation in declaring him a heretic; others were not so sure. Two, both clerics, held there was no truth in any of the charges against him, one asserting that "they proceed more from hate than from a spirit of love." The document merits careful study, but the only point I wish here to make is that, in the course of a hearing, testimony in favor of the accused might sometimes be heard. But such categorical statements as those of the two clerics are not usual.

I have indicated as a further disability of the defendant before the court his lack of counsel. Innocent III in 1199 had forbidden advocates to represent heretics and notaries to prepare legal papers for them. Were this rule infringed, they would make themselves liable to prosecution and deprivation of the right to practice longer their professions. Six years later, in the bull *Si adversus*, he was even more explicit in his insistence that no lawyer or notary should serve any heretic or one of their believers, defenders, or protectors. Since this prohibition was specifically against those who were "still in their contumacy and error" the presumption is that it would not apply to the counseling of suspects before the court of the Inquisition, after its establishment a generation later, at least until their heresy had been proved. That this is the correct interpretation is implied in a letter of Gregory IX, written in 1234 to the papal legate and five bishops of southern France, advising them to investigate certain charges made by Count Raymond of Toulouse against inquisitors in his lands. Among these was the claim that "certain men, proceeding to make inquest in his lands about the said crime [of heresy], put aside normal legal procedure . . . and . . . on their own authority deprive those concerning whom inquest is being made of all means of defense and advice of counsel." It may be inferred, also, from a formulary of the Inquisition, drawn up about 1245. In this the authors, two inquisitors, state that they deny to no one proper defense; their procedure accords with that of other courts except in their refusal to divulge the names of witnesses. Since in other contemporary courts counsel was permitted, and even under certain conditions provided, it seems reasonable to conclude that there was no existing law forbidding counsel to suspects before the Inquisition. In the actual records of the Inquisition, however, no evidence of the presence of advocates before the court, either to advise the accused or actually to argue the cases, appears prior to the third decade of the fourteenth century. Indeed, it would have been a courageous man who would have accepted the risk involved in representing one charged with heresy, and by this incurring the threat of implication in heresy. By the middle of the century theory was, rather, in the other direction. The business of the court should be carried on "simply and directly without the loud speaking and sophistry of lawyers and the ordinary courts of law." With the fourteenth century we see indication of an amelioration of this rule. In 1323 the Inquisition, in the person of Jacques Fournier, bishop of Pamiers, had under consideration the case of one Bernard Clerc, which had already been before the court over a period of two years and was to continue for one and one-half years longer before its final disposition. To Bernard was granted the right to have "an advocate, or advocates, if he so desired, in accord with the form of law and the manner and practice of the court of the Inquisition." A decade later, in the trial of Raymond Amelius, to which reference was made above, the same privilege was accorded by the inquisitor in substantially the same terms.

The whole question seems to turn on the meaning of the phrase "juxta juris formam ac stylum et usum officii inquisitionis." The fact of its insertion into the record of these trials seems again to indicate that allowing advocates to the accused was, under certain conditions, normal procedure, though no other cases have, to my knowledge, come to light, except from a later period. Bernard Clerc, however, found that no lawyer would represent him except by formal order of the court. When one was finally appointed he devoted himself largely to attempting to persuade Bernard to plead guilty and thus gain the mercy of the court. Vidal, in his discussion of this case, concludes that the "stylum et usum officii inquisitionis" consisted in the court designating a lawyer as advocate for the defendant. He was not expected to appear before the court, but confined himself to advising the accused and aiding him in drawing up any papers he might wish to present to the court. He was to be constant in his endeavor to induce the defendant to tell the truth. And he must dissociate himself from the case the moment he became convinced of the guilt of his client. Vidal concluded that the counsel of Bernard Clerc was rather the advocate of the court than of the defendant. Bernard refused his aid on these terms and resigned any attempt at defense. Eymeric clarifies somewhat this situation. He argues that if the accused confesses his fault, whether or not he has been convicted by the testimony of witnesses, the services of counsel are useless, but where there is doubt of his guilt or he insists upon defending himself he may have counsel, "honorable, beyond suspicion in the eyes of the law, with knowledge of both laws, and zealous for the faith." Such a man may be given a complete record of the trial, with names of witnesses and accusers suppressed if there be threat of danger, otherwise they also are given. Elsewhere he holds that the inquisitor may proceed against advocates or notaries who render aid to heretics. Thus his position is that a man may be assisted by counsel so long as valid proof of his guilt is lacking, but when guilt has been established there is no further utility in allowing such assistance. He bases his judgment upon *Si adversus* of Innocent III, to which reference has been made above, and seems to be fully in accord with the principle there laid down.

The actual procedure of the inquisitorial courts during the thirteenth century was, however, not in accord with this principle. Indeed, at almost the same time that Bishop Fournier was allowing counsel to a suspect before his court, Bernard Gui was writing his *Practica inquisitionis*, wherein he states procedure without the delay and irritation of advocates to be one of the prerogatives of the inquisitor. We may conclude, therefore, that during this period of approximately seventy-five years the inquisitors, under stress of the urgent need to root out heresy and with the acquiescence of popes and councils, departed from the normal procedure of the courts in the matter of counsel and only returned when, in the early fourteenth century, pressure was relieved through the decline of the Catharist heresy.

We have now come to the last point under discussion, that of the anonymity of informers and witnesses. This was much debated at the time and has been the subject of sharp criticism on the part of modern historians. From the earliest days of the Inquisition it appears to have been a sore point. Prior to the founding of that tribunal the custom in both lay and ecclesiastical courts was to make known the names of accusers and witnesses. Defendants before the court were allowed to confront their accusers. It was difficult enough, at best, for a man accused of heresy to present a useful defense, given the reluctance or absolute refusal of witnesses to testify in his behalf, the difficulty if not impossibility of securing counsel, and his lack of knowledge of the exact nature of the charges against him. To keep him in ignorance also of the names of those who had given evidence against him and to deprive him of all opportunity to cross-examine them may well have seemed an intolerable handicap.

The matter arose in 1229 in connection with the Council of Toulouse and those there brought under suspicion of heresy by Guillaume de Solerio. When these were cited before the pope's legate to answer the charges, some readily admitted their guilt and were reconciled with slight penances; others with "tougher minds" resisted for a time, but finally sought absolution; a third group elected to defend themselves against the charges and asked for the names of those who testified against them, "because," they said, "mortal enemies might be among them to whose testimony no credence should be given." The names the legate refused to divulge, though they importuned him from Toulouse to Montpellier, because he feared for the safety of the witnesses. But he finally yielded to the point where he let them have a single list including the names of all those who had testified against any of the suspects. This proved of no value, since no individual could tell from the list who had testified specifically against him. Hence they felt themselves unable to prepare a proper defense and in disgust abandoned the attempt.

The question was not then settled, however, for five years later we find Pope Gregory IX writing to the legate and bishops in southern France asking them so to conduct themselves, and so to watch over the process of uprooting heresy in the lands of the count of Toulouse, that "innocence may not suffer and iniquity may not remain unpunished." On the particular point under discussion he wrote: "It has been made known to us by our beloved son, the noble count of Toulouse, that certain men, proceeding to make inquest in his lands about the said crime [of heresy], put aside normal legal procedure, hear witnesses concerning heresy in secret, and, entirely withholding the names and testimony of the witnesses, on their own authority deprive those concerning whom inquest is being made of all means of defense and advice of advocates. From this it comes about that sometimes those conscious of guilt turn to shrewd falsehoods and denounce to the Inquisition those men of good repute, by whom they fear that they may be anticipated in bringing accusation. At times, forsooth, in secret confessions they freely accuse their own enemies, and thus it often happens that the innocent are condemned and wickedness is passed over without punishment." It would not be accurate to present this as typical of Pope Gregory's attitude toward heresy and the means taken to uproot it. It probably reflects rather the criticisms of Raymond VII of Toulouse, with whose mood the pope for the moment was in sympathy. It does, however, make clear some of the objections already being raised against inquisitorial procedure, and specifically this question of the difficult position in which a suspect was placed before the inquisitor's court.

The Training of a Knight

SIDNEY PAINTER

The knight in shining armor is mostly a figment created by medieval romance writers and refurbished and given new impetus by nineteenth-century authors. The real knight lived a life not so far removed in its material aspects from that of prosperous contemporary peasants. He was almost constantly on the move, living the hard life of a traveler and engaging in tournaments or real campaigns. The rules governing his life, so embellished by the romance poets, were largely responses to the demands of his existence and served to make its hardships bearable. Most of the rules evolved out of the conditions of feudal warfare and regulated the treatment of prisoners taken in combat and the relations between the ranks in the feudal army. In the constant round of fighting, one week's victor might be next week's victim, and the economics of knightly life dictated a refined treatment of captured knights. A dead knight was not worth very much, but a live one might ransom himself at a considerable price. If a knight was one of the majority in his class who did not possess any landed estate and therefore had no stable income, collecting ransoms constituted a livelihood. Other aspects of the chivalric code, as the rules were called, aimed at preserving the social and political structure of feudalism, although these too were related to military activities. The feudal system depended on the loyalty of vassals to their liege lords, and this loyalty was the cohesive element of the feudal army. Loyalty was won and kept by open-handedness, so generosity too was a knightly virtue.

It is important to study the training of a knight in order to understand the character of the class. In this selection, we observe the early training of William Marshal, a man who achieved the ideal of knighthood according to the writings of his time. He was born about 1146 in England, the fourth son of a petty baron, John, who was marshal for King Henry I. The marshal was originally in charge of the royal stables and the provisioning of the household, but by John's day these duties had been delegated to others, and the marshal was a hereditary post in the king's entourage. William, as a younger son, had little chance of inheriting his father's position, but he was trained as a knight anyway, since he could make his way in the world as a feudal soldier. As it turned out, his talent won him one of the premier places in the feudal hierarchy of England.

There were several stages in the life of a successful knight. In his early youth, he was taught to ride and perhaps given the rudiments of his education in chivalry. But his real training began around the age of thirteen, when he was sent to a relative's or lord's household as a squire. There he learned to handle a knight's weapons and to be part of a feudal army. He also learned the details of the life style he was expected to adopt. After the squire became a knight, he began an often long period of itinerancy, traveling from tournament to tournament and joining in real campaigns when the opportunity arose. Sometimes knights errant, as such men were called, joined the entourage of great lords or kings and became part of their "team" in the tournaments. William became a member of Prince Henry of England's (son of Henry II) entourage and quickly rose to a preeminent position within it. In William's time, the tournaments were not the controlled combats of the later Middle Ages so often described in popular literature. They were virtual free-for-alls in which knights teamed up and fought as armies. One of these melees is described in this selection.

For the knight who did not inherit a position within the feudal hierarchy, the period of errancy often lasted until he was past forty. At this point, if he was lucky, he would marry into the hierarchy. William achieved this goal in 1190 when Richard I of England (son and successor of Henry II) permitted him to marry the heiress of the great earldom of Pembroke. The marriage made William one of the first lords of England, and when Richard's successor, John, died in 1216, William became one of the regents of the realm. He himself died in 1219.

William's career demonstrates that there was mobility within the feudal ranks during the twelfth century. He was clearly the outstanding example of the possibilities that existed, but many others had similar if not so illustrious careers. In the later Middle Ages, the possibility of rising in the ranks became increasingly restricted as the feudal elite found its position challenged by the kings on one side and by the burghers on the other. In its heyday, the knightly class exhibited vitality and adaptability. Once it was forced to take a defensive stance, it became rigid and regressive in its social, economic, and political attitudes.

William Marshal was the fourth son of John fitz Gilbert and the second of those born to the castellan of Marlborough by the sister of Earl Patrick of Salisbury. Our knowledge of William's youth is confined to a few brief glimpses through the fog of time—scenes which made so vivid an impression on his mind that he could recount them years later to his squire and biographer, John d'Erley. The earliest of these recollections concerned a comparatively unimportant incident in the contest between Stephen and Matilda. In the year 1152 King Stephen at the head of a strong force suddenly swooped down on John Marshal's castle of Newbury at a time when it was inadequately garrisoned and poorly stocked with provisions. The constable, a man both brave and loyal, indignantly refused the king's demand for the immediate surrender of the fortress. When the garrison successfuly repulsed an attempt to take the place by storm, Stephen prepared for a regular siege and swore that he would not leave until he had captured the castle and hanged its defenders. The constable, realizing that his lack of provisions made an extended resistance impossible, asked for and obtained a day's truce so that he might make known his plight to his lord, John Marshal. This was the

From Sidney Painter, *William Marshal* (Baltimore: The Johns Hopkins Press, 1933), pp. 13–29. Reprinted by permission of The Johns Hopkins Press.

customary procedure for a castellan who found himself in a hopeless position. Once granted a truce, he would inform his master that unless he were relieved by a certain day, he would be forced to surrender. If no assistance appeared within the specified time, the commander could surrender the castle without failing in his duty to his lord. The besieging force was usually willing to grant a truce in the hope of obtaining the castle without long, wearisome, and expensive siege operations. When John Marshal learned of the predicament of his garrison of Newbury, he was sadly perplexed. As he could not muster enough men to drive off Stephen's army, his only hope of saving his fortress lay in a resort to strategy. John asked Stephen to extend the truce while he sought aid from the Countess Matilda in whose name he held the castle. The king did not trust his turbulent marshal, but he finally agreed to give the garrison of Newbury a further respite if John would surrender one of his sons as a guarantee that he would observe the terms of the truce. John was to use the days of grace to communicate with Matilda—the hostage would be his pledge that he would not reinforce or provision the castle. Acceding to Stephen's demand, John gave the king his son William as a hostage. Then he promptly sent into Newbury a strong force of knights, serjeants, and archers with a plentiful supply of provisions. Newbury was prepared to withstand a siege—the cunning of John Marshal had saved his castle.

His father's clever stratagem left William in an extremely precarious position. By the customs of the time his life was forfeited by his father's breach of faith. Stephen's entourage urged him to hang William at once, but the king was unwilling to execute the child without giving his father a chance to have him by surrendering Newbury. But John Marshal, having four sons and a fruitful wife, considered the youngest of his sons of far less value than a strong castle. He cheerfully told the king's messenger that he cared little if William were hanged, for he had the anvils and hammers with which to forge still better sons. When he received this brutal reply, Stephen ordered his men to lead William to a convenient tree. Fearing that John planned a rescue, the king himself escorted the executioners with a strong force. William, who was only five or six years old, had no idea what this solemn parade portended. When he saw William, earl of Arundel, twirling a most enticing javelin, he asked him for the weapon. This reminder of William's youth and innocence was too much for King Stephen's resolution, and, taking the boy in his arms, he carried him back to the camp. A little later some of the royalists had the ingenious idea of throwing William over the castle walls from a siege engine, but Stephen vetoed that scheme as well. He had decided to spare his young prisoner.

For some two months William was the guest of King Stephen while the royal army lay before Newbury. One day as the king sat in a tent strewn with varicolored flowers William wandered about picking plantains. When the boy had gathered a fair number, he asked the king to play "knights" with him. Each of them would take a "knight" or plantain, and strike it against the one held by the other. The victory would go to the player who with his knight struck off the clump of leaves that represented the head of his opponent's champion. When Stephen readily agreed to play, William gave him a bunch of plantains and asked him to decide who should strike first. The amiable king gave William the first blow with the result that the royal champion lost his head. The boy was vastly pleased with his victory. While Stephen, king of England, was playing at knights with the young son of his rebellious marshal, a servitor whom Lady Sibile had sent to see how her son fared glanced into the tent. As war and enemies meant nothing to William, he loudly welcomed the familiar face. The man, utterly terrified, fled so hastily that the pursuit ordered by the king was fruitless.

This story of William and King Stephen is, no doubt, merely reminiscence recounted years later with the embellishments usual in such tales, but it bears all the ear-marks of veracity. It serves to confirm the statements of the chroniclers as to Stephen's character—that he was a man of gentle nature, far too mild to rule the barons of England. Furthermore the incidents of the tale are essentially probable. It was quite customary to give young children as hostages to guarantee an agreement and equally so to make them suffer for their parents' bad faith. When Eustace de Breteuil, the husband of a natural daughter of Henry I, put out the eyes of the son of one of his vassals, the king allowed the enraged father to multilate in the same way Eustace's daughter whom Henry held as a hostage for his son-in-law's good behavior. Again in the year 1211 when Maelgwyn ap Rees, prince of South Wales, raided the marches, Robert de Vieuxpont hanged the prince's seven-year-old son who was in his hands as a pledge that Maelgwyn would keep the peace. The fact that Earl William of Arundel is known to have taken part in the siege of Newbury and might well have twirled his javelin before the fascinated William tends to confirm this story still further. Hence one can accept as essentially true this pleasant and very human picture of a dark age and an unfortunate king.

When peace was finally concluded between Stephen and Henry Plantagenet, William was returned to his parents who, according to the *History*, had been very unquiet about him. While John Marshal had probably counted to some extent on Stephen's notorious mildness, he had had plenty of justification for any fears he may have felt for his son's safety. Meanwhile the boy was growing rapidly. Within a few years the Marshal family would be forced to consider his future. If the romances of the time are to be believed, it was customary for a baron of any importance to entrust his sons' education to some friendly lord. John Marshal decided to send William to his cousin, William, lord of Tancarville and hereditary chamberlain of Normandy. The chamberlain was a powerful baron with a great castle on the lower Seine and ninety-four knights to follow his banner. Being himself a well known knight and a frequenter of tourneys, he was well fitted to supervise the military education of his young kinsman and to give him a good start on his chivalric career. When he was about thirteen years old, William started for Tancarville attended by a *valet*, or companion of gentle birth, and a servant. The fourth son of a minor English baron was setting forth to seek his fortune.

For eight years William served as a squire to the chamberlain of Tancarville. During this time his principal duty was to learn the trade of arms. The squire's body was hardened and his skill in the use of weapons developed by frequent and strenuous military exercises. While the chain mail of the twelfth century was far lighter and less cumbersome than the plate armor of later times, the mere wearing of it required considerable physical strength. To be able, as every squire must, to leap fully armed into the saddle without touching the stirrup, was a feat which must have required long and rigorous training. The effective use of the weapons of a knight—the spear, sword, and shield—was a highly intricate science which a squire was forced to master if he wished to excel in his chosen profession. In addition a knight should know how to care for his equipment. A squire spent long hours tending his master's horses and cleaning, polishing, and testing his arms and armor. William's success in battle and tourney will show how thoroughly he mastered these fundamentals of his profession. But while it was essential that a knight be brave and skilful in the use of his weapons, other quite different qualities were also expected of him. God and Woman, the church and the troubadour cult of Courtly Love, were beginning to soften and polish the manners of the feudal aristocracy. For a long time the church had demanded that a knight be pious, now ladies were insisting that he be courteous. If a squire hoped to be acceptable to such devotees of the new movement as Eleanor of Aquitaine and her daughter, Marie of Champagne, he must learn some more gentle art than that of smiting mighty blows. If he could not write songs, he could at least learn to sing them. Finally the professional creators and distributors of the literature which embodied these new ideas, the trouvères and the jongleurs, were formulating another knightly virtue—generosity. Their existence depended on the liberality of their patrons, and they did not fail to extol the generous and heap scorn on the penurious. Every time the squire confessed to a priest, he was instructed in the church's conception of the perfect knight. As he sat in the great hall of the castle while some trouvère or jongleur told of Tristan and Iseut or of Lancelot and Guenevere, he was imbued with the doctrines of romantic chivalry. The squire himself might be expected to while away the leisure hours of his lady and her damsels with one of the gentle songs of the troubadours. Possibly William owed his love for singing which remained with him to his death to the advanced taste of the lady of Tancarville.

By the spring of 1167 William was approaching his twenty-first year. As a squire he seems to have given little promise of future greatness. He gained a reputation for drinking, eating, and sleeping, but for little else. His companions, who were jealous of the favor shown him by the chamberlain, made fun of his appetite, but he was so gentle and debonnaire that he always kept silent and pretended not to hear the remarks. A hearty, healthy, good natured, and rather stupid youth was young William. The author of the *History* furnishes a personal description which probably belongs to this period of William's life. "His body was so well formed that if it had been fashioned by a sculptor, it would not have had such beautiful limbs. I saw them and remember them well. He had very beautiful feet and hands, but all these were minor details in the ensemble of his body. If anyone looked at him carefully, he seemed so well and straightly made that if one judged honestly, one would be forced to say that he had the best formed body in the world. He had brown hair. His face even more than his body resembled that of a man of high enough rank to be the Emperor of Rome. He had as long legs and as good a stature as a gentleman could. Whoever fashioned him was a master." Is this a purely conventional portrait or a true one of William Marshal as he reached man's estate?

In a military society, be it that of the early Germans or the feudal aristocracy, the youth comes of age when he is accepted as a full-fledged warrior. Every squire burned to end his apprenticeship by receiving the insignia of knighthood. The squire followed his master to battles and tournaments, cared for his horse and armor, nursed him if he were wounded, and often guarded his prisoners, but he himself could not take an active part in the combat. Being simply an attendant, the squire had no opportunity to win renown. As eight years was, at least according to the testimony of contemporary romances, a rather long time to remain a squire, William must have been extremely impatient for the day when he would be admitted into the chivalric order. He longed for the time when the approach of a promising war or a great tourney would move the chamberlain to dub him a knight and give him a chance to show his worth.

The occasion for which William had hoped came in the summer of 1167. King Henry II was at war with his suzerain Louis VII of France. While Louis himself occupied Henry's attention by ravaging the Norman Vexin, the French king's allies, the counts of Flanders, Boulogne, and Ponthieu, invaded the county of Eu. Count John of Eu, unable to hold his own against the invaders, was forced to retire to Neufchatel-en-Bray, then called Drincourt. There he encountered a force of knights which Henry had sent to his assistance under the command of the constable of Normandy and the lord of Tancarville. The chamberlain decided that this was an auspicious time for knighting William. A goodly array of Norman barons was at hand to lend dignity to the occasion, and the future seemed to promise an opportunity for the young knight to prove his valor. William's induction into the order of chivalry was attended by little of the ceremony usually associated with the dubbing of a knight. Dressed in a new mantle, the young man stood before the chamberlain, who girt him with a sword, the principal emblem of knighthood, and gave him the ceremonial blow.

William had not long to wait for an opportunity to prove himself worthy of his new dignity. As Drincourt lay on the northern bank of the river Bethune at the southern extremity of the county of Eu, it was directly in the path of the army which had been ravaging that district. Count John of Eu and the constable of Normandy had no desire to await the advance of the enemy. On the morning following William's knighting they left Drincourt by the road which led south toward Rouen. Before they had gone very far, they were overtaken by a messenger with the news that the counts of Flanders, Boulogne, and Ponthieu, and the lord of St. Valery were marching on Drincourt at the head of a strong force of knights and serjeants. As the two barons halted their party to consider what they should do, they saw the chamberlain followed by twenty-eight knights of his household riding toward them from the direction of Drincourt. As soon as he was within speaking distance, the chamberlain addressed the constable, "Sire, it will be a great disgrace if we permit them to burn this town." "You speak truly, chamberlain," replied the constable, "and since it is your idea, do you go to its defence." When they saw that they could hope for no assistance from either the count of Eu or the constable, the chamberlain and his knights rode back toward Drincourt. Between them and the town ran the river Bethune. When they reached the bridge which spanned this stream, they found it occupied by a party of knights under the command of William de Mandeville, earl of Essex, who, lacking sufficient men to dispute the enemy's entrance into the town, had retired to hold the passage of the Bethune. The chamberlain hurried to join Earl William, and William Marshal, anxious to show his mettle, spurred forward at his leader's side. The chamberlain turned to the enthusiastic novice, "William, drop back; be not so impatient; let these knights pass." William, who considered himself most decidedly a knight, fell back, abashed. He let three others go ahead of him and then dashed forward again until he was in the front rank.

The combined forces of the chamberlain and the earl of Essex rode into Drincourt to meet the enemy who were entering the town from the northeast. The two parties met at full gallop with a thunderous shock. William's lance was broken, but, drawing his sword, he rushed into the midst of the enemy. So fiercely did the Normans fight that they drove the French out of the town as far as the bridge over the moat on the road to Eu. There the enemy was reinforced, and the Normans were pressed back through Drincourt to the bridge over the Bethune. Once more the Normans charged, and once more they drove the French before them. Just as their victory seemed certain, Count Mathew of Boulogne came up with a fresh division. Four times the enemy beat their way into the town, and each time the Normans drove them out again. Once as William turned back from a charge, a Flemish serjeant caught him by the shoulder with an iron hook. Although he was dragged from his horse in the midst of hostile foot-soldiers, he managed to disengage the hook and cut his way out, but his horse was killed. Meanwhile the good people of Drincourt had been watching from their windows the fierce battle being waged up and down the streets of the town. Hastily arming themselves, the burghers rushed to the aid of the Norman knights, and the enemy was completely routed.

That night the lord of Tancarville held a great feast to celebrate the victory. The burghers of Drincourt were loud in their praises of the chamberlain and his knights. While the constable and the count of Eu had deserted the town, the chamberlain and his household had saved it from burning and pillage. As the revelers discussed the incidents of the battle, someone remarked that William had fought to save the town rather than to take prisoners who could pay him rich ransoms. With this in mind the earl of Essex addressed the young knight—"Marshal, give me a gift, a crupper or an old horse collar." "But I have never possessed one in all my life." "Marshal, what are you saying? Assuredly you had forty or sixty today." The hardened warrior was gently reminding the novice that war was a business as well as a path to fame.

The war was soon brought to an end by a truce between King Henry and Louis of France. As their services were no longer needed, the chamberlain and his entourage returned to Tancarville. Since no true knight would willing rest peacefully in a castle, the lord of Tancarville gave his followers leave to seek adventure where they pleased. William now found himself in a most embarrasing position, for he had lost his war horse at Drincourt, and the cost of a new one was far beyond his resources. While he still had his palfrey, this light animal could not be expected to carry him in full armor through the shocks of a battle or tourney. The chamberlain, who normally would have seen to it that William as a member of his household was properly equipped, felt that the young man should be taught to take advantage of his opportunities to capture horses in battle and hence showed little sympathy for his predicament. By selling the rich mantle which he had worn when he was dubbed a knight, William obtained twenty-two sous Angevin with which he purchased a baggage horse to carry his armor, but while this arrangement allowed him to travel in comfort, it would not enable him to take part in a tourney. One day word came to Tancarville that a great tournament was to be held near Le Mans in which the knights of Anjou, Maine, Poitou, and Brittany would oppose those of France, England, and Normandy. The chamberlain and his court received the news with joy and prepared to take part in the sport, but William, who could not go without a horse, was very sorrowful. The chamberlain, however, decided that his young cousin had had enough of a lesson in knightly economy and promised to furnish him with a mount. After a night spent in making ready their arms and armor, the knights gathered in the castle court while their lord distributed the war horses. William received a splendid one, strong and fast. He never forgot the lesson taught him by the chamberlain and William de Mandeville. Never again did he neglect to capture good horses when he had the opportunity.

On the appointed day a fair sized company assembled to take part in the tournament. King William of Scotland was present with a numerous suite while the chamberlain himself took the field at the head of forty knights. This tourney was not to be one of those mild affairs in which everything was arranged beforehand even to the price of the ransoms, but a contest in which the vanquished would lose all they possessed. After the knights had armed in the refuges provided at each end of the field, the two parties advanced toward one another in serried, orderly ranks. William wasted no time in getting about the business of the day. Attacking Philip de Valognes, a knight of King William's household, he seized his horse by the rein and forced him out of the mêlée. Then after taking Philip's pledge that he would pay his ransom, William returned to the combat and captured two more knights. By his success in this tourney William not only demonstrated his prowess, but rehabilitated his finances as well. Each of the captured knights was forced to surrender all his equipment. William gained war horses, palfreys, arms, and armor for his own use, roncins for his servants, and sumpter horses for his baggage. His first tournament had been highly profitable.

This success sharpened William's appetite for knightly sports. When word came to Tancarville of another tourney to be held in Maine, he asked the chamberlain, who had decided to stay at home, to allow him to attend. He arrived at the appointed place just as the last of the contestants were arming in their refuges, and leaping from his palfrey hastened to put on his armor and mount his charger. In the first onslaught the young knight handled his lance so skillfully that he was able to unhorse one of his opponents, but before he could complete the capture of the fallen knight he was attacked by five others. Although by drawing his sword and smiting lusty blows on every side William managed to beat off his enemies, he received a stroke on his helmet which turned it around on his head so that he could no longer breath through the holes provided for that purpose. While he was standing in the refuge repairing this damage, two well known knights rode past, Bon Abbé le Rouge and John de Subligni. "Sir John," said the first, "who is that knight who is so capable with his weapons?" "That is William Marshal" replied the other. "There is no man more true. The device on his shield shows that he hails from Tancarville." "Surely," said Bon Abbé, "the band which he leads should be the gainer in valor and hardiness." Much pleased by these words of praise, William put on his helmet again and reentered the contest. So well did he bear himself that he was awarded the prize of the tourney—a splendid war horse from Lombardy.

William now felt that he was well started on his chivalric career. He had achieved the dignity of knighthood and had shown his prowess in the combat at Drincourt and in two tournaments. It was high time that he visited England to parade his accomplishments before his admiring family. John fitz Gilbert had died in 1165 while William was still a squire at Tancarville. Of his two sons by his first wife the elder had outlived him but a year, the younger had predeceased him. Hence John, the eldest son by Sibile of

Salisbury, had inherited the family lands and the office of marshal. When William sought the chamberlain's permission to go to England, the lord of Tancarville feared that his young cousin, being the heir presumptive to the family lands, might be tempted to settle down at home. He gave him leave to go, but urged him to return as soon as possible. While England was a good enough country for a man of mean spirit who had no desire to seek adventure, those who loved the life of a knight-errant and the excitement of the tourney should stay in Normandy and Brittany where such pastimes were appreciated. If one were to acquire the prizes of battle, one must live in a land of tourneys. England seemed to the chamberlain to be an orderly, dull, spiritless country. Carried across the channel by a fair wind, William traversed Sussex and Hampshire on his way to his Wiltshire home. At Salisbury he found his uncle, Earl Patrick, who received him joyfully as a gallant young knight and his own sister's son.

William's vacation in England was destined to be a short one. In December 1167 Earl Patrick was summoned to the continent to aid the king in suppressing a revolt of the nobles of Poitou led by the counts of La Marche and Angoulême and the house of Lusignan. Being in all probability heartily tired of his quiet life in England, William was only too willing to follow his uncle to Poitou. King Henry captured the castle of Lusignan, garrisoned it, and then turned north to keep an appointment with Louis VII in the Norman marches near Mantes. His wife, Eleanor, who was by right of her birth duchess of Aquitaine and countess of Poitou, stayed at Lusignan with Earl Patrick. Their position was far from comfortable. Of all the restless nobility of Poitou none were more turbulent than the five de Lusignan brothers, and none played so great a part in the history of their day. Two of the brothers, Hugh and Ralph, became respectively counts of La Marche and Eu, while Guy and Aimery, expelled from Poitou for their perpetual rebellions, both attained the throne of Jerusalem. Such a family was unlikely to stand by quietly while an enemy held their ancestral castle, even if that enemy was their liege lord. One day near Eastertide as the queen and Earl Patrick were riding outside the castle, they were suddenly confronted by a strong force under the command of Geoffrey and Guy de Lusignan. Although Patrick and his men were unarmed, the earl was unwilling to flee. Sending Eleanor to shelter in the castle, he called for his war horse and ordered his followers to prepare for battle. Unfortunately the de Lusignans were not sufficiently chivalrous to wait while their foes armed. Just as Earl Patrick was mounting his charger, a Poitevin knight killed him with a single blow at his unprotected back. Meanwhile William had donned his hauberk, but had not had time to put on his helmet. When he saw his uncle fall, he jumped on his horse and charged the enemy, sword in hand. The first man he met was cut down at a single stroke, but before he could satisfy his thirst for vengeance on the slayers of his uncle, a well directed thrust killed his horse. When he had freed himself from the saddle, William placed his back against a hedge to fight it out on foot as the loss of his horse made flight impossible. For some time he managed to hold his own by cutting down the chargers of his opponents, but at last a knight crossed the hedge, came up behind, and leaning over the barrier, thrust his sword into the young man's thigh. Disabled, William was easily made prisoner.

His captors mounted him on a mare and set off. No one paid any attention to William's wound, for, according to the *History*, they wanted him to suffer as much as possible so that he might be the more anxious to ransom himself. William took the cords which bound his braies and tied up his wound as best he could. Dreading the king's vengeance, the rebel band kept to the wooded country and made its halts in secluded spots. Henry Plantagenet was not a monarch who would permit the slayers of his lieutenant to go unpunished. One night while they were resting at the castle of one of their partisans, a lady noticed the wounded prisoner. She cut the center out of a loaf of bread, filled the hole with flaxen bandages, and sent the loaf to William. Her kindness enabled him to dress his wound properly. Another evening William's captors amused themselves by casting a great stone. William joined in the game and defeated all the others, but the exertion reopened his wound, and as he was forced to ride night and day with little rest, he grew better very slowly. Finally Queen Eleanor came to his aid. She gave hostages to his captors to guarantee that his ransom would be paid, and he was delivered to her. To recompense him for his sufferings, she gave him money, horses, arms, and rich vestments.

The Poitevin campaign had a far-reaching effect on William's life. In it lay the origins of his intense hatred for the house of Lusignan and his close personal relationship with the Plantagenet family. To understand his bitter feud with the Lusignans one must realize that the killing of Earl Patrick, which seems to us a normal act of war, was in William's sight a dastardly crime. The author of the *History* calls the earl's slayer felon and assassin. Not only did he strike down an unarmed man, an unknightly act in itself, but he slew the lieutenant of his feudal suzerain. The first of these offences probably did not trouble William greatly. Some years later when Richard Plantagenet was in rebellion against his father, William came on that prince when he was unarmed and slew his horse. William afterward insisted that it would have been no crime had he slain Richard himself. To attack an unarmed man was at worst merely a breach of knightly courtesy. But for a rebel to kill the representative of his suzerain was the most serious of feudal crimes—treason. William held Geoffrey de Lusignan responsible for his uncle's death. Whether he simply blamed Geoffrey as the leader of the party and responsible for his men or whether he believed him the actual slayer is not clear. Geoffrey himself denied his guilt, and one chronicler places the blame on his brother, Guy. One is inclined to believe that the two de Lusignan brothers were in command of the party, but had no intention of killing Earl Patrick. Some careless or over-enthusiastic subordinate struck down the earl whom the leaders were simply hoping to capture. This view is confirmed by the care exercised by the rebels to take William alive when, as he was fighting without his helmet, he could have been killed easily. But, rightly or wrongly, William never forgave the house of Lusignan.

The same brief combat which made William the mortal enemy of the de Lusignans brought him to the attention of Queen Eleanor, the ideal patroness for a young knight. The richest heiress of Europe by reason of the great duchy of Aquitaine which she had inherited from her father, Eleanor had at an early age married Louis VII of France. Divorced from him, she had promptly given her hand to Henry Plantagenet. As ruler of more than half of the homeland of the troubadours, as patroness of such artists as Bernard de Ventadour, and as the mother of the countesses of Champagne and Blois whose courts were centers of romantic literature, Eleanor was the high priestess of the cult of courtly love. Unfortunately little is known of William's relations with this great lady. One cannot say whether she became interested in him because of his fondness for singing and his knightly courtesy, or simply because he had undergone hardships in her service. But whatever its origin, her favor was an invaluable asset. Normandy and England were full of brave young knights, but there were few who could say that they had suffered wounds and imprisonment in the service of Queen Eleanor and had been ransomed and reequipped by her.

When William Marshal left Poitou in the autumn of 1168, he may well have considered with satisfaction the accomplishments of his twenty-two years. While he had followed what the contemporary romances tell us was the usual course of a young man's education, he had done so with rare success. At the age of thirteen he had left home to seek his fortune in the service of William of Tancarville. At the chamberlain's court he had served his apprenticeship in the trade of arms and from his hand he had received the boon of knighthood. In the combat at Drincourt and in at least two tourneys he had shown himself a brave and capable warrior. The campaign in Poitou had not only given him a taste of the hardships of a soldier's life, but had gained him the favor of Eleanor of Aquitaine. William could with justice believe that he was on the high road to fame and fortune.

Traveling the Roads
in the Twelfth Century

URBAN T. HOLMES, JR.

The importance of roads in Western history has varied. The Greeks seem to have done the bulk of their traveling by ship, and they planted their colonies along the shores of the Mediterranean. Road systems connected these cities with their hinterlands, but none of the networks was very extensive or impressive. The Romans made the road a central part of their transportation and communications systems, and their roads are justly famous for their engineering. But the Roman road was designed for the specific purpose of military communications and movement, and it went straight to its goal without regard to the convenience of travelers. The military engineers paid no attention to the needs of commerce and built narrow roads that were often ill suited for carts or even pack animals. Often the Roman roads ran precipitously over ridges and mountains instead of following the valleys and winding over the plains. The army, however, needed well-built roads. Over a foundation of large stones went one or more layers of gravel topped by large paving stones. A large supply of slave labor was needed to repair the cracking and settling that was common in the rigid pavement. By the Middle Ages, lack of care and theft of the paving blocks for roadside construction had stripped the Roman highways to their foundations. They have remained in this condition since that time and have continued to be used up to the modern era.

In Roman times, there were severe restrictions on land transport that had nothing to do with the character of the roads. Until the ninth century, draft animals were unshod and could not travel long distances without damaging their hooves. The weakness of horses' feet virtually eliminated them from any serious use and thus deprived the Romans and their German successors of potentially their best animal power. At the same time, the collars used in pre–ninth-century harnesses severely limited the weight of loads. If an animal pulled much more than its own weight, the soft collar would constrict its windpipe and choke it. When the rigid collar was introduced in Carolingian times, it became possible for animals to haul very large loads even though there were few roads and not enough of an economy to make use of the new technology.

That traveling any distance by road in the Middle Ages was a formidable feat is proven by the comments of men who did it. As one tenth-century traveler remarked of his journey from the Greek city of Lepanto to Constantinople (with some exaggeration perhaps), "On mule-back, on foot, on horseback, fasting, suffering from thirst, sighing, weeping, lamenting, I arrived after forty-nine days." No wonder the chief means of transport in medieval Europe was the river system, which, while often indirect and difficult, was easily maintained and permitted the shipping of heavy and bulky loads.

By the thirteenth century, however, the road had again become a major avenue of commerce and communication in Europe. An English law of 1285 indicates the importance of the road system by requiring the clearing of trees, large rocks, and other possible hiding places for robbers to a distance of 200 feet on either side of the country's main roads.

The roads of the Middle Ages were considerably different from the ancient Roman roads. On the whole, medieval roads followed foot and animal paths that had been worn between the fields. Since these roads led from village to village, they were a boon to the commercial traveler, who was thus provided with easy access to the region's markets. At the same time, many of the remains of Roman roads were controlled by feudal lords who demanded tolls. The traveler kept costs down by avoiding these highways, and this economy was important not only to the merchants but also to the many noncommercial travelers who used the roads from the twelfth century on.

One of the scholars who regularly traveled from one school to another in the late twelfth century has left an account of his experiences. Urban T. Holmes used the account of Alexander Neckam (1157–1217) as the basis for a description of the trip from southern England to Paris. Alexander made the journey in 1177, and his experiences were typical of those encountered by most people who traveled to the famous schools of Paris in this period.

The trip to London was an easy one along the somewhat battered Roman pavement of Watling Street. A traveler who rode seriously could average some thirty-five miles a day, making six miles an hour on his horse or mule. He would mount in the morning at six-thirty or seven, modern time, and would ride until the dinner hour at eleven. Usually he rested immediately after this meal. It would be nearly three o'clock, after *relevée*, before the traveler would once more mount his steed, and this time he would continue till nearly six o'clock. In the time-reckoning of the twelfth century we would say that the rider began his journey at *basse prime*, or at break of day, and went on till dinner at *haute tierce*. After *relevée* he continued till Vespers.

Alexander was a cleric in lesser orders, or perhaps he had only the simple tonsure. We will assume that his mount was a mule, borrowed for the occasion, to be left at the Augustinian priory of St. Bartholomew's in Smithfield, London. The harness worn by such an animal was not unlike what we know today. The headstall was of cloth strips, or perhaps of leather. Like modern harness, the chin strap of this headpiece was slipped under the animal's chin and the metal bit was placed in his mouth. The upper strap looped

From Urban T. Holmes, Jr., *Daily Living in the Twelfth Century* (Madison: The University of Wisconsin Press; © 1967 by the Regents of the University of Wisconsin), pp. 19–25.

over the ears. But, unlike what we see today, the headband continued around the head and was tied in the rear with long loose ends. Alexander describes the harness of a palfrey or mule, but his language is not very specific:

> Let the horse's back be covered with a canvas, afterwards with a sweat pad or cloth; next let a saddle be properly placed with the fringes of the sweat cloth hanging over the crupper. The stirrups should hang well. The saddle has a front bow or pommel and a cantle. . . . Folded clothing may be well placed in a saddlebag behind the cantle. A breast strap and the trappings for the use of someone riding should not be forgotten: halter and headstall, bit covered with bloody foam, reins, girths, buckles, cushion, padding . . . which I intentionally pass over. An attendant should carry a currycomb.

We can do better than this, at eight hundred years' distance, by describing what we find in illuminations and sculptures of the time. The bit was always single, but double reins were attached to it. A *culière*, or crupper, passed under the horse's tail and fastened to the cantle of the saddle. The traveling pack was tied onto this. Over the seat of the saddle a third cloth was usually draped. This was called the *baudré*, and we are told that it was often of a rich brown material, well embroidered. It could be very long, almost touching the ground. The bows of the saddle were of wood and, more often than not, were ornamented with plates of ivory, hammered metal, or elaborately painted leather. Supposedly such decoration should be added after purchase from the saddler, but John of Garland mentions the sale of painted saddles. Precious stones could be soldered onto the surface of the pommel and cantle, producing, in our modern eyes, a very tawdry effect. Alexander refers to buckles on the saddle girths, usually two. In the illuminated Bible page of the Morgan Library, the girths of Absalom's saddle seem to have hard knots at the end which slip into openings on the two straps hanging down from under the right side of the saddle. In brief, metal buckles existed, but it is evident that they were expensive enough to be avoided when possible. Metal pendants or little bells jangled from the *peitrel*, or breast strap, of the mount. Women had a sidesaddle (*sambue*), but whether they used it invariably is not clear.

Alexander lists also the clothing that was best worn by a traveler:

> Let one who is about to ride have a *chape* with sleeves, of which the hood will not mind the weather, and let him have boots, and spurs that he may prevent the horse from stumbling, jolting, turning, rearing, resisting, and may make him *bein amblant*, "possessed of a good gait," and easily manageable. Shoes should be well fastened with iron nails.

Most of the traveling at this date was done at a good walk. There are excellent examples of the twelfth-century spur in both Cluny and the British

Museum. It had a single prong or prick, which could give the horse quite a wound if improperly used. The heavy shoe worn by a traveler might have a high top of soft leather, when it was called a boot (*heuse or ocrea*). This is the type of footwear which Alexander has in mind. A peasant, however, might wear a heavy shoe of undressed leather (*revelins*) and drape his legs in baggy cloth which he would then bandage on with leather thongs. This arrangement also could be referred to as *ocreas*. Men of all classes often wrapped their legs with spiral puttees, which are visible to us in hunting scenes or on the legs of knights. As a clerk in minor orders Alexander would have worn dark clothing, perhaps black, and his hair was cut shorter than was customary among the laity. It was nonetheless a little shaggy about the neck and ears. A simple tonsure, or small shaven spot, was visible on the crown of his head. His face was more or less clean shaven. He could have worn a peaked felt hat, with a very narrow rolled brim, but it is not likely that he did. We will picture him as bareheaded.

Although Alexander was traveling without a retinue, he must have made chance acquaintances along the road. When traveling on a walking mule there was ample time for companionship. For our story's sake we will assume that Alexander fell in with a Scot who likewise was on his way to London town. This man, like all his countrymen, wore "Scottish dress and had the manner of the Scot." He frequently shook his "staff as they shake the weapon which they call a *gaveloc* at those who mock them, shouting threatening words in the manner of the Scots." Alexander "closely examined his clothes and boots . . . and even the old shoes which he carried on his shoulders in the Scottish manner." We should like some details on these Scottish peculiarities of dress and manner, but Jocelin of Brakeland, whom we are quoting, gives nothing further. Englishmen were considered "cold of disposition" inwardly.

As the two rode along they would be joined by others, and they would continue conversing in the "commun language" of England, the Anglo-Norman dialect of French. This tongue was careless in its use of cases, and cultivated speakers were ashamed of this laxity; they yearned to improve their speech by a sojourn on the Continent. Like most members of the clerical class, Alexander lapsed freely into Latin when he had complicated thoughts to express. Years of habit in the schools had brought this about. But the Norman speech was his mother tongue and he enjoyed speaking it with the "simple gent," and on occasion with brother clerics. Living in England as he did, Alexander could understand a little English, but the memories of it which remained from childhood, when he spoke it with his nurse and the kitchen knaves, had grown rusty. A few common words such as *welcomme* and *drinkhail* were used by everyone, often for comic effect. Alexander could barely understand the Scottish phrases and oaths with which the Scottish traveler frequently salted his remarks.

It was customary to travel in company for two reasons. First, there was the matter of protection from wild beasts and bad men. Both of these annoyances sometimes appeared out of the woods, which came down to the very edge of the road. The region to the north of London was rather heavily forested. A second reason was one of pride. Much importance was placed on external appearances. One of the greatest compliments that could be paid was to say that a man looked *fier*. This meant that he looked every inch a man of quality. A person traveling by himself did not attract much attention, and his dignity could be slighted. We assume, therefore, that as Alexander rode along Watling Street he drew together with other voyagers.

On such an occasion it was customary to sing. "He came sitting on his horse, a song echoing to his voice; in the manner of travelers he thus shortened his journey." If the company were friendly enough, they might exchange tales. The common types of song were the *virelai*, the *rondeau*, and the *rotrouenge*. Such verse forms had considerable repetition of melody and lines, which made it possible for all to join in. The *virelai* ran *AbbaA*, capital letters indicating repeated words or refrain. The *rondeau* had the form *ABaAabAB*. The repetition in the *rondeau* was so considerable that it lent itself admirably to group participation. The English members of Alexander's traveling party probably thought of singing in unison, but the Scotsman, if we are to believe Giraldus, would break forth into a free separate part in his quavering treble. Alexander, like Giraldus, would be astonished at the ease with which those who dwelt north of the Humber could chime in with a free organum, or second moving part. They learned to do this as children. If there had been Welshmen in the company, they would have added a third, and even a fourth part, but we will not burden our company with all those Celts. Welsh music was frequently not pleasant to English ears.

Alexander's mule sometimes had to pick its way carefully over the worn Roman pavement, which was in frightful repair. Too often a neighboring farmer would have removed a few flat paving stones to build him a wall or the corner of his house. This kind of theft left a layer of rubble which was hard on an animal's feet. An occasional hole was deep enough to cause a broken neck. Along this road to London were scattered clearings, and a village or two. Groups of detached houses, usually of wood (unpainted), and rarely of small stones cemented together, stood along the road. Farmyards were seldom, if ever, contiguous to the houses. These yards were detached enclosures, walled with pales or tall wooden stakes, squared and sharpened at the top. Briars or other thorn branches were intertwined over the entire surface of such a fencing, to keep out intruders. The yards were built sufficiently near to the house to allow the tenant to hear any disturbance among his chickens or his cattle. The houses themselves consisted of little more than a doorway and one window. The roof was thatched with straw or reeds. A large wooden shutter, hinged at the top, perhaps with leather thongs, was held open by a stick placed between it and the sill. Because of the constant wear of feet, each house was apt to have a depression in the unpaved ground before its door. This was too often filled with stagnant water. Houses such as these were occupied by villeins and bordars (serfs). Well-to-do peasant farmers would occupy manor houses of a kind set farther back from the highway.

The Rise of the Universities

CHARLES H. HASKINS

Institutions of higher education originated in the Academy founded by Plato and in the philosophical schools formed as rivals to the Academy. This great tradition of education lasted until the Academy was finally closed by Justinian in 529 A.D. By that time the established schools had largely been replaced by scattered masters who taught in the cities of the empire. St. Augustine was such a master, teaching rhetoric in Milan and Rome as well as in North Africa. But by the sixth century, even these masters were disappearing in the West, and Cassiodorus, private secretary of the Gothic king Theodoric and a contemporary of St. Benedict, set up a monastery on his country estate at Bari in Italy for the purpose of preserving ancient learning. Under Cassiodorus' guidance, the monks of the Vivarium, as the institution was called, copied and studied ancient texts. Cassiodorus himself tried to condense ancient culture into a manageable form so that the men of his chaotic age might at least achieve a rudimentary classical education. In time, the monasteries that followed the famous rule of St. Benedict took up the task of Cassiodorus' Vivarium and became the centers of education and culture in the early Middle Ages. As the monastic scholar Jean Leclercq has pointed out, the monks pursued learning as one means of achieving their spiritual goal. In the sacred texts and commentaries, they found their faith and its explication. In the poetry of the liturgy, they placed themselves before God.

Monastic schools were among the most famous educational institutions of the early Middle Ages. It was only in the eleventh and twelfth centuries that they lost their preeminent position. The rebirth of the cities led to the rise of cathedral schools that became centers of new learning and instruction in the liberal arts and of professional studies in law and medicine. The shift from monastery to cathedral was in fact accelerated by the reform of the monastic orders themselves. Under the auspices of such reformers as St. Bernard of Clairvaux, the monasteries closed their schools to all but monks. The new cathedral schools flourished wherever a great master taught. The masters held positions in the episcopal administrations and were often the chancellors of their sees. In the early twelfth century, the fame of their masters made Paris, Reims, Laon, Chartres, and Orleans stand out. The death of a master could lead to the eclipse of the school; in fact, of the schools named, Laon and Orleans were short lived.

As the twelfth-century renaissance progressed, more and more students flocked to the great masters. In some places, particularly Paris and Bologna, the number of masters also increased. By the middle of the century, both Paris and Bologna had far surpassed other cities as seats of learning, and the majority of the masters teaching in these cities were independent of the cathedral. They were supported by the fees of those who came to their lectures. At Bologna the primary subject was law, both Roman and canon law, while at Paris, philosophical and theological studies predominated. The major scholastic centers quickly became important cultural institutions, and by the late twelfth century they were becoming established as tangible organizations attempting to free themselves from the power of the episcopal chancellors. It was a long struggle of the type that academic faculties have always waged against outside authorities. Other permanent features of university life were evident from the beginning—for example, the friction between town and gown. Our earliest evidence of the existence of universities comes from records of battles between the townspeople and students.

In this selection, Charles H. Haskins discusses the origins of the universities. The institution he describes contains much that is familiar to students and faculty members today, but some characteristic features of the modern university did not arise until later. The origins of some of these features will be the subject of J. M. Fletcher's "Rich and Poor in the Late Medieval Universities" in Part 5 of this volume.

Among all these indications of considerable bodies of masters and students and of vigorous intellectual life, we find very little evidence of formal university organization. Even the name university eludes our search before the thirteenth century, when it appears incidentally in 1208–09 in the letters of a former student, Pope Innocent III. Here, as so often in the history of institutions, the name follows after the thing itself. But while we cannot find in the earlier period such full-fledged institutions as the four organized faculties, the nations, or the rectorship, we can discern some traces of common university life. The subjects of study are grouped by faculties, whether or not the faculties themselves existed, and the students seem to live in local groups, even if these are not yet technically the nations of later times. The first college also appears about 1180. There is some suggestion of fixed terms of study, while for all schools a canon of the Lateran Council of 1179 requires free admission of competent candidates to the rank of master. Herein at Paris lay the germ of university organization, in the control of teaching by the chancellor of the cathedral, who alone conferred the right to teach, *licentia docendi*, and in the gild of the licensed masters or professors which became the university. Already in Abaelard's time there are traces of such supervision of teaching on the part of the cathedral, as illustrated by his difficulties with the authorities at Paris and at Laon, and the control of the body of teachers over formal admission to their ranks grew as the century advanced. Inasmuch as such a development was necessarily gradual, we cannot say just when Paris ceased to be a cathedral school and became a university, or give any special date for the university's foundation. Like all the oldest universities, it was not

Reprinted by permission of the publishers from Charles Homer Haskins, *The Renaissance of the Twelfth Century* (Cambridge, Mass.: Harvard University Press, 1927), pp. 381–87. Copyright 1927 by Charles Homer Haskins; 1955 by Clare Allen Haskins.

founded but grew. The growth, too, was partly physical, from the precincts of the cathedral which housed the earliest school to the Little Bridge on which masters and scholars lived—the "philosophers of the Little Bridge" even form a group by themselves—and thence to the Left Bank which has ever since been the Latin Quarter of Paris.

While the University of Paris thus originated of itself, it came to depend upon royal and still more upon papal support, and with papal support came papal control. The first specific document of the university's history belongs to the year 1200, the famous charter of Philip Augustus from which the existence of a university is sometimes dated, though such an institution really existed years earlier. There is here no suggestion of a new creation, but merely the recognition of a body of students and teachers which already exists: the *prévôt* and his men had attacked a hospice of German students and killed some of their number, including the bishop-elect of Liége; the king disciplines the *prévôt* severely and provides that students and their chattels shall have justice and be exempt from the jurisdiction of lay courts. The name university is not mentioned, but the assembly of scholars is recognized as the body before which the royal officers shall take oath. In 1208 or 1209 the earliest statutes deal with academic dress and funerals and with "the accustomed order in lectures and disputations," and the Pope recognizes the corporate character of this academic society, or university. Its right to self-government is further extended by the papal legate in 1215 in a document which gives the earliest outline of the course of study in arts. With the great papal privilege of 1231, the result of another town and gown row and a prolonged cessation of lectures, the fundamental documents of the university are complete. Indeed, the chancellor has begun to complain that there is too much organization and too much time consumed with university business: "in the old days when each master taught for himself and the name of the university was unknown, lectures and disputations were more frequent and there was more zeal for study." Paris has already fallen from the traditions of the good old times!

By the thirteenth century Paris has become the mother of universities as well as the mother of the sciences, counting the first of that numerous progeny which was to comprise all the mediaeval universities of Northern Europe, in Great Britain and in Germany as well as in Northern France and the Low Countries. An even wider field is suggested in a letter of 1205, in which the new Latin emperor of Constantinople asks for aid from Paris to reform the study of letters in Greece. The eldest daughter of this large family was Oxford, mother in turn of English universities.

Just why the first English university or indeed any university should have arisen at Oxford, nobody knows. Oxford in the Middle Ages was not a cathedral city, nor was it one of the greatest towns of the realm. Saxon in origin, it had a Norman stronghold, a monastery at St. Frideswide's and three monasteries in the neighborhood at Abingdon, Oseney, and Eynsham, and a royal castle not far distant; but if one were seeking a likely site for a future university, one would be more apt to choose a better established centre such as London, York, Winchester, or Canterbury. London, particularly, whose university dates only from 1836, might seem intrinsically to have had as good a chance as Paris. As Dean Rashdall concludes, "Oxford must be content to accept its academic position as an accident of its commercial importance," and, we may add, of the ease of access which goes with trade.

Nor can any one say just when a university first arose at Oxford. Time was indeed when Oxford seemed so necessary and ancient a part of the established order that its origin was ascribed to King Alfred or the Greek philosophers brought by the first British king, Brutus, grandson of Aeneas; the memory of man ran not to the contrary. Oxford could not have "just grown," like Paris, for we cannot discern anything out of which it grew. Theobald of Étampes, who taught there before 1117, was an isolated master, not the head of a school, and we do not know that he had a definite successor, or that the schools of Oxford in the twelfth century differed from those of many other places, as, for example, the London schools of whose disputes FitzStephen has left so vivid a description toward the close of the century. The fact seems to be that in some unexplained way Oxford profited by the recall of English students from Paris about 1167 so as to become their chief place of resort, and that it rose quickly into the position of a university, or *studium generale*, attended by students from foreign countries as well. By 1197 King Richard is supporting a clerk of Hungary in its schools. We must not, however, think of these foreign students as the nucleus of the *studium*; while it seems to have drawn the model of its organization from Paris, the material was English, the masters and students in whom the England of Henry II abounded and of whom we have seen many at Paris, but who henceforth remain in large numbers at home. Ca. 1180 the presence of a considerable community of scholars is shown by the appearance of a bookbinder, a scribe, two parchmenters, and three illuminators as witnesses of a conveyance of land near St. Mary's church. Ca. 1188 the irrepressible Giraldus Cambrensis, "in the most flattering of all autobiographies," tells how he publicly read his latest book at Oxford, "where the clergy in England chiefly flourished and excelled in clerkship," the reading consuming three successive days in the course of which he entertained in his hostel all the doctors and scholars, "a costly and noble act which renewed the authentic and ancient times of the poets, nor does the present or any past age recall anything like it in England." Alexander Neckam, who died in 1217, mentions Oxford along with Paris, Bologna, Montpellier, and Salerno, but says nothing of its characteristic studies, which did not differ notably from those of Paris.

Nevertheless, as compared with Paris and Bologna, Oxford in 1200 was only an inchoate university. It had as yet no famous masters, it lacked charter and statutes. Its first privilege, the legatine ordinance of 1214, in which the chancellor is first mentioned, came as the result of a town and gown riot, which, five years previously, had scattered its masters and scholars—to Cambridge, among other places—and produced a real crisis in the history of Oxford. Not until the second half of the thirteenth century do we meet with the earliest colleges, Balliol, Merton, and University, an institution which had sprung up first on the Continent but was destined in time to prove the most distinctive in English university life. Cambridge, the other modern home of the collegiate system, was quite unknown before the migration from Oxford in 1209, nor can we explain on any inherent grounds why it should have become the site of the other historic English university. In any case its origin and history lie beyond our period.

The Workday of a Bishop

from THE REGISTER OF EUDES OF ROUEN

The Operation of a Monastery

from THE CHRONICLE OF JOCELIN OF BRAKELOND

The Church of the Middle Ages grew slowly during the first millennium of Christian Europe. The apostles spread out through the Roman Empire, establishing Christian communities in its great cities. At the end of the third century, the successors of the apostles, the bishops, emerged as the rulers of the Christian communities, patterning their government of the Church on the imperial system established by Diocletian. The diocese and its bishop became the basic unit of ecclesiastical organization. From the reign of Constantine on, the great decisions concerning the life of the Church—the definition of its faith and the establishment of its discipline—were made in general councils of bishops.

The centers of episcopal power were in the cities. Only very slowly did Christian preachers penetrate the countryside, where the conservative peasant population held to its pagan religion. Each bishop had a *familia*, a group of helpers who gradually formed the clerical orders of the Church and who administered the diocese under the bishop's direction. The *familia* lived with the bishop in the city, but as the Church made progress in rural areas, the *familia* divided into two groups. One group continued to help the bishop in the diocesan administration, while the other spent more and more of its time in the outlying areas, preaching and ministering to the peasants. This arrangement might have persisted if the development of feudalism had not taken place. In the chaos created by the breakdown of the Carolingian government and the Viking invasions, feudal lords saw in the Church a tool for controlling their territories and extracting from them all the financial resources they possessed. By building local churches in their villages, lords could use the Church's ancient tithing powers to their own advantage. They appointed their own men to these "proprietary churches" and paid them a pittance out of funds produced by the ecclesiastical taxes. Ecclesiastical ordination was a mere technicality in the appointment of village priests.

This system of private churches, the basis of the parish church system that still exists, strengthened the hold of Christianity on the peasants, but it also created a corrupt and incompetent clergy. Feudal lords were not interested in providing well-trained and honest pastors for their churches, and although the parishes were ostensibly subject to the bishops, the bishops themselves were the appointees of great lords and kings. By the eleventh century, the use of the Church by secular rulers had brought the hierarchy to one of the lowest points in its history. This situation in turn produced one of the Church's most powerful reform movements, the Gregorian reform of the eleventh century. After a long struggle with the secular powers, a new ecclesiastical hierarchy was able to return the elaborate system of churches and bishoprics to the cause of religion. In the twelfth and thirteenth centuries, churchmen still played an important role in the political life of the secular kingdoms, but they also spent considerable time fulfilling their role as pastors.

The register of Archbishop Eudes of Rouen is a monument to the bishop as pastor. Rouen was one of the greatest dioceses of Europe, the primatial see of Normandy. Eudes, bishop from 1242 to 1267, was a conscientious administrator, and in his register we can see the pattern and character of his activities. He traveled constantly to check up on his clergy, and he seems to have had periodic obsessions with certain aspects of clerical misbehavior—concubinage, gluttony, drunkenness. From his record, it is clear that although Eudes held a spiritual office, he was an effective ruler of the community contained within his diocese. There was also a secular ruler, and one of the most interesting questions raised by the register is how the roles of the secular and ecclesiastical rulers were distinguished in the day-to-day life of the community.

The second of the two selections presented here comes from the other major sector of the Church, the monastic orders. The earliest monks were desert-dwelling anchorites in Egypt and Syria. By the middle of the third century, there were hundreds, perhaps thousands, of such men, many of whom were not even Christian. The increasingly burdensome obligations placed on city-dwellers by the Roman government drove men of all creeds away from their homes. Cenobitic—that is, communal—monasticism first arose in Egypt during the third century, when the monk Pachomius formed a community of monks on an island in the Nile. He wrote down the monastic traditions of the anchorites as a guide for his monks. From the beginning, the ideals of these communities consisted in helping men achieve an easier path to God through withdrawal, asceticism, and prayer. Pachomius and his successors tempered the extreme asceticism practiced by some of the most famous anchorites and instead aimed at a moderate standard to which all might aspire.

Withdrawal, prayer, and asceticism continued to be the aims of monastic life when it was transported to the West. Romans, including members of the ecclesiastical hierarchy, did not immediately accept the monastic ideals; but gradually the monks brought western Europeans to understand and sympathize with their spiritual program, and by the sixth century monasticism was well established in the western part of the empire. In the first part of the sixth century, St. Benedict of Nursia (490–540) wrote his rules for monastic communities, the end product of the development begun by Pachomius and the basis of Western monasticism since that time. Benedict stressed an orderly pattern of prayer, manual labor, poverty, and withdrawal and created a community based on humility and paternalistic authority. His simple constitution is one of the great communal plans in Western history.

The Benedictines, as followers of Benedict's rule are called, began almost immediately to attract attention. Under the auspices of Pope Gregory the Great (590–604), the Benedictines spread through Europe. Although time and growth changed and sometimes corrupted Benedictinism, the movement produced periodic reform groups that revitalized its ideals and gave it new life. The monks had a varied and profound effect on European society. They withdrew to wild areas and became expert and progressive farmers who significantly improved Europe's agricultural technique. They built great churches and advanced the art of building. They patronized art and developed a rich musical tradition to go along with their liturgical activities. They preserved the Latin classics for posterity and produced a prodigious literature of their own to which all Western literature owes a great debt. And they attracted to their ranks some of the most forceful and brilliant men in their society. For a long time, the monasteries were the seat of Europe's intellectual and administrative talent, and when the Church began the general reform movement of the eleventh and twelfth centuries, the monasteries furnished the men who led it.

Thus, the monks withdrew from the world only to find that the world had come with them. The regular round of prayer and fasts became only the background pattern of a communal life focused on the monastery's responsible position in the world. The monks found that wealth and power were two of the results of their holiness.

The monastic chronicle—"diary" might be a more accurate term—written by the monk Jocelin of Brakelond reflects the focus of monastic life in a great congregation. Jocelin was a member of Bury St. Edmund's in England, and he presents a picture of life in the great monastery at the juncture of the twelfth and thirteenth cenuries. He portrays a highly organized community complete with internal struggles and complex relations with its abbot on the one hand and the king on the other. Jocelin's eye is keen and his judgment good. His chronicle fills a large gap in our knowledge of monastic life in the Middle Ages.

THE WORKDAY OF A BISHOP

1249

June 30. We visited the deanery of Meulan at Chars. We found that the priest at Courdimanche has occasionally celebrated Mass though he is under suspension and that he has kept a concubine; he rides horseback dressed in a short mantle, and he runs about too much. Item, the priest at Courcelles does not keep residence well nor is he in the habit of wearing his gown. Item, the priest at Hérouville only rarely wears a gown. Item, the priest at Valmondois sells his services; he is noted for having money, is contentious, and is given to drinking. Item, the priest at Vaux is a trader and had, and still has, a certain vineyard which he holds as security from a certain wastrel to whom he has loaned his too precious coins; he does not say his Hours well and sometimes he comes to Mass straight from his bed. Item, the priest at Chars is ill famed of a certain widow; he runs about too much. Item, the priest at Courcelles does not keep residence well, nor does he wear a gown.

From *The Register of Eudes of Rouen*, edited by J. F. O'Sullivan, translated by S. M. Brown (New York: Columbia University Press, 1964), pp. 43–46, 292–95, 514–16. Reprinted by permission of the Columbia University Press.

Item, the priest at Longuesse is ill famed of Eugénie, his parishioner, and has had children by her; he promised us that if he should be ill famed of these matters again he would regard his church as resigned.

We spent the night at Sérans, at our own expense.

July 1.   We visited the priory at Parnes.

July 2.   At Parnes. We visited the priory and received our procuration from it. They have but one chalice and one missal. They do not confess every month as required by the Statutes of Pope Gregory; we enjoined them to confess as the said Statutes require. They have an income of two hundred pounds; they owe about fifteen pounds. They use meat; we prohibited the eating of meat altogether, saving as the Rule permits. They use feather beds; we forbade the use of these, except in cases of necessity.

This day we visited the deanery of Magny, at Magny. We found that the priest at Lainville is a drunkard and incontinent. Item, the prior of Magny is grievously ill famed of a certain woman who is known as "The Mistress" and of the wife of a knight at Etres. The priest at Magny is ill famed of drinking too much, especially with laymen, and of incontinence, and about a year ago he begot a child because of it. Item, the priest at Genainville is ill famed of drunkenness and is useless to his church. The priest at Lierville does not attend the synods. Item, the priest at St. Clair is publicly known for drinking too much at the tavern. We warned them.

This day we visited the priory at Magny. There are three canons there, and they have made profession in their order. They do not observe the fasts of the Rule very well. They receive money for clothing. They have an income of eighty pounds and are in debt up to eighty pounds. The prior is publicly known for incontinence, as we have already been informed by several priests during our visitation of the deanery of Magny. This day we visited the priory at Magny; there were three canons there. They do not observe the fasts of the Rule; they have money to buy clothes. They have an income of eighty pounds of Paris; they owe about eighty pounds.

From the prior of Magny, whom we found grievously ill famed of incontinence, we have a letter stating that if any further ill fame should arise against him and is supported by the truth, or is of such a nature that he cannot purge himself, he will regard his priorate as resigned by that very fact. And this he swore to us. Item, he also swore to set out for Rome before the octave of the Assumption of the Blessed Virgin and to bring us a letter from any one of the Lord Pope's penitentiaries which made mention of this matter, and furthermore, neither to remain in the said priory nor to return to it until recalled by us.

July 3.   We visited the priory of Notre-Dame-de-Chaumont. Only two monks are there, and there should be three. They do not confess every month as the Statutes of Pope Gregory require. They have no written copy of their Rule, nor a copy of the Statutes. They do not hold chapter, nor do they receive the minor penances. They do not keep the fasts of the Rule; they eat meat when it is not necessary. They use feather beds, though we had warned them about this before. Instead this time, and in the presence of their own abbot of St-Germer, we enjoined them with firmness to correct their deficiencies. They have an income of one hundred pounds; they owe about thirty pounds.

July 4.   We visited the priory at Liancourt. Three monks are there. They have an income of one hundred twenty pounds; they owe seventy pounds of Paris. We found some things amiss, to wit, that they eat meat and use feather beds though we had prohibited these things before. This time we forbade them more severely. They owe us a procuration fee of only four pounds of Paris.

July 5.   We visited the monastery of St-Martin-de-Pontoise, where there are twenty-five monks. They have nine priories, and two monks are in each. On Sundays, women and laymen enter the cloister, marching in procession; we forbade them to enter henceforth. They owe pensions up to sixteen pounds of Paris. They have the patronage of thirty churches. In the outside priories they eat meat at any time. We enjoined them to abstain from the eating of meat, save as the Rule permits. They owe about twelve hundred pounds; they have an income of one thousand pounds. We spent the night there and received our procuration. . . .

1256

October 22.   We visited the chapter of St.-Sépulcre-de-Caen. One dignitary is there, that is to say, the dean. There is as yet no certain number of canons. Luke, called Capet, runs about the town disgracefully and gets intoxicated very easily; but then he is weak in the head. Total for procuration: nine pounds, fourteen shillings, six pence.

October 23.   We visited the monastery of nuns at La-Trinité-de-Caen. The abbess was in England at the time. We found seventy-two nuns there. One does not accuse another [in chapter]. The rule of silence is not well observed; we enjoined them to correct this. They take three vows at the time of their being blessed; to wit, the vows of obedience, chastity, and poverty, but no other vow. The young nuns keep larks, and at the feast of the Innocents they sing their Office with farcical improvisations; we forbade this. They have paid three hundred fifty marks to the Roman Curia. About as much is owing to them as they owe. Total for procuration: seven pounds, six shillings, four pence.

October 24.   We visited the abbey of St-Étienne-de-Caen, where there are sixty-three monks. All but three are priests. In one of the priories there are rabbit dogs; we forbade the monks who are staying there to become hunters. There are some who do not confess every month; we enjoined them to correct this. It used to be their practice that all those ministering [to the celebrants] at all Masses, save those [Masses] for the dead, received Communion, but this practice, through negligence, has gradually been abandoned;

we enjoined the abbot and prior to have this custom more fully observed by all. The cloister is badly kept; we enjoined them to correct this. Traveling monks do not observe the fasts of the Rule; we enjoined them to correct this. In the priories they do not observe the fasts of the Rule and they eat meat freely; we enjoined them to correct this. They owe fifteen hundred pounds, but about as much is owed to them; they have an income of four thousand pounds. Total for procuration: seven pounds, ten shillings, ten pence.

October 25. We visited the Maison-Dieu at Caen. Seven canons are there. The prior was not there. The brethren receive Communion and confess twice a year, to wit, at Advent and at Lent. They have an income of one thousand pounds and another five hundred for daily alms; they owe two hundred pounds, and they have their annate money on hand.

This day we spent the night at Troarn, at our own expense.

October 26. We visited there, finding forty monks. All but six are priests. Those who are not priests receive Communion every Sunday. Traveling monks do not observe the fasts of the Rule. In the priories they do not observe the fasts of the Rule, and they eat meat freely; we enjoined them to correct this. They owe about four hundred pounds; they have an income of about three thousand pounds. Total for procuration: eight pounds, twelve shillings, eight pence.

When we were visiting in the diocese of Bayeux, we warned Brother Henry, prior of Cahagnes, of the diocese of Bayeux, to receive us for visitation and procuration, but he refused to do this, stating that he was not under obligation to do so, and alleged in justification that, in his time, the bishop of Bayeux had never visited him, nor had he ever received procuration there from him nor, as far as he knew, from any of his predecessors. However, the prior swore to abide by our decision in this matter, and we, after diligent investigation, discovered that the bishop of Bayeux had visited there many times and had received procuration. This being the case, we peremptorily cited the said prior to appear before us at Troarn on the Thursday before All Saints to hear our judgment, and the said prior having come before us at the said time and place, we gave orders that the prior and his successors should be obliged to receive us there for visitation and procuration. We ordered the prior to pay us a fine for having given us offense by unjustly refusing to receive us on the aforementioned business. Present were: Peter, archdeacon of Grand-Caux; Richard of Sap, canon of Rouen; the prior of Ste-Barbe; Hugh, rector at Foucescalier; Reginald, rector at Giverny; Morel of Us; Robert Scansore; . . . [*lacuna in MS*], the abbot of Troarn; and many others. Thereupon, and at the said time and place, the said prior recognized that he was obligated to the foregoing and to the payment of full procuration if we should desire to exact it. He agreed to pay whatever fine we should desire for the offense shown to us. However, we forbore to exact this penalty until such time as we should think best. Present were the aforesaid archdeacon, Richard; William, the prior of Troarn; Brother Harduin of the Friars

Minor; and Morel and Robert, our abovementioned clerks. The said prior, before the aforementioned witnesses, swore that he would pay the said fine to us, whenever we should ask him to do so.

October 27. At Pont-l'Evéque, at our expense. *October 28.* At Pont-Audemer. *October 29.* At Bourg-Achard. *October 30.* At Déville. *October 31.* At Rouen. *November 1.* At Rouen. We celebrated the feast of All Saints. *November 2–5.* At Déville. *November 6.* We held the sacred synod at Rouen, and spent the night at St-Matthicu. *November 7–8.* At Rouen. *November 9.* At Frênes. *November 10.* At St-Germer-de-Flay. *November 11.* At Bulles. *November 12.* At Gournay-sur-Aronde. *November 13–23.* At Noyon, on the business of the inquest held on the body of St. Eloi. *November 24.* At Verberie. *November 25.* At Louvres, in the diocese of Paris. *November 26–28.* At Pontoise. *November 29.* We received procuration at Gasny. Total for procuration: one hundred nine shillings, three pence. . . .

1262

January 26. With God's grace we visited the priory at Bures. There was a certain monk from Pré, near Rouen, there, not as prior, but acting as a custodian for the prior of Pré. He holds the administration at the prior's pleasure. There should be at least two monks there. We did find two who had arrived with the said custodian, to convalesce, and with the prior's permission. They used feather beds and ate meat when there was no need, nor did they observe the fasts of the Rule very well. They owed nothing, nor was anything owed to them, since the prior of Pré collected everything and kept what remained after paying for the sustenance of the monks and the household. We received procuration there this day. Total: . . . [*lacuna in MS*].

January 27. We visited the house at Nogent, near Neufchâtel, and spent the night at Neufchâtel, where the lessee of the abovementioned house gave us procuration. Total for procuration: eleven pounds, nine shillings, five pence.

This day we visited the local Hôtel-Dieu, or hospital, where were two canons with their prior. One of them, to wit, Hugh, called Dominus, was useless and broken down by age, wherefore we were pleased to order him [the prior] to receive into the hospital and give the habit to two suitable men as soon as possible; he [the prior] should receive Communion at least once a month. There were three lay brothers and six lay sisters there. The prior has the cure of all those in residence. They have an income of two hundred pounds and more; they owed fifty pounds; more than one hundred pounds was owed to them. With the exception of wine, they had sufficient provisions to last out the year.

January 28. To wit, Septuagesima Sunday. With God's grace we celebrated Mass and preached at St. Mary's church at Neufchâtel. We spent the night at Mortemer-sur-Eaulne, where we received procuration from the lessee of the local house or priory. Total for procuration: thirteen pounds, eleven shillings.

January 29. We visited the said house, where there were two monks from Lewes. They receive twenty shillings of Tours every week for their sustenance from Master Eudes of St-Denis, who holds the said house for life.

This day we spent the night at Aumale, at our own expense.

January 30. With God's grace we visited the abbey of this said place. Nineteen monks were in residence; three were in England. All but four were priests. One did not accuse another [in chapter]. Four lay brothers were there; we ordered the abbot to urge them to make frequent confession and to see that they confessed and received Communion four to six times a year. Silence was badly observed; we ordered this corrected. Item, we gave orders that lay folk be kept out of the cloister and that some monk be appointed to guard the cloister gate so that women and laymen could not have free access as they had had up to this time. Item, we expressly forbade anyone to remain away from Compline or to drink after Compline. Item, we ordered them to dismiss their present baker and to secure some one else who would be more upright and suitable. Item, we ordered the abbot to inspect and take away all keys of coffers and boxes of the monks before Ash Wednesday, lest they should be in the possession of any property. He had been negligent in this matter. Item, we ordered them to have the income written down in registers. They owed five hundred pounds; they had sufficient provisions for the year, and at present some eighty pounds from last year's wool was still owed to them. We advised them to increase both their alms donations and the number of their monks, if they could do so. The abbot's sister sometimes dined with him at the abbey, a thing which displeased us. We forbade him to invite her in the future. He may invite his brother-in-law without his wife. Item, we expressly forbade him, as well as all the monks of the place, and as we had done before, to allow any secular clerics, priests, or laymen to dine in the refectory as had been the custom. Item, we enjoined the monks to obey their abbot in all legitimate and proper things as they were bound to do, or that otherwise we would severly punish those whom we should find guilty of disobedience. Item, Ralph of St-Valery was suspected of owning property; we ordered the abbot to have a careful investigation made into the truth of this, and then to take such action as seemed fitting under the Rule. Item, we found that Enguerrand, the prior, was defamed and that an evil report had been raised against him; but since we were not at that time able to get any definite evidence concerning the truth of the matter, we ordered the abbot to make an inquiry into the evil report as well as into the truth of the matter, as cautiously and honestly as he could, and then to handle it in a proper manner. Furthermore, we were much displeased that the abbot had promoted the said E[nguerrand], as prior, for he had been behaving badly for many years, and an evil report of long standing had never been cleared up. We received procuration there this day. Total for procuration: nine pounds, eight shillings.

THE OPERATION OF A MONASTERY

I have been at pains to set down the things that I have seen and heard, which came to pass in the Church of St. Edmund in our days, from the year in which the Flemings were taken prisoner outside the town, that being the year in which I assumed the religious habit, and Prior Hugh was deposed and his office given to Robert; and I have included certain evil things for a warning, and certain good as an example to others. At that time Abbot Hugh was grown old and his eyes waxed somewhat dim. Pious he was and kindly, a strict monk and good, but in the business of this world neither good nor wise. For he trusted those about him overmuch and gave them too ready credence, relying always on the wisdom of others rather than his own. Discipline and religion and all things pertaining to the Rule were zealously observed within the cloister; but outside all things were badly handled, and every man did, not what he ought, but what he would, since his lord was simple and growing old. The townships of the Abbot and all the hundreds were given out to farm; the woods were destroyed, the houses of the manors threatened to fall in ruin, and day by day all things went from bad to worse. The Abbot found but one remedy and one consolation—to borrow money, that thus at least he might be able to maintain the honour of his house. No Easter nor Michaelmas came round during the eight years before his death but that one or two hundred pounds were added to his debt; the bonds were continually renewed, and the interest as it grew was turned into capital. This infirmity spread from the head to the members—from the superior to his subjects. And so it came about that each obedientiary had his own seal and bound himself in debt to Jews and Christians as he pleased. Often silken copes and flasks of gold and other ornaments of the church were placed in pawn without the knowledge of the Convent. I saw a bond given to William FitzIsabel for one thousand and forty pounds, and have never known the why or the wherefore. I saw another bond given to Isaac the son of Rabbi Joce for four hundred pounds, but I know not why; and yet a third to Benedict the Jew of Norwich for eight hundred and fourscore; and the cause of this last debt was as follows: our chamber was fallen in ruin, and the Sacrist, willy-nilly, undertook to restore it, and secretly borrowed forty marks at interest from Benedict the Jew and gave him a bond sealed with the seal that used to hang from the feretory of St. Edmund, and with which the instruments of the guilds and fraternities used to be sealed: it was broken up afterwards, at the bidding of the Convent, but all too late. Now when this debt had increased to one hundred pounds, the Jew came with letters from our lord the King concerning the Sacrist's debt, and at last that which had been hidden from the Abbot and the Convent was revealed. The Abbot was angry and would have deposed the

From *The Chronicle of Jocelin of Brakelond*, edited and translated by H. E. Butler (London: Thomas Nelson & Sons, 1949), pp. 1–5, 7–9, 20–23. Reprinted by permission of The Clarendon Press, Oxford.

Sacrist, alleging a privilege granted him by the Lord Pope, enabling him to depose William his Sacrist when he would. But someone came to the Abbot and speaking on the Sacrist's behalf, so deluded the Abbot that he allowed a bond to be given to Benedict the Jew for four hundred pounds, to be paid at the end of four years, to wit, for the hundred pounds already accumulated at interest and another hundred pounds which the said Jew had lent the Sacrist on the Abbot's behalf. And the Sacrist undertook in full chapter to repay the whole debt, and a bond was given sealed with the Convent's seal: for the Abbot dissembled and would not set his seal to the bond, as though the debt was no concern of his. But at the end of four years there was not the wherewithal to pay the debt, and a new bond was made for eight hundred and fourscore pounds, to be paid off at stated times at the rate of fourscore pounds a year. The same Jew also held a number of bonds for smaller debts and one that was of fourteen years' standing, so that the total debt due to him amounted to twelve hundred pounds not counting the accumulated interest. And R. the almoner of our lord the King came and made it known to the Abbot that a rumour had reached the King concerning these great debts. So after the Abbot had taken counsel with the prior and a few others, the Almoner was brought into the Chapter; and, while we sat by in silence, the Abbot said: "Here is the King's Almoner, my lord and friend and yours also, who led by his love of God and of St. Edmund, has told us that our lord the King has heard something untoward concerning us, and that the affairs of our Church are ill-managed both within and without. Wherefore it is my will, and I charge you on your obedience that you should say and openly acknowledge how matters stand." The Prior therefore arose, and speaking as it were on behalf of us all, he said that the Church was in good state, and that the Rule was well and religiously observed within our house, while without our affairs were well and wisely handled, though none the less we had incurred some small amount of debt, like others of our neighbours; but that there was no debt of sufficient magnitude to be a burden to us. Hearing this the Almoner replied that he was very glad to have heard the testimony of the Convent—that is to say, the Prior speaking as he did. The Prior said the same thing on another occasion, and with him Master Geoffrey de Constantine, both of them speaking and excusing the Abbot, when Archbishop Richard came to our Chapter in virtue of his office as legate, before we possessed such exemption as we now enjoy. But at that time I was a novice and, when the opportunity offered, I spoke concerning these matters with my master, who used to teach me the Rule and to whose care I had been assigned—to wit, Master Samson, who was afterwards Abbot, "What is this," I said, "that I hear? Why are you silent, who see and hear such things as these, you who are a cloister monk and have no desire for office and fear God more than you fear man?" But he made answer and said, "My son, a child newly burned dreads the fire; thus it is with me and many others. Hugh the Prior has of late been deposed from his priorship and sent into exile.

Denys and Hugh and Roger of Hingham have but lately returned from exile. I like them was imprisoned and afterwards sent to Acre, because we had spoken on behalf of the common good of our Church against the will of the Abbot. This is the hour of darkness; this is the hour in which flatterers prevail and are believed; their power is made strong and we can do nothing against it. We must for a time shut our eyes to these things. Let the Lord behold and judge."

A rumour reached Abbot Hugh that Richard, Archbishop of Canterbury, desired to come to us and hold a scrutiny in our Church, by virtue of his authority as legate; and after taking counsel the Abbot sent to Rome and obtained exemption from the power of the said legate. When our messenger returned from Rome, we had not the wherewithal to pay the sums that he had promised the Lord Pope and the cardinals, except, under the circumstances, the cross that was above the High Altar and the little image of the Virgin and that of St. John, which images Stigand the Archbishop had adorned with a great weight of gold and silver, and had given to St. Edmund. Some of our brethren who were close friends of the Abbot went so far as to say that even the feretory of St. Edmund ought to be stripped of its plating to pay for such a liberty as this, not noting the great peril that might arise from such a liberty. For if there should arise some Abbot of ours who desired to dilapidate the property of our Church and to treat his Convent ill, there will be no man to whom the Convent will be able to complain of the wrongs done by the Abbot, who will fear neither Bishop or Archbishop or Legate, and his impunity will make him all the bolder to do wrong. . . .

In the twenty-third year of his abbacy it came into Abbot Hugh's mind to go to the shrine of St. Thomas to pray; and on his way thither upon the day after the Nativity of the Virgin he had a grievous fall near Rochester, so that his knee-cap was put out and lodged in the ham of his leg. Physicians hastened to him and tortured him in many ways, but healed him not; and he was carried back to us in a horse litter and devoutly received as was his due. To cut a long story short, his leg mortified and the pain ascended even to his heart, and by reason of the pain a tertian fever laid hold on him, in the fourth fit of which he died and gave up his soul to God on the morrow of the day of St. Brice. Before he died, everything was pillaged by his servants so that nothing was left in his house but three-legged stools and tables which they were unable to carry off. The Abbot himself was scarce left with his coverlet and two old torn blankets which someone had placed over him after removing those that were whole. There was nothing worth a single penny that could be distributed to the poor for the benefit of his soul. The Sacrist said that it was no business of his, asserting that he had found all expenses for the Abbot and his household for a whole month. For the tenants of the townships refused to give anything before the appointed time and his creditors would lend him nothing, when they saw that he was sick even unto death. None the less the tenant of Palgrave found fifty shillings for distribution to the poor, since he entered on his tenancy of Palgrave on that day. But those fifty shillings were later given back to the King's bailiffs who demanded the whole rent on behalf of the King.

When Abbot Hugh had been buried, it was resolved in the Chapter that a messenger should announce his death to Ranulph de Glanvill, Justiciar of England. Master Samson and Master R. Ruff, monks of our house, crossed the sea and bore this news to our lord the King: and from him they secured letters to the effect that the property and revenues of the Convent, which were separated from those of the abbot, should be wholly in the hands of the Prior and the Convent, while the rest of the Abbey should be in the hands of the King. The custody of the Abbey was given to Robert de Cockfield and Robert de Flamville, our Steward, who straightway placed under gage and pledge all the servants and kinsfolk of the Abbot, to whom he had given anything before he fell sick or who had taken anything from his property; and they did this even to the Abbot's chaplain, one of our monks, for whom the Prior stood security: and entering our vestry they caused an inventory to be made of all the ornaments of the church.

While the abbacy was vacant, the Prior was above all things zealous for the maintenance of peace in the Convent and the preservation of the honour of our Church in the entertainment of guests, desiring neither to disturb anyone or provoke any to anger, so that he might keep all men and all things in peace. Yet none the less he shut his eyes to certain things that deserved correction in the conduct of our obedientiaries, above all of the Sacrist who, during the vacancy, as though he did not care what he did with the sacristy, paid not a single debt nor built anything at all, but oblations and chance incomings were foolishly squandered. Wherefore the Prior who was the head of the Convent was thought blameworthy and called remiss. And our brethren spoke of this among themselves, when the time came for the election of an Abbot. . . .

But the Prior and the twelve with him, after much toil and delay, at length stood before the King at Waltham, a manor of the Bishop of Winchester, on the second Sunday in Lent. Our lord the King received them kindly and, declaring that he wished to act according to God's will and for the honour of the Church, he commanded the brethren by the mouth of his intermediaries, Richard Bishop of Winchester and Geoffrey the Chancellor, afterwards Archbishop of York, that they should nominate three of our Convent. Whereupon the Prior and the brethren went aside, as though to speak on this matter, and drew out the seal and broke it, and found the names in the following order: Samson the sub-sacrist, Roger the Cellarer and Hugh the third prior. Whereat the brothers who were of higher rank blushed. Moreover, all marvelled that the same Hugh was both elector and elect. But since they could not change the facts, by common consent they changed the order, putting Hugh first, because he was third prior, Roger the Cellarer second, and Samson third, making, on the face of it, the first last and the last first. But the King, after first enquiring whether those nominated were born in his realm and within whose domain, said that he did not know them and ordered that three others of the Convent should be nominated as well as those three. This being agreed, William the Sacrist said, "Our Prior should be nominated because he is our head." This was readily allowed. Then said the Prior, "William the Sacrist is a good man." The same was said of Denys, and it was allowed. These being nominated without delay before the King, he marvelled saying, "They have done this quickly; God is with them." Afterwards the King demanded that for the honour of his realm they should nominate three more from other houses. Hearing this the brethren were afraid, suspecting guile. At length they agreed to name three, but on this condition that they should accept none of them without the counsel of those of the Convent who remained at home. And they nominated three: Master Nicholas of Wallingford, later and at the present time Abbot of Malmesbury, Bertrand, Prior of St. Faith, afterwards Abbot of Chertsey, and the Lord H. of St. Neots, a monk of Bec, a man of great religion and very circumspect both in matters temporal and spiritual. This done, the King thanked them and gave orders that three out of the nine should be struck off the list, whereupon the three aliens were at once removed, to wit, the Prior of St. Faith afterwards Abbot of Chertsey, Nicholas, monk of St. Albans, afterwards Abbot of Malmesbury, and the Prior of St. Neots. William the Sacrist withdrew of his own free will: two of the remaining five were struck off by order of the King, and then one of the three remaining, two only being left, namely the Prior and Samson. Finally the intermediaries of our lord the King whom I have mentioned above, were called in to take counsel with the brethren. And Denys, speaking for us all, began to commend the persons of the Prior and Samson, saying that both were literate, both good, both of praiseworthy life and of unblemished reputation; but always in the corner of his speech thrusting Samson forward, multiplying the words he uttered in his praise and saying that he was a man strict in his behaviour, stern in chastising transgressions, a hard worker, prudent in wordly business, and proved in divers offices. The Bishop of Winchester replied, "We understand clearly what you mean; from your words we gather that your Prior seems to you to be somewhat slack and that you desire him whom you call Samson." Denys replied, "Both of them are good, but we should like, God willing, to have the better." The Bishop made answer, "Of two good men you must choose the better. Tell me openly, do you wish to have Samson?" And a number, making a majority, answered clearly, "We want Samson," not a voice being raised against them, though some of set purpose said nothing, because they wished to offend neither the one or the other. Samson then having been nominated in the presence of the King, and the latter having taken brief counsel with his advisers, all the rest were summoned, and the King said, "You have presented Samson to me: I do not know him. If you had presented your Prior, I should have accepted him; for I have seen him and know him. But, as it is, I will do what you desire. But have a care; for by the very eyes of God, if you do ill, I will be at you!" He then asked the Prior, if he agreed to this and desired it. The Prior answered that he did desire it and that Samson was much more worthy of honour. The elect therefore fell at the King's feet and kissed them, then rose in haste, and in haste went to the altar with the brethren, singing "Miserere mei, Deus," his head held high and his countenance unchanged. And when the King saw this, he said to those who stood by, "By God's eyes, this elect thinks himself worthy to be the guardian of his Abbey."

The Role of a Baron's Wife

MARGARET LABARGE

Historians have assumed that women of the medieval noble classes were little better off than their Roman counterparts described by M. I. Finley in "The Silent Women of Rome" (in Part 1 of this volume). Little space is devoted to women in the standard histories of the Middle Ages, and it is often said that only literature gave them an escape from the restrictions and drudgery of their lives. In fact, some scholars have suggested that the literary genre of courtly love romances was created for women by the *jongleurs* (minstrels) of the twelfth century. During the long absences of their husbands, who were occupied with the rounds of tournaments and wars, women sought entertainment by patronizing the singers who naturally catered to the dreams of their audience. But while the romances do place the woman in an unaccustomed position of importance, they also focus on the men and their exploits, and they were popular with men as well as with women. In addition, recent research has indicated that the wives of barons did not conform to the stereotype presented by the romances or by those trying to imagine the character of their audiences.

Women of the peasant class undoubtedly worked hard alongside their husbands, and while there were differences in the work done by the sexes, those differences were dictated more by the demands of the job than by socially defined sex roles. An assessment of the position of upper-class women, however, is more difficult. In the eleventh and twelfth centuries—at about the same time that the romance literature came into being—aristocratic women emerged from the shadows and began to play an active role in politics. Agnes of Poitiers (c. 1024–77), wife of Henry III of Germany, was an active queen who was regent of her kingdom for almost ten years after the death of her husband in 1056. Countess Mathilda of Tuscany (1048–1115) governed one of Italy's most populous and richest provinces for more than four decades and held the difficult middle ground between the papacy and the German empire during the Investiture Contest. Another Mathilda (1102–67), daughter of the English king Henry I (1100–35), waged a long civil war in England on behalf of her son Henry II. Henry II's succession to the largest domain in Europe in 1154 was largely due to the persistence and abilities of his mother. Henry's power was also significantly increased by his marriage to the famous Eleanor of Aquitaine (1122–1204), heiress to the largest duchy in France. It might be that mention of such women in contemporary documents resulted not from a new status for women, but from the growing literacy of the aristocratic class during the twelfth-century renaissance. It is certainly possible, however, that the rise in the cultural level and the relative stability of the European communities did affect the position of women for the better.

Political activity was not, of course, the normal occupation of medieval women—as it was not the normal occupation of medieval men either. Women spent the bulk of their time running the household and administering the landed estates of their families during the frequent absences of their husbands. These tasks could be formidable. The baronial household was a large and complex organization almost always on the move or getting ready to move because large supplies of food and forage could not be transported appreciable distances in the Middle Ages, and so large households were forced to move from manor to manor, eating up their yearly wealth in produce. In the book from which this selection is drawn, Margaret Labarge used the household accounts of Simon de Montfort and his wife Eleanor, sister of Henry III of England. The accounts come from the 1250s, when Simon was leading a baronial rebellion against the king and was constantly away from home. Eleanor not only managed a large household, but also participated in the struggles between her husband and her brother. The position of her family and its political involvement greatly complicated Eleanor's job and made her situation more difficult than that of most of her contemporaries. Yet her story can teach us much about the administration of baronial households and about the place of baronial women in their society. In the following selection, Ms. Labarge takes an overview and extrapolates from Eleanor's experience to the experience of other women of her time.

If it is difficult to think of the castle as a home, it is even harder to estimate fairly the position of the lady of the house. The evidence is varied and conflicting. On the one hand, the moralists and the writers on manners underline the basic, divinely-ordained subordination of women; they emphasize their foolishness and the need of their obedient submission to man in the person of their husbands. On the other, the romances present the ideas and standards of courtly love; they describe amazing heroines for whose supercilious smile any right-minded knight would brave death innumerable times. But the ladies of the romances generally seem to be only cardboard figures, cut to an identical pattern. The description of the heroine of *Jehan et Blonde* illustrates the accepted type.[1] Blonde was the ideal heroine with hair of shining gold, dark, straight eyebrows, and white unwrinkled skin. Her tiny mouth had full red lips over little white teeth, and her breath smelt pleasantly sweet. Her throat was so long and white that the author poetically insisted that you could

---

[1] *Jehan et Blonde*, by Philippe de Beaumanoir, was one of the most popular French romances of the thirteenth century. It has a special interest for English readers because its central situation, of a French younger son gaining love and fortune in England, parallels the true life story of Simon de Montfort. The author probably formed part of Simon's household for a time, and certainly was familiar with English ways. This romance was a product of his youth, when he was known as Philippe de Remi; many years later, as sire de Beaumanoir, he wrote *Coutumes de Beauvaisis*, the most famous lawbook of thirteenth-century France.

From Margaret Labarge, *A Baronial Household of the Thirteenth Century* (London, Eyre & Spottiswoode, 1965), pp. 38–52. Reprinted by permission of Eyre & Spottiswoode (Publishers) Ltd. and Curtis Brown Ltd.

see when she drank red wine. The catalogue goes on, but even this brief sample is sufficient to illustrate the medieval requirements for the fashionable beauty.

Neither the moralists' nor the romancer's descriptions of women had much relation to reality, for the chroniclers quite incidentally provide occasional glimpses of women who did not fit into these stock categories. There was Nicolaa de la Hay, for example, who held the castle of Lincoln for the boy king Henry during the desperate siege of 1216. The redoubtable countess of Arundel, who in 1252 reproved Henry III for his refusal to do justice to his barons and taunted him with his failure to keep his oaths to uphold the Great Charter, was a woman of great force, praised for her outspokenness. Even more impressive was Blanche of Castile, queen and regent of France and the backbone of French administration for a quarter of a century. These women were obviously neither cardboard beauties nor foolish, submissive sheep. Indeed the roster of independent, active and capable women could be greatly extended at many levels of the social scale. Contemporary evidence affords considerable insight into the actual relation of the female stereotype to the reality, and enables us to evaluate more accurately the true place of women in thirteenth-century society.

It must be remembered that there was an enormous gulf between the occupations and status of the young girl and the married woman. At this time fourteen was generally considered the normal marriageable age for a girl. An important heiress, or a royal relative, who served as a pawn in the absorbing game of feudal politics, might be betrothed much earlier. The Countess Eleanor had been married at the age of nine in the hopes of assuring the loyalty of her first husband, Earl William Marshal the younger. Her elder sister Joanna had been betrothed at the age of four, as part of a peace settlement between King John and the Lusignan family of Poitou. Even the less well born unmarried girl was likely to be both young and foolish, and often in need of all the stringent protection the moralists insisted on. The single girl had no real tasks and little social standing; she therefore looked forward to marriage which brought her prestige and an independent establishment. The married woman was charged with the considerable responsibility of directly supervising the affairs of the household. This was particularly true in less extensive establishments than that of the countess of Leicester. The initiative and ability of the wife of a lesser baron were at once more obvious and more necessary.

Apart from her domestic responsibilities, the woman had a recognized legal position; though her lands and goods were theoretically under the control of her husband, she was in fact the equal of a man in all matters of private law. Frederick Maitland, the great legal historian, puts the matter most clearly:

The woman can hold land, even by military tenure, can own chattels, make a will, make a contract, can sue and be sued. She sues and is sued in person without the interposition of a guardian; she can plead with her own voice if she pleases; indeed—and this is a strong case—a married woman will sometimes appear as her husband's attorney. A widow will often be the guardian of her own children; a lady will often be the guardian of the children of her tenants.

Thus the wife of any great baron would expect to cope with her own property and lands; also to understand and carry on the many legal and financial affairs of the barony during her husband's absence or after his death. Robert Grosseteste, the great bishop of Lincoln, wrote a brief treatise on administration for the countess of Lincoln after her husband's death in 1240. He took for granted her ability to supervise the seignorial and manorial officials, as well as her own immediate household, and merely wrote down some instruction on the accepted methods. The best evidence for the independence and initiative of women is to be found in the numerous court cases in which they figure. Countess Eleanor's legal struggle for her full dower rights, which dragged on for over forty years, is only a particularly long-drawn-out instance of the persistent litigiousness of both sexes in thirteenth-century society.

Obviously the wife of a great baron often played an extraordinarily important part in the marriage partnership. Her varied activities were such an accepted fact that contemporary writers usually ignore them as too ordinary for comment. Nor do they refer to the bond of unity and affection which frequently developed in medieval marriages, even though these were primarily arranged to increase wealth or power. Husband and wife often worked together in a common purpose, and showed a mutual respect which was not echoed by the woman-hating moralists.

Surprisingly these didactic writers seem blinded by their clerical animus, and singularly remote from practical affairs. They pay little attention to the legal and financial responsibilities of a baron's wife, or the important position of middle-class women in many of the town trades. Instead they fall back on the trite statement that a good wife is man's greatest gift from heaven, although they hasten to add that this is only true if she behaves herself and obeys him.

The writers of the treatises on etiquette are equally conventional and uninformative. Stephen of Fougères, chaplain of King Henry II and later bishop of Rennes, had a narrow conception of the proper employments of a great lady. To judge by his praise of the countess of Hereford, the best way for a gentlewoman to occupy her time was in building chapels, decorating altars, caring for the poor, and honouring and serving high personages—to which the bishop thoughtfully added, "especially churchmen." One wonders what he thought of the extremely secular activities of Eleanor of Aquitaine, Henry II's indomitable queen. Fortunately not all the didactic writers were quite so pious, or so limited. Robert of Blois,[2] for example, breathes a welcome air of common sense in his discussion of the matter. He admitted that he would like to teach ladies how to behave, but he realized that it was very difficult for a lady to conduct herself well in the world.

> If she speaks, someone says it is too much. If she is silent, she is reproached for not knowing how to greet people. If she is friendly and courteous, someone pretends it is for love. If on the other hand she does not put on a bright face, she passes for being too proud.

The problem of contradictory advice to women is obviously not a modern development.

About 1265, Philip of Novara[3] wrote a little treatise called the *Four Ages of Man* in which he dealt with the proper education of upper-class boys and girls. His work provides convenient clues to what the age expected of them. Philip, like most other medieval writers, emphasized the importance of largess as the prime virtue of kings, princes and the nobility. Generosity could cover a multitude of sins, and any man with pretensions to noble blood must practice it as part of his duty to his class and himself. However, largess was not a suitable virtue for a girl, or even a woman. A maid had no need to make gifts, Philip thought, and he quoted approvingly the common saying, "poorer than a maid." His disapproval of gift-giving by married women stemmed from strictly practical reasons:

> If the wife and husband are both generous, it is the ruin of the house, while a wife's greater generosity shames her lord. The only kind of largess suitable for a woman is the giving of alms, provided she has her husband's permission and the household can afford it.

In Philip's opinion, obedience and chastity should be a girl's main virtues, and were the only ones strictly required. They were aided by a "fair countenance," that is, the habit of looking straight ahead "with a tranquil and measured air, not too high and not too low, modestly and without affectation." This question of a woman's style of walking and regarding others was one on which all the writers on manners laid great emphasis. Ladies were to walk erect, with dignity, said Robert of Blois, neither trotting nor running, nor dallying either, with their eyes fixed on the ground ahead of them. They were to be particularly careful that they did not regard men as the sparrow-

[2] Robert of Blois was a French poet who wrote in the middle of the thirteenth century. His treatise on manners has perhaps some element of satire in it but generally echoes the accepted requirements of the times.

[3] Philip of Novara was a Lombard crusader who settled in the East and wrote a chronicle favourable to the Ibelin family. His treatise on manners was written when he himself was seventy-five.

hawk does the lark. Anger and high words would also inevitably injure their reputations.

The feminine range of accomplishments was not expected to be very great. Every girl should learn to spin and weave, Philip of Novara insisted, because the poor will need the knowledge and the rich will better appreciate the work of others; but should not be taught to read and write unless she was to become a nun. Many evils, said Philip disapprovingly, have come from the fact that women have learnt such things, for then men dare to write follies or supplications which they would not dare to say or send by messenger. Philip ended his injunctions with the rather patronizing remark that even old women might be useful, for "they can manage and watch their houses, raise the children and arrange marriages." At least, the good ones occupied themselves in these ways, but the bad "plaster their faces, dye their hair, waste their patrimony in seeking love when they are old."

The requirements for the ideal woman put forward by such writers as Robert of Blois and Philip of Novara probably have as much relation to the realities of their time as the formalities of present-day writers on etiquette have to ordinary social life. They mirror the contemporary French ideals of polite behaviour carried to extremes. But, in the thirteenth century too, a good wife was rather more than the bloodless embodiment of the virtues preached by the moralists, or even the competent administrative helpmeet. The Knight of La Tour Landry, in the prologue of his fourteenth-century book of deportment for his daughters, describes most eloquently the bond of love and respect that bound him to his dead wife. According to the Knight, she was:

> Both fair and good, which had knowledge of all honour, all good, and fair maintaining, and of all good she was bell and the flower; and I delighted so much in her that I made for her love songs, ballads, rondels, virelays, and diverse things in the best wise I could. . . . And so it is more than twenty years that I have been for her full of great sorrow. For a true lover's heart forgetteth never the woman that once he has truly loved.

This was indeed a noble compliment, although perhaps influenced by literary convention. It is a useful counterbalance to the belief that marriage and love were quite incompatible in the Middle Ages.

The countess of Leicester did not altogether conform to the patterns laid down by writers on morals and manners. Her character and activities can afford one example of how thirteenth-century theory about the place of women was carried out in practice. Certainly the countess was no cipher. Eleanor brought Simon de Montfort great wealth, as she was the widow of one of the greatest earls of the realm; also great prestige because she was the king's sister. These two facts alone would have ensured her importance. In addition her character was assertive—she was not the meek, submissive, dovelike type so highly praised by the moralists. Several years earlier, the Franciscan Adam Marsh had found it necessary to write to her reprovingly, suggesting that she lay aside all contentions and irritating quarrels and act in a spirit of moderation when she had to counsel her husband. Obviously a high-spirited woman, she was also unfailingly loyal to Earl Simon through good times and bad. She shared many of her husband's travels—to Italy, France, and Gascony, but she was also capable of handling their many concerns alone. The evidence of the household account shows the countess at a period when she was, of necessity, in charge. The earl was away, engaged on his campaigns, and the management of all their affairs lay in her hands. The role of the countess at this time was more than ever that of the woman of affairs. Even the sober items of the account show how much political initiative Eleanor displayed, and how the executive ability and practical foresight of a capable woman were extended to their furthest limits.

On the domestic side the countess had many officials to take care of the immediate requirements of the household, though she herself had to oversee their accounts and agree to their expenditures. For female companionship she had certain women, who also served as ladies-in-waiting and were referred to as the countess's damsels. Her daughter Eleanor was now almost thirteen, but she still had her own nurse and took an unimportant place in the life of the household.

Indeed the medieval magnates had surprisingly little to do with their children. Almost immediately after birth, they were handed over to the care of a nurse whose duties, as described by Bartholomew the Englishman,[4] included not only the physical care of the child, but also the display of affection which is now considered essentially maternal. According to Bartholomew the nurse's duties were very extensive. She was ordained to nourish and feed the child, to give it suck, to kiss it if it fell, and comfort it if it wept, and to wash it when it was dirty. The nurse was also to teach the child to speak by sounding out the words for him, to dose him with medicines when necessary, and even to chew the toothless child's meat so that he could swallow it. The mother must have been a rather remote figure. Discipline was always considered the father's primary duty. Bartholomew specifically insisted that the father must treat his child with harshness and severity. He should teach him with scoldings and beatings, put him under wardens and tutors, and, above all, show "no glad cheer lest the child wax proud." The old adage of "spare the rod and spoil the child" was firmly entrenched in all medieval treatises on the proper upbringing of children.

The earl and countess of Leicester had taken care to put these precepts into practice. In 1265 they had six living children, ranging in age from twenty-

---

[4] Bartholomew the Englishman was a thirteenth-century Franciscan who wrote an immensely popular encyclopaedia, *Concerning the Nature of Things*. He dealt with a multiplicity of subjects, ranging from the nature of God and the angels to the size of the cooking pots. His work was widely used as a textbook until the sixteenth century.

six to thirteen. Two of their sons had been sent when young to the household of Bishop Grosseteste to be instructed in good manners and some learning. It was a recognized medieval practice to send both boys and girls away to more important or more learned households as a way of furthering their education. Now the two eldest boys, Henry and Simon the younger, had been knighted and were a valued part of their father's army. Guy was also a fighting man with his father. The fourth son, Amaury, was a clerk; he had profited handsomely by his father's success for he had been appointed, at the age of twenty-one, to the rich office of treasurer of York. Richard, the youngest of the sons, is a shadowy figure who flits briefly through the records before his departure for Bigorre in September when he disappears completely. The only daughter, Eleanor, remained with her mother during this period, but her father was busy trying to arrange a marriage for her with Llywelyn, prince of Wales. Earl Simon hoped to reinforce the alliance between the baronial troops and the wild Welsh tribesmen. However, the catastrophe of Evesham changed all this. Young Eleanor accompanied her mother into exile in France, and the betrothal to Llywelyn was postponed. Finally the countess succeeded in having it carried out by proxy in France just before her death in 1275. Even then complications of policy forced a further postponement of three years before Eleanor's marriage was solemnized and, at the age of twenty-six, she was finally free to join her Welsh prince.

It seems to have been the usual practice for each child in an important household to have his own nurse. In the countess's account, besides the payment for young Eleanor's nurse, there is also mention of the nurse of William de Braose.[5] This multiplicity of nurses is also evident in the household of young Henry, the son of Edward I. There were three children in that household: Henry himself, his elder sister, Eleanor, and their cousin, John of Brittany; each of these children had his own nurse. These ladies were of some standing, since their robes, a considerable addition to their annual wages and a gauge of social position, were of the same value as those of the official guardian of the household. Henry's account also underlines the fact that it was the nurse, not the mother, who was constantly present. The queen sent messengers enquiring after the health of the sickly lad, but affairs of state and the pattern of behaviour of the time kept them apart even in his final illness. The thirteenth century regarded children's deaths as a frequent, and inevitable, example of the inscrutable will of God.

It is obvious that the duties of the countess, or of any great baron's wife, were not restricted to her home and family in the sense in which later centuries have understood these terms. A great magnate's wife was not expected to be a very domestic woman—her duties dealt with a wider sphere.

---

[5] William's place in the household remains in doubt. Probably he was a relation of the famous marcher family to which Earl Simon's great-aunt, Countess Loretta of Leicester, belonged, and may have been a hostage for father or uncle, as a William de Braose holding lands in Dorset and Kent was a vigorous loyalist.

The account shows very clearly two fields in which the countess's personal initiative was particularly important. Eleanor entertained a great number of people, both at Odihom and Dover, during the spring and summer of 1265; she also had an extraordinarily wide range of correspondence.

Visitors were a common and welcome feature of medieval social life. Indeed one of the primary duties of the gently-born, and especially of the heads of a household, was to greet all their guests with enthusiasm and courtesy. Grosseteste counselled the countess of Lincoln that all guests, secular and religious, should be received "quickly, courteously, and with good cheer," and then they should be "courteously addressed, lodged, and served." It is an interesting peculiarity of the Montfort household account that the clerk each day listed by name those guests of importance who ate with the countess. This gives us valuable clues to the nature of people who came on varying errands, and, with the marshal's daily accounting for the number of horses, shows the fluctuations in size of the countess's household.

A considerable number of visitors were listed—over fifty names are mentioned in the seven months of the account—and many of them were accompanied by large retinues. However, it should be remembered that everyone whose normal place was not in the countess's household was specified on the roll as an outsider. For example, when Earl Simon came with his own large army to spend the two weeks before Easter at Odiham, he was listed as a visitor; so, too, were the elder sons, on their occasional appearances to see their mother. Others who appear frequently are the senior officials of the household, whose business led them back and forth between the earl and the countess, wherever they might be, and also took them up and down to London for purchases.

The true guests were of many types: royal officials, knights of the shire who were staunch supporters of the earl, and men who had previously served as local officials for the earl and now had a share in the administration of the country. It is interesting to note that in a period which might reasonably seem to discourage unarmed travellers, the countess also entertained a large number of religious personages. Some were definitely friends of the Leicesters and supporters of the baronial cause, such as the abbot of Waverley, the Cistercian abbey so close to Odiham. Others, such as the prioress of Wintney and the prioress of Amesbury, seem to have been trying to complete business for their convents.

But nuns were not the only women travelling, either for business or for pleasure. Some of the greatest ladies of the realm were among the countess's visitors. Isabella de Fortibus, for example, spent the Easter weekend at Odiham, and the countess of Oxford visited in May. Her appearance is less surprising since her husband was a strong supporter of Earl Simon.

The titled and the wealthy are easily classifiable, but sometimes it is possible to trace the lines of self-interest and feudal relationship which lie behind the unexplained and unfamiliar names in the roll. Margery de Crek is a particularly good example of the many possible ties. Margery came to visit the countess at Odiham in March, travelling with a retinue of twelve horses. She was almost certainly a widow. Her husband, Bartholomew de Crek, had been in Ireland in 1224 in the service of William Marshal, the Countess Eleanor's first husband, and in 1232, after the earl's death, was described as Eleanor's yeoman. By 1235 he had married Margery, held lands in Norfolk and Suffolk and, like many others richer than himself, was deeply in debt to some Jews of London. His upward social climb was ultimately crowned by knighthood. The date of Bartholomew's death is not ascertainable, though his name disappears from the records after 1251. Margery, however, lived many years as a widow, dying in 1282 when she must have been at least in her sixties. By this time she had retired with a fairly large household to the Augustinian convent of Flixton. She was quite a wealthy woman, and her will disposed of many of her goods in favour of the Flixton community. Her son John died seven years after his mother, still holding Creake in Norfolk of the earl marshal, and Combe in Suffolk of the king in chief. The original connection of Margery and Bartholomew de Crek with the countess of Leicester was undoubtedly due to Bartholomew's service of William Marshal, who may have rewarded him with his original landholding. In any case ancient acquaintance, and perhaps the hope of present favours, kept Margery in friendly touch with the Countess Eleanor in the troubled year of 1265. This one case, in which the connecting links are reasonably easy to uncover, illustrates very clearly the involved tangle of political self-interest, feudal relationships, and even natural human companionship which formed the fabric of thirteenth-century feudal society.

Apart from her overnight guests, the Countess Eleanor seems to have been well aware that hospitality could serve political ends. During her trip from Odiham to the greater safety of Dover she entertained the burgesess of Winchelsea as she passed through their town. Only three days after she arrived at Dover she invited the burgesses of Sandwich to dinner, and both groups of burgesses were again asked to dinner at Dover castle in July. The reason for these invitations is abundantly clear, as the support of the important townsmen of the Cinque Ports was essential for the baronial cause. It was imperative that Eleanor should keep them loyal to Earl Simon, for they could guard the coast against French invasion, and keep out mercenaries recruited for the king overseas.

Correspondence, as well as hospitality, was put to political uses. An analysis of the Countess Eleanor's correspondents shows very clearly the wide-ranging interests of a great magnate and his wife, though its unusual extent was influenced by their extraordinary situation. The frequent use of letters was nothing new, for in more peaceful years Eleanor and Simon had corresponded with Bishop Grosseteste and Brother Adam Marsh, who was a fluent, if enigmatic, letter-writer. In the spring and summer of 1265 an unusual number of messages went back and forth between husband and wife.

These were undoubtedly accounted for by the exigencies of the political and military situation. Indeed the messengers who carried the letters were among the busiest members of the household. Besides her husband, the countess corresponded with Richard Gravesend, bishop of Lincoln and enthusiast for the baronial cause, Thomas Cantilupe, the baronial chancellor, and her officials and favourite merchants among many others. Nor was this activity limited only to England. Messengers went back and forth between England and Bigorre, where the earl still claimed the title of count, and Laura de Montfort, Earl Simon's niece, wrote from the family castle at Montfort-l'Amaury. The frequent entries on the account are sufficient to show that the countess was extremely active in many fields, and that constant communication was possible whenever political or personal needs required it.

After the earl's defeat and death at Evesham, the countess's role was even more important and demanding. The responsibility for salvaging any fragment of the Montfort fortunes was hers alone. The account shows how she armed her intercessors with letters for her unforgiving brother the king when he held his first parliament after his return to unfettered power; and how she also wrote, with greater success, to Richard of Cornwall to ensure his good will and promise of assistance. Not only did she arrange the departure of her youngest son for Bigorre, she also seems to have succeeded in smuggling 11,000 marks out of England to France. In a final agreement made at Dover with the Lord Edward, Eleanor ensured the return to grace and favour of most of her household, though she herself had to leave the kingdom. All these various achievements illustrate the many facets of the countess's executive ability and capacity for planning.

The household account gives glimpses of a great lady's many activities. From its evidence it is easy to see that many, in fact most, of her occupations were not particularly domestic, or even feminine in the restricted sense. The primary duty of a great baron's wife was to produce the heir necessary to carry on the line, and then to serve as an active partner with her husband in the many enterprises of feudal life. She might even, when necessary, take sole charge. The purely domestic routine of the lady of the house in such a vast establishment was discharged by a well-planned and carefully detailed organization which was responsible for the smooth running of the domestic machinery.

The Late Middle Ages, 14th Century

Many studies of social life in premodern Europe focus on the fourteenth century, and there are two main reasons for this. First, during the late thirteenth and early fourteenth centuries, record-keeping by governmental and private institutions became a standard practice. Studies of rural society, which are so dependent on records of landholding, naturally end up focusing on this record-rich period. Studies of the cities follow the same pattern, and even legal history assumes a new dimension when it concerns itself with the period of the Yearbooks—reports of cases brought before the royal court in England, which were first circulated in 1292. Second, war and pestilence profoundly disrupted fourteenth-century society throughout Europe. The Hundred Years' War, originating in sporadic conflicts between England and France in the early fourteenth century, created a new nationalism in Europe's kingdoms and caused destruction on a scale that could not fail to affect the character of both rural and urban communities. The Black Death, recurrent in Europe throughout the second half of the century, drastically reduced the population at all levels and created instability throughout the society. The selections in this part reflect both the record-keeping proclivities of fourteenth-century institutions and the effect of war and plague on those institutions.

William Bowsky's "Keeping the Urban Peace" reveals the development and early character of urban police forces in Italy. The urban communes were small, self-contained units with a highly varied population living in close quarters. Competition for power within these communities and troubles derived from jealousy among the social classes were persistent problems. The reaction of the authorities to threats against the peace was to establish security forces that doubled as watchmen whose function was to protect the town from common criminals.

Other problems of city life are the subject of Philip Ziegler's "Hygiene in Fourteenth Century London." Here the focus is on the health problems of the cities just before the first epidemics of plague hit them. (This theme was also treated in A. H. M. Jones' "Sanitation and Safety in the

Greek City" in Part 1.) In "Family Life in the Cities," Lewis Mumford assesses the quality of urban family life, filling out the description of city life in the premodern era.

Thomas B. Costain's "The Peasants in Revolt" and H. J. Hewitt's "Feudal War in Practice" concern the disruption caused by war and plague during the fourteenth century. Costain describes the peasant rebellions, which were among the most important results of the plague. These rebellions occurred throughout Europe and were caused by labor shortages and other disruptions that followed the mass deaths. The rebellions appear at first to be wars between the classes, but close study shows that they were inspired by limited aims and grievances. In "Feudal War in Practice," Hewitt revises traditional ideas about the character of war during the period and shows how the military conflicts affected combatants and noncombatants alike.

Bibliography

On the government of the Italian cities of the late Middle Ages, see William Bowsky, "The *Buon Governo* of Siena (1287–1355): A Medieval Italian Oligarchy," *Speculum*, Vol. 37 (1962), pp. 368–81, and Marvin Becker, "A Study in Political Failure: The Florentine Magnates 1280–1343," *Mediaeval Studies*, Vol. 27 (1965), pp. 246–308. For good general studies of individual cities, see David Herlihy, *Medieval and Renaissance Pistoia* (New Haven, 1967), and Gene Brucker, *Renaissance Florence* (New York, 1969).

For further material on the rebellion in England, see Charles Oman, *The Great Revolt of 1381* (Oxford, 1906), and Bertie Wilkinson, "The Peasants' Revolt of 1381," *Speculum*, Vol. 15 (1940), pp. 12–35. On the relation of the plague to peasant unrest, see Eileen Power, "The Effects of the Black Death on Rural Organization in England," *History*, Vol. 3 (1918), pp. 109–16, and B. H. Putnam, *The Enforcement of the Statute of Labourers* (New York, 1908). On the insurrections throughout Europe, see Edward P. Cheyney, *The Dawn of a New Era, 1250–1453* (New York, 1936). See also Steven Runciman, *The Sicilian Vespers* (Cambridge, Eng., 1958), Chaps. XII and XIII.

Besides H. J. Hewitt's general work on England's organization for war, *The Organization of War Under Edward III* (Manchester, Eng., 1966), from which "Feudal War in Practice" is taken, see his book *The Black Prince's Expedition of 1355–57* (Manchester, Eng., 1958). For a general history of the Hundred Years' War see Eduard Perroy, *The Hundred Years' War* (London, 1957). On another aspect of English military power, see F. W. Brooks, *The English Naval Forces 1199–1272* (London, 1962). The standard history of medieval warfare is Charles Oman, *A History of the Art of War in the Middle Ages* (London, 1924). See also John Beeler, *Warfare in England 1066–1189* (Ithaca, N.Y., 1966).

For broader studies of medieval cities, see J. W. F. Hill, *Medieval Lincoln* (Cambridge, Eng., 1948) and G. A. Williams, *Medieval London*

(London, 1963). On the planning and founding of towns in the Middle Ages, see M. W. Beresford, *New Towns of the Middle Ages* (London, 1967), and F. Haverfield, *Ancient Town Planning* (Oxford, 1913). On those who lived in the city, see A. H. Hibbert, "The Origins of the Medieval Town Patriciate," *Past and Present*, Vol. 3 (1953), pp. 15–27, and Florence E. de Roover, "Andrea Banchi: Florentine Silk Manufacturer and Merchant in the Fifteenth Century," *Studies in Medieval and Renaissance History*, Vol. 3 (1966), pp. 221–86. Fritz Rörig surveys the whole urban population in *The Medieval Town* (Berkeley, 1967).

Keeping the Urban Peace

WILLIAM BOWSKY

The revival of urban life in the twelfth century was accompanied by a long struggle between the burghers, led by the merchant class, and the feudal lords who had taken control of the towns in the course of the feudalization of Europe. The burghers sought autonomy that would give them control over their commercial activities and over the institutions that served the urban economy, such as the town market. The struggle went on for centuries, but one indication of the extent of the burghers' success was the popularity of the slogan, "City air makes one free." As the independence of the cities was established, they ceased to be an integral part of feudal society and thus migration—or escape—to a city came to mean withdrawal from the dominant form of social structure.

The townspeople gradually won control over their communities, and by the late Middle Ages the organization of city life was controlled by the merchants rather than by the feudal lords. The ruling class of the cities established institutions suited to commerce. Merchants had no time for the slow procedures of the feudal courts, and they did not want to undergo ordeals to prove or disprove the existence of commercial debts. Feudal law and the legal system of the feudal court were replaced by municipal courts that meted out quick and rational justice. The law of the cities was clearly an advance over the law of the manor. But the same legal system that was quick and rational in resolving civil suits was quick and harsh in its treatment of criminals. Because the warehouses and markets had to be protected and general peace and quiet had to be maintained if trade were to prosper, the cities developed means of policing their populations. In this selection, William Bowsky analyzes the Sienese approach to the peace-keeping problems of the urban communities.

Rarely does the medievalist treat a theme of such contemporary interest as that of this paper. We need only recall how recently a major candidate for national office made the problem of crime in America's cities a significant public issue, or recollect the riots in Detroit and elsewhere. Yet even medieval historians have paid little direct attention to the specific problem of internal violence, particularly in Italy.

This article is a case study—an examination of police power and public

From William Bowsky, "The Medieval Commune and Internal Violence: Police Power and Public Safety in Siena, 1287–1355," *American Historical Review*, Vol. 73 (1967), pp. 1–17. Reprinted by permission of William Bowsky.

safety in the heart of a Tuscan city-state from the late thirteenth through the mid-fourteenth century, when an oligarchy called the Nine ruled the Sienese commune. What follow are suggestions and tentative findings concerning Sienese urban police power that arose during preparation of a forthcoming general study of Siena under the Nine.

In order to bring the issue into the clearest focus, the concentration will be upon the mother city of Siena itself, to the exclusion of the *contado* or state bordering the city and governed by it. Nor can this be an examination of justice in the broadest sense, including criminal law, courts, and their jurisdiction and procedure. Rather it is an examination of the problem of the protection of the community from lawbreakers: their detection, apprehension, and detention—strictly police functions.

Basic questions must be posed, even though there is not always sufficient documentation to provide the most satisfactory answers. How did communal authorities conceive of the problem of police power? To what extent and degree did it concern them? How did the government deal with the problem? With what results? And what might such an examination contribute to our knowledge of other facets of life, values, or problems in a late medieval or early Renaissance commune?

The commune was in fact vitally concerned with the seizure, punishment, and removal from circulation of lawbreakers. Its prisons were foul, dank, and crowded. This is not surprising as the commune "farmed" the custody of its prisons to Sienese citizens or companies, who, in turn, in the manner of tax farmers, sought to recoup their expenses and to extract a profit from the prisoners. The result was no overgenerosity in the treatment of prisoners who were regularly chained to the walls to prevent attempts at escape.

The government took considerable interest in the prisons. In 1330 new communally owned institutions were completed beneath the great Communal Palace, and prisoners were transferred to them from jails that the commune had rented in a private palace—jails in which over sixty prisoners had died during only the preceding two years.

Communal prison regulations of 1298, still unpublished, illuminate the attitudes of the governing classes toward crime and the bases for the distinctions made in the treatment of prisoners. The regulations provided for the division of the jails into three principal sections. The first consisted of two rooms, one of which served for the detention of those convicted of the so-called "enormous crimes," among them homicide, treason, arson, kidnaping, rape, poisoning, mutilation, torture, highway robbery, perjury, wounding and drawing blood, and breaking into a home for the purpose of theft. Another room held those convicted of lesser crimes. The second major section also had two rooms: one for convicted debtors and the other for women, regardless of the offense. Confined in the third section were those not yet sentenced but undergoing investigation or trial, with one significant exception: nobles and *boni homines* under investigation for any crime that did not entail the death penalty could live in a special house of detention, or, if they provided the highest communal magistrate (the podesta) with surety for good conduct, they could even leave the house of detention.

Thus, while the commune made what we would consider a wise distinction between accused and convicted, it made two additional distinctions: one relegating women to a separate category, and another providing special, lenient treatment for the commune's most powerful, wealthy, and politically important elements, both noble and popular, so long as they were the well-to-do citizens of good reputation generally understood by their fellow Sienese to be comprehended within the term *boni homines.*

Well might the government concern itself with public safety, for this was an age characterized by rapid resort to violence despite the centuries-old teachings of the Church. Inadequate documentation prevents an accurate estimate of the numbers of persons seized and confined, but an incomplete register shows over seventeen thousand persons from the city and *contado* fined for criminal acts from mid-1270 to mid-1296, while in a brief three weeks in 1298 only one judge for a single third of the city heard seventeen criminal cases. Almost every six months from two to fifty or more prisoners were released as religious offerings. And records do not give us the number of those who eluded capture.

No single class of society possessed a monopoly on violence. To expand upon the numerous episodes involving members of powerful noble families would belabor the obvious. Published chronicles alone are replete with tales of their murders, assaults, and minor battles. And wool manufacturer and woolworker, shopkeeper and manual laborer, all are among those seized and sentenced. It might, however, be particularly timely to add in fairness that the students who frequented the Sienese *Studio* or university were quite law abiding, particularly as compared with their counterparts at the University of Bologna and elsewhere.

The clergy were not exempt from the proclivity to resort to violence. Episcopal provisions of 1297 envisioned clerics committing every imaginable sort of crime from sedition and sodomy to brawling and breaking bones. And despite its generally good relations with the Sienese church, the commune adamantly enforced its own police jurisdiction against criminous clerics, even when this meant lengthy and expensive litigation and threats of excommunication.

The fairer sex produced its share of mayhem and bloodshed and for good measure seems to have been well equipped with sharp tongues, for whose use many were seized and punished. Not without interest is a sentence of 1342 against a woman who had struck a man on the forehead with a lantern and drawn blood. Her fine was increased because of her contumacy, but halved "because a woman against a man," doubled again "because at night," and doubled once more "because she struck him in his house." Like other townsmen, the medieval Sienese was no stranger to the idea that a man's home is his castle.

Crime and violence were not only common, but involved every sort of activity from the so-called "enormous crimes" to drunken brawling. The commune had to contend, moreover, with violence that erupted as a result of special situations it was not always able to prevent, particularly food riots. These occurred during the famines and food shortages that plagued Tuscany on several occasions during the first half of the fourteenth century. One such riot in 1329 cost the commune over L. 667 to reimburse only for stolen grain.

Such nonviolent crimes as bearing unauthorized weapons, breaking curfew, gambling, and frequenting taverns required law enforcement. Some offenses such as blasphemy and sodomy entailed what today seem to be disproportionately severe penalties, penalties that at times were executed. Thus in 1336 a blasphemer who failed to pay a weighty fine within ten days of being sentenced had his tongue cut out. The medieval Sienese was most horrified of and angered by sodomy, fearing the unleashing of divine wrath against the community that permitted it. The sodomite, or procurer for a sodomite, who did not pay three hundred lire within a month of sentencing was, read a statute, "to be hanged by his virile members in the principal market place, and there remain hanging . . . for an entire day."

Communal authorities especially feared those acts of violence that could develop from a private fracas into a threat to the regime itself. Most troublesome were certain games that appealed so greatly to the Sienese that despite numerous prohibitions they were frequently played in the Campo, beneath the windows of the Communal Palace wherein resided the Nine and the podesta. Such games often began as simple fist fights, but progressed to the hurling of stones, the use of staves, spears, and knives, and rapidly degenerated into pitched battles. Yet they were so popular that on at least one occasion (1291) the City Council felt itself compelled to grant permission for "a game or battle of *elmora* in the Campo."

The heated and confused combat could easily turn the games into an attack upon the palace itself, whenever the participants felt sufficiently aggrieved against the regime or when groups conspiring the government's overthrow engineered the shift from game to open rebellion. Thus in early February 1325 various conspirators (including powerful Tolomei nobles) plotted to turn a game of *pugna* into open rebellion. The Sienese government was indeed well served by two hundred gold florins that it paid at the end of that month "to a secret accuser who revealed to the war captain the treason, conspiracy, and plot that had been arranged against the office of the Lords Nine . . ." as recorded in a register of communal expenditures.

Police were also directly involved in efforts to quell such outright rebellion and insurrection as that of early October 1311 to which its plotters had perhaps been emboldened by Henry of Luxemburg's victorious conclusion of the siege of Brescia, and hence the prospect that an imperial army swelled with Ghibelline exiles and warriors would soon pass temptingly close to Guelph Siena as the Emperor-elect journeyed southward to Rome and the imperial coronation.

Prior to the regime's final collapse the only major rebellion that placed it in mortal danger was that of October 26, 1318. In a pitched battle in the Campo that took many lives, at least 269 mercenary infantry, 81 mercenary cavalry, and over 20 crossbowmen defended the government. Beside them, 84 of the 100 *birri*, or police, of the Nine and commune valiantly battled and later received generous rewards for their efforts.

The manifold needs for law enforcement were as obvious to the medieval Sienese as they are to the modern historian, and the commune resorted to varied methods in efforts to provide such protection and to curb violence. Like other cities, Siena was subject to a strict curfew, and only such authorized persons as night guards, visiting physicians, and garbage collectors could appear on the streets at night without special permits. Others found outside their houses after the sound of the so-called "Third Bell" had rung two hours after sunset were subject to a fine of 20s., one such fine being collected from that lively Sienese poet and correspondent of Dante, Cecco Angiolieri.

Another method of enforcement, already referred to, was reliance upon secret accusers who denounced to communal authorities those who they knew had violated specific laws. In return, an accuser's name was kept secret (much to the historian's annoyance), and he received one-fifth, one-fourth, or even one-half of the fine depending upon the offense, while the City Council granted even larger sums to those disclosing treason plots.

The principal instrument of law enforcement, however, was the police. What then of the police force, or rather, forces?

Most police duties were entrusted to hired foreign policemen. Their sheer number in proportion to the size of the urban population strikes the historian. By the mid-1330's there was a foreign policeman for each 145 inhabitants of Siena, men, women, and children, lay and cleric, if the reader accepts my recent population estimates. (Reliance upon previous estimates would yield a ratio of about 1 policeman per 73 Sienese.)

For the sake of illustration and contrast only, we may note that in the midwestern city of Lincoln, Nebraska, with a population of about 135,000, there is 1 policeman per 1,000 inhabitants. New York City (not without its crime problem) has a ratio of approximately 1 to 285. These obviously are modern cities, with methods of communication and control unknown in the thirteenth and fourteenth centuries, but the contrast remains striking.

More useful might be a comparison with a medieval Tuscan commune, but this problem has yet to engage the serious attention of historians. A ratio of 1 to 800 suggested for Florence during the first half of the fourteenth century is based on scanty research. More important, it fails to reveal what may have been the significance of this disparity between Florentine and

Sienese police forces. Was there, for example, less need for police protection in the Arno city, were its organization and legislation more effective than that of Siena, or did the Sienese devote greater attention than their Florentine contemporaries to the problem of lawlessness and internal violence?

We should not speak of *the* police force. Even in the late thirteenth century the principal foreign magistrates in Siena, the podesta and the captain of the people, each had a group of police in the entourage or "family" that accompanied him into office and was paid by him from his own salary. Another police force served "the Nine and the Commune." Two new police forces were created during the following century: the police who formed a part of the "family" of the war captain—a new official whose office was regularized in the 1320's—and, in 1334, the *Quattrini,* particularly charged with the daytime custody of the city. This brought to five the number of foreign police forces.

The government was aware then of the need for police protection. It was also aware of inadequacies in the police system, and that system became the object of a mass of regular legislation. The regime experimented continuously with the size, organization, distribution, tours of duty, and jurisdictions of its police units.

The smallest force was that of the captain of the people: generally no more than 20 men in the late thirteenth century, 10 during the fourteenth. Its size reflects accurately that magistrate's decreasing authority in all areas of activity. The podesta's police ranged from a high of 60 to a low of 20 men, and the number was set at 40 by statutes of the late 1330's. The war captain's police, originally 50, were set at 100 by the same statutes, again a good measure of that official's increasing importance. There was considerable experimentation with the force of the Nine and commune, but usually it was 90 or 100. The *Quattrini* too were the object of experimentation: increased from 60 to 100 within months of their creation, 150 two years later, and then 100 from 1338 until the abandonment of the force.

The jurisdictions of these forces ordinarily overlapped and were the object of constant legislative attention. To select only a few measures at random, provisions of 1299, 1300, and 1306 assigned night watch particularly to police of the podesta and of the captain of the people, while entrusting the podesta alone with supervision of the day watch. An act of 1308 charged the podesta with both day and night watch, and for this purpose granted him the disposition of some of the police of the captain of the people and many of those of the Nine and commune in addition to his own.

Provisions of 1334 for the custody of the city at night allocated a separate third of the area to the podesta, war captain, and captain of the people, but the first two could also investigate conditions in each of the remaining sections. The war captain and the captain of the people each received the same authority as the podesta to have the city searched for persons bearing prohibited arms and to hear, define, and terminate their cases. The *Quat-*

trini too sought all types of delinquents. Another act of 1334 ordered all foreign officials, their families, and all mercenaries to pursue and seize malefactors and deliver them to the podesta—except that the war captain's men were to deliver their prisoners to him.

Despite variations in size, composition, and jurisdiction, the foreign police forces had much in common, beginning with the overlapping jurisdiction itself. At the request of communal officials all forces were subject to official review in order to determine whether all were present, properly armed, and if any unauthorized substitutions had been made in personnel. Violators were fined. In addition to receiving regular salaries, foreign police capturing and delivering a prisoner who was either already wanted or was later convicted received a cash reward. But, while effective service was rewarded, policing was to be a full-time task. A provision for the *Quattrini*, for example, forbade them from engaging in any trade or manual labor in the city under the penalty of a fine of twenty-five lire, almost five months' salary. And like foreign magistrates the police could not fraternize with the local populace. The nature of police duty too was the same for all forces: separated into groups of two or more men they patroled assigned portions of the city. Common characteristics marked the hiring of these forces. The policemen were not hired separately; rather the commune contracted for six-month terms with their captains or with the foreign official in whose entourage they were included.

Nor did the police have any special police training prior to entering Sienese service or while in that service. They were, in fact, nothing but foot soldiers or infantry hired for police duty, and in many documents they are referred to interchangeably as *birri*—police—or as *fanti* or *pedites*—infantrymen. Indeed it seems that the same type of men, at times even the same men, who served Siena as police at other times served Siena and other communes as mercenary infantry, even under the same captains. This phenomenon might be investigated by future historians of the origins and development of the *Compagnie di Ventura*, the Free or Mercenary Companies, and of the *condottieri* who attained such notoriety during the high Renaissance.

The government also took a strong and continuing interest in the type of men hired for police duty: all were hired (through their captains) by the commune's highest signory, the same signory that selected the podesta, captain of the people, and war captain. For the signory wanted more than skilled fighting men as police; police had to have the correct political persuasions. Statutes declared, for example, that the captains of the police of the Nine and commune were to be Guelph counts or barons, friends of the Church, and, especially, friends of the Sienese commune. They could not come from the Sienese state or from the cities of the podesta or captain of the people who would be in office at the same time, a wise precaution against the concentration of power in the hands of a single foreign official. This concern for the political leanings of the police is readily understandable when we recall how crimes of violence could become a political menace, and that police forces composed of trained infantry functioned indiscriminately in both areas.

The same lack of distinction between military and police functions and the same emphasis upon political coloration are evident when we examine the few police activities performed by the inhabitants of Siena.

The commune called upon members of the companies of the city for night watch, companies that had resulted from a fusion of military companies and companies of the society of the people, analogous to the situation in Pisa. Under the Nine the companies not only served in Siena's armies, but assisted in quelling fighting that involved the city's powerful noble families and in quashing major riots and rebellion. Their members swore to uphold the existing regime.

These companies supplied a pool of 600 men a month for night watch, with about 120 actually serving during any month. After 1324 the commune remunerated the men of the companies for these services. During the next decade this night watch was made directly responsible to the war captain (not, we may note, to the companies' traditional leader, the captain of the people).

Two members of each company selected by the Nine for a six-month term performed other police functions. Called *paciarii* or peace officials, they reported to high communal officials infractions of private peace agreements and acts of oppression and injuries that occurred among the members of their companies. The remaining police function performed by Sienese was assigned for six-month terms to representatives of the *contrade* or *lire*, the city's administrative and tax districts. Each district had one official or *sindaco* salaried by the commune whose task it was to report to the podesta crimes and law violations that occurred within his district, under the penalty of heavy fines for the neglect of duty. (And it is self-evident that the areas allotted to the military companies with their *paciarii* overlapped and duplicated the *lire* with their *sindaci*.)

We have seen something of how the communal authorities conceived of and dealt with the problems of internal violence, police power, and public safety. But how effective were their measures? It should be noted at once that the state was cognizant of some of the limitations upon its ability to secure and maintain internal peace and order. There are numerous indications of this awareness.

Like Florence, its more powerful northern neighbor, Siena still recognized the legality of the vendetta. Lacking the strength to eliminate the vendetta, the government concentrated upon limiting its application and narrowing the circle of persons who could practice it and against whom it could be waged. A timorous attempt of May 1306 to isolate the actual offender by forcing his relatives to renounce the possibility of protecting him with a vendetta against possible avengers served only to demonstrate the commune's weakness: the measure was not retroactive, and it exempted those most likely to become involved—the culprit's father, sons, and blood brothers.

More serious was the continued recognition in public law of the so-called "instrument of peace" (*instrumentum pacis*)—a notarized document secured by an offender from an injured person (or his heirs), granting that offender peace and thus eliminating the possibility of a legal vendetta. An instrument of peace was necessary before one convicted of a crime of violence could be freed at a religious festival or take advantage of special or general amnesties or compositions. So important was this document that the state dropped all criminal action if a defendant could produce such a peace document even during the course of a trial. Here, in effect, a public crime was reduced to the status of a private concern. (Nor was it a major advance in public law when in 1350, in order to prevent the state from being deprived of its fine by collusion between offender and offended, it was ordered that henceforth even those producing peace instruments would not be given peace by the commune until they paid 5 per cent of the fine for the crime of which they had been accused.) While one may wish to interpret this attachment to the peace instrument as a desire to reinforce the commune's decisions with private agreement, it seems rather to be a confession of the state's inability to confer complete protection upon those who committed acts of violence.

The general amnesties, compositions, and commutations of sentences were themselves more than a device for filling communal coffers or for fulfilling some idea of justice; they were also an indication of the commune's recognition of its inability to capture and confine all lawbreakers. Many benefiting from such acts had never been captured. I have been able to discover no less than ten general amnesties and compositions enacted from 1302 to 1354, and they benefited well over five thousand persons from the city and *contado*, perhaps even double that number. Other individuals gained the same advantages as a result of private bills passed by the City Council.

The effectiveness of law enforcement against some of the greatest offenders, members of powerful, wealthy, and numerous noble *consorterie* or family federations seems particularly imperfect when we find that some nobles who benefited from general amnesty legislation were freed of four or more death sentences, each imposed for a different offense. Most impressive is the case of Messer Deo di Messer Guccio Guelfo Tolomei, acknowledged leader of the Tolomei *consorteria*. A leader of the rebellion of October 26, 1318, he had fled the city, captured the *contado* castle of Menzano in 1320, yielding it only when the war captain threatened to execute four innocent Tolomei, and in 1322 and 1323 played as much the role of the leader of a Free Company as that of a Sienese rebel as he ravaged the Sienese Valdichiana and Valdorcia with a large company that included Aretines and mercenaries in Florentine pay. He nonetheless benefited from a general act of 1339 and purchased the cancellation of five separate death sentences at the bargain rate of a thousand gold florins, for the price was the same regardless of the number of death sentences canceled. While such cases are rare, their very existence is significant.

On several occasions, when many members of some of the greatest noble *consorterie* engaged in acts of violence, rather than rely upon normal police legislation, Siena, like other communes, resorted to persuading them to conclude private truces. Those truces then received official government sanction, and violators were threatened with the severest penalties. The Nine forced the conclusion of such truces several times during the prolonged enmity between the Tolomei and the Salimbeni, and at least once during a Malavolti-Piccolomini dispute.

Following the precedent established by earlier regimes, the Nine licensed the possession of arms in the city through the sale of arms permits, though it limited these to the less dangerous weapons. Nonetheless they could not prevent men from appearing in public prepared for violence, and at any time well over a hundred men possessed such permits. While the government tried to restrict the area of the city where one could appear so armed, and this during the daytime only, it is alarming that, by the mid-1330's, eligibility for such permits had been extended even to foreigners. And we need scarcely emphasize that the existence of this system of arms permits was not justified by such reasoning as that which underlies our own Bill of Rights; it was rather an admission by the Sienese government of its inability to provide absolute protection for all of its subjects and to prevent them completely from exercising their more violent proclivities.

But while the commune could not completely control all of its subjects' violent tendencies, it could and did resist attempted intrusions into its jurisdiction. Thus in 1307 and 1311 it engaged in major disputes with the inquisitor in Tuscany, the Franciscan Phillip of Lucca, who claimed the right to issue arms permits to persons not in his regular retinue, even to private Sienese citizens.

The recognized imperfections of the Sienese police system should not, however, be viewed against a backdrop of absolute perfection—a standard not attained by any human society. Nor should we forget that the communal prisons were always well tenanted; that even members of the greatest noble families such as the Piccolomini, and of families represented on the Nine, ended with the hangman and at the executioner's block; and that the commune did, in fact, destroy houses and palaces of convicted criminals of the highest station, including Tolomei.

The onslaught of the Black Death in 1348 seems to mark a watershed. The plague struck Siena with exceptional severity, and the disorder and confusion that it left in its wake combined with a lack of available police to make the problem of police protection even more difficult and to strain the commune's every ability.

Already in the years immediately preceding the plague, marauding Free Companies had attacked the Sienese state. In 1342 the "Great Company" of Werner von Urslingen, self-styled "Enemy of God, of Piety, and of Mercy," visited it and could even embarrass the government by waylaying a war captain and his judge but a few miles from the city walls as they came to take office, robbing them of cash, lawbooks, armor, and silver vases worth at least five hundred gold florins. But such problems were dwarfed by the burning, murder, rapine, and extortion of the famous Fra Moriale during the summer of 1354. And before Siena bought him off with over thirteen thousand gold florins it even suffered the humiliation of paying him damages for horses killed by Sienese who had resisted him!

It comes as no surprise that the city itself was not immune from the increased violence of the postplague years. In 1350 the City Council lamented that there was a great increase in the number of crimes of violence, including bloodshed, brawling, and homicide, being committed within the city, and that criminals now acted with "ever-growing impunity" as it was simple for them to flee the city and evade capture. The commune's continued inability to cope with the deteriorating situation led it in 1352 to create a new "official for the custody of the city," complete with notary and family, to share the podesta's powers for guarding the city. A Ser Nuto of Città di Castello held the new office for a two-month term, but as he accomplished little or nothing, the experiment was quickly abandoned.

During 1313 and 1314 the commune had imposed a truce on all citizens having mortal hatreds or enmities, allegedly because the commune was threatened with foreign invasion. The same reason was alleged for a similar measure in 1351, but, although it was extended to 1353 and its implementation assigned to the powerful war captain, it had little or no effect. And would the government have waited thirty-seven years to repeat such a device if it had originally been successful? There had certainly been sufficient threats of foreign invasion upon which to draw for justification: the advent of the Emperor Louis the Bavarian and the incursions of Pisa, to name but two. The truce of 1351 seems at least as much a measure of desperation as of inspiration.

Public safety was further jeopardized in these dangerous postplague years by the abandonment of the force of *Quattrini* and by the reduction of the police of the Nine and commune from one hundred to eighty men—men retained, however, at increased wages owing to the lack of reliable, trained mercenary infantry for hire.

The atmosphere of increased violence, and the commune's decreased facilities for coping with it, was but one factor that contributed to the success of the rebellion that finally overthrew the regime of the Nine in 1355, but it should not be overlooked.

Throughout the history of the Nine, police power and public safety were major concerns to the highest communal authorities. Aware of the dangers of uncontrolled internal violence, they evolved a vast and complex body of police legislation and continually sought new approaches and solutions with admirable inventiveness and persistence. Even while admitting some of the commune's limitations they staunchly defended its right of sole police jurisdiction.

Before the plague the problem of crime control and police protection was generally kept within manageable limits, with a few striking, but temporary, exceptions. But during the postplague years immediately preceding the fall of the Nine the situation got increasingly out of hand.

Part of the difficulty was the tendency of all elements of society to resort to violence upon what we would consider insufficient provocation, and the persistence of the belief that personal vendetta was superior to recourse to public authority for the redress of private grievances of personal insult or injury. These factors alone necessitated a numerous police force.

But was not the problem of maintaining public safety increased by the existence of several police forces having overlapping and conflicting jurisdictions? These could lead to neglect of duty or to bitter distrust, suspicion, and rivalry in the competition for the rewards of successful captures. Perhaps, too, the failure to distinguish between violence wreaked by one citizen upon another and attacks upon the regime in power, between ordinary police functions and the need to defend the government militarily against violent overthrow, hindered further sophistication of police work.

Granted these complexities and the lack of modern means of communication and specialized police training, the system long functioned well. Its study offers insights into the nature and role of internal violence, and, in part, its relation to other aspects of life. Together with numerous analyses for other cities, it should provide material for a much-needed study of internal violence in the medieval and early Renaissance city-state.

The Peasants in Revolt

THOMAS B. COSTAIN

France in 1251 and 1358; Sicily in 1282; Flanders in 1255, 1267, 1275, 1280, and 1302; and England in 1381 all experienced violent lower-class rebellions. And these are only the major uprisings; there were many others. In 1251, Louis IX of France, on a crusade in Egypt and recently defeated at Cairo, sent home a call for help. All over France, peasants rose to form a huge army that would bring succor to the king, but within a short time segments of this army forgot their mission and went rampaging through manors and cities. Under Louis's mother, Blanche of Castille, the royal government had at first supported the peasant army, but when Blanche and her counselors recognized the anarchic character of the movement, they acted in concert with city authorities and feudal lords to put a bloody end to it. In 1358, after twenty years of war with England and several plague epidemics, the peasants of France again rose in revolt. The immediate cause of the uprising was an order that the hard-pressed peasants must help rebuild the castles and manor houses of the rich in preparation for further fighting. The rising was incredibly vicious and bloody on both sides.

In Flanders, the rebellions were mostly urban since that area was, and still is, one of the most densely populated regions in Europe. The weavers and other lower-class groups in the cities rose against the patriciate, which had allied itself with the hated French king. The worst of these uprisings was the Matins of Bruges, which took place on May 17, 1302. When the town's church bells sounded matins, the first prayer service of the day at 2 a.m., the population rose to slaughter the French garrison and officials. Under the leadership of the Count of Flanders, an army of weavers and workers devastated a French army sent to put down the rebellion. All the rebellions of Flanders were tied up with the political competition between the count and the French king. During the Hundred Years' War, the count sided with the English and further deepened the political divisions.

The Sicilian Vespers was also a popular uprising with political overtones. The people rose to drive out the French conquerors of the island, leaving the way open to Spanish intervention. But politics and social grievances were inexorably mixed up in the rebellion, and hundreds of French citizens, including women and children, lost their lives. Castles and other buildings occupied by the ruling class were also destroyed.

The most written-about insurrection, however, was the Peasants' Rebellion of 1381 in England. There had been unrest among the lower classes of the country for years following the plague. The drastic population decrease caused a severe labor shortage and led to a general disruption of the economy. Workers demanded higher wages, peasants left their farms to seek higher paying jobs in the cities. The nobility, whose income depended on the rents received from peasant farmers, and the merchants, whose profits were being squeezed, took action against this movement in the Statutes of Laborers, which fixed wages and prohibited migration from the farms. That these provisions were not effective is shown by the complaints brought out in the parliaments of the period. Thomas B. Costain captures the experience of the rebellion in this selection from his book *The Last Plantagenets*.

Four years had passed since the little king lost his shoe. He was growing into a handsome and confident boy, and measures were being taken already to find him a princess for a wife. The council governed the kingdom, and the queen mother (who was now a heavy load for any palfrey) governed the council. If the war against France was going on at all, it was going on badly. The treasury, as was always the case with Plantagenet kings, yawned with emptiness. And at this moment, in June 1381 to be exact, there came about one of the most dramatic, significant, and dreadful events in English history— the rebellion of the peasants.

Historians have found many words to apply to this upflaring of class discontent, including "mysterious." It is true that it had many elements of mystery, particularly the suddenness with which it began and its almost instantaneous spread across the southern and eastern counties like a stubble field afire. Had the seeds of rebellion been carefully planted in advance? Had it been possible to do this with such secrecy that villeins by the tens of thousands were ready and waiting while their masters had no inkling of impending trouble?

The discontent was due to the land laws which held a large proportion of the peasants in a state bordering on peonage. They were called villeins and were allowed to cultivate some acres of land belonging to the lord of the manor, paying in lieu of rent by giving a portion of their time to the land reserved for the lord himself. The was called the *corvée* and it would not have been entirely unfair except for the "boons," the right of the owner to call on them for extra work without remuneration at anytime he saw fit, particularly if rain were expected and he wanted his crops harvested in time. The boon in that event might mean that the poor villein's own crops would be beaten down by the autumnal storms and go unharvested. There were other class restrictions under which the peasant labored. He was bound to the land and could never leave without his lord's consent. His children were bound also. Nor were they allowed to marry save with seignorial approval.

The grim harvest of the Black Death had intensified these conditions. The villeins died in such numbers that it was no longer possible to cultivate all the land. At first this benefited the workmen because they could demand better terms for their labor but it did not take the law long to step in. It was stipulated that a man could not seek new employers and demand what he

From pp. 37–38 and 40–46 of *The Last Plantagenets* by Thomas B. Costain, copyright © 1962 by Thomas B. Costain. Reprinted by permission of Doubleday & Company, Inc.

wished. He must remain on the demesne where he was born and work for his own lord *on the terms which had prevailed before the coming of the plague.* This was the worst kind of injustice because the shortage of crops had sent up the cost of living.

It also rankled in the minds of the yeomen that it was the longbow (even the least expert of them might have shot the plume off a French helmet at a hundred yards) which had won the great victories in France, not the armed knight on horseback. Had they not proven their worth? Should the sons of men who had drawn a stout bow at Crécy be subjected to such unfair laws?

Finally, because of the cost of the abortive struggle against the French, there had come the poll tax. Parliament had decided that a certain number of groats, which the common people called "thickpennies," should be paid by everyone, the lowest rate being three groats for all over fifteen years of age. The peasants found this an intolerable burden on top of the penny on every hearth which had to be paid for the Romescot (Peter's Pence). Already on the verge of starvation, they refused to be taxed further.

It should not be assumed that the peasants were involved in a solidly knit and secret organization. It was more certainly a deep-seated conviction they held in common, a bitterness of desire for full freedom, which led to the sudden outburst. Any discussion of what happened when this discontent reached the breaking point must begin with the story of a hedge priest named John Ball. . . .

To say that John Ball was a hedge priest meant that he had no church and no charge, nor any post which linked him to the established order. Neither had he house nor table under which he could place his feet to partake of the loaf, the joint, and the jug of wine to which, surely, every good priest was entitled. It was equally true that he had no bed in which to sleep, no cell in monastery, no snug corner in a deanery. As his feet carried him hither and yon according to what he deemed to be the Lord's will, he slept for the most part under hedges. Sometimes he preached boldly at village crosses but more often cautiously in thick woods by moonlight.

For twenty years he wandered over the face England. Three times he was confined in the prison of the archbishop and finally he was put under a ban of excommunication. This made no difference, for he never ceased to preach what he believed, and what he believed sent his hearers into transports of wonderment and anticipation. His feet deserted early the relatively solid ground of Lollardy and carried him up high into a spiritual world where all men were equal. He always left hope behind him in the minds of those who had hung on his words. They must bide their time and be in readiness. When the right moment came, he, John Ball, would sound the bell.

This was heady stuff and some word of the gospel of unrest that he was spreading inevitably reached the ears of authority, hence his imprisonments. It is said that only the most courageous among the brawny tillers of the soil committed themselves to taking a part and that they found it wise to maintain strict conspiratorial silence. When one man who was pledged met another, whose sympathies were unknown, he would not resort to any of the usual artifices, a certain gesture, a low catchword, or perhaps a special manner of handshake. Instead he would whisper,

John the Miller grinds small, small, small.

The other, if he also believed in the message of John Ball would answer,

The King's son of heaven shall pay for all.

This may sound clumsy and even nonsensical but it must be borne in mind that this was an age of deep faiths and that men had a hunger for the poetic and the mystical which made such phrases sound warmly in their ears. There is nothing in the records to indicate that the use of these words ever led to any break in the seal of silence which had been imposed.

It is generally assumed that the messages in rhyme, which were distributed throughout the country, and were clearly the work of the bold hedge priest, did not get into circulation until the rising began. It seems more likely, however, that some of them at least had been used to strengthen the faith of the unhappy villeins through the years when the yoke rested heaviest on their shoulders and the day of reckoning seemed to get no closer. Otherwise the uprising would have lacked the spontaneity which brought the peasants out in tens of thousands in a matter almost of hours.

When the missives were written, and how they were distributed, must remain part of the mystery. All that can be set down as certain is that they came from the pen of John Ball and that they struck straight to the hearts of the common people.

> "Help truth and truth will help you," he wrote.
> "Now reigneth pride in price,
> And covetise is counted wise,
> And lechery withouten shame,
> And gluttony withouten blame."

A more direct appeal could be found in some of them, particularly the verses signed by such names as John the Miller, Jack Carter, and Jack Trewman. In these missives, or tracts as they soon came to be called, occurred such phrases as "make a good end of that ye have begun" and "now is the time," which made it clear that these at least were issued after the insurrection had started.

The rebellion flared up first in green and richly fertile Kent, where villeinage had never been introduced. The scene was the village of Dartford, which lay seventeen miles southeast of London. It was a busy place and served as first stop on the famous pilgrimage road between the capital and

Canterbury. Here a tegheler, or tyler named Wat was so incensed at the indecency of a poll-tax collector who insisted that the man's daughter was old enough to pay the tax, and had proceeded to strip off her clothes to prove it, that he seized a hammer and knocked the collector's brains out. Whether this indignant father was Wat the Tyler who later became leader of the march on London seems uncertain. There were two men of that name, one of them from Maidstone, and some historians claimed it was the latter who assumed command of the peasant army. To this day, however, the site of Wat the Tyler's house in Dartford is pointed out to visitors.

The incident threw the little Kentish town into an uproar. By nightfall hundreds of men had gathered, some with bows over their shoulders, some carrying pikes or oak quarterstaves, some armed only with flails and bill hooks or the crude handles of plows. Many had come from all the villages thereabouts and a contingent of hundreds had heard of what had happened and marched in from the Channel shore.

The next morning they marched south instead of north and came to Maidstone on the Medwige (Medway) River, a distance of more than twenty miles. The reason for this long detour was plain to all of them. John Ball was being held in the archbishop's prison in Maidstone and, as he was the spiritual leader of the forces of discontent, he must be released before anything more could be done.

There was an archbishop's palace of considerable size and beauty in Maidstone, which was said to have been built and presented to the episcopal see during the term of Stephen Langton of immortal memory. It was a graceful building of the native ragstone, with two Norman towers and a cluster of steeply angled roofs. It stood between the square-pillared church of St. Mary's and the squat and gloomy prison where offenders against clerical law were held.

It is stated in one chronicle that when John Ball was last sentenced in the archbishop's court he had cried out, "I can summon twenty thousand friends to win me free!" and that the somewhat sour-faced officials had paid no heed. There is nothing in the record of John Ball, who had wandered for so many years over flinty roads and rough forest paths to carry comfort to the common people of the land, to lend any substance to a charge of boastfulness. In addition to the improbability of such open bravado, it must be taken into account that he would not thus betray the strength of the movement, which had been kept under cover so carefully and for so long.

If he had been guilty of such an utterance, however, he would have found proof on this day that his friends were indeed rallying in sudden and almost unbelievable strength. There was no exercise ground for the inmates and the prison looked down directly on the street. Nevertheless, it would take a tall man to see through the small high windows. William Morris pictures the itinerant priest as "tall and big-boned, a ring of dark hair surrounding his priest's tonsure," so perhaps he could look out on the main road of Maidstone, which was the widest in all of England, and see the peasants pouring in, their improvised weapons over their shoulders; thousands of them, shouting, cheering, and calling for John Ball; many of them bare of torso and of leg, for who would risk damage to a jerkin at such a time? From this he would have realized that circumstances had forced his hand, that this uprising of the embattled sons of the soil would precipitate the inevitable conflict. Secrecy was no longer possible or necessary.

When the prison gates had been broken open and he had come out, a free man again, he consulted with those who had assumed leadership of the brawny peasants and they proceeded at once to arouse the villeins everywhere. Messengers were sent out over the whole arc of west, north, and east, as far away as Cornwall and the Humber in the north. They were sent to all parts of Kent and Sussex, to Essex, Suffolk, Norfolk, and Cambridge, to Hertford, Hants, and Somerset, to York, Lancashire, Lincoln, and Durham. The message was the same to all:

John Ball hath rungen thy bell.

In all accounts of this amazing outbreak the emphasis is laid on the men of Kent under Wat Tyler and John Ball. But there had been trouble earlier in Essex. Before Whitsuntide, which fell that year on June 2, the men of three communities, Fobbing, Corringham and Brentwood, had been haled into court because they refused to pay the poll tax. Violent scenes resulted and the angry people had rallied under the leadership of a common priest who took the name of Jack Straw. A number of the court officials and the jury had been killed and their heads carried on the ends of pikes in wild scenes of mob hysteria.

Here again taxation had been the main issue. A specific demand had been made to allow the villeins the use of land at a rent of fourpence an acre and to have the *corvée* abolished.

It was quite a different situation in Suffolk and all of East Anglia where the men of the towns as well as the tillers of the soil had been at war with the abbey of St. Edmundsbury for nearly a century. The abbots had been granted charters which gave them a despotic hold on the countryside. They held the gates of Bury St. Edmunds, they owned a large part of the land, they were hard masters of the *corvée*. They had even been given the wardships of all orphans in the district and had not hesitated to collect good fees from the estates. To add the final touch of dissension, the abbey had gone into the lending of money and the archives were stuffed with bills against all the substantial citizens. When the stern overlordship of the monks was called into question, the abbot of the moment could always go back to his papers and produce charters which supported his pretensions.

The archives of St. Edmundsbury had become synonymous with sinister power. Whenever the victims of the monastic maw got together they would whisper bitterly that "the abbot's papers have a sharper edge than the headsman's ax."

And so in 1327 the abbey had been burned by an infuriated mob. The charters and bills had been seized and torn into shreds, to be tossed about jubilantly like stage snow. Troops had been sent, of course, to put down the uprising and twenty of the rioters had been hanged. The charters had been replaced and the old tyranny had begun again. Hate and discontent had continued to smolder. And so when the word reached Suffolk of the ringing of the bell, the people were ready to respond.

It happened that the post of abbot was vacant and that Prior John of Cambridge was temporarily in charge. This Prior John was a precise and thin-lipped man with the shrewd head of a lawyer on his narrow shoulders. He fluttered his white and well-tended hands most effectively during services, but the townspeople muttered darkly that his thumbs were callused from the tightness with which he applied the screws to all debtors. The sweetness of voice with which he chanted the prayers changed to the habitual whine of the usurer when matters of money were at stake. Prior John was cordially hated.

He happened to be in his manor house at Mildenham. Suddenly an infuriated clamor broke out and the gardens were filled with a mob which had come to settle scores with him.

Prior John tried to escape but it is said that his household servants had small reason to love him and that they betrayed him to the angry people. A mock trial was held and without a whisper of dissent he was sentenced to die. They took him out to the gardens where his head was cut off. His naked body was tossed on a dunghill.

Returning to town, the mob broke open the abbey gates and demanded again that all charters and bonds be turned over to them. The frightened monks produced everything they could find and there was another scene of exuberant demolition.

The madness was now spreading like a forest fire. The townspeople of Cambridge burned the charters of the university. In Norfolk a man named Geoffrey the Litster, or Dyer (the revival of dyeing was a recent development in England) emerged from the reek of his copperas vats and set himself up as leader of the people. He proceeded to introduce some elements of comedy into the tragic scene. Believing himself inspired to command the movement, he selected for himself the title of "King of the Commons." Riding a horse, and with bay leaves sewn into his greasy hat, he led the hastily assembled mob to the work of destruction. However, he insisted that none of the nobility who fell into his hands were to be killed. Instead he forced them to serve him at meals; on their knees, no less. One of the barons had to act as official food taster for this self-made master.

Geoffrey the Litster was one of the maddest of the worthless rogues who inevitably rise to the top under such circumstances. More will be told about him later.

At St. Albans, also, the uprising was directed against the abbey. One of the prime grievances of the people was that no one was allowed to grind his own corn or even to take the grain to a miller. The abbey held a monopoly and with an eye perhaps to security had set up the millstones within the sheltering shadow of the cloisters. Breaking their way in, the townspeople smashed the stones into such small pieces that each one was able to carry away a fragment as a memento of the day.

The men of East Kent rose early and laid seige to the tall castle which looked out over the walls of Rochester to the mouth of the Medway. The besiegers had been reinforced by levies from Essex and in some chronicles it is said that they numbered 30,000 men. What happened at Rochester would be duplicated centuries later when the *sansculottes* of Paris attacked the Bastille; sheer mass strength would triumph over high stone walls. The peasants used the trunks of trees to break in the doors and then smothered the garrison in hand-to-hand fighting. The governor capitulated when he found himself and what was left of his men penned in the upper reaches of the Keep.

And so it went in every part of southern and eastern England. Hatreds of long standing caused instantaneous explosions, in the course of which the common people struck, furiously and blindly, at institutions and people associated in their minds with oppression and injustice.

Feudal War in Practice

H. J. HEWITT

There are many books and articles on warfare in the Middle Ages and many studies of individual battles and campaigns, but the great majority of these works focus on the art of war rather than on the actual conduct of operations. The military predominance of the heavily armed knight and the great body of contemporary literature promulgating the ideal of knightly life have influenced the historiography of warfare so as to emphasize the role of the knight and the battle of mounted soldiers. The natural proclivity of medieval chroniclers to recount the stories of the battles and leave the rest of the campaign to the imagination of their readers has contributed to the relative lack of concern that historians have had for a major part of every foray, the time between battles.

In the selection that follows, H. J. Hewitt attempts to right the balance by focusing on the whole war effort of the English armies during the first phases of the Hundred Years' War. This war is among the best recorded of the Middle Ages and has yielded striking statistics about the conduct of war in that period. H. S. Denifle, a French historian of the nineteenth century, did a monumental study of the ecclesiastical buildings destroyed during the war and provided ample evidence that riding into battle well plumed and well oiled was only a small part of the activities of the knightly contingents that fought in the war. Hewitt's studies confirm the impression created by Denifle's findings: destruction, systematically carried out, was the principal aim of the military leadership.

The men who landed in France were shortly to spend much of their time and energy in the destruction of property, in the forcible seizure of food and forage, and in plundering. These three operations were of course illegal in their own country. They were, however, normal and purposeful accompaniments of war; they were diametrically opposed to the lives and interests of the people of the invaded regions; and they could be carried to lengths which exceeded military necessity, military advantage or even good sense. At times, therefore, it would fall to a commander to set limits to his soldiers' activities and enforce his orders—if he had sufficient control over the men to do so. Before dealing with these activities in detail, it is appropriate to consider briefly the background to the discipline of the armies.

From H. J. Hewitt, *The Organization of War Under Edward III* (Manchester, Eng.: Manchester University Press, 1966), pp. 93–118. Reprinted by permission of the Manchester University Press.

Recruits were animated, as would be expected, by such divers motives as the honourable pursuit of the profession of arms, the attainment of fame, the desire for adventure or for the spoils of war, and the need to gain pardon for crime. There were also men raised by the commissions of array. And in most, if not all, of the *chevauchées*, they were joined by non-English elements—Gascon subjects or Flemish allies or miscellaneous volunteers—attracted largely by hopes of plunder. But the differing motives could not alter the nature of war which at that period consisted very largely of military pressure involving the destruction of the means by which life is maintained.

The men carrying out this work had to act corporately and needed therefore principles of conduct for battle, for the march, for the camp and for relations with civilians in the invaded areas. It was—as always—necessary to gain both obedience to commands for action and compliance with prohibitions.

With the discipline of the battle and the march we are not here directly concerned. As for the discipline of the camp, the arrival of the army at a given town meant the diversion from the local population of as much food as the commander decided to take. Since the economical use of food might govern the length of the stay—if a stay was desired—maladministration or misuse of victuals was a serious breach of camp discipline. But it is with conduct in relation to the civil population and especially with restraints on conduct that we are chiefly concerned.

The morale of a modern army is the fruit of months and even years of training of officers and men. Now it might be maintained that fourteenth-century armies had neither training nor instruction. Archers, for example, were chosen, tested and arrayed, and leaders were appointed, but between the issuing of orders for the array and the date by which the men were expected to be available for the journey to the port of embarkation, the period was often no more than two months. Training, if any, could hardly have lasted more than one month. It must usually have been much less than that and more probably spent in archery than in cultivating that trained submission to Authority which ensures prompt compliance with orders or prohibitions. It is true that there was commonly a delay at the port which might have been used for training, but there is no evidence that it was so spent.

English soldiers, therefore, crossed the seas and were soon on the march in a foreign land. That they were engaged day after day in looting, destruction and burning, the chroniclers both English and French make certain. That in some—probably very many—instances there was maltreatment of non-combatants there can be no doubt.

For a considered judgement on their conduct, the following factors must be borne in mind. The slowly evolving general practices which would gradually develop into a system and become known as international law, did not yet distinguish between combatants and non-combatants. Customs of war were gathering round such recurrent events as the siege and surrender of towns, and the capture, treatment and ransoming of prisoners. Humanity to civilians was not yet a prevailing principle though, as we shall see, it was sometimes commanded.

Moreover, the obligation to take food for man and horse at one stroke regularized theft, while the ordained destruction of villages and towns led to disregard of the sanctity of "enemy" property of any kind. The remoteness of the enemy's force for days, and even at times for weeks, rendered strict discipline unnecessary. There may occasionally have been some unclearness in men's minds respecting the chain of authority when they were enrolled, paid by, and answerable to, knights who were subcontractors of an earl who had raised his quota of men by agreement with the king.

Further, though Froissart's narrative affords so many pictures of knights rejoicing in the business of war, the greater part of the armies were not knights. The men-at-arms, archers and foot soldiers included, as we have seen, many men who had been indicted of murder and no doubt others termed in the Patent Rolls "evildoers." Desertion before embarkation was not uncommon. Even from the king's army in Normandy, there were deserters. Wellington knew the effect of wine-drinking on English soldiers. In the fourteenth century, they used their opportunities in France. Finally, in all campaigns there were a few men of the kind Froissart described as "rascal and other followers of the host."

We are not therefore considering solely the practices of knights pledged traditionally to certain standards of behaviour, but the conduct of ordinary men—good, bad and indifferent—loosed from their domestic moorings, temporarily following the trade of war in a foreign land, ignorant of its language, not subject to its laws, and probably at first contemptuous of its people. "Dog of a Frenchman," a French poet puts into an English soldier's mouth, "you do naught but drink wine."

For the maintenance of discipline during a voyage, the admirals were authorized to chastise mariners. During campaigns on land, effective punishment was notoriously difficult to impose. Froissart records the king's resort to hanging for disregard of orders. Between that ultimate expedient and mere reprimand, there were few practicable deterrents. In the armies, strict discipline must have been difficult to maintain.

A few instances of success and of failure are revealed in the narratives of the chevauchées. Routine operations, as we shall see, were fourfold: marching, getting food, pillaging and destroying. The first two were necessary; the second two were not necessary, but commonly permitted or even ordered. It was over these latter activities that crises in discipline might occur, for pillage was profitable to the soldier, and destruction sanctioned unlimited licence. Yet they took time, lowered morale and might be contrary to the overriding interests of the campaign. For reasons of military necessity or diplomatic prudence or respect for the church or respect for non-combatants, a commander might prohibit pillage or/and destruction. The first ground needs no elaboration; the others can be illustrated. Pauses in destruction for prudential reasons occurred in the Black Prince's campaign in Gascony, the most important being when he journeyed westward through the lands of the influential count of Foix who had neither helped nor opposed him. A meeting between the prince and the count was arranged. On the preceding and succeeding days, the usual operations were carried out, but on the day of the prince's visit there was no burning.

More frequently it was respect for the church that led to a prohibition. This was not uncommon before the period we are studying. During his campaigns in Scotland, Edward had destroyed Dunfermline but spared the abbey (1333); he had devastated lands in Elgin but avoided burning the town of Elgin "because of the Trinity in whose honour stood a pleasing church." When Bassoue in Gascony surrendered to the prince, he allowed only the victualling officers to enter, because it belonged to the church. In 1339, the king directed that no harm should befall the abbey of Mount Saint Martin; in 1346, as he burnt and ravaged within sight of Paris, he issued an order that on the feast of the Assumption there should be neither spoiling nor firing; in 1359 at Pontigny, the burial place of a former archbishop of Canterbury, he commanded the whole host on pain of life and limb and forfeiture of goods, to spare the abbey. In each case his orders were observed.

And at times, he is represented as a humane commander keeping a tight hold on the discipline of his troops when they were in contact with civilians. "In kindly consideration of the deficiencies of (Normandy)," says a chronicler, "he made an order for his army that no man should presume to burn towns or manors, despoil churches or holy places, harm little children or women in his kingdom or France; such as attacked other persons—men excepted—or did evil of any kind would do so under pain of life and limb. He ordered also that if anyone violating this order were brought to him, a reward of forty shillings would be paid." At Caen says the same chronicler, he "had it proclaimed throughout his army that no one should imprison women, children, nuns, monks, or harm their churches or houses."

Edward was not as kindly as these orders might suggest. In practice, he was stern both with opponents and with his men, but there were times when his orders were disregarded. At Carentan in 1346, much of the town was burnt in spite of his commands, and he was not able to prevent the burning of a religious house at Messien near Beauvais, but he showed his determination to ensure respect for the church by having a score of men hanged. The Black Prince also saw his orders violated. In his campaign of 1355, against his will, Seissan was fired and could not be saved; in several places church property was destroyed and conspicuously at Carcassone where he had given explicit instructions that it should be preserved. Whether punishment followed is not stated. It must of course be allowed that once a block of wooden buildings had been set alight, a whole town was likely to burn in spite of intentions to save some parts. As for humanity to non-combatants, the chroniclers offer practically no evidence—for this period.

The broad conclusions are that the troops were unaccustomed to restraint imposed by authority; that they were often acting—as we shall see—under circumstances in which restraint would be very unnatural; that while the army was on the march, punishment short of death could not readily be imposed; that discipline could be, and probably often was, strong enough to prevent attacks on church property; that some destruction by burning may have resulted from mischance rather than design. But on very many occasions, no orders for restraint appear to have been given and the terrible work of war proceeded in the customary way. That the French, the Scots and the Flemings, when occasion offered, spread the work by the same means is evident to any student of the chronicles.

That they and the English regarded themselves as engaged in war none of them would have disputed, but the word used for a campaign of this kind was usually *chevauchée*, that is to say a ride. The increased use of horses was rendering armies more mobile. Not only knights and men-at-arms but also archers were often mounted. *Chevaucher* became ambiguous. Sometimes it was clarified by adding à *l'aventure* to describe the activities of the *routier*, or by adding *de guerre* to describe a specifically military operation. But in certain contexts it could be used alone meaning to ride out to war—usually with a relatively small force. In 1359, when king John of France announced the extension of the truce between the French and the English, he stated that men on both sides would continue in their existing positions till 24 June *sans faire guerre ou chevaucher*. The distinction need not be laboured for, by the fourteenth century, *chevaucher* covered not only simple fighting and the pillaging already associated with it, but also the destruction which had become an important part of campaigning. It follows that the modern English use of "raid" as a translation of *chevauchée* is not wholly satisfactory. The *chevauchée* moved swiftly and might include the driving away of cattle, but the concept is wider than that of "raid."

We proceed to the army's typical activities. Having brought an armed force to the Anglo-Scottish border, or having landed on the coast of France, or led an army from Sluys or Bordeaux to the French frontier, what was the commander's aim?

It was not, as might have been supposed, to seek out the enemy and bring him to decisive combat. Notwithstanding the ideals of chivalry, the Orders of the Garter and of the Star, the romance of the Round Table, the Fight of the Thirty; notwithstanding the laudable desire of young knights to display prowess, the king, the prince and Henry of Lancaster were not—or not usually—bent on that critical conflict of arms, nor did they refer to such an aim in their reports, nor did adulatory chroniclers attribute that aim to them.

The commander's purpose was to work havoc, to inflict damage or loss or ruin or destruction on the enemy and his subjects by devastation. Commonly the word used was *damnum* (usually spelt *dampnum*) or *damnificare*. In 1346, king Philip pointed out to the king of Scotland that he had a favourable opportunity for inflicting on England very great damage (*maximum damnum*). He offered Edward a place and date for a battle and asked him in the meantime not to commit further havoc (*damna*), burning and looting. A few years later, the seneschal of Gascony reported that John of Claremont, marshal of France, had ridden into the English dominions working havoc (*damnificando*). The town of Millau placed on record that the king of England was about to work havoc (*damnificare*) in the land of France. The Black Prince decided in 1355 that his army should proceed to inflict damage (*demolicionem*) on the county of Armagnac, and Delachenal regarded the prince's campaigns of 1355 and 1366 as aimed solely at the pillage, devastation and ruin of the lands through which he passed. Eustache Deschamps summed up a sad little poem with "*La guerre est damnation.*"

Exerting pressure by devastation is, however, only one of the army's activities. It has to live on the country, that is to say it has to gather from the invaded region enough food and forage to sustain man and horse. It has also to move forward at quite short intervals. It will often be more profitable to seize cattle, poultry and bags of corn than to destroy them. It will also be more congenial to the soldier to seize certain goods than to destroy them. These circumstances do not alter the fundamental aim of working havoc; but they complicate the procedure for, although the army may often find villages from which the inhabitants have fled in terror, it will also arrive at towns where the people offer furious resistance not only to the soldiers' entry to the town, but also to every act of appropriation or destruction. Victualling, looting and destroying, though routine activities in principle, are not invariably carried out with quiet efficiency by well disciplined troops. On the contrary, between hungry, thirsty, weary or drunken soldiers on the one side and desperate "civilians" on the other, there will be scenes of high drama and great violence.

For the sake of clarity, it is necessary to consider the three concurrent activities separately. We begin with the accumulation of food. The provisioning of English armies serving overseas is a subject large enough for a study in itself. The general principle that an army had to "live on the country" must, of course, be qualified since armies varied in size and speed of movement, and countries varied very much in the wealth of their resources. Of few campaigns was the principle wholly true. Edward I had lightened the task of conquering North Wales by having supplies sent by sea to the Dee estuary, and for some of his campaigns in Scotland food was transported from England. When Edward III proceeded to Scotland or to Flanders, vessels carrying stores—as we have seen—augmented local resources. For many years, Stirling, the port of Calais and the region round Bordeaux needed victuals from English sources. And no army could prudently land on a hostile shore or cross a frontier without food or forage for a few days' subsistence.

Broadly, however, the principle is true. The maintenance of a line of communications from a distant base to the theatre of operations was quite impracticable. A small quantity of food was carried to meet emergencies. Day-to-day supplies had to be gathered wherever they could be found—in national territory by payment, in invaded territory by seizure. Under dire compulsion, owners of victuals might sometimes deliver their goods. Far more frequently, they had fled. The army had therefore to organize a body of men to seek out and transport some kinds of victuals to the columns.

The means of transport—not all of them being required for food—were classified by one chronicler as "sumpter horses, vehicles and carriers of victuals." Others refer to the "carts bearing victuals" and to "carts and heavily laden wagons." The army started with many such carts and wagons and seized others according to its needs. For the expedition of 1359, a large number were made in England. The position of the "baggage train" in the column of march grew important when quick movement was necessary. It might, for example, be necessary to start it on the evening preceding the march of the main body lest it should impede progress at a bridge.

Of the men at their work, ransacking farm buildings and other stores, no chronicler gives any description nor have I found any pictorial illustration. They must have ranged very far from the column or columns, for an army often moved along more or less parallel routes and was divided among two or more villages at nights. (Indeed the repeated emphasis on the width of the track devastated probably implies the carrying off of stores before the destruction of buildings.) They would collect not only corn and flour, but also cheese, bacon, salted meat, salted and fresh fish, butter, eggs and fruit.

They would also round up cattle and sheep and drive them to suitable places for slaughter. Scottish forces raiding Northumberland, Cumberland and Durham almost invariably carried off cattle not solely for their immediate needs but also for the sustenance of their countrymen north of the border. Some indication of the extent of Scottish raiding may be seen in an official warning in 1345 that a Scottish invasion was imminent and that men of the northern counties should drive their cattle to the forests of Knaresborough and Galtres.

When an army was stationary—for example the king's during the siege of Calais, and subsequently the English garrison within that city, and the prince's in winter quarters in 1355—bold raids into French territory procured numbers of live cattle for the troops. Henxteworth's account shows a large payment to Sir John Chandos and his fellows early in 1356 for 215 head of cattle they had gained as booty.

By one means or another, then, an army usually contrived to "live on the country," and there are occasional glimpses of the soldiers' satisfaction at the amount of victuals available. A raid on St. Amand (1340) produced a great quantity of provisions. At Carentan, at St. Lo, at Caen and at le Crotoy (1346), food and drink were in good supply. Carcassonne (1355) was well stocked with wine and food. At Tonnerre (1360) the army found a great quantity of good wine which "was of great service" to them, and at Flamingy (1360) and in the surrounding region, the supply of provisions enabled the army to stay in one place for an unusually long time.

But the stores accumulated in any one place were quickly consumed and, quite apart from the aim of inflicting further damage, the army was obliged to move forward to obtain supplies. The *chevauchée* could not afford luxurious living for the troops. Conditions during the king's march of 1346 are reflected in a letter from Calais at the beginning of September: "the king hath sent to you for victuals and that too as quickly as you can send; for from the time that we departed from Caen, we have lived on the country to the great travail and harm of our people, but thanks be to God, we have no loss. But now we are in such plight that we must in part be refreshed by victuals" (that is victuals from England). In contrast with the ample plenty of some districts in Languedoc were the poverty and discomfort of others through which the prince's men passed in November 1355, districts in which they had no water for the horses or for cooking, where food was scarce and nights were wet and cold, and swollen rivers had to be crossed without the aid of bridges. And the king's armies during the winter of 1359–60, notwithstanding the provisions brought from England and those found in Burgundy, endured "the grievous labours of this campaign . . . subsisting all the time upon the [resources] of the country, sometimes in plenty, at other times according to what they could find in a country wasted and raided before their coming by the above-mentioned English . . ."

Forage also was necessary. During summer campaigns no doubt the horses ate the grass at night and, in the winter, wherever it was practicable, they consumed the stores of provender accumulated in the ricks and barns of the monasteries. But scarcity of food influenced army movements. The king himself, for example, as the seige of Cambrai dragged on with slight prospect of success, was prevailed on to push forward into France where both forage and provisions would be more abundant. And in 1360, on the memorable day when the worst storm in living memory wrought such damage on his army, the reason for marching in such weather was the lack of fodder.

The general situation may be illustrated and summarized by two contrasting sentences taken from Froissart. "They found the country plentiful for there had been no war of a long season." "The country was so wasted that they wist not wither to go for forage." In a region that had not been invaded, a commander might be able to sustain his men for a quite short period, but though their stay might be no more than a single night, the stores accumulated for a whole winter were consumed, carried off or destroyed. When the soldiers had also stolen his treasures and set fire to his house, the "civilian" had lost his all.

We turn to plundering. The practice of seizing goods belonging to the enemy is, of course, very old and must have been universal. The Old Testament abounds in references to spoils; the Romans made much of booty; Villehardouin and Joinville deal at length with plunder gained by the Crusaders; and, in the French plan, drawn up in 1339, for an invasion of England, arrangements were made for the collection and division of the booty to be taken by the sailors manning the transports.

As with victualling, so here with plunder, we are treating separately one of three concurrent activities. So closely related were these activities that cattle might be seized for victuals, driven away as plunder or simply destroyed. Goods similarly might be looted or destroyed.

Now while the main aim of the *chevauchée*, havoc, could not be attained without the forcible seizure of cattle, corn and forage, it could, in theory at least, be achieved without plunderings of household goods and money. Yet plundering of this kind was very widely practised by all armies. It may be regarded as enlarging the havoc since it increased impoverishment and sadness among the enemy. On the soldier the effect was threefold: the lure of booty (as well as good pay) aided recruitment; the prospect of treasure helped to maintain cheerfulness on a dreary march; but just as the desire to capture prisoners for ransom, even during an encounter, diverted men from the supreme aim of battle, so the search for private booty might hinder the work of destruction and even the progress of the march. A further effect was evident in some wars. When soldiers' pay was greatly in arrears, plunder became a substitute for wages. In all wars of the period, in the absence of specific prohibition, leave to plunder was probably taken for granted.

The scope of such work varied greatly. The towns of France were more attractive than the march of Scotland but a large town might prove disappointing. At Carcassonne, for example, and at Narbonne—both flourishing cities—the inhabitants fled to their great citadels before the prince's troops arrived. With them, it is clear, they took their money and much of their portable valuables. As conditions at each place were unfavourable for a siege, the army had to move on without the rich spoils that might have been expected. Many smaller towns, however, were easily denuded of valuables. Occasionally a religious house was despoiled. Panic-stricken people might leave their goods anywhere. The Black Prince himself is reported to have alluded to the "splendid spoils" Englishmen had gathered in France.

For the chroniclers, plundering of goods was so common that they usually record it in a single word. The illuminators of manuscripts ignore it. From Froissart, however, we may quote a few descriptions of scenes:

The French in 1339:

. . . knights and soldiers on the French side desired nothing but that they might pass in Hainault to pillage and profit . . . so the French went in and found the people, men and women, in their homes; they took them as they would and all their goods, gold and silver, cloth, jewels and cattle; then they set fire to the town and burnt it so clean that nothing remained but the walls. Within the town was a priory . . . The Frenchmen robbed the place and burnt it to the ground and with their pillage returned to Cambrai.

The English in Normandy in 1346. A general picture a few days after the landing:

. . . the country [was] plentiful of everything, the granges full of corn, the houses full of riches, rich burgesses, carts and chariots, horses, swine, muttons and other beasts: they took what them list and brought it into the king's host; but the soldiers made no count to the king nor to none of his officers of the gold and silver that they did get; they kept that to themselves.

At Barfleur:

. . . there was found so much riches that the boys and villains of the host set nothing by good furred gowns.

A specific industry:

. . . the king came to St. Lo, a rich town of drapery and many rich burgesses. . . . Anon the town was taken and clean robbed. It was hard to think the great riches that there was won, in clothes especially; cloth would have been sold good cheap, if there had been any buyers.

An anonymous chronicler describing the sack of Caen says:

The English desiring spoils brought back to the ships only jewelled clothing or very valuable ornaments.

The Anglo-Gascon force in Languedoc in 1355:

The wanton:

they took what they liked and burnt the rest.

The discriminating:

they disregarded clothing and went only for silver plate and cash.

The indiscriminate:

nothing of value remained. They carried off everything, especially the Gascons who are very grasping.

Just one pictorial illustration of looting has been found. It shows soldiers removing valuables from a house, carrying out the money coffer, drinking wine and smashing the wine vats.

No such detailed sketches, verbal or pictorial, are available for the looting by Scots in the north of England. The chroniclers say tersely that they took much booty. But there are instances of Englishmen paying the Scots sums of money as an alternative to suffering spoliation.

It would be interesting to know how the material booty (as distinct from the cattle) was shared among the troops. The individual soldier needed answers to two questions—"How soon may I begin (to gather goods)?" and "May I keep all I can gain?" Answers to these questions had been provided long before the fourteenth century. They were indeed hardening into customs but they were not yet invariable, for the share which commanders might expect in the light of custom, or insist on as a right, or wish in practice to take, was not fixed; and even if a system had been universally accepted, its operation would depend on the state of discipline prevailing in any given unit at a given date.

Light is thrown by Villehardouin and Joinville on the principles underlying the sharing of booty in the later Crusades. They refer to strict orders to bring every article seized to a central place, to the guarding of the accumulated treasure, to the equal or proportionate distribution of the spoils and to the strong tendency among the soldiers to dishonest concealment of their finds. Stern penalties were visited on defrauders. Oliver de la Marche, in the fifteenth century, describes the taking of a town which had not offered resistance: the control of the soldiers till a given moment, then the rush for booty, the order to bring everything—gold, silver, copper, cloth, leather work—to the booty officers, the well-conducted public auction of the goods and the rumour that the booty officers made a profit for themselves.

It is, of course, necessary to distinguish between single episodes, common practices, military regulations and jurists' declarations. There was evidently a general trend towards a controlled, equitable and pre-determined distribution of spoils. In the French plan of 1339 for the invasion of England, the sailors transporting the French army were to share the booty:

> No armed man shall go out to plunder, but there shall be chosen in each ship a certain number of the men at arms and they shall pillage and get booty and bring away the beasts. Also in each ship shall be chosen two men [who] shall receive all the booty and profit and it shall be parted as well among the men of arms as among those which shall abide in the ships, and those which shall part it, according to the condition of the persons.

This appears to be the clearest statement of principle on the French side for the brief period under consideration.

A pre-determined but less controlled plan is recorded of a French attack on Roche Derrien when held by the English:

> The lord of Craon (sent by the French king) offered a purse of fifty écus d'or to the first man who should enter the town. It was won by a Genoan . . . and then any who would, entered . . . for it had been laid down in advance by the captains that the goods in the town should be common and abandoned to all those of the army who should be able to gain them.

Other references, for example, "The French . . . went to Auberton and there divided their booty," are too brief for guidance.

On the English side also the evidence is not abundant. At Newcastle-upon-Tyne in 1319, as he prepared for an expedition into Scotland, Edward II had "granted to each man as much of the enemies' goods as he could seize up to a hundred pounds" without the risk of restitution being negotiated in a truce. It is, however, clear that in campaigns on the Continent, the leader had a share of the booty. In 1340, when Edward III returned from Flanders he "distributed the spoils among his earls." Walsingham says of Henry of Lancaster's campaign of 1345 that his "liberality and munificence attracted recruits. They found it pleasant to go to war under his command for when he took a town, he kept very little or nothing for himself but let the army have it all." Of the earliest phase of the campaign of 1346, we have the illuminating statement already quoted: vehicles and cattle were brought into the common fund; gold and silver were kept by individual soldiers. But in recording that "they made no account to the king nor to none of his officers . . . ," Froissart probably implies that the soldiers' conduct was contrary to current practice or in disobedience of an order. From then onward, though the chroniclers refer many times to pillage, they have little or nothing to say about the division of spoils.

Honoré Bonet (born c. 1340) says "the law on the matter is involved and by no means clear." He insists on the right to take plunder, allows that men may have to "hand it over to the duke of the battle," and adds that "the duke should share the spoils out among his men, to each according to his valour."

When allowance has been made for some picturesque exaggeration, the quantity of goods taken by English invaders from French towns must have been very considerable. Froissart says of the prince's campaign of 1355 that the baggage train returned to the base loaded with plunder, and the chevauchée brought "much profit"; and he records that in 1356 the prince's army came back to Bordeaux "laded with gold, silver and prisoners." There is moreover other evidence of valuables found in the French tents near the battlefield of Poitiers.

As for the ultimate end of the riches seized, Froissart, ever mindful of cash values, has a comment on the prince's men in winter quarters near Bordeaux in 1355: they "spent foolishly the gold and silver they had won." No doubt for one reason or another, a good deal of the looted material remained in France. But in 1346 large quantities were brought from Normandy to England. Baker says that the spoils seized were transferred to the ships which followed the army along the coast. Froissart says the ships were "charged with clothes, jewels, vessels of gold and silver . . . and prisoners." And Walsingham adds that by 1348 much of it had been dispersed in England; "there were few women who did not possess something from Caen, Calais or other overseas towns, such as clothing, furs, cushions. Table clothes and linen were seen in everybody's houses. Married women were decked in the trimmings of French matrons and if the latter sorrowed over their loss, the former rejoiced in their gain."

Scarcely anyone, says a guide for priests, was prepared to admit (to a priest) the sin of plundering, but if one did, then "modern confessors and especially those of the mendicant orders . . . having altogether no power to absolve such a sinner in this case, if some part of the plunder or something else is given to them, absolve *de facto* the plunderer and his adherents . . ."

We turn to the third regular activity of the invading forces and the main purpose of the expeditions, namely devastation. The leaders' own reports relate their achievements to that aim. In 1339, the king sent word to his son Edward that he had begun operations near Cambrai on the appointed day and that there had been much destruction. A fortnight after his landing in Normandy in 1346, he informed the archbishop of Canterbury of the destruction he had caused, and when the long march ended, it was officially summarized in these words: "He passed through France to Calais, wasting and destroying." Henry of Lancaster briefly described his campaign of 1345 and summed it up as a "fine chevauchée." "We took our road," the Black Prince reported of his campaign of 1355, "through the land of Toulouse where were many goodly towns and strongholds burnt and destroyed," and Wengfeld, his chief secretary, commented: "Since this war began, there was never such loss nor destruction as hath been in this raid." Such reports might be regarded as claims intended to justify the various expeditions but, as will be seen, in many places the damage done was very great.

We have stressed the aim of the invader, for, although it is a commonplace to all who study the chronicles and records, it receives slight recognition in the military histories, and still less in the political and other studies, of the period. Oman dismisses the prince's autumn campaign of 1355 in two sentences. Of the king's work in Normandy in 1346, Lot has not one word on destruction. And A. H. Burne finds difficulty in explaining the purpose of the devastation near Cambrai in 1338, but adds "it was a very usual custom for an invading army not only to pillage but to burn a hostile country." Writers who exclude devastation from the study of medieval campaigns, or regard it only as a "custom," may deal adequately with the *art* of war. They cannot portray the *practice* of war.

For medieval war did not consist wholly or mainly in battles and sieges with the marches necessary to effect encounters. It consisted very largely in the exertion of pressure on the civil population, and this pressure took the form of destruction, of working havoc. The ends sought in twentieth-century warfare by blockade and aerial bombardment had to be sought in the four-teenth century by operations on the ground. That in recent periods civilians suffered in mind, body and estate and were intended to suffer, is universally allowed. The circumstances of the fourteenth century, though not wholly parallel, are sufficiently similar to enable us to infer the purpose and the effect of the devastation carried out in that period.

In such phrases as "utterly destroyed," "wholly devastated," the terse narratives state comprehensively the result without referring to the means employed. Devastation called for neither skill nor courage nor strength. It afforded no opportunity for personal distinction. Much of it was no more than arson. City walls, castles, armour, weapons remain to this day as evi-dence of the apparatus of war. Devastation by its nature has left no material evidence. It needed no detailed description in the chronicles and no entry in the administrative or financial records of the attacker. Unfortunately also, it is extremely rare to find it portrayed in illuminated manuscripts.

The principal agent was, of course, fire, but several other means of working havoc were available. The trampling of growing corn, the damaging of vines, the slaughter of unwanted cattle and the smashing of vats of wine are occasionally, but not frequently, mentioned. The manual destruction of buildings is perhaps reflected in such contemporary verse as

> And by assaut he won the citee after,
> And rente adoun both wall and sparre and rafter.

But the breaking of bridges is frequently recorded—usually not as devastation, but as a defensive measure. When the king approached the Seine in 1346, he found the bridges down, and was driven to march many miles in search of a crossing. The destruction (by the French) and repair (by the English) of the bridge at Poissy form an important incident in his march. As the Black Prince moved toward the great curve of the Garonne in 1355, Jean d'Armagnac had all the bridges destroyed except the one in the city itself; and on his westward journey a few weeks later, the prince found the bridges over the tributaries of the Garonne had also been cut. That the English also broke bridges is extremely likely. Whether the work was done by one side or the other, the economic effect would be serious.

The most useful means of destruction was fire, for it was all-consuming, and its ravages in France at this period have formed the subject of vivid pic-tures and strong comment by writers of later centuries. It must, however, be seen in the perspective of history. Fire was not an extraordinary means of destruction, nor was its use peculiar to the fourteenth century, nor was it used solely by the English. Fire had been an agent and accompaniment of war almost since the dawn of recorded history. Troy had been reduced to ashes. Burning was sufficiently common in the inter-state wars of Greece for Plato to question the propriety of burning homesteads. Carthage and Jerusalem had been destroyed by fire. If it be objected that these were great, walled cities whose resistance infuriated the besiegers, whereas the English fired quite small towns and even villages, it may be replied that the Romans burnt villages in Palestine; the Danes burnt houses and corn; William the Conqueror used fire extensively in France as well as in England; the Crusaders used it; and the Scots burned buildings wherever they could reach south of the Cheviots.

It was certain therefore that fire would be used in the Hundred Years' War. It had two obvious limitations. In the first place, since its property is to destroy combustible matter, it was an instrument of attack rather than of defence. Denifle's dictum that "fire was the constant ally of the English" needs qualification, for fire was the ally of any army that could use it to advantage. On French soil, the English were almost always the attackers and their use of fire is the more conspicuous. When on the other hand, the French attacked the southern ports of England, they too invariably used fire. And occasionally they applied the policy subsequently known as "scorched earth," burning their own towns on the coast of northern France that the English might not with advantage land there.

A second limitation lay in the need for the attackers to get very near combustible material in order to start a conflagration. A captured town could be set alight from within, but the high stone walls of a city or a castle usually afforded an effective defence against fire from without. The English "brent clean hard to the gates all the suburbs" of Beauvais, says Froissart, but the city itself escaped major damage. It was in the unwalled towns and the villages that havoc was wrought most easily.

A third aspect of fire, though it did not limit its use, led to contemporary blame and subsequent condemnation. It is an undiscriminating agent and may get out of control, destroying—as we have seen—property a leader intended to preserve.

Concerning the methods used to start or spread a conflagration, most of the chroniclers are completely silent. Since fire was needed and probably maintained for cooking (and at times for shoeing horses), it would be inferred that burning material could be carried away for destructive purposes. In towns of any size, the operation would need to be organized. Two writers throw a little light on the means employed. Of Narbonne, Baker says the town was set alight by "burning carts" and of Caen, an anonymous chronicler says the "burners" (*combustores*) "scatter" (*spargunt* [without an object]) "all around them as they do their work."

The effect would be speedy. Where houses, churches, shops, stables, barns, granaries, mills, windmills and storehouses of every kind were built wholly or largely of wood, where wood was stacked for fuel, for building purposes, for the making of barrels, dairy and domestic utensils and agricultural implements and carts, where most of the roofs were of thatch, where hay and straw were stacked, where ripe corn was standing in the fields—in all such places, once a fire had been started, it would be impossible to extinguish it. Ships in harbour with their tackle and cargoes were fired. So were carts and wagons conveying weapons and victuals.

For the most part, the chroniclers treat the matter in the same laconic way as they treat pillaging. They merely record events which needed no description for their contemporaries. Typical formulae are "burning and pillaging," "laying waste and burning," "destroying and burning," "burning and exiling the country." A distinction could be made between route-burning in which the army destroys as it proceeds, and region-burning in which destruction is spread systematically over a limited area—the devastation near Cambrai was a full week's work—but the methods and results differ only slightly. Baker reveals his satisfaction in the thoroughness of the work done by his fellow countrymen especially in Languedoc. In his narrative, this or that town, he says, was "burnt," "consumed by fire," "reduced to ashes," "burnt out," "given to the flames." *The Anonimalle Chronicle* shows that in the march of Scotland, the work was of the tit-for-tat order. Froissart associates Scots' burning with its current evidence: the English "followed the Scots by the sight of the smoke they made with burning." On another occasion, the smoke from burning hamlets came into the town of Newcastle-upon-Tyne. Still later, "tidings came in that the Scots were abroad and that they might well see by the smoke abroad in the country."

The most vivid impressions however are those experienced in darkness. Baker describes the scene near Cambrai one very dark night in 1339 when Geoffrey le Scrope took a French cardinal to the top of a lofty tower. The whole countryside was lit up for miles with the fires still burning from king Edward's work. "Your Eminence," Scrope said, "does it not seem that the silken thread which girdles France is broken?" The cardinal is said to have been so overcome that he fainted. Our anonymous chronicler, dealing with English fires near Caen, says "the sky appeared to the eyes of onlookers as if it were of fire," and a few nights later, "they set alight the homes so that whichever way a man turned his eyes, his face was lit up by the brightness of the fire."

Smoke by day, glowing lights by night marked the route of the *chevauchée*. For many months—in some instances for years—across the countryside lay a track several miles wide without habitation for man or beast and (except for grass and fruit) without food for either. This was the "desolation," the achievement of the leader's aim. Great material damage had been inflicted and the consequences were inescapable. Homeless people crowded into other localities; the carrying off and destruction of food raised prices; for lack of means, rents were not paid; and, directly or indirectly, public revenues were diminished.

Devastation is the typical military operation of the period and, in some campaigns, almost the only significant one. War consists in military pressure applied at those points, that is to say in those regions, where it may be most effective. The regions chosen are those in which provincial loyalties are as strong as or stronger than national loyalties, or in which other particularist forces are working against the consolidation of the French kingdom. The two kings are competing for provincial allegiances, and the theatres chosen by Edward for military operations are designed to impress provincial opinion.

But what impression is it intended to make? On the one hand, we have the general circumstances of the period and the events set in motion by design—all incompletely known, of course. On the other hand, we have to try to divine the motives of the English king, the state of mind of the not wholly loyal provincials, the hopes, fears, capacity and temperament of the French king. And we seek to define the function of devastation—the destruction of the means by which life is maintained—as understood by king Edward and his army leaders.

A few Englishmen—perhaps rationalizing or seeking to justify what in their hearts they deplored—offered their own explanation: the aim, they said, was to provoke the French king to fight. That probably seemed plausible to many people, but in the light of all the circumstances, it is inadequate. Devastation was not a new feature in war requiring justification to rational minds. It was a very old accompaniment of war, feared but expected, in the marchlands of most states. Further, in most wars—as was well understood at the time—fast-moving raiders operating at selected points could inflict damage with slight risk to themselves. The aim was damage itself, independently of provocation. Finally, though common reasoning would suggest that on grounds of political prudence there was a degree of endurance beyond which a king would be compelled to fight, experience was showing that such reasoning was not necessarily valid. The prince of Wales' march through some 600 miles of French territory in 1355 and the king's march of some 500 miles in 1359–60 amounted to provocation indeed. Yet French forces had not opposed them. On the two occasions when French kings had been provoked to fight—at Crécy and Poitiers—the results were so disastrous to the French that their government resolved to endure rather than to fight.

Some further explanation is called for. Edward may at times have believed that the French king would be provoked to give battle. Tentatively, however, we suggest two other lines of thought. The campaigns, particularly those of 1345, 1346, 1355, 1356, 1359, were demonstrations of English might. This might was not directed against the knight or his warhorse, the archer, the castle or the engine of war. Its weight, its ruinous effect fell on the people whom a later generation would call "civilians." That fact was perfectly understood by the leaders of the invading forces. For the sufferers—the French people at large, including the rich—the only conceivable reaction proper in a king was defence or retribution in kind. Where defence was effectively organized (as it was against the Scots in 1346) or retributory devastation was promptly inflicted (as the Scots discovered in 1355–6), a king was respected. Where there was neither defence nor retaliation, loyalty might be very seriously undermined. The ultimate aim was of course political. The means for the attainment of that end (that is to say the military commander's immediate aim) was devastation. It demonstrated the power of the English king and the feebleness of the French king.

Secondly, since it was impracticable to occupy France, the war was becoming one of attrition: the enemy was to be weakened by the destruction of his resources. Devastation was a negative, economic means for the attainment of the ultimate, political end.

Thus devastation, which the military historians find so difficult to fit into the art of war, takes its place in the practice of war. King Edward could "cry 'Havoc!' and let slip the dogs of war." Knights and men, when the occasion arose, would acquit themselves well. If however the occasion did not arise, their march would not have been in vain, for havoc was itself an important means to his end.

Hygiene
in Fourteenth Century London

PHILIP ZIEGLER

Family Life in the Cities

LEWIS MUMFORD

There is a currently prevalent image of medieval and early modern city life as being characterized by crowded, noisy streets, filth, and a lack of sunlight and open space. This image has been engraved on our minds by films like *Becket*, *The Lion in Winter*, and *Tom Jones*; the filmmakers took their notion of the city from historians who themselves had based their descriptions on engravings of cities produced in the sixteenth and seventeenth centuries. The impression is reinforced when we enter the older parts of European and some American cities, where the streets are narrow, crooked, and apparently laid out in a haphazard pattern. Compared with the gridlike plans favored by modern city planners, these remains of earlier urban life seem confused and crowded; but the builders of premodern cities were not abdicating their duties, and they were not incompetent. The picture of their towns should be much brighter than it is painted.

Cities were planned for two purposes—defense and trade. In most cases, these two functions together determined the plans, but defensibility was the greater value. Study of most European cities will reveal a plan radiating out from the central point that once contained, and sometimes still contains, the fortress. In some cities, the cathedral usurped the position of the citadel, since the bishops were the lords of the towns. Thus, in Toledo or Chartres or Durham the cathedral holds the heights and could, with its strong walls and high towers, function as a fortress when necessary.

Not only were medieval cities well planned for their needs, they were also full of open spaces. The urban population grew rapidly from the twelfth century on, but houses were built close together, leaving gardens and even pastures within the city walls. The new urban families came from the countryside (mostly from the area immediately surrounding the town), and it took some time for them to lose their penchant for farming. City dwellers supplemented their diets by growing their own vegetables and milking their own cows; "truck farming" was rather primitive in most places. The open spaces were gradually filled, however, and the cities became increasingly crowded despite efforts in some places to limit the population by law. It was only the plague that brought an end to the growth, and the population decline continued long after the epidemics subsided. It is estimated, for example, that between 1494 and 1520, one-eighth to one-seventh of the houses in Freiburg were demolished and turned back into gardens.

The picture of the city as a beehive did fit some places, of course, and one of them seems to have been London, by far the largest and most prosperous city in England. It would be wrong to assume that the houses of fourteenth-century London were built on top of one another, but there was a hygiene problem in the city that was conducive to the spreading of disease. The first of the two selections presented here concerns this problem. Philip Ziegler provides a lively description of London before the plague struck in the mid-fourteenth century. In the piece from Lewis Mumford's *The City in History*, the focus is on the home life of the medieval and early modern burghers. What is said in these selections is valid for most European cities of the premodern era.

HYGIENE IN FOURTEENTH CENTURY LONDON

London seems to have grown more rapidly and more consistently than any of its rivals. Though the city was not included in the Domesday Book, at that time it probably had some fifteen or sixteen thousand inhabitants. By early in the thirteenth century, Professor Russell calculated, this figure must have doubled and, by 1348, doubled again to a population of some sixty thousand within the city wall. The immediately outlying villages, integrated with the city in many ways and certainly part of the same unit from the point of view of the spread of the plague, must have added another ten or fifteen thousand to the total.

It would be inappropriate [here] to attempt any profound or detailed analyis of day-to-day life in a medieval city. Nevertheless there is much about the state of London, as for that matter about Paris or Florence, which is directly relevant to any study of the plague, since there were certain built-in features in the Londoner's pattern of life which contributed directly to its successful spread. Perhaps the most relevant of these was the overcrowding. Privacy was not a concept close to the heart of medieval man and even in the grandest castle life was conducted in a perpetual crowd. Hoccleve writes of an earl and countess, their daughter and their daughter's governess who all slept in the same room. It would not be in the least surprising to know that they slept in the same bed as well if, indeed, there was a bed. In the houses of the poor, where beds were an unheard of luxury, it would not have been exceptional to find a dozen people sleeping on the floor of the same room. In the country villages, indeed in many urban houses as well, pigs and chickens and perhaps even ponies, cows and sheep, would share the common residence. Even if people had realised that such a step was desirable it would have been physically impossible to isolate the sick. The surprise is not how many households were totally wiped out but, rather, in how many cases some at least of the inhabitants survived.)

The dirt and inadequate sanitation of these hovels was, strictly speaking, less revelant to the spread of the Black Death. No one was going to become infected with bubonic plague by drinking tainted water or breathing foetid air. But, equally, it is true that the plague found its work easier in bodies weakened by dysentery, diarrhoea or the thousand natural shocks that the unclean body is particularly heir to. Still more important; warmth and dirt provide the ideal environment for the rat. The eventual victory of the brown rat over the plague-bearing black rat was in part due to the physical superiority of the former, but, at least as important, was a tribute to the rise in the standard of living and the substitution of brick for clay and wood which deprived the black rat of his sustenance and favourite way of life. The medieval house might have been built to specifications approved by a rodent council as eminently suitable for the rat's enjoyment of a healthy and care-free life.

What one might call the cinematic image of a medieval town is well known. Lanes barely wide enough to allow two ponies to pass meander between the steep walls of houses which grow together at the top, so as almost to blot out the light of day. The lanes themselves—they seem indeed more drains than lanes—are deep in mud and filth; no doubt to be attributed to the myriad buxom servant-wenches who appear at the upper windows and empty chamber pots filled with excrement on the passers-by. No street corner is without the body of a dead donkey and a beggar exhibiting his gruesome sores and deformities to the charitable citizens. Clearly one is in a society where hygiene counts for nothing and no town-council would waste its time supervising the cleaning of streets or the emptying of cesspools.

The picture, though of course over-drawn, is not entirely false. A medieval city, by modern standards, would seem a pretty filthy and smelly spot. But it would be unfair to suggest that citizens and rulers were indifferent to the nuisance or did nothing to remedy it. Thanks to the researches of Mr. E. L. Sabine and others, we now know much about conditions in London and the activities of the mayor, alderman and common council. Though London, as the largest city of England, had the most serious problems, so also it had the greatest resources with which to deal with them. The overall picture of London's filth or cleanliness will be more or less valid for most of England's towns and cities.

Sanitary equipment, it need hardly be said, was scarce and primitive. In monasteries or castles, "garderobes" were relatively common. Since 1307, the Palace of Westminster boasted a pipe between the King's lavatory and the main sewer which had been installed to carry away the filth from the royal kitchen. But this was probably unique in London; usually the privies of the aristocrats jutted out over the Thames so that their excrement would fall directly in the river or splash down the face of the castle wall. The situation was worse when the privies projected, not over a free flowing river but above a shallow stream or ditch. An inquest into the state of the Fleet Prison Ditch in 1355 revealed that, though it should have been ten feet wide and deep enough to float a boat laden with a tun of wine, it was choked by the filth from eleven latrines and three sewers. So deep was the resultant sludge that no water from Fleet Stream was flowing around the prison moat.

Occasionally citizens tried to dispose of their filth by piping it into the common drain in the centre of the street. A more ingenious technique was exposed at an Assize of Nuisances in 1347, when it was found that two men had been piping their ordure into the cellar of a neighbour. This ploy was not detected until the neighbour's cellar began to overflow.

Normally those fortunate enough to possess a private latrine would also have their own cesspool. In theory these had to be built to certain minimum standards; placed at least two and a half feet from a neighbour's land if they were stone-lined and three and a half feet if they were not. But there were many cases of seepage into adjoining properties and the contamination of private or public wells. Nor were these the only perils inherent in a cesspool, as the unfortunate Richard the Raker discovered when he vanished through the rotten planks of his latrine and drowned monstrously in his own excrement. Most blocks of tenement houses had their own privies though this was not invariable. But even where such facilities were lacking the chances were that there would be a public latrine not too far away.

Though sewers and cesspools were perhaps the most important of the common council's responsibilities, they provided by no means the only field in which the authorities saw reason to intervene. The three city butcheries of St. Nicholas Shambles near Friars Minors in Newgate, the Stocks Market near Walbrook and East Cheap were subject to strict regulations. The years just before the Black Death, when cattle murrain was rife in the South of England, gave rise to many such prosecutions for selling meat described as "putrid, rotten, stinking and abominable to the human race." Offenders ran the risk of being placed in a pillory and having the putrid meat burnt underneath them.

The disposal of offal and other refuse was a serious problem. At the time of the Black Death the butchers of St. Nicholas Shambles had been assigned a spot at Seacoal Lane near the Fleet prison where they could clean carcases and dispose of the entrails. But, under pressure from the Prior of St. John of Jerusalem, the site was moved and subsequently moved again, to a choice of Stratford or Knightsbridge; both suitably remote spots outside the city wall. "Because," as the royal instruction read, "by the killing of great beasts, from whose putrid blood running down the streets and the bowels cast into the Thames, the air in the city is very much corrupted and infected, whence abominable and most filthy stinks proceed, sicknesses and many other evils have happened to such as have abode in the said city, or have resorted to it; and great dangers are feared to fall out for the time to come unless remedy be presently made against it . . . " The final solution was to build a house on a pier above the Thames and dump the offal directly in the river during the ebb tide.

Even with such precautions the state of the streets was far from satisfactory. The tenement buildings, in which each story projected two or three feet beyond the one below, seemed designed for the emptying of slops, garbage and soiled rushes into the street. The gutters, which ran down the centre of the narrower streets and both sides of the wider ones, were generally inadequate to carry away the litter, augmented as it was by the dung of the innumerable domestic animals which lived in the centre of the city. The open sewers which ran down to the river were better able to manage the load but even these were often blocked and inadequate, especially in times of drought, to clear away all that was put in them.

To deal with these problems the common council appointed a number of "scavengers" with instructions to "remove all filth, and to take distresses, or else fourpence, from those who placed them there, the same being removed at their cost." By 1345 the penalty for defiling a street had risen to two shillings and every householder was deemed responsible for a mess outside his house unless he could prove his innocence. At least one city raker was appointed for each ward and there seem to have been between forty and fifty carts and horses. The householders, knowing that they would be the ones to suffer if a street was allowed to grow filthy, could generally be relied on to support the efforts of the authorities. Sometimes, indeed, their aid seemed over-enthusiastic as when a pedlar threw some eel skins to the ground in St. Mary-le-Bow and was killed in the resultant struggle.

But though refuse might have been removed with some efficiency from the city centre, too often the system subsequently broke down. Large dumps were established on the banks of the Thames and the adjoining lanes. In 1344 the situation had become so bad, especially around Walbrook, Fleet Stream and the city ditch, that a comprehensive survey of all the lanes was ordered. But though there was some improvement it does not seem to have lasted long. Thirteen years later the King was complaining bitterly that his progresses along the Thames were being disturbed by the "dung, lay-stalls and other filth" which were piled up along the bank.

The overall picture, therefore, is of a city squalid and insanitary enough but aware of its deficiencies and doing its best, though with altogether inadequate tools, to put things right. The records reveal many cases of behaviour in wanton defiance of the rules of hygiene but the very fact that such behaviour was commented on and sometimes prosecuted shows that the picturesque excesses, so dear to the heart of the antiquarian, were not permitted to flourish unchecked. A responsible city council and a population on the whole aware of its civic duties did quite a good job of keeping London clean.

But the Black Death proved altogether too much for the public health services. In 1349, the King wrote to the mayor to remonstrate about filth being thrown from the houses so that "the streets and lanes through which people had to pass were foul with human faeces and the air of the city poisoned to the great danger of men passing, especially in this time of infectious disease." The mayor was helpless. Not only had many of the efficient cleaners died or deserted their post and the machinery for the enforcement of the law been strained beyond its capacities but also the technical problem of transporting something over twenty thousand corpses to the burial grounds had imposed an extra and unexpected burden on the skeleton force which remained. Even ten years later the service was far from normal; in the year of the Black Death itself, the most lurid imaginings of a romantic novelist would hardly have done justice to reality.

FAMILY LIFE IN THE CITIES

In most aspects of medieval life, the closed corporation prevailed. But compared to modern life, the medieval urban family was a very open unit; for it included, as part of the normal household, not only relatives by blood but a group of industrial workers as well as domestics whose relation was that of secondary members of the family. This held for all classes, for young men from the upper classes got their knowledge of the world by serving as waiting men in a noble family: what they observed and overheard at mealtime was part of their education. Apprentices, and sometimes journeymen, lived as members of the master craftsman's family. If marriage was perhaps deferred longer for men than today, the advantages of home life were not entirely lacking even for the bachelor.

The workshop was a family; likewise the merchant's counting house. The members ate together at the same table, worked in the same rooms, slept in the same or common hall, converted at night into dormitories, joined in the family prayers, participated in the common amusements. Chastity and virginity were still the ideal states, as Saint Paul had proclaimed them, but the reader of Boccaccio or Chaucer will not exaggerate their prevalence. The guild itself was a sort of patriarchal family, which kept order in its own household, fining and penalizing smaller offenses against the brotherhood quite apart from the municipality. Even the prostitutes formed guilds: indeed, in Hamburg, Vienna, and Augsburg the brothels were under municipal protection. When one remembers that syphilis did not make its definite appearance, at least in virulent form, until the fifteenth century, even prostitution constituted a smaller threat to bodily health than it did in the following centuries.

From pp. 281–97 of *The City in History,* © 1961 by Lewis Mumford. Reprinted by permission of Harcourt Brace Jovanovich, Inc. and Martin Secker & Warburg Ltd.

The intimate union of domesticity and labor, surviving now in the city only in petty shops or in the household of an occasional painter, architect, or physician, dictated the major arrangements within the medieval dwelling house itself. Naturally, between the rude huts and bare stone enclosures of the tenth century and the elaborate merchant houses that were built from the eleventh to the sixteenth centuries, there was a difference as great as that between a seventeenth-century dwelling and a metropolitan apartment house today. Let us attempt, nevertheless, to single out certain common factors in this development. Some of them left a permanent imprint, down to the twentieth century.

Houses—only two or three stories high at the beginning—were usually built in continuous rows around the perimeter of their rear gardens; sometimes in large blocks they formed inner courts, with a private green, reached through a single gateway on the street. Freestanding houses, unduly exposed to the elements, wasteful of the land on each side, harder to heat, were relatively scarce; even farmhouses would be part of a solid block that included the stables, barns, granaries. The materials for the houses came out of the local soil, and they varied with the region, now wattle and daub, now stone or brick, now with thatched roofs (which were fire hazards), now with tile or slate. Continuous row houses forming the closed perimeter of a block, with guarded access on the ground floor, served as a domestic wall: a genuine protection against felonious entry in troubled times.

The earliest houses would have small window openings, with shutters to keep out the weather; then later, permanent windows of oiled cloth, paper, eventually glass. In the fifteenth century glass, hitherto so costly it was used only for public buildings, became more frequent, at first only in the upper part of the window. In the sixteenth-century painting of the Annunciation, by Joos van Cleve (Metropolitan Museum), one sees a double window, divided into three panels: the uppermost panel, fixed, is of diamond-paned glass; the next two panels have shutters that open inward; thus the amount of exposure to sunlight and air could be controlled, yet on inclement days, both sets of shutters could be closed, without altogether shutting out light. On any consideration of hygiene and ventilation this type of window, which was common in the Low Countries, was superior to the all-glass window that succeeded it, since glass excludes the bactericidal ultraviolet rays. Even more definitely, it was superior to the sealed glass wall which current architectural fashion has lately foisted on a supposedly enlightened age, in defiance of every scientific precept of hygiene or physiology.

By the sixteenth century glass had become cheap and widely available; so the popular saying in England about Hardwick Hall—"more glass than wall"—was equally true of the burgher houses. But strangely enough, in England ventilation was often inadequate. Did not Erasmus of Rotterdam suggest in a letter to Wolsey's physician that English health might be better if bedrooms had windows on two or three sides?

In the North Sea area a broad bank of windows would extend across the whole house at each story, front and rear, thus making up in effect for the tendency to deepen the house. But in the southern parts of Europe, the oppressive summer heat put a brake on this development, for all but the living room areas. Though medieval interiors, accordingly, were often subdued in lighting, if not dark, by our standards, their builders acted boldly to achieve light when they needed it: the old houses of the weavers, in Sudbury, England, have extra-large windows on the upper story, to give light to the loom; and when not enough light was available by that means, the workers would move outdoors, as the ancient lacemakers of Bruges still do, sitting by their doorsteps.

Heating arrangements steadily improved. This fact partly accounts for the outburst of human energy in the north; winter gradually ceased to be a period of stupefied hibernation. The open hearth in the middle of a stone floor, scarcely as effective as the arrangements in an Indian tepee, gave way to the fireplace and the chimney. Fireproofing went along with this development, for originally, lacking proper materials, the poorer burghers were tempted to experiment with wooden chimneys: an unduly optimistic practice repeated in the early settlements of New England and Virginia. In 1276 Lübeck passed an ordinance enforcing the use of fireproof roofing and the fireproof party wall; and in London, after the severe fire in 1189, special privileges were given to people building in stone and tile; while in 1212 thatched roofs were ordered to be whitewashed, the better to resist fire.

As for the plan of the house, it varied with the region and the century; yet certain features remained common. Viollet-le-Duc has shown us the ground plan of a French house, with a shop on the ground floor, connected by an open galley with the kitchen in the rear. The two formed a court, where the well occupied a corner. There was a chimney in the kitchen and in the living room, or *grande salle*, above the shop; from the latter there was access to the dormitories above. Moritz Heyne's plan of an old house in Nürnberg is not essentially different; but, as in the surviving houses of the seventeenth century, there are more interior rooms, a kitchen and a smaller room on the ground floor, a heatable room above the kitchen, and a number of chambers, with a toilet on the second floor directly above that on the first.

In Italy, a desire to be comfortable in summer, perhaps combined with an innate love of grandeur or a Roman sense of scale, raised the ceiling above any reasonable height, in Genoa or Florence, from the sixteenth century on; but the buildings that have survived from the thirteenth century, like Dante's dwelling, indicate more modest dimensions, better suited to year-round living. In the development of the house, rising manmade temperatures go along with an expansion of interior space and a raising of the ceilings, but heating rarely caught up with winter cold in Italy. The "brutalist" scale of so many sixteenth and seventeenth century palaces was as brutal to the body as to the eye. The low-ceilinged servants' floors must have been more comfortable, at least in winter, than the drafty masters' quarters.

The only form of modern hallway was the open gallery or the narrow, usually winding, stairs. The gallery was a common feature in dwelling houses, and it survives in the design of ancient inns, where a means of circulation was specially necessary, and the internal hall, because of the absence of artificial light, was not an attractive solution—until the whole inner court could be covered by a skylight, as in some nineteenth-century mansions and hotels. The main outlines of this type of house lasted right down through the seventeenth century, even later.

As one went downward in the economic scale, arrangements would be less differentiated and the space more constricted. The one-room apartment for a whole family in a multiple story dwelling, still common among the poor in many countries, possibly had its origin in the more industrialized cities of the later Middle Ages: even in the countryside, where there was no scarcity of land, Coulton records a family house for three people twenty-four feet long and only eleven feet wide. Both in city and country, the lack of space itself sprang from sheer poverty.

The fact that the burgher house served as workshop, store, and counting house prevented any municipal zoning between these functions. The competition for space between the domestic and the working quarters, as business grew and the scale of production expanded, was doubtless responsible for encroachment over the original back gardens by sheds, storage bins, and special workshops. But there is still a brewery in Bruges which now occupies almost one whole side of the Walplaats, built on the same scale as the residence alongside it: the loading is done in the courtyard behind. Here the storehouse, sheds, and garage have ample space—but are still on a medieval scale. Except where the industry was small and noisy, when it was often put at the edge of the town or outside the walls, this intimate connection of industrial and domestic life long remained normal: the exact antithesis of the segregated, legally sterilized residential quarter of today.

Mass production and the concentration of looms in great sheds was indeed known in Flanders in the fourteenth century, and operations like milling, glass-making, and iron-making required a more isolated type of workshop, sometimes surrounded by related workshops, as with fulling, dyeing, weaving, and shrinking. In these industries came the earliest break between domestic life and work, both in space and function. But at first the family pattern dominated industry, just as it dominated the organization of the Benedictine monastery. Survivals of this regime lingered on in every historic European city: the habit of "living in," long retained by London drapers, with the men and the women divided into dormitories, was a typical holdover from the Middle Ages.

In the disposition and the specialization of rooms in the Middle Ages, the ways of the aristocracy filtered down but slowly to the rest of the population. Comforts that were enjoyed by lords and ladies alone in the thirteenth century did not become popular privileges until the seventeenth century. One might see in this another instance of the "law of cultural seepage": the making of innovations by a favored minority and their slow infiltration over the centuries into the lower economic ranks. The first radical change, which was to alter the form of the medieval house, was the development of a sense of privacy. This meant, in effect, withdrawal at will from the common life and the common interests of one's fellows. Privacy in sleep; privacy in eating; privacy in religious and social ritual; finally, privacy in thought. This came about with a general clarification and separation of functions that even extended, by the seventeenth century, in France, to cookery.

In the castles of the thirteenth century, one notes the existence of a private bedroom for the noble owners; and one also finds, not far from it, perched over the moat, a private toilet: the first hint of the nineteenth-century luxury of a private toilet for every family, or the extravagant American demand for a private toilet for every bedroom. In 1362 Langland, in "Piers Plowman," chided the tendency of the Lord and Lady to withdraw from the common hall for private meals and for private entertainment. He must have foreseen the end of that reciprocal social relation between the stationary upper and lower ranks of the feudal regime: a relation that had mitigated its oppressions, since they shared the same quarters. The desire for privacy marked the beginning of that new alignment of classes which was to usher in the merciless class competition and individual self-assertion of a later day: for once consciences become tender, it is easier to practice inhumanity upon those you do not see.

The separation of the kitchen from the dining room is not characteristic, probably, of the majority of the houses in any country today: indeed, in America, thanks to the absence of domestic servants, the visual and functional union of these two parts is rapidly being restored. Such a separation had taken place in the monastery because of the scale of the preparations, and it was copied eventually in the manorial hall, the college, and the fine town house. But the common quarters offered this incentive to social living: they alone were usually heated. That the medieval house was cold in winter, hardly less in the south than in the north, perhaps accounts for the development of inner rooms, insulated from the outer walls by air, as it surely does for the development of the alcove for the bed, or of curtaining around the bed, to make the enclosed heat of the bodies warm the stale air.

Yet the cold could not have been unendurable, or else people would have worn nightdresses or kept on a shift, instead of "going to their naked bed," as numberless illustrations depict them. Privacy in bed came first in Italy among the upper classes: witness Carpaccio's "Vision of St. Ursula," in a bedroom one would still find adequate and charming today. But the desire for it seems to have developed almost as slowly as the means. Michelangelo, on occasion, slept with his workmen, four to a bed. As late as the seventeenth century, maidservants often slept in trundle beds (rolled under the big bed by day) at the foot of that of their master and mistress, while three centuries earlier, Thomas Hoccleve refers in a poem to an earl, a countess, their governess, and their daughter all sleeping in the same room.

Until the curtained bed was invented, sexual intercourse must have taken place for the most part under cover, and whether the bed was curtained or not, in darkness. Privacy in bed preceded the private bedroom; for even in seventeenth-century engravings of upper-middle-class life—and in France, a country of reputed refinement—the bed still often occupies a part of the living room. Under these circumstances, the erotic ritual must have been short and almost secretive, with little preliminary stirring through eye or voice or free movement. But sex had its open seasons, no doubt, especially spring; for the late medieval astrological calenders, which depict this awakening, show the lovers having intercourse in the open with their clothes on. In short, erotic passion was more attractive in the garden and the wood or under a hedge, despite stubble or insects, than it was in the house, on a mattress whose stale straw or down was never quite free from musty dampness or fleas.

For lovers in the medieval house, the winter months must have been a large wet blanket. But as against this somewhat unfavorable interpretation, one must, in honesty, quote the contrary judgment of the medieval poet François Villon:

> They boast of sleeping near the woodland tree.
> Doth not a chair-flanked bedstead better please?
> What say you? Does it need a longer plea?
> No treasure is like living at our ease.

To sum up the medieval dwelling, one may say that it was characterized by a general absence of functionally differentiated space. In the cities, however, this lack of internal specialization was offset by a completer development of domestic functions in public institutions. Though the house might lack a private bake-oven, there was a public one in the nearby baker's or the cook shop. Though it might lack a private bathroom, there was a municipal bath-house in the neighborhood. Though it might lack facilities for isolating and nursing a diseased member, there were numerous public hospitals: so that Thomas More, in his Utopia, could even conceive that in his ideal commonwealth people would prefer to be looked after in such an institution. And though lovers might lack a private bedroom, they could "lie between the acres of the rye," just outsides the city's walls—with a hey! and a ho! and a hey-nonny-no!

Plainly, the medieval house had scarcely an inkling of two important domestic requirements of the present day: privacy and comfort. And the tendency in the late Middle Ages to deepen the narrow house under the pressure of congestion progressively deprived those who stayed most steadily indoors, the mother, the domestics, the young children, of the necessary air and light which country dwellers in much cruder hovels could have.

Mark this paradox of prosperity. As long as conditions were rude—when people lived in the open, pissed freely in the garden or the street, bought and sold outdoors, opened their shutters and let in full sunlight—the biological defects of medieval housing were far less serious than they were later under a more refined regime. As for its virtues, the house by day was no sexual isolation ward: women had an intimate part in all family and business concerns, and woman's constant presence, if sometimes distracting, probably had a humanizing influence on the working life: an influence raised to ideal heights in the thirteenth-century cult of the Virgin.

With motherhood itself valued and elevated, child care improved. It was no lack of concern for children that made the infant mortality records of the medieval period so black, so far as we may estimate them. The cradle, the hobby horse, and even the toddler, for the child who had not yet learned to walk, are depicted in sixteenth-century prints. These cherubs were treated with love: it was for a children's home in the Piazza SS. Annunziata in Florence that Andrea della Robbia did some of his most charming ceramic sculptures.

But the domestic environment, under the pressure of crowding and high rents at the end of the Middle Ages, became increasingly defective; and such diseases as are spread through either contact or respiration must have had a maximum opportunity for sweeping through the family in the late medieval house. The urban dwelling was, indeed, the weakest link in medieval sanitary arrangements, once the natural open spaces were pushed farther away with the growth of the town, and the inner ones got built over. In other respects, the standards were far more adequate than most Victorian commentators—and those who still echo their prejudices and blandly repeat their errors—believed.

PART 5

The
Renaissance-Reformation,
15th–17th Centuries

The cultural and religious movements that give their names to the Renaissance-Reformation period occurred against a social background that has become familiar through studies of late medieval and Renaissance Italian cities and of the northern kingdoms. The increasing urbanization of Italy made people more aware of their connections with earlier ages, when civilization and empire were based on the cities. It also made the urban communities the arena in which the social classes struggled with one another and in which individuals in search of higher status waged their personal campaigns. The effect of changing the social arena from rural to urban was greatest for the noble class. John Gager's "Preserving the Noble Class" describes a pattern of noble life in sharp contrast to that described in Sidney Painter's "The Training of a Knight" (in Part 3), where William Marshal's rise to prominence is followed. In both the twelfth and the sixteenth centuries, marriage played an important role in the system of social mobility, but its importance in the later period was significantly greater than it had been earlier.

The Renaissance was a period of expansion for European power and influence. For centuries, the crusading movement had brought Europeans into contact with powers in North Africa and the Middle East. Now, European sailors began a series of explorations that led ultimately to the colonization of large areas throughout the world. The success of these seamen was founded on the long tradition of Mediterranean shipping. In H. F. M. Prescott's "Touring the Holy Land," the experience of travelers and sailors in the Mediterranean is brought to life.

In J. M. Fletcher's "Rich and Poor in the Medieval Universities," we return to the universities and follow their development into the institutions we know today. The amorphous body of scholars and students that made up the twelfth- and thirteenth-century universities gradually became more established. Many cities attempted to create universities in order to attract the large student population to their communities—and their shops. At the same time, the connection between the Church and the universities was weakened, and university education became more common among merchants as well as among churchmen and bureaucrats. Fletcher's selection describes the effect of the new pressures and new role of the universities on their institutional growth and their life.

Assessment of the changes taking place in sixteenth-century Europe depends on their effect on individuals. As the older institutions broke down and new ones had to be constructed, individuals were forced to make difficult choices and to take decisive actions that wrenched them from the security of established society. In "Young Man Luther," Erik Erikson focuses on the principal leader of the religious revolution, Martin Luther, and at the same time raises questions about how historians ought to approach the writing of biography.

Just as the changing consciousness of individuals is revealed in their actions and the articulation of their ideas, society as a whole reveals its consciousness through its art and works. In the final selection, the emergence of a new consciousness of the family in European society is described. This study raises methodological problems about the use of the sources and historiographical problems about the relationship between changing social attitudes and great religious and cultural movements.

Bibliography

For a closer look at aristocratic society in Italy, see Paul Coles, "The Crisis of Renaissance Society: Genoa 1488–1507," *Past and Present*, Vol. 11 (1957), pp. 17–47. There is important comparative material in Eduard Perroy, "Social Mobility among the French Noblesse in the Later Middle Ages," *Past and Present*, Vol. 21 (1962), pp. 25–38, and Laurence Stone, *The Crisis of the Aristocracy 1558–1641* (Oxford, 1965), which focuses on England.

There is a study of ships in the period of Friar Felix's journey in M. E. Mallett, *The Florentine Galleys in the Fifteenth Century* (Oxford, 1967). Mallett includes a ship's log from the period as well. See aso E. L. Guilford, *Travel and Travellers in the Middle Ages* (New York, 1924). On the pilgrimages of the Middle Ages, see A. Kendall, *Medieval Pilgrims* (London, 1970). See also Robert S. Lopez, "The Evolution of Land Transport in the Middle Ages," *Past and Present*, Vol. 19 (1956), pp. 17–29. Irving Agus, in *Urban Civilization in Pre-Crusade Europe* (New York, 1965), includes an entire section on travel. His material focuses on the period from the ninth to the eleventh centuries, when political conditions kept most people off the roads.

Hastings Rashdall, *The Universities of Europe in the Middle Ages*, ed. by F. M. Powicke and A. B. Emden (Cambridge, Eng., 1936) is helpful for the late medieval period as well as for the origins of the university. See also Kenneth Charlton, *Education in Renaissance England* (Toronto, 1965), and two articles by Joan Simon—"The Reformation and English Education," *Past and Present*, Vol. 11 (1957), pp. 48–65, and "The Social Origins of Cambridge Students 1603–1640," *Past and Present*, Vol. 26 (1963), pp. 58–67.

For a comparison with Erikson's approach to Martin Luther, see R. H. Fife, *Young Luther: The Intellectual and Religious Development of Martin Luther to 1518* (New York, 1928). See also H. Boehmer, *Road to Reformation* (Philadelphia, 1946), and A. G. Dickens, *Martin Luther and Reformation* (London, 1967). Roland Bainton criticizes both Erikson and Boehmer in *Studies on the Reformation* (Boston, 1963), Chap. 8. His own approach is presented in *Here I Stand: A Life of Martin Luther* (New York, 1950). See Erikson's *Childhood and Society* (New York, 1963) for a broader consideration of the problems analyzed in the context of his study of Luther. See also William Langer's discussion of the use of psychological and psychoanalytical techniques in historiography, "The Next Assignment," *American Historical Review*, Vol. 63 (1958), pp. 283–304.

Studies of the family in premodern Europe are not numerous. See George C. Homans, *English Villagers of the Thirteenth Century*, Book II (Cambridge, Mass., 1941), for a study of the peasant family. Part III of Marc Bloch, *Feudal Society*, 2 vols. (Chicago, 1961), describes kinship ties. Joan Thirsk has reviewed and summarized recent French studies on the family in "The Family," *Past and Present*, Vol. 27 (1964), pp. 116–22. See also Sidney Painter, "The Family and the Feudal System in Twelfth Century England," *Speculum*, Vol. 35 (1960), pp. 1–16. For more information about Philippe Aries' artistic sources, see V. Egbert, *The Medieval Artist at Work* (Princeton, N.J., 1967) and Emil Mâle, *The Gothic Image* (New York, 1958).

Preserving the Noble Class

JOHN GAGE

With the rise of the cities in the twelfth century, there arose a new aristocracy to challenge the feudal aristocracy that held power in the countryside. The new aristocrats based their position on the wealth being produced by their growing commercial interests, but soon they were attempting to get into the old aristocratic hierarchy. The struggle of the old aristocratic families against the merchant nobles is a well-known aspect of the social history of the upper classes, but there is another struggle not as familiar and yet in many ways more important and interesting than that one. Within the cities themselves, there was a constant shifting of power and sometimes a nearly complete realignment that depended on shifts in economic prosperity and the locus of economic power. The flux of circumstances created a behavioral pattern in the upper classes designed to preserve nobility or gain it. The heart of this pattern was marriage. To marry well—meaning to marry money if you were an impoverished noble or to marry status if you were *nouveau riche*—became a major preoccupation of the upper classes. This struggle for survival is perhaps best seen in the Italy of the late Middle Ages and Renaissance, where urban life had a more constant existence than it had in the North, and where its revival progressed more quickly and more completely than elsewhere. As John Gage shows in this selection, the governmental power of the Italian cities was used to protect the noble class from the consequences of internal competition as well as from competition with the other urban classes.

In his handbook of courtesy, *The Book of the Courtier*, written in north Italy in the first quarter of the sixteenth century, Baldesar Castiglione put forward a theory of the nobility of blood, based on a quasi-biological idea of heredity, which was dear to many Italian Renaissance writers. A Veronese jurist, Cristoforo Lanfranchini, writing in 1497 on whether it is preferable to be a knight or a scholar, spoke of the sort of nobility "deriving from a man's ancestors, continuing in the persons of their successors who lead praiseworthy and well-mannered lives," which "leaves no doubt that they are nobles and will be regarded as such for all time, so long as they do not degenerate . . . or practise any low profession. . . ." Neither virtue nor office, according to another Veronese jurist of the period, could confer nobility on a man "unless it was in his forebears." "Virtue," or mental and spiritual qualities, played their part in nobility, but in general the burden of these views ran counter to another, better-known conception, represented in a treatise *On Nobility* by the Florentine humanist Poggio Bracciolini, who held that it depended solely on "virtue" and was therefore "at the disposition of all." Castiglione was no more definite on this point than many other writers, and he qualified his opinion by stating that those poorly endowed by nature could remedy their defects by study and effort. But in the political life of the period it was certainly birth and wealth which were decisive in determining who ruled; as much in the so-called Republics of Florence and Venice as in the kingdoms and the duchies of Naples and Milan; and Bracciolini's diatribe against the aristocratic pastimes of the chase corresponded in no way with ideals and habits of the political classes, whose views on their hereditary prerogatives tended to harden throughout the fifteenth and sixteenth centuries.

In Naples it was the town nobility, the *Seggi*, almost exclusively who administered the kingdom; and when in the 1490s the French invader Charles VIII was surprised that a deputation of them should represent the whole city, they replied that they alone were people, bourgeois and nobles and that all the other inhabitants of Naples were foreigners. In the countryside the old feudal barons still ruled, as they did in Lombardy, where a new ducal family like the Sforza in Milan could control them only loosely. In 1483 the lieutenant of Castel San Giovanni refused to open the town gates in response to ducal letters, claiming that he was beholden only to the feudatory, Count Piero dal Verme. It was chiefly in Lombardy that the ancient Guelph (papal) and Ghibelline (Imperial) factions revived most strongly at the beginning of the sixteenth century, with their cult of emblems and the blood-feud which had been so characteristic of the later middle ages in Italy. In Genoa, too, where the old feudal magnates were still strong, they sought to retain power after the popular revolutions of the fourteenth century by playing off the Guelph and Ghibelline merchant families against one another. Although the Genoese nobles formed only one twelfth of the population, half of the government offices were reserved to them; and they were favoured successively by the Milanese and French authorities who gained political control in the city. It was not until after 1503 that the merchant element began to predominate in political life.

Naples with its king, Milan with its duke and Genoa with its Doge were, throughout the Medici period, essentially in the control of single men; but in Venice the office of Doge had become all but symbolic by the fifteenth century. No ducal portrait or family emblem was to be exhibited in public places; and the ducal income of 3500 ducats was only a little above that of the Grand Chancellor. Venice was now technically a Republic: political power was vested in the Grand Council; but this had become more and more the preserve of a few leading families after its "closing" (*serrata*) at the end of the thirteenth century. In 1423 the legal suppression of the Popular Assembly was the last act confirming this tendency; and from now on the Venetian patricians were able, like the Neapolitan nobility, to refer to Venice constantly as their "own state." These conceptions Venice transferred to the old communes of her hinterland, where she built up an empire throughout the fifteenth century. In Padua, where the anti-magnate legislation of the fourteenth century had already been eroded under the Carrara Signory, Venetian constitutional reforms of 1420 brought most of the old families back. In the second quarter of the century, out of a population of rather less than 20,000 members from only 149 families were elected to government office; and of these, 42 families filled half the seats in the Assembly. Later attempts to limit the power of these families were easily evaded. At Verona which was also under Venetian domination, the Council of 1495 comprised 140 citizens from 79 families; and 13 families controlled more than one third of the seats. Similarly, at Belluno in the early fifteenth century the ruling group of families decreed that only those of noble stock and a family tradition in politics could exercise power; and in 1450 seats in the Council were to be restricted to candidates whose families had been members for three generations.

The government of Florence seems at first sight to be an exception to this general tendency for power to be concentrated in the hands of a few noble families. Since the popular unrests of the fourteenth century the magnates (*Grandi*) had been denied political office, although in 1433 some civil and military posts had been re-opened to them. But the designation *Grandi* was a very flexible one. Before their banishment in 1433, the Medici, who had never been magnates, were declared *Grandi* so as to be more readily deprived; and on his restoration the following year, Cosimo de' Medici gave to the old magnate families who had not opposed him the status of *popolani*, or popular families, so that they could be enfranchised. In the event, however, this was not effective, since none of their names appeared subsequently in the electoral urns, and they continued to enjoy only a small share in government. Nonetheless an analysis of the names of candidates from the Major Guilds eligible for the three major state offices in 1484 shows two thirds from old magnate or *populani* families, and only one third from families who had qualified for office since the Medici restoration in 1434. Since the close of the fourteenth century political exile and the amalgamation of offices had concentrated power into the hands of fewer and fewer families; and fears of the popular domination of government voiced by contemporary critics were generally unfounded. When in 1448 it was said, "into the electoral bags came [the names of] many new people, unused to governing, to the great scandal of the government and the displeasure of the many good citizens (*popolani*) accustomed to political office," there was in fact only a one percent increase of new families since the last electoral census. In 1440 in the city electoral district of S. Giovanni 25 families had 65 percent of the tickets of eligibility for the Signory or Government Committee, and 80 percent of those for the chief office of Gonfaloniere of Justice. The Medici policy of concentrating power increasingly in their own hands, by augmenting the competence of the selec-

tors of eligible names, and extending the duration and hence the powers of
the emergency committees (Balìe), had the effect, too, of reducing the number of politically active families. The manipulation of the official as opposed
to the elected seats in the Assembly enabled them to circumvent a restriction
of one or two elected members per family. In the Balìa of 1438, from the S.
Giovanni district the Medici had five members, five other families had three
each, and ten others two. In the 1450s there was a slight shift to candidates
from the Minor Guilds among those eligible for the three major state offices;
but throughout the period the "popular" government of Florence was so only
in name; in 1495 only about 3200 from a population of some 100,000 had
political rights at all. When in 1458 the Signory summoned all citizens over
the age of 14 to come unarmed to the heavily guarded public square to ap-
prove a law establishing a new Balìa, "since only few understood what Ser
Bartolommeo [the state notary] was saying, for he cannot speak loudly, only
few citizens answered with yea"—and yet the law was passed.

As in Venice, so in Florence, political office was itself the most tangible
token of social worth. "You are hardly a man," wrote the patrician historian
Francesco Guicciardini, "unless you have served in the Signory at least once";
and when Carlo di Salvestro Gondi heard that his name was on the list of
those put forward for the office of Gonfaloniere of Justice in 1458, he was
overjoyed even though he was disqualified for tax-arrears, "because I wanted
this honour, which seemed to me to give an enormous impetus to our family."
But aristocracy and political power implied wealth. Apart from very backward
areas like Venetian Dalmatia, where the nobility was generally poor and yet
politically strong, wealth and power were inseparable. In Venice itself there
were poor nobles called sqizari, to whom it was considered honourable to
give alms, and whose votes in council were bought by the richer patricians.
In 1499 the nobleman Antonio Contarini pleaded before the Signory that he
had nine sons and an income of only 16 ducats a year, no profession, debts
amounting to 60 ducats, and had held no office for 16 years. Office was itself
a means to wealth: complaints from the Venetian subject territories against
nobles who exploited their political positions for personal gain were common;
and it is clear that no one without other resources could live from the 15
ducats a month allowed officially to some criminal officers in Venice, or the
six allowed to councillors. The Doge of Genoa himself received in 1489 15,000
lire out of a total government expenditure of only 50,000. The politically active nobility in Genoa and Venice were in fact all engaged in business and
had large private fortunes. Titles to nobility itself, in Venice, Modena, Padua
and Verona, were bought and sold; Lanfranchini ridiculed those "knights of
our age of gold," who "every day stand in the squares and behind their coun-
ters exercising some base profession; and there are many who do not know
how to put their arms on. . . ." The Florentine bookseller and biographer
Vespasiano da Bisticci made wealth and lavishness almost the condition of
nobility when he wrote of a Spanish count at the court of Naples: "He had

one habit which becomes a gentleman, that is at the end of the year he would have spent all his income and sometimes would have entrenched upon the next year's."

One source of wealth and influence that bore especially political fruits was the practice of the law, which provided a sort of *noblesse de robe*. In Florentine usage knights and lawyers were addressed with the formal *voi*; merchants and less with the familiar *tu*; and Florentine history provides examples of men whose political power came not from family or conspicuous wealth, but from successful legal practice. In Bologna, the sumptuary law of 1474 defined gentlemen as those who had exercised no profession for 30 years and who had either a knight or a doctor of law in the family. The medical profession enjoyed a similar status: in the Veronese Council of 1495 the only members with named professions were six medical doctors, three notaries and one lawyer; and at Treviso in 1469 the doctors and lawyers claimed from the nobility the right to a voice in the superior councils, which was granted at least in part. At Padua the threat of lawyers and doctors to the political power of the old nobility was parried only when this nobility took over the Colleges of Jurists, doctors and philosophers, and were careful only to elect their own.

The financial profits to be had from the law were enormous. Sanuto records the case of a man in 1504 who begged the governor of Bergamo for seven soldi to have his shoes repaired, and yet who had legal expenses of 200 lire; and at Modena some years later a citizen was so constantly engaged in litigation that he married the daughter of a jurist so as to have a useful supporter in the family. The more humble legal profession of notary was equally lucrative: the Noceto family of notaries in Genoa became within three generations honorary citizens of Lucca, and through the patronage of Popes Nicholas V and Pius II the holders of rich benefices. One son became Papal ambassador in France and married into an old noble family; the eldest was secretary to two cardinals and died with a fortune of 400,000 ducats, more than 15 times that of his father. Both were made counts by the Emperor Frederick III in 1451, and by 1528 the family was ranked with the chief of the Genoese nobility The Noceto family is a striking contradiction to the mournful observations of the Florentine patrician and humanist, Leon Battista Alberti that his own, and other Florentine families like the Peruzzi, the Spini and the Ricci had taken the opposite course and declined in three generations from wealth to poverty.

If nobility, political power and wealth itself were fruits of the family, it is clear that in the Italian Renaissance the upholding of family values was the driving force of social endeavour. An intense concern for the family, past, present and future runs through all the forms of Renaissance life: its learning, its festivals, its art. Great pains were taken to discover and display what the family had been. Carefully listed in the inventory of the Florentine silk merchant Luca da Panzano's household effects was his family tree; and in the chronicle of the Paduan Alvise Businello the writer solicitously derives his family from a galaxy of great names: the della Torre, Lords of Milan; the Emperor Charlemagne, and, at the fount, a natural son of Priam of Troy, called Franco. In Florence Buonacorso Pitti lamented that a relative had removed and dispersed old family papers, so that he could not go back with certainty beyond the magic cycle of three generations. Many Florentine families owned copies of Villani's fourteenth-century *Chronicle*, where they might find information about their own forebears, and a list of political officers; and many others compiled their own. Alberti quotes a man so anxious about the fate of his family papers that "he kept them locked away in my study, almost like a consecrated and religious object." A characteristic family chronicle began:

> Because so far there is nothing written in this book, I wanted, I, that is Giovanni of Pagolo of Bartolommeo of Morello of Giraldo of Ruggieri, or Walter, of Calandro of Benamato of Albertino of the Morelli, to write of our clan and ancient state and what will become of us, as far as I can and shall remember; and this to pass the time and so that our family shall learn something about itself, as nowadays everyone traces their foundations to the earliest ages, and so I am going to show the truth of our great antiquity.

Family values did not go untreated by the theorists: Alberti's *Four Books on the Family* was written in the 1430s as a direct consequence of his feelings for the misfortunes of his own house, impoverished and scattered as it was by political unrest and business necessity. Alberti laid down four principles governing family prosperity: a steadily increasing number of male children and wealth; respect for the good name of the house; the avoidance of enmity and the cultivation of friendship and benevolence. In the treatise most of these arguments are reduced to economic ones. The family should keep together because it is less expensive to run one household than several; it is far less costly and more agreeable to draw one's servants from the family circle; it is hard for a man to have spent years amassing wealth and then have no heirs to whom to leave it. Alberti's analysis was largely true in practice: the family unit was the *casato*, or all those eating under one roof; and it included servents and slaves as well as blood relations. A *casato* might number as many as 50 "mouths," each of whom was allowed a certain rebate in the tax returns of the head of the household. In Genoa, the family groups, or *alberghi*, were even larger. All members, even freed slaves, took the family name; and in 1465 there were 400 men, youths and male children in Genoa bearing the name Doria. An observer noted: "in general all citizens of the same family and lineage live in the same street or square; there they have a common church and a loggia where all the members of the family gather each day to amuse themselves or deal with serious business."

These family groupings were fully recognised at law. They were established by notarial contract, and all additions were similarly contractual. When

in the 1460s Leonardo Scotto joined the Cattaneo *albergo*, it promised "to accord him all the honours, rights, prerogatives and all the other advantages
which they enjoy, and to treat him as a man of the name, relationship and
albergo of the Cattanei"; and he in return promised "to call and recognise
himself as of the *albergo* in all things, as much for its honours as on all occasions to wear its insignia and its arms." In Florence and Tuscany generally
the liability for a crime committed by any member of a family fell upon the
group as a whole; and it was recognised as an exceptional act of the Medici
in 1434 that they did not expel the whole of the rival Albizzi family from
Florence, but allowed one of the brothers to stay and even hold political
office. The statutes of the Florentine Silk Guild held that, in the case of a
worker's being too poor to meet a fine for filching, the money was recoverable
from his family, or even his girl-friend (*amica*); and that the husbands and
sons of women workers were responsible for the activities of their wives and
mothers.

The most extreme legal form of family coherence was reflected in the
vendetta, which was recognised at law, although the authorities were continually attempting to restrict its scope, so that the relatives not actually connected with an offence might be safeguarded. In the 1470s Florence tended to
banish rather than execute murderers, so as to avoid reprisals; and at Modena
in the mid-sixteenth century a murderer could compound with the sons and
daughters of his victim by paying a dowry and financial compensation. Nonetheless the vendetta was widespread, and often conducted with startling cool-
ness. "The Doge Foscari: my debtor for the death of my father and uncle,"
wrote the Venetian Jacopo Loredano in his ledger; and when his revenge was
complete he added "Paid." Luca da Panzano recorded in his diary how in
March 1420 he fasted in honour of the Virgin "for the remission of my sins
and those of our forebears." In May he procured permission from the Florentine Signory and Guilds to leave the city for one month and go to Naples
against "our enemy." He was back in June having accomplished the vendetta,
which he described in great detail; and in July he learned that the man who
had offended him (for what he does not say) had died of his wounds, "so that
we have carried out our vendetta, through the grace of God." A Dominican
writer on the family held that numerous children were chiefly useful for
making the house great, "or to inspire fear, or to carry out a vendetta."

Children, that is male children, were in fact the chief object of family
policy. The first duty of a wife, wrote Alberti, was to bear children, and only
the second to be a companion to her husband; and S. Bernardino of Siena in
a sermon admonished his congregation: "Take a wife, a beautiful wife, well-
built, good-tempered, wise, and one who will give you many children. Sad is
the life of a man who stays alone." It was indeed the duty of every young man
to marry and have children. Alberti advised a father to disinherit his son if he
did not take a wife at the appropriate time—not before he was 25, potent and
mature; and in fact at Lucca in 1454 no public office could be held by a man

who was still unwed at the age of 27. The commune awarded premiums for
every marriage concluded to the public officials who arranged them. Another
writer held that 21 was the ideal age for a man to marry, "so that he does not
hinder his growth," and that a girl should not be too young, "so that she gives
birth to a weak child; and she is at the greatest danger in childbirth." A case
is recorded of the papal dispensation for the annulment of a marriage where
the husband was too young to consummate. Officially girls were marriageable
at 12, but in practice 15 or 16 was the customary age, recognised institution-
ally by the Florentine Dowry Bank, which paid back investments made by a
father when his daughter had reached this age.

Marriage and childbed had their own important rituals and inspired
their own art. The emphasis of the marriage ceremony was not on the sacra-
ment but on the consummation, which in some cases was regarded as the only
token that a marriage had taken place. Until the Council of Trent in the
sixteenth century, the intervention of a priest and the holding of a religious
service was unnecessary to a marriage; and a case in Venice in 1443 shows how
casual the whole arrangement could be. A merchant passing through a street
called up to a widow sitting at a window:

> "Woman, find some servant-girl for me."
> "Fool," replied the widow, "do you want me to play the bawd?"
> "I don't mean that," said the man, "I mean as my wife."
> "Well then," returned the widow, "by God's faith, I'll find one for you.
>   Come back tomorrow."

The merchant returned the following day and found a girl, Maria, with
a witness, who asked the couple whether they wanted to be married, "as God
and Holy Church command." They both agreed and gave hands, took a wedding breakfast with the household and consummated the marriage. One of
the mildest rites was the putting of the bridal pair to bed by the groom's
family, of which we have an account in 1491 on the return of Anna Sforza
and Alfonso d'Este to Ferrara after their wedding. In the evening, wrote a
correspondent to the bride's father,

> we stood talking for a while, and then the bride and groom were put to bed,
> and we all went up with them right to the bed, laughing at them. On don
> Alfonso's side was the Marquis of Mantua with many others who taunted
> him, and he defended himself with a piece of stick; it seemed strange to
> both of them to see so many people around their bed, all saying some pretty
> thing as they usually do in these cases. We left, and the following morning
> we wanted to know how things had gone, and found that they had both
> slept very well, as indeed we believed they ought to have done.

Marriages by proxy were solemnised by the proxy's sitting with the bride
on a bed and touching her bare leg with his own. When Galeazzo Maria

Sforza wedded Bona of Savoy in Paris, his brother Tristano acted as proxy, and the prince was pleased that the ceremony had been carried out "on a bed with you on one side and her on the other." He was also reassured, however, that, even had the two been closer "you would have behaved only as befits a good brother."

From the point of view of the conservation of the family this anxious emphasis on the procreative function of marriage was wholly just, for the rate of infant mortality was staggeringly high. Pope Pius II in his autobiography recorded that his mother "was so fruitful that she often gave birth to twins, and by her [his father] had eighteen children, though there were never more than ten living at once . . . the cruel plague finally carried off all but Enea [Pius himself] and his sisters Laodamina and Caterina." This precariousness of the family situation makes more comprehensible the prevailing Italian attitude towards legitimacy, which was far more liberal than in other parts of Europe. It was accentuated by the Church's prohibition of divorce. Not that usage was uniform throughout Italy. In Venice, where bastards were sometimes called, incongruously, "spiritual sons" in wills, a law of 1430 forbade even legitimised natural sons to sit in the Great Council; and with the increasing concern for purity of noble blood a register of legitimate births was established there in 1506. Bastards were given another paternity, and at baptism their real names were concealed under the formula *Not allowed to be named in this place*. But in Tuscany there was much less rigidity. In 1456 Antonio Guinizzi de' Rizzi successfully petitioned the Archbishop of Florence to legitimise his son by a slave, since his wife had given him no heir. Here the slave girl was not freed; but the Prato merchant Francesco Datini did enfranchise at the same time as he legitimised his children by them; and one of these children, Ginevra, was cared for by his childless wife "as if she were my own, as indeed I consider her." She was given a handsome dowry of one thousand florins and married to a respectable wool merchant. Illegitimate children were included in the *casato*. In 1433 a Florentine brought home his bride to find already installed in the house his slave and the two sons she had had by him. They all continued to live together. Bastard sons were indeed often a most important element in the family, and it is noticeable that they were far more frequently legitimised than girls. Federigo Duke of Urbino obtained papal briefs for the legitimisation of two natural sons before the death of his childless first wife; and in the remarkable case of Cardinal Alessandro Farnese, later Pope Paul III, and the last of his line, "so that such a distinguished family should not decline for want of sons," ran the official account, "he had by a noble and free lady, later married to a baron, several children, whom he was able to legitimise."

The general concern with births was, however, confined to male children. A message from the French singer Jacques de Marville to Cosimo de' Medici was as specific as it was sycophantic: "God preserve you and arrange that the first night you sleep with your noble and illustrious wife, you may conceive a male child." When Alfonso d'Este's wife bore him Beatrice, he forebade any celebrations, "because he had wanted her to be a boy"; and Baldesar Castiglione's mother rated him in a letter because "it seems doubtful to me that I shall live long enough to see a son of yours; five years ago I expected to see one nine months later, and I went on feeding on fine words and promises; what other mother would have tolerated the absence of a single son?"

Girls were not able to pass on the family property, of which they inherited no more than a small portion, since a man's estate passed to his brothers in the absence of sons. It was sons alone who were regarded as the conservators of the family patrimony. Worse, girls were a great liability, since they had to be furnished with dowries. Sanuto wrote that families were made or ruined through the dowries they received or gave. According to Roman marriage law, which prevailed from the fourteenth century, the dowry represented a girl's inheritance from her father; and it was doubtful whether a girl marrying without her father's consent had a right to one at all. If her husband died, she could claim it back in full, but if the couple were separated through her adultery her husband kept it. In the fourteenth century dowries had been largely in goods, but later money portions became the rule; and they were carefully regulated according to the social status of the parties. A Venetian law of 1420, made in order to prevent nobles from having to send all their daughters to convents rather than bear the expense of marriages, restricted dowries to 1600 ducats, two thirds of which were to be in money, and one in goods; but non-noble girls marrying into noble families could bring up to 2000 ducats. By the end of the century Sanuto records dowries of 3000 ducats, and in 1517 a Capello girl brought her husband 15,000 ducats, plus 500 in credits in Government Stock and another 500 in clothes and jewelry. An early sixteenth-century bourgeois dowry in Venice averaged 1000 ducats.

In Naples the average fifteenth-century noble dowry of 1200 ducats had nearly doubled by the following century; and in Rome, where a statute of 1469 limited dowries to 800 cameral florins (the Medici had just received 6000 there), they similarly rose to above 3000. In Genoa, 3000 lire was already common among the nobility in the early fifteenth century; and a figure of 4500, plus 500 lire in trousseau is recorded for 1461.

Florence, however, offers the most interesting cases of dowry inflation, for the great social need led to the founding of a Dowry Bank in 1425, to provide in the first instance emergency finance for the war against Milan. Stock was purchased in the name of the daughter, and matured at the end of 15 years. By 1470 this fund accounted for more than half of the Florentine revenue; and when in 1477, in the wake of a series of financial crises, the payment of dowries was more than 16 months in arrears, a contemporary noted: "There is a great deal of outcry and infamy in the city. If no remedy is found, this institution, which is so needful to the city, will be ruined." As the Venetian ambassador noted in 1527, the Bank was a sure profit to the state, "an alchemy, so to speak," since many girls died before reaching marriageable age, or went into convents, in which case their stock was forfeit.

Yet even this useful and profitable expedient did not remove the anxieties of Florentine parents, for here, as everywhere, dowry inflation was rampant, and Allessandra Macinghi Strozzi noted in the third quarter of the fifteenth century that even artisans expected a thousand florins. When in 1447 she settled her daughter Caterina, the letter to the girl's brother expressed all the solicitude and complication of a Florentine betrothal:

> we have placed our Caterina with the son of Parente di Pier Parenti, who is an upstanding young man, virtuous and a bachelor, rich and 25 years old, with a silk workshop. They have some property, and it is not long since the father was in the government. And so I am going to give her a dowry of 1000 florins; that is 500 that she will have from the Fund in May next year, and the other 500 I have to give her in cash and the trousseau when she joins her husband, which I think will be in November, God willing. This money is partly yours and partly mine. If I had not taken this step she would not have been married this twelvemonth, for he who takes a wife wants cash, and I could not find anyone prepared to wait for the dowry in 1448 and a part in 1450, so that, as I am giving her this 500 in cash and trousseau, the 1450 instalment will also fall to me, if she lives. This step has been taken for the best, for she is 16 and there was no time to be lost marrying her off. We did have the chance of putting her in a better position and with more gentility, but with 1400 or 1500 florins, which would have been the ruin of both of us, and I don't know how the girl would have liked it herself. . . .

The marriage-settlement was a great family responsibility; the Neapolitan humanist Tristano Carracciolo had to endow all his sisters before he was able, in his thirties, to marry himself. The dowry payment could be a long-standing family commitment, even where the Dowry Bank provided as much as was intended (and by 1478 repayments had sunk to a quarter of the sum due). When the Florentine patrician Cino Rinuccini married in 1460, his wife brought him a dowry totalling 1400 florins, 1000 from the Fund, 200 when he took her to wife, in cash and goods (including an *Hours of the Virgin* in a cover embroidered with silver and pearls, and a pair of scissors), and 200 which was to be paid by his brother-in-law within eight years. The difficulties of recovering the balance could be numerous, and Alberti advised small dowries in ready money rather than large ones spread over a period of time. He painted a vivid picture of the behaviour of the in-laws:

> As the bride is sitting in your house, in the first year nothing seems to be allowed but confirming the relationship with frequent visits and junketings. Perhaps it is thought to be insensitive, among the relatives and festivities, to take a firm line and litigate; so new husbands tend to ask with slow and restrained words so as not to affront the still tender relationship; and it seems

that every little excuse must be accepted. And if you demand satisfaction more boldly, they produce an endless catalogue of their own needs, lamenting their ill-fortune, blaming the times, taking men to task. . . . [They are] generous in promising to satisfy you, in so far as it is in them, at a later date, pleading with you and winning you over. . . .

In these circumstances it was an act of conspicuous charity to provide poor girls with dowries. Pope Sixtus IV would send the girls he thus endowed in procession, with jewelled gowns, and attendants with mules bearing their trousseaus. Michelangelo write to a rich nephew that the charity shown in demanding no portion from his wife would relieve him of the obligation to humour "the luxuries and whims of women," and her health and temper were far more valuable assets. The appallingly grave financial and family consequences of a mistaken match make understandable the universal arrangement of marriages by the parents, often many years in advance.

I write to inform you [said Bernardo Ruccellai to Piero de' Medici's wife in 1477] that your Lorenzo has given in marriage to my Cosimo [his nephew, aged eight] . . . a daughter of the Marchese Gabrielle Malaspina [aged five]. This connection as you will understand, is most suitable in every way, and is much grander than we might have expected.

But the problem was common to the middle classes to, and in 1480 Machiavelli's father was at some pains to unmake a love-match involving his daughter, which had been made without his consent and was impossible because the dowry had not yet matured in the Fund and there was no other money available for a provisional settlement.

These dominant interests and pre-occupations with family solidarity were fully shared by the Medici, who had understood them long before their emergence as a political force in Florence in 1434. The family had been prominent in Florentine banking since the thirteenth century and already about a century later one of their members, Veri di Cambio, was one of the 16 richest men in the city, and had married into the old aristocratic house of the Strozzi. In 1385, Cosimo il Vecchio's father brought the largest dowry of the century, 1500 florins, into the family; and he married two sons, including Cosimo himself, into the ancient Florentine families of the Bardi and the Cavalcanti-Malaspini. As early as 1373, when the family was numerically in decline as a result of successive plagues, one of them could write in his memorandum:

I urge you . . . to conserve not only the possessions but also the status acquired by our ancestors, which is great, and was still greater in the past, and which began to decline as a result of the lack of valiant men . . . so great were we that there was a saying, "You are like one of the Medici," and all men feared us.

Cosimo's father, Giovanni di Bicci, deliberately kept out of politics and built up the family fortune which established their prosperity in the fifteenth century. When Pope Martin V made him Count of Monteverde in 1422, he refused to assume the title. Cosimo likewise preferred to play down his political interests and consolidate the family business, so that where Giovanni di Bicci had died in 1428 as the third richest man in Florence, by 1457 the family was by far the richest of all, although some branches of it were still poor, including the heirs of that Veri di Cambio who had amassed such a fortune in the previous century. Knowing the deep Florentine distrust of through financial pressures, in which they were helped by an electoral system magnates, Giovanni di Bicci and Cosimo preferred to work more subtly through financial pressures, in which they were helped by an electoral system which made solvency a qualification for political office. Cosimo was only three times a Gonfalonier of Justice and held only ten other important government posts in his long career; but for long periods in the 1440s and 1450s he was, significantly, an official of the Public Debt, still the chief financial resource of the state. In his political faction were to be found new families like the Cocchi Donati and the Pucci, who had major holdings in government stock. On his deathbed Cosimo appealed for a modest funeral and tomb; and it was only foreigners unfamiliar with Florentine political conventions who interpreted his rôle as that of a despot.

His eldest son, Piero the Gouty, head of the family between 1464 and 1469, was distinctly less reticent. His lavish activities as a patron of art were the expression of aspirations far beyond those of a merchant, brilliant though he was in the management of the Medici Bank. His marriage of his son Lorenzo (later called The Magnificent) into the old Roman noble family of the Orsini in 1468, is a first sign of the really Continental aspirations of the clan; and the manner of its arrangement shows to what extent they had already socially arrived.

> Everything has been agreed in the following fashion [reported the Archbishop of Pisa to Piero] that they shall give a dowry of 6000 Roman florins in money, jewels and dresses; which they stipulate should return to their heirs should she not have children or dispose of it by will. They agree that you should not give her the fourth part of the dowry as is customary here; and in this and in all other matters the Florentine custom and usage is to be followed, save in the restitution of the dowry if she dies *without sons and intestate.*

The ceremonies in Florence were, however, according to an eye-witness,

> prepared for a marriage rather than for a magnificent feast, and I think this was done . . . as an example to others not to exceed the modesty and simplicity suitable to marriages, so that there was never more than one roast. . . . Of silver plate there was but little. No sideboards had been placed for

the silver . . . there was none for the guests save the basins and jugs for the washing of hands. . . . The common folk were not invited.

With Lorenzo's accession to power in 1469 the political dominance of the family was an open fact.

The second day after my father's death [he wrote in his memoirs] though I was very young at the time, not more than 21, the chiefs of the state came to our house and . . . requested me to undertake the charge of the state, as my grandfather and father had done; which request, from a weighty sense of my youth, and of the great responsibility and danger of the task, I acceded to very reluctantly, and only for the sake of being in a position likely to keep our friends and ourselves secure; for in Florence there is no living without the support of the government.

Even during the lifetime of his father the 16-year-old boy had been petitioned by a member of an old Florentine family: "I pray you will help me in the way [the bearer of the letter] tells you, for with four words you can give me a place in the world again. Lorenzo, I will be your slave for ever."

A comparison of ambassadorial letters to Lorenzo with those to the government committee show that it was far more important to keep him well informed than they, although he never actually held office in the Signory itself. Like Cosimo, however, he was long an official of the Funded Debt, and frequently in the important office of selector of names for election, a post whose development at the expense of the traditional system of lots had been one of the chief means of Medici power. Well might he advise his son Piero, on embassy to Rome in 1484, to respect the other ambassadors, "for although you are my son, you are still no other than a Florentine citizen, as they are too." The facts of the situation were long clear; and a few years later he asked the Florentine ambassador in Rome to find for the same Piero a fine jewel so that he might appear at some festivities "more honourably" than the rest.

With Lorenzo and his son the Medici fortunes went into a commercial and political decline from which they never recovered. But they had established themselves as perhaps the leading Italian family, and in token of this, as a symbol of their international status, were the two Popes, who came in quick succession from their ranks. When Giovanni de' Medici, later Pope Leo X, became a cardinal at the unprecedented age of 14 in 1488, his father Lorenzo wrote a characteristic memoir of the fact, "because it is the greatest thing that our family ever did," and in a long letter of admonition to the boy he emphasised that his first duty was to the Church, but the second was to his city and his family, "for the family goes with the city." It was because the last, illegitimate, scion of this Medici line, the Duke Alessandro, had not married before he was assassinated in his late twenties, that the fortunes of the family passed irretrievably to an older and more obscure branch of the family in 1537.

Touring the Holy Land

H. F. M. PRESCOTT

From late imperial times, pilgrims traveled to shrines throughout Europe, and from the eleventh century on, many of them went to Jerusalem and the holy places in its vicinity. The establishment of the Latin Kingdom of Jerusalem after the First Crusade (1099) facilitated the movement of pilgrims to that area, and in the twelfth century, the first of several knightly orders was formed to protect pilgrims on their way to and in the Holy Land. The first order was the Knights Templar and they, in conjunction with other orders formed later, built a series of fortresses along the pilgrimage routes. Many of these still stand today.

In early times, pilgrims were probably the most numerous travelers in Europe —along with some Jewish merchants whose activities are the subject of Irving Agus' "Jews in a Christian Society" in Part 2. By the later Middle Ages, commercial travelers were by far the most important group, although the number of pilgrims had also increased dramatically. The pilgrims followed the trade routes and in fact became an important part of the traffic going through the great Italian commercial centers. The seriousness with which the city fathers of Venice and other cities regarded the pilgrim trade is demonstrated by the elaborate controls they imposed on those who transported the travelers. It is clear that ship captains in the Italian cities maintained a regular transportation service for the pilgrims and that the authorities wanted to ensure the continuation of the flow of pilgrim-tourists through their ports.

In turn, the pilgrims have helped historians by leaving many accounts of their journeys across the Mediterranean. These travel diaries are the principal source of our knowledge of the conditions of transport and travel in the fifteenth and sixteenth centuries. The longest of the fifteenth-century accounts is by Friar Felix, a Dominican from Ulm in southern Germany who made two trips, one in 1480 and one in 1483. Felix's diary serves as the basis of the following description by H. F. M. Prescott.

In the year 1480, just at that season in which, as Chaucer knew, men long to go on pilgrimage, namely on April 14, Felix, having preached his farewell sermon, mounted his horse, and with Prior Ludwich Fuchs set out for Memmingen, where he should meet "Master George." Of the start from the convent at Ulm he says nothing; the parting from Fuchs was what mattered; at Memmingen next morning the two friends kissed, not without tears,

From H. F. M. Prescott, *Friar Felix at Large* (New Haven: Yale University Press, 1950), pp. 36–61. Reprinted by permission of Collins-Knowlton-Wing, Inc. Copyright © 1950 by H. F. M. Prescott.

the Prior insisting that Felix should promise to remember him at the Holy Places, to write (if he might find a messenger), to come back soon. "Then sadly he left me, returning with the servant to Ulm, to his sons, my brothers there." That parting took away at a stroke all Felix's courage and all his delight in pilgrimage. "And I raged at myself for having entered upon it. All who would have dissuaded me I thought of now as my best counselors and true friends; those who had led me into it I reckoned my deadly enemies. At that moment I had rather look on Swabia than on the land of Canaan, Ulm was sweeter to me than Jerusalem; I was more frightened than ever about the sea, and . . ." (this is a most honest traveler) "if I had not been ashamed I should have hurried after Master Ludwig and gone back to Ulm with him, for that was what then I most longed for."

Shame, however, did prevent that flight from the unknown; Felix, with the young man and his servant, set out for Innsbruck, and by the time they reached the Alps the Friar is able to use one of his favorite words, for already they were traveling "merrily," having discovered, as they came to make each other's acquaintance, "that we and our tastes agreed well together." So that though they had lost their way, and though, having no common language with the people of the inn, they could use only signs, their night at Bassano, with as much of the local red wine as they liked to drink, must have been cheerful.

So much, without any information about mileages, or rates of exchange ("let those who want such, read other books of pilgrimages"), without even a mention of relics seen and revered upon the way, is all that Felix says of this first stage in their pilgrimage, which landed them at that great port of pilgrim travel—the city of Venice.

Even before the fifteenth century Venice had monopolized the pilgrim traffic to Jerusalem, and, as with her other concerns, had organized it with a thoroughness and precision which belong rather to the modern than to the medieval world, the state itself often fulfilling the functions both of the shipping company and the travel agency, and when allowing individual enterprise, minutely and jealously controlling it.

Directly he reached Venice the pilgrim found himself the object of almost fatherly care on the part of the state. There were inns for him to put up at, and license to keep such an inn must be sought from the Senate. But it was not enough that his lodging should be respectable; the crowds of pilgrims which poured into Venice each pilgrimage season must be shepherded about the strange city and protected from those who would exploit them. For this purpose, since a time long before that of Felix's pilgrimage, the Venetian State had regularly appointed officials called *Cattaveri*, and, under them, a number of "Piazza Guides." At the beginning of the century two of the twelve Piazza guides must be on duty during every week, keeping, from dawn to dusk, their station either on the Rialto or in the Piazza of St. Mark, and these two must have command of more than one foreign language between them. Human nature being what it is, these guides at one time began to make a practice of taking the dinner hour off. This would not do; it was enacted that while one dined the other must remain on duty; later the Senate softened, and the dinner hour was allowed.

The business of these officers was to interpret for the pilgrims, to help them to obtain the correct exchange for their money, to see that they were not fleeced in the shopping so necessary for the next stage of their journey, to bring them into contact with the captains of the pilgrim galleys, and to a certain extent advise them in the agreements which were then made. Over all these activities the Cattaveri kept a sort of watching brief; appeal could be made at any time to them, the contract between captain and pilgrims must be handed in at their office three days before it was signed.

The records of the Venetian Senate show what vigilance and ingenuity were needed in order that the profiteering tendencies of innkeepers and guides might be thwarted. But the battle against their peccadilloes was as nothing to that against the greed and insubordination to statute of the captains; all of them of the great noble houses of Venice, and by the circumstances of the case removed for the greater part of the voyage from supervision by the state.

From as far back as the early years of the thirteenth century the Senate had laid down regulations which, if observed, should insure the safety and comparative comfort of their pilgrim clients. Every pilgrim galley sailing from Venice must have a cross painted at a certain level on the hull; this served the same purpose as our Plimsoll mark, lading with relation to this cross being graded according to the age, and hence the seaworthiness, of the vessel. So many sailors, so many rowers, must be shipped; sailors in the earlier century, and again during the dangerous times of the Ottoman advance, must be provided with arms, must be over eighteen, must take an oath to look after ship and tackle, and not to steal more than five small soldis' worth. Captains must be at least thirty years old. In order to prevent these noble captains from merely painting up ancient and unseaworthy craft, the magistrates were instructed to send experts to inspect these before sailing, and the Venetian governors at various ports were made responsible for seeing that the captains of the pilgrim galleys did not load them up with any more merchandise than was agreed upon between captain and pilgrims. But this list of provisions, regulations, prohibitions could be prolonged almost indefinitely. Let us sum it up by saying that no possible opportunity seems to have been lost by the Venetian captains for making something "on the side" out of the pilgrim traffic, and that such sharp practice was nosed out and forbidden (as we shall see, vainly forbidden) by the state, through a period of more than three hundred years.

The great flow of Jerusalem pilgrims to Venice was accommodated for the journey in three different classes of vessels. For the rich, the "V.I.P.'s" of the period, there was the galley, hired out by the Venetian State to the noble pilgrim. For the poor there was the sailing ship. For the vast mass of pilrgims there was the regular service of galleys, timed to leave Venice at two seasons of the year, that is to say soon after Easter and soon after Ascension Day.

The practice of hiring a galley to persons of wealth and importance was considered by the Venetian State as part of their foreign policy. With the enlightened self-interest fitting in a nation of splendid shopkeepers, the Senate in 1392 declared that it was "wise and prudent to oblige the princes of the world . . . having in view the facilities and favors which our merchants trading in those ports may receive and obtain."

Though so candid about their motive, the Fathers of the State seem to have been less truthful about the terms of their bargain in this case. The minutes of their meeting state that the galley in which Henry of Lancaster, later Henry IV, passed oversea to the Holy Land was lent, furnished, and stocked free. The earl's account books tell another tale; a payment of 2,785 ducats goes down under the heading of "Skippagium" for the hire of the galley. However the Signory voted 300 ducats to be spent on a farewell entertainment before Henry sailed and another 100 for a similar function on his return. And, one way or another, the sprat caught its mackerel, for when Henry of Lancaster became Henry King of England in 1399 he promised to treat all Venetians as his own subjects.

Lancaster was by no means the only great noble to whom the Senate hired out their galleys for the Jerusalem journey. His enemy, Mowbray of Norfolk, in 1399; a Portuguese prince in 1406; and others throughout the fifteenth century made the pilgrimage in this way.

While the great went overseas, each with his own household, in a galley, lent or hired by the Venetian State, the poor would travel most cheaply in a sailing ship. When the writer of the *Informacōn for Pylgrymes* sailed with "Luke Mantell" each of forty-six pilgrims on board paid as he could afford 32, 26, or 24 ducats for his return fare to Jatfa, with food included. Devout captains sometimes carried friars "for the love of God." The less devout took them at a reduced rate, charging 15 to 20 ducats for the voyage out and back.

But the ordinary run of pilgrims traveled in the regular service of pilgrim galleys, though even among these ordinary pilgrims there were often to be found great men who, whether from motives of humility or parsimony, arrived in Venice and took their passage without advertising their wealth and rank. This practice caused the Signory considerable anxiety, ". . . on account of the abominable way in which princes, counts and other foreign noblemen who went disguised as pilgrims, to the Holy Sepulchre, on board our galleys, had been and were actually treated" by avaricious galley captains. What such treatment could be we shall see later, for Felix and his companions sailed with a captain notorious for his avarice and bad faith. The Venetian State, acutely sensitive to the opinion of such great persons, ". . . considering how much they can injure or aid those of our merchants and citizens who pass through their countries," could only continue its unending battle against the erring captains.

Apart from keeping constant watch over the condition of the pilgrim galleys, and this might mean, as in 1473, the condemning of a vessel which had seen twenty years' service, the state did what it could to protect the pilgrims in the formal contract, made between them and whatever captain was to carry them overseas. Enactment and re-enactment follow each other in the minutes of the Senate; but in spite of all, at the end of the century it was necessary to decree that captains must find four sureties to be bound to the amount of 250 ducats each for the observation of the contract; the injured pilgrims should be compensated by the sureties, and the defaulting captain punished by the state.

The pilgrims themselves, profiting by the long experience that lay behind them, did what they could, in these contracts, to safeguard themselves, and there is a common form which the contract usually follows. The fare was more or less fixed by custom. Surian, in 1500, says that pilgrims were charged according to their quality, and that the sums ranged from 30 to 60 ducats, with 13½ ducats for sight-seeing expenses in the Holy Land. In 1483 Bernhard von Breydenbach's party, which sailed with Agostino Contarini, paid 42 ducats each; Felix and his company, in the ship of Pietro Lando, paid 40. The *Informacōn for Pylgrymes* on the other hand says that you must pay 50 ducats for "freight and for meat and drink . . . for to be in a good honest place, and to have your ease in the galley and to be cherished." Casola, fourteen years later than Felix, but traveling with the captain of Felix's first pilgrimage, paid 60 gold ducats. But this was to cover his keep "by sea and land" and a place at the captain's table.

This fare covered more than the transport to and from Jaffa. On board ship the captain was to provide a hot meal twice a day with good wine (but, said the pilgrims, there was always plenty of water in it), and "to each of us a bicker or small glass of Malvoisie" every morning before breakfast. In port, on the voyage, pilgrims provided their own food, unless it were an "uninhabited harbour," where the captain must feed them. Once arrived at Jaffa it was the duty of the captain to arrange and pay for the transit of the pilgrims to Jerusalem; that is to say "all dues, all money for safe-conducts, and for asses and other expenses, in whatever names they may be charged . . . or in whatever place they have to be paid, shall be paid in full by the captain alone, on behalf of all the pilgrims without their being charged anything . . ." The anxious precision of the clause indicates what pitfalls were known to lie in the path of overconfiding pilgrims.

This "lump sum" payment, satisfactory in one way to the pilgrim, had its drawbacks. It was necessary to stipulate that "the captain shall let the pilgrims remain in the Holy Land for the due length of time, and shall not hurry them through it too fast . . ." The "due time" was a fortnight from landing to departure, and as we shall see, Felix in his first pilgrimage was denied even this short period.

Other clauses, among the twenty or so which may appear, seek to insure the pilgrims against the captain keeping them waiting, and wasting their money in Venice; against his calling at unnecessary, unusual, and strange ports on his way; against his trying to prevent them going out of Jerusalem to the Jordan. It is stipulated that he shall protect the pilgrims from the galley slaves; shall, if a pilgrim die on the journey return half the fare to his executors; shall not interfere with the goods of the dead man; and shall, if possible, put into port for the burial. A sick pilgrim shall be given a place to lie out of the "stench of the cabin"—but that might mean no better refuge than one of the rowers' benches. Not only the pilgrims but the Venetian State itself tried to prevent the captains of the pilgrim galleys from adding to their legitimate profits by private trading on the homeward run. In 1417 two captains were prosecuted for crowding the pilgrims with their merchandise; next year, though it was admitted that the officers and oarsmen had the right to trade, their merchandise must not overflow into the ship but must be contained in boxes; in 1440, and again twelve years later, trading was forbidden to the captains. But prohibitions and prosecutions were in vain.

On his first pilgrimage Felix sailed in the galley of one of the most notorious of these patrician profiteers. Agostino Contarini, Agostino dal Zaffo ("of Jaffa") as he came to be known, had already begun his long career as a pilgrim captain, and had begun it badly, since in his voyage of 1479 he had found himself succeeding to the inheritance of a nasty quarrel between the captain of the previous year and the Saracens. That had meant loss instead of profit; even in 1480 he thought it wiser to bring as a present to the Saracen governor of Syria one of the famous glass vessels of Murano. He was therefore determined to recoup himself. The state allowed him to raise his charges to 55 golden ducats for each pilgrim and throughout the voyage he saw to it that wherever he might he would spend a little less on, or wring a little more out of, the pilgrims; or would cheat the Saracens; or would do a little private trading on his own account.

At Ramle, when he must pay dues to the Saracens for every man who went up to Jerusalem, he tried to pass off fifteen of the pilgrims (without their knowledge of the deal) as sailors of the galley's crew, ". . . so that he should pay for them only half the tribute, although he had had from each 55 ducats. And certain of the pilgrims passed as crew, and the others were refused . . . and thus the said captain's trick failed, although he made a lot on those who passed."

At Jerusalem the pilgrims fell foul of him again, for he would not provide them with an escort to make the Jordan expedition, though this, they insisted, had been included in the contract. At Ramle on the way home he demanded a ducat and 8 *marcelins* from each of them for the hire of donkeys;

those stouter spirits who refused, and who continued to refuse, were brought to order at Jaffa by the threat that they would be left behind.

When all were on board he kept the ship waiting at Jaffa from "Thursday to Friday evening" in order to trade; and his merchandise must have added to the discomfort of the pilgrims, for already "our whole galley was cluttered with the 600 or 800 ducats' worth of good Jaffa cotton" which was the result of the trading ventures of the officers and crew. Nor was the captain yet satisfied, for at Cyprus he loaded up with ". . . lovely salt, white as crystal . . . in fine pieces like tiles, four or six fingers thick . . ." from the salt lake at Larnaca.

Fourteen years later Agostino dal Zaffo, still in the pilgrim trade, had not changed his ways. Casola, a friendly critic, thought that the amount of Cyprus carob beans brought to the galley at Limasol was "stupendous. . . . sufficient to supply all the world . . ." At Crete, on the homeward run, the pilgrims, "satiated with so much malmsey and muscatel . . . began to say to the captain that he must take them away from there, and that if he wanted to trade in malmsey or anything else he could do it at his good pleasure, provided he sent the company to Venice."

Apart from the momentous affair of their agreement with the galley captain the pilgrims' most serious business in Venice was shopping for the voyage. It is remarkable and I think curious, that Felix himself, even in the full flood of his reminiscences of his second pilgrimage, says little of this, though quite a lot when he comes to describe the setting out from Jerusalem of the pilgrims for Sinai that same year. At Venice he briefly remarks that "we went to the market and bought all that we should need on our galley for the voyage—cushions, mattresses, pillows, sheets, coverlets, mats, jars, and so forth . . . I bade them buy a mattress for me stuffed with cows' hair, and I had brought woollen blankets with me from Ulm . . ."

Other pilgrims are far more particular in their lists and earnest in the advice that they give. You must have a feather bed and bedding, pillow slips and two pairs of sheets. You should buy the bed mattress and pillows from a man near St. Mark's. They will cost you 3 ducats, and when you come back you can sell them again, even if "broken and worn," for half that. You should also buy a chest and see that it has a lock and key. Buy barrels, two for wine and one for water. The best water for keeping is to be drawn at St. Nicholas, and when that is used up fill the barrel again at any port of call. As for wine, there is none so good for the voyage as that of Padua, "which is a little wine, bright red, and not strong." The wines that you will find on the voyage are so strong that they cannot be drunk (fearful things are said of the effect upon the inner man of Cyprian wine: drunk neat it will burn up the entrails, therefore dilute it with anything up to four quarts of water). A wise man will keep his Paduan wine to drink on the return voyage. It is well to have "a little caldron, a frying pan, dishes . . . saucers of tree [wood], cups of glass [an unexpected refinement] a grater for bread . . ."

Although the pilgrims while on board ship were provided with two meals a day by the captain, they did not build much upon these, "for some time ye shall have feeble bread and feeble wine and stinking water so that many times ye will be right fain to eat of your own." So, besides flour and firewood they would buy hams or salt ox-tongues; Englishmen took bacon; Italians would take "good Lombard cheese" and sausage; all would take cheese of some sort, eggs, bread, and biscuit, ". . . that is bread twice baked which keeps without going bad, and it is so well baked that it is as hard three days after as it is at the end of a year." Fruit was important, dried apples and dates, figs and raisins, spices too, unless you were prepared to eat tasteless food, so take "pepper saffron cloves and maces a few as ye think need, and loaf sugar also."

An Italian adds such refinements as sugar "of the best quality" and above all fruit syrup, ". . . for it is that which keeps a man going in that great heat . . ."; some syrup of ginger to be used, but with discretion, after seasickness; quinces, unspiced; "aromatics flavoured with rose and carnation," the necessity for which is made sufficiently clear by an Englishman's vivid description of the lower deck on a galley as a place "right evil and smoldering hot and stinking." The Italian adds also, with startling modernity, "some good milk products."

Besides all these it was well to "hire you a cage for half a dozen of hens or chickens to have with you . . . And buy you half a bushel of millet seed at Venice for them." Nor would even this bulk of provision be sufficient: wherever the ship touches on the voyage the pilgrim "should furnish himself with eggs and fowls, bread, sweetmeats and fruit, and not count what he has paid to the captain, because" (it is a wealthy Italian speaking) "this is a journey on which the purse cannot be kept shut." In addition to all that he brought the rich and influential pilgrim might, while at Venice arrange, as von Harff did, for letters of credit.

Having provided as far as possible for all needs, the pilgrims almost always found themselves forced to wait upon, as they were convinced, the pleasure of the captain, or, as he regularly maintained, a favorable wind. This delay, during which the pilgrims fretted, and which the anxious state tried by successive legislation to restrict to reasonable dimensions, the pilgrims would fill in by sight-seeing, sacred or secular. But in 1480 Felix, still numbed by the "temptation" of homesickness, which "caused me to be dull and stupid both in viewing places of note . . . and also in writing accounts of them," says nothing at all about the beauties of that city, which his fellow pilgrim, the clerk from Paris, describes with such enthusiasm. Neither the curiosity and fascination of water instead of roadway, "the little barks and boats [which] go through the streets," nor the "twelve to fifteen hundred bridges, big and little, of stone or wood," nor "the fair houses which they call palaces," drew from Felix a word of notice. It is the Paris pilgrim who so carefully explains and so palpably admires the splendors of mosaic work: "the little pieces and bits of glass the size of a small silver penny . . . in gold and azure and other right rich colors . . . of these little bits are made the vaults and walls of the churches, all showing characters of the Old and New Testaments, and to each of these characters a writing, which describes the character, and the writing is made of the little bits, and the pavement is made up of small pieces of stone of all colors, in the shape of beasts, birds, and other most beautiful designs." It is the Paris pilgrim who describes the massed splendors of the treasure of St. Mark's, displayed at Ascensiontide, the "images, angels, chalices, patens, vessels, and chandeliers, all of gold, huge, thick, massive, and garnished with precious stones of price inestimable and of every color." While the Paris pilgrim climbed the campanile and looked down upon "the sea and the town," and "round about the town, towers, castles, churches, abbeys, houses of Religious, monasteries, hospitals, and villages . . . all in the midst of the sea"; while he visited the Arsenal, and stared at the reception of the Turkish ambassador and admired the nightly illuminations on the towers of Venice, Felix, for all we know to the contrary, moped in the inn of St. George, yet making friends, in spite of his melancholy, with Master John, the innkeeper, and Mistress Margaret, and with the big black dog, all of whom were to welcome him so warmly on his arrival at Venice three years later.

With this heavy mood upon him Felix passes by his first visit to Venice without a word. He and Master George came there, made their agreement with Agostino Contarini, and waited for the day on which they might sail, as all the rest of the pilgrims then gathered in Venice must wait. This company, scattered as yet among the many inns, included noblemen of various countries, "priests, monks, laymen, gentle and simple, from Germany . . . and France, and especially two Bishops, that is of Orleans and of Le Mans," besides English, Scots, Spanish, and Flemings. To the disgust of some of the noblemen there were as well no less than six wealthy matrons, who, though "through old age scarcely able to support their own weight . . ." intended the pilgrimage.

When at last the ship was ready to sail, news came which, to the expectant pilgrims, was a heavy, almost a disabling blow. A ship arriving in Venice reported that the Grand Turk was besieging the Knights in Rhodes and that the seas of the Levant swarmed with his ships. Whether to go or stay became the question which sowed "troubles, discord and quarrels" among the pilgrims, especially as the Venetian Senate refused to guarantee in any way the safety of the pilgrims themselves, though it did not prohibit the voyage, the galley being covered by the Turkish safe-conduct.

It was therefore after a period of painful indecision that on Thursday, June 7, "just before dinner time, all the pilgrims aboard, and the wind fair, the three sails were spread to the sound of trumpets and horns and we sailed out to the open sea . . ."

When he came to write his book for the stay-at-home brethren at Ulm, Felix dealt thoroughly with the subject of ships, and from his account and that of Casola we learn much of the disposition of the pilgrim galleys and the routine of life aboard.

Felix, according to his custom, goes right back to the elements, and enumerates three kinds of ships "which are great, middle-sized and small ones," refers to the reputed invention of the first ship, and so, working his way gradually onward to the present and the particular, declares that he will deal only with the galley, "an oblong vessel which is propelled by sails and oars."

But here it is necessary to explain what is only implicit in the descriptions of the Friar and of Canon Casola. The pilgrim galleys formed part of the merchant fleet of Venice, and by this time were vessels of much greater draft than the fast war galleys. A large merchant galley could load two hundred and fifty tons of cargo below deck, so that she rode low in the water, and must depend for the greater part of the voyage upon her sails, being, in fact, practically a sailing ship, with the added convenience of oars for use in entering and leaving port. So Casola will state, though without explanation, that during his voyage the oars were little used, and Felix will remark that "when the sun rose, the galley slaves began to work the galley along with their oars," or that "before it was fully light the slaves rowed the galley out of the harbour as far as the corner of the mountain, where we committed her to the wind."

Again, though both Casola and Felix mention biremes and triremes, and Felix explains that one is "rowed by pairs and pairs of oars" and the other "by threes and threes of oars, because on each bench it has three oars and as many rowers," neither he nor Casola makes it clear that these benches were set at such an angle with the ship's side that the oar of the rower at the inboard end entered the water aft of that of his neighbor, and this man's oar aft of that of the rower nearest the gunwale.

Apart from this the two landsmen give a fairly exhaustive description of the galley. They speak of its narrow build, of the three masts, of the iron prow "made something like a dragon's head, with open mouth . . . wherewith to strike any ship which it may meet." Both were especially impressed by the ropes, "many, long, thick, and of manifold kinds. It is wonderful to see the multitude of ropes and their joinings and twinings about the vessel." Casola learnt with respect the price of the great anchor cable, and doubted whether "two Milanese waggons with two pairs of oxen to each could have carried all the ropes" in the galley.

Starting from the prow, with its small forecastle and sail, the two mention the rowers' benches, with the wide gangway between, laid upon chests of merchandise and running from prow to poop. Felix alone concerns himself with the rowers, most of them, he says, slaves of the captain, though there were others, wretched enough but free, from Albania, Macedonia, Illyria. They lived, ate, slept on the benches, if necessary chained there in port lest they should escape. "They are all big men; but their labours are only fit for asses . . . They are frequently forced to let their tunics and shirts hang down by their girdles, and work with bare backs . . . that they may be reached with whips and scourges. . . . They are so accustomed to their misery that they work feebly . . . unless someone stands over them and beats them like asses and curses them." When not at work they would gamble with cards or dice, shocking the good Friar with the incessant foulness of their language. Some were craftsmen, plying such trades as that of the tailor or shoemaker; all were traders, keeping their merchandise under their benches to sell when the ship made harbor, or to the pilgrims; they sold, says Felix, excellent wine.

At the galley's stern rose the tall, three-storied poop, upon which "the flag is always hoisted to show which way the wind blows." When Casola made his pilgrimage the "castle" was hung with canvas and with curtains of red cloth embroidered with devices of the Holy Sepulcher and the Contarini arms. In a latticed chamber in the topmost story was the steersman "and he who tells the steersman how the compass points, and those who watch the stars and winds, and point out the way across the sea." Below, on the deck level, was the captain's cabin, and the place where "the tables are spread for meals." Below again, when Felix made his first pilgrimage, "the noble ladies were housed at night," and the captain kept his treasure. Casola describes this lowest compartment as without windows, and says that it was used for sleeping and for storing arms and tackle.

A little forward of the poop, toward the starboard side, was the captain's food store. Between this and the ship's side stood the kitchen, open to the air, with its "large and small cauldrons, frying-pans and soup-pots—not only of copper, but also of earthenware—spits for roasting and other kitchen utensils." There were three or four cooks, very hot-tempered men, said Felix, but excusably so, considering the restricted space, the number of pots and things to be cooked, the smallness of the fire, and the shouting that went on outside as men clamored to have things made ready; "besides that the labor of cooks is always such as moves one to pity." Close and handy to the kitchen were the pens for the wretched animals, carried for food, but so ill nourished that by the end of the voyage they were little but skin and bone.

The pilgrims' cabin, "a kind of hall . . . supported by strong columns," was reached by four hatchways, and with ladders of seven steps, from the rowers' deck. It was spacious but unlighted, and here the berth space of each pilgrim was chalked out on the deck; one and a half feet was looked on as a fair allowance. In two long lines, at the feet of the pilgrims, stood each man's chest, but in the daytime mattress, pillows, and all must be rolled up, roped, and hung from a nail above the berth.

Below the pilgrims' cabin was the sand ballast, and this the pilgrims found a convenience, for they could lift the planks and bury in the sand wine, eggs, or anything that needed to be kept cool. Quite a different matter was the bilge water below, the stench of which was a sore trial to the pilgrims. But it was only one trial in many, for besides this they must suffer such inconveniences as smoke from the kitchen, rats, mice, fleas, and other vermin, but not (Providence being merciful in this to sailors) scorpions, vipers, toads, poisonous snakes, or spiders.

Comfort, and even peace, were rare on shipboard. Meals were a scramble for all except those noblemen who had their own servants and ate either on deck near the mainmast or by lantern light in the cabin. The ordinary pilgrim, when the four trumpets sounded for meals, must "run with the utmost haste to the poop," if he wanted to get a place at the three tables laid there; if he came late he must be content with a place on the rowers' benches "in the sun, the rain, or the wind." Even those at table were served in a hurry; they had malvoisie as an apéritif, and with the meal "as much wine . . . as one can drink, sometimes good, sometimes thin, but always well mixed and baptized with water." The food was, of course, cooked Italian fashion; at dinner a salad of lettuce in oil if there was any greenstuff to be had, then mutton, and some sort of pudding of meal, bruised wheat or barley; or else panada and cheese. On fast days salt fish with oil and vinegar took the place of meat, and there was a spongecake and a pudding. There was fresh bread only in harbor, or for the few days after; otherwise that biscuit of which the Paris pilgrim spoke, and which Felix describes as "hard as stones."

No sooner had the pilgrims finished eating than the trumpets sounded again, and they must get up from table so that this could be cleared and laid again for the captain and the other Venetian noblemen on board; who, though their fare was more frugal than that of the pilgrims, ate from silver, "and his [the captain's] drink is tasted . . . as is done to princes in our own country."

In between mealtimes pilgrims often found time hang heavy on their hands. "Some . . . go about the galley inquiring where the best wine is sold, and there sit down and spend the whole day over their wine. This is usually done by Saxons, Flemings, and other men of a low class. Some play for money [it was the Frenchmen who, according to Felix, were "gambling morning, noon, and night"] . . . Some sing songs, or pass their time with lutes, flutes, bagpipes, clavichords, zithers and other musical instruments. Some discuss worldly matters, some read books, some pray with beads; some sit still and meditate . . . some work with their hands, some pass almost the whole time asleep in their berths. Others run up the rigging, others jump, others show their strength by lifting heavy weights or doing other feats. Others accompany all these, looking on first at one, and then at another. Some sit and look at the sea and the land which they are passing, and write about them . . ." a feat of concentration upon which one at least of our authors, Santo Brasca, was rightly congratulated. *Mutatis mutandis*, the description would not be unapt for the passengers of many a liner today. One occupation, however, these later travelers are spared, which in Felix's day "albeit loathsome, is yet very common, daily, and necessary—I mean the hunting and catching of lice and vermin."

On deck, even in daytime, and whatever his occupation, the pilgrim must be on his guard. He must not meddle with ropes; he must not sit where a block will fall upon him; during this very voyage the chief officer himself was killed by a falling spar. Above all the landsman must not get in the way of the sailors, or, be he lord, bishop, or even officiating priest, they will throw him down and trample on him, so urgent is work at sea, to be done, as it were, "with lightning speed." If he sits down on the rowers' benches he is liable to be assaulted by these rough and desperate fellows.

His property, as well as his person, is always in danger. The rowers steal whatever they can lay hands on, but this is not so surprising as the strange habit of thieving which attacks even honest men at sea, "especially in the matter of trifles, such as kerchiefs, belts, shirts . . . For example, while you are writing, if you lay down your pen and turn your face away, your pen will be lost, even though you be among men whom you know . . ." And there are other lesser perils. The pilgrim must be careful "where he sits down . . . for every place is covered with pitch, which becomes soft in the heat of the sun." He must beware if he leans on the edge of the galley not to let anything of value slip from his hand into the sea, or he will lose it, as a nobleman talking to Felix lost a rosary of precious stones and Felix himself his Office Book.

If the day is full of discomforts and anxieties the night is worse. There is a "tremendous disturbance" while all are making their beds, with dust flying and tempers rising, till in disputes about the boundary for each man's berth "whole companies of pilgrims" take part, sometimes with swords and daggers. Even when most have settled down to sleep there will be latecomers who keep the rest awake by their talk and the lights they bring, which lights Felix had seen hot-tempered pilgrims extinguish, impolitely but effectively, with the contents of their chamber pots. And when all lights were out there were some incorrigible talkers who would "begin to settle the affairs of the world with their neighbours," continuing till midnight, and perhaps causing a fresh outbreak of noise and quarreling if some outraged companion called for silence.

For a man used to the quiet of his own cell rest was almost impossible. When all others slept Felix would be kept awake by the snoring of his fellows, the stamping of the penned beasts, and the trampling of the sailors on the deck above. The narrow bed, the hard pillow, the close proximity of his neighbors, the foul and hot air, the vermin, would drive him at last on deck, braving even the danger of being taken for a thief, to sit, "upon the woodwork at the sides of the galley, letting his feet hang down towards the sea, and holding on by the shrouds . . ."

There, though waking, the pilgrim found some good moments, at least in fair weather, for "the ship runs along quietly, without faltering . . . and all is still, save only he who watches the compass and he who holds the handle of the rudder, for these by way of returning thanks . . . continually greet the breeze, praise God, the Blessed Virgin and the saints, one answering the other, and are never silent as long as the wind is fair." Their chant reminded the Friar of the cry of the night watchmen at home, "which cry hinders no one from sleeping, but sends many restless folk to sleep."

But the freedom from anxiety necessary for the enjoyment of such rare moments cannot have been possible for the pilgrims who sailed from Venice at Ascensiontide in 1480, bound for Corfu, where they should find the Venetian Captain of the Sea and ask his permission to proceed on their pilgrimage. At Parenzo, their first port of call, they heard "horrible tales about the Turks." At Zara they dared not touch, for they heard there was plague there. Lesina (Hvar) they passed by in order to take advantage of a good wind, which changed presently and brought them to an uninhabited harbor on the Croatian coast; going ashore for diversion they found upon the beach "a corpse cast up by the sea, putrid and rotten"; a sign, so the sailors at once declared, of approaching disaster. Yet when, three days later, and after many unsuccessful attempts, a fair wind took them from that inhospitable coast they learnt from a passing Venetian war galley which they spoke that the contrary winds that had beaten them back into port had saved them from falling in with the Turkish fleet, even then on its way to sack Otranto.

The fear of the Turk was everywhere. At Curzola (Korčula) and Ragusa (Dubrovnik) they found that folk had either fled from, or hastily fortified, their towns. On the hills at night they saw the alarm beacons lit, and as they sailed along the wooded Albanian coast they might remember the strong places which Venice had held there, now in Turkish hands, and regret the days when timber from those forests was used to build Venetian galleys, but now served for the ships of the infidel. When they came to Corfu the Captain of the Sea called them fools for their pains, advised them to turn back, and threatened that if they persisted they must make shift for themselves, for he would not allow a galley of St. Mark's to go into such dangers as those which lay ahead.

Small shame to the pilgrims had they yielded to such pressure. Many did yield, among whom were two of the greatest of the German nobles and the two French bishops. The rest, foolhardy or courageous but certainly obstinate, after a week of wrangling ignored both advice and prohibition. They had come, they told the captain, ". . . from France, Spain, England, Scotland, Flanders, Germany, and other regions and countries at great cost and outlay, determined to accomplish their pilgrimage or die, according as it was the will of God . . ." They then made ready to leave and defiantly carried into the galley all that they had bought, but once on board, being solemnized by their peril, they took an oath not to gamble, swear, or quarrel any more, but to have litanies sung by the clerks on board. Next morning the trumpets were blown, the moorings cast off, and "with joy and singing" they left the harbor, where the other pilgrims laughed at them from the quay, those turning back being, doubtless, embittered by the fact that of each man's 55 ducats Contarini had repaid only 10.

Upon the remainder of the voyage out we need not linger. At Crete even the Turkish merchants trading there charitably advised them not to put to sea. They persisted, passed the dangerous proximity of Rhodes on a favorable gale, touched at Cyprus, and so on the third day out of Larnaca got their first sight of the Holy Land and came safe to Jaffa.

They had dared and suffered much but, as it proved, to little purpose. At Ramle Agostino Contarini was seized and kept in prison for four days, which time he, on his enlargement, took care to subtract from the pilgrims' time in Jerusalem, so that "we did not spend," says Felix, "more than nine days in the Holy Land, and in that time we rushed round the usual Holy Places in the utmost haste, making our pilgrimages both by day and night, and hardly given any time to rest . . . When we had hurriedly visited the Holy Places . . . we were led out of the Holy City, by the same road by which we had come, down to the sea where our galley waited."

That was all, after six weeks at sea and many perils. Felix's first pilgrimage would have been a miserable failure but for one thing. When at Jerusalem the Friar "firmly determined that I would return again." It was this resolve which prevented him at once undertaking the journey to Mount Sinai in company with two English pilgrims who were setting out thither—that and not the fact that he and the Englishmen had no common language. It was also, I think, this resolve which restored Felix to himself, so that on the journey home he was able to observe, to savor experience, and to laugh.

He had in any case sufficiently recovered himself to be equal to snubbing an ecclesiastical superior, though certainly the occasion was just and the provocation extreme. The pilgrims, sick and weary for home, were held up for three days in the open roadstead of Lanarca; they were told that the galley must wait for two bishops of Cyprus who were to be passengers. When these arrived, with a great cavalcade and much gear, the pilgrims, crowded enough already, found themselves worse off than ever, and what made their discomforts harder to bear, they could not like their new companions. One of the two dignitaries Felix passes over in silence, but upon the other his eye was fixed with disapproval and growing indignation. For the bishop of Paphos, though a friar of Felix's own order, was "a young man, beardless and lady-faced, and behaving like any woman too." He wore a friar's gown, but it was of costly cloth, and colored "with a tail at the back like a woman"; his fingers were covered with jeweled rings; round his neck was a golden chain. Besides all this his manners were bad; he squabbled constantly with his servants and looked down on everyone, especially the pilgrims, whom he would not allow to sit down with him.

One day "a certain priest, chaplain to one of the pilgrim knights,"—the anonymity is not so consistently kept but that we may not recognize Felix himself—"a certain priest" asked the young man "to move up a little from where he sat." The bishop's only answer was a disdainful look. The priest, calling to mind how dearly he had paid for his berth and passage, determined to resist encroachment, and for a minute priest and bishop leaned heavily and angrily against each other in silence.

Then said the bishop, "How, you ass, can you dare to contend with me? Don't you know who I am?"

"I," replied Felix, "am not an ass but a priest. It would be wrong for me to scorn a priest or despise a bishop, but I know a proud monk and an irregular friar when I see one, and I will contend against such with all my might."

At this point the bishop, forgetful of episcopal dignity, made that gesture with his thumb, "which the Italians use when they want to be rude to anyone." This brought in "the priest's knight" and other young knights with him, all shouting and swearing, so that the bishop, choosing the wisest course, fled to the captain's cabin, and came no more among the pilgrims.

Felix certainly needed all his courage for the voyage that was before him. Worn out by their labors, by the heat, by having to sleep out-of-doors. By lack of wine and of good bread, by the hurry of their tour, the pilgrims returned to the galley in such a state that it "became like a hospital full of wretched invalids," and it was the old women who, of tougher fiber than any man, nursed those who had scorned their company.

Worse suffering was to come. Contrary winds kept them at sea even when, knowing that the Turk had given up the siege of Rhodes, they tried to make that port. Water ran short; the sailors now could sell any that was not foul, "albeit it was lukewarm, whitish, and discoloured," at a higher price than wine. Soon "even putrid stinking water was precious and the captain and all the pilots were scared that we should run out even of . . . that." No water at all could be spared for the beasts; and Felix watched them with pity as they licked the dew from the ship's timbers.

"During those days of suffering," says he, "I often wondered how any man living on earth can be so pampered as to worry almost the whole year about the Lent fast, and the bread and water of Good Friday." (Was it Felix himself who so worried?) Now he found himself longing for that "white bread, fresh and good, and for the water, clear, cold, sweet and clean . . . Often I suffered so from thirst, and so greatly desired cold water, that I thought, when I get back to Ulm I will climb up at once to Blaubüren and there sit down beside the lake which wells out from the depths until I have slaked my thirst." At last, however, they made the coast of the island, the sailors rowed ashore for water, the pilgrims drank, and at once, "like parched plants," revived.

They were held up in Crete by damage to the rudder. But Felix did not object to the delay. For one thing there was plenty for the pilgrims to watch. They might hang over the side and see the man who was to mend the rudder strip to his breeches and sink down into the water with hammer, nails, and pincers, to come up again, long after, with the work marvelously completed below the surface. Besides everything was cheap here, and especially that famous Cretan wine, malvoisie, "so we did not mind staying there, but enjoyed it."

That same Cretan wine was responsible for a number of laughable accidents which Felix recorded, because "as I promised . . . I often mix fun and amusement with serious matters." So, when the evening trumpet blew to recall the pilgrims to the ship, those already on board might be diverted by the sight of their fellows lined up on the quay, too drunk to risk the steps down to the boats. Once Felix enjoyed the spectacle of a drunken servingman who pitched headlong from the steps into the harbor; he had been carrying on his back his master's gear, and though he himself was soon fished out by the boatmen, "the loaves of bread and all that he was carrying floated over him, and were all utterly ruined."

Even ecclesiastics, losing their dignity, provided entertainment for the rest of the company. A Dalmatian priest with whom Felix had become friendly, returning late and "lit up" to the galley, lingered on deck till it was almost dark; then, deciding to go below, he made for the nearest hatchway, and, forgetting that the ladder was always removed at sunset, stepped down. At the crash of his fall "the whole galley shook, for he was a big man and fat," and for a moment the rest of the pilgrims, lying in their beds below, talking, were silent in horror, till they heard his voice, angry and stammering, but not that of one seriously injured.

"There!" said he, "I had the ladder under my feet and I went down three steps, and someone dragged it from under my feet and I fell down." He was told, "The ladder was taken away an hour ago," but he persisted. "That's not true, for I had gone down three steps already, and when I stood on the third it was dragged from under me."

At that the others began to laugh, and Felix loudest of all, for joy, he explains, that his friend had taken no harm in so great a fall.

"There!" cried the Dalmatian, "now I am sure that it was you, Brother Felix, who dragged the ladder from my feet. Be sure that I shall pay you out before you leave the galley," and the more Felix tried to clear himself the angrier grew the other, swearing to have his revenge the very next day. But, says Felix, by next morning all was forgotten, so potent is the wine of Crete.

After the pleasant days in Crete the pilgrims had yet another trial to face. Beyond Corfu they ran into a terrible storm, with wind and rain, lightning and thunder. Yet even here it is possible to discern in Felix that priceless gift, the enjoyment of mere experience.

"The rain . . . fell in such torrents as though entire rainclouds had burst and fallen upon us. Violent squalls kept striking the galley, covering it with water, and beating upon the sides of it as hard as though great stones from some high mountains were sent flying along the planks. I have often wondered when at sea in storms how it can be that water, being as it is a thin, soft and weak body, can strike such hard blows . . . for it makes a noise when it runs against the the ship as though millstones were being flung against her . . . Waves of sea-water are more vehement, more noisy, and more wonderful than those of other water. I have had great pleasure in sitting or standing on the upper deck during a storm, and watching the marvellous succession of gusts of wind and the frightful rush of the waters." But, as well as the interest of the thing, this storm drove them fast upon their course, so, though "our beds and all our things were sopping," bread and biscuit spoiled with salt water, no fire in the galley, the kitchen awash, and all the pilgrims seasick, they bore it with patience.

And, except for one bad time when the anchor dragged and they nearly fell upon the rocky Dalmatian coast, the storm was the last of their ill fortune. After five days at Parenzo, on Friday, October 21, "we reached the city of Venice and broke up our company, every man going to his own home," though Felix, ill and exhausted, spent a fortnight in bed at Venice and did not reach Ulm till November 16.

Rich and Poor
in the Late Medieval Universities

J. M. FLETCHER

We are accustomed, in the post–World War II period, to regarding the university as a significant social and political institution. The number of students has grown so astronomically in that period that the university experience is becoming a common one. Governmental agencies have poured millions of dollars into research facilities and projects. Academic degrees have become licenses for entrance into business as well as into the traditional professions. Professors are being drawn into government by political leaders. The university, in other words, is becoming again what it was during the first two centuries of its existence; for in the thirteenth and fourteenth centuries, the great university communities like Paris, Oxford, and Bologna played an important role in society and politics. Kings took an active interest in university affairs and relied on the universities for the civil servants who built their bureaucratic regimes. University-trained teachers began to dominate the growing educational system of Europe and participated in the spread of literacy. The universities even acted as arbiters in local and international disputes within the Church, and they concomitantly reflected those disputes in their own functioning. The apex of the universities' political involvement in the Church occurred during the great schism of the late fourteenth century.

In a less formal way, the university system provided an avenue for social mobility in the late medieval community—a community in which the lines of class division were progressively hardening. The values of the educational system cut across economic and social-class lines, although it would be wrong to overestimate the egalitarianism of the system. There were a significant number of poor boys in the schools and universities, but for individual members of the lower classes, gaining entry to the university must have appeared a formidable task whose successful completion depended on luck and really extraordinary ability. The contrast between rich and poor students in the German universities of the fifteenth and sixteenth centuries is one of the focal points of the following article by J. M. Fletcher. By that time, the obligations and social relationships between the various groups of students had become well established and in many cases were written into the constitutions of the university.

The second object of Fletcher's study is the relationship between rich and poor faculty members. In nearly all medieval schools and universities, professors were paid directly by the students who took their courses. The unpopular lecturer did not last long, and the resultant uncertainty for the masters made the whole system very difficult to maintain. Gradually, teaching shifted to the residential colleges that were being set up by patrons. The heads of the houses were usually masters who were thus supported independently of their teaching and could escape the perils of the university lecture halls.

By the fifteenth century, university teaching was declining rapidly and something had to be done to maintain it. The first endowed chair at Oxford was established by Lady Margaret, mother of Henry VII, in 1497 and under Henry VIII the number of such chairs increased significantly with the creation of the Regius Professorships. At the same time, tenured and high-paid faculty positions were being created in universities elsewhere in Europe, and this development profoundly altered the nature of the universities. On the one hand, it created a tension between rich and poor members of the faculties and on the other, it allowed professors to pursue their interests regardless of the interests of their students and the community. The analogy between the modern—that is, post-renaissance—university and the monastery is certainly too strong, but the growth of tenured faculty in the universities did help to remove them from the world that had always determined their character and that had exerted constant pressure for change and development, if not for truth and beauty. The history presented by Fletcher thus raises questions and issues with which we are still wrestling.

Throughout the medieval period the number of students of noble birth entering the German universities remained small. The fame of the celebrated law schools of northern Italy and the increasing popularity of the "New Learning" drew many ambitious nobles south. Nevertheless, German universities attempted to attract influential students by allowing special privileges to the nobility. Their motives were not at all altruistic. A rich nobleman not only brought fame to the university, but while studying could be compelled to spend money lavishly to maintain his privileged position, and in his future career would be expected to support the university in any legal or political difficulty. To ingratiate itself with Frederick I, the university of Heidelberg was even prepared in 1474 to allow his son to hear lectures for the B.A. degree in the electoral castle. The future prosperity of the university was so closely associated with its support of the electoral house that requests for privileges such as this could hardly be rejected.

The young nobleman learned very soon after his entry to the university that his enjoyment of a special status was closely associated with his ability to support the university financially. At matriculation many German univerities demanded higher enrolment fees from noblemen. The statutes of Tübingen, for example, provide for special charges for nobles, prelates, and those wishing to be placed "on the front rows." References to this special, reserved seating for rich scholars attending lectures and important ceremonies appear frequently in university documents. At Basel privileges were given to

From J. M. Fletcher, "Wealth and Poverty in the Medieval German Universities," in J. R. Hale, J. R. L. Highfield, and B. Smalley, eds., *Europe in the Late Middle Ages* (Evanston, Ill.: Northwestern University Press, 1965), pp. 411–14, 417–27, 435–36. Reprinted by permission of Northwestern University Press and Faber and Faber Ltd.

those "with a particular place on the benches" and at Freiburg to those "who are allocated the highest benches." Special seating in churches used by the university was also provided for noblemen. Respect for wealth could affect academic standards. A decision at Freiburg to compel all masters of arts to attend daily lectures in the higher faculties was not imposed on noblemen "because of their distinction and the high level of their scholarship." More striking was the preference given to the nobility at degree examinations. Successful candidates for the B.A. degree at Tübingen were to be placed in the same order as they had in the Matricula, but noblemen were to be preferred to all others. The examiners for the M.A. degree, on the contrary, were to place the successful applicants in order of merit. Here again nobility and the prospect of an important career were influential. In deciding the place to be occupied in the list by a successful candidate, the examiners were to consider not just his knowledge, manner of life and his ability to express himself, but his chance of future promotion and his noble birth.

The rich nobleman could not be expected to live under the same restrictions as the ordinary students. He usually had with him a retinue of servants whose entry to one of the burses, the halls of residence for the students, would have dislocated the communal life practised there. He would also have found the simple food served there inadequate to his tastes. Many rich young men were able to employ their own private tutors and, therefore, had less need of the special instruction provided in the burses. Accordingly, university statutes expressly exempt noblemen from the requirement of residence in a burse. It was usually sufficient for them to obtain permission from the university for their lodging in a private house, although at Vienna the statutes also insisted on the appointment of someone to live with such students and be responsible to the authorities for their good behaviour. In recognition of the nobleman's rank, the universities also allowed him to wear distinctive clothing. At Freiburg, he was exempted from the punishment decreed for students "who go about in tunics that have no girdle" and allowed to wear the *birretum*, a privilege usually confined to bachelors of the higher faculties. Should a student, able to spend annually more than thirty florins, obtain the master's degree at Leipzig, he was expected to maintain the dignity of the university by purchasing within six months the proper academic dress. The relative liberty allowed to a nobleman concerning his dress could be abused. In July 1470 the rector at Freiburg was instructed to call before him certain nobles guilty of wearing improper dress. They were to be "piously warned" but also informed that any minor breaches of the statute regulating the dress of students would be tolerated.

During the ceremonies that accompanied the award of a degree the university regents took this final opportunity to extort as much as possible from the successful candidate. Gifts of money, offerings of clothing, and invitations to expensive banquets were required. The rich man at this time was especially vulnerable; as an act of charity he frequently paid for the *prandium*

Aristotelis, the degree feast, on behalf of poorer scholars. At Cologne the university officially appointed a rich man to undertake the duty of providing this banquet, and in return endowed him with the honorary title of *primus universitatis*. In such ways, the German universities attempted to impose obligations on their wealthy students to benefit both the university itself and its poorer scholars.

The noblemen attending the universities were too few to affect fundamentally their development in the medieval period. They were a small group with interesting but exceptional privileges. Of more importance were the rich, salaried lecturers within the teaching body of the university itself, who formed a permanent pressure group with their own special interests. Although the earlier German universities attempted to reproduce the regency system of Paris, whereby all official teaching was done by those who had qualified for a degree and had been accepted into the corporation of masters, the smaller universities found that they could not attract lecturers of sufficient standing by this method. Universities such as Freiburg or Rostock never had sufficient students to provide an adequate salary from lecture fees alone for an ambitious master. The higher faculties in particular could never be certain of attracting sufficient students to reward adequately a highly qualified lecturing doctor. Nor did the prestige of a regent's position compensate for loss of income as it did, to a certain extent, in the larger and more celebrated universities. To solve this problem many German universities created a number of lectureships in all faculties which were financed directly or indirectly by the university itself and which were allocated annually a fixed sum. The money for these lectures was usually donated by local noble patrons of the university or by town councils. In either case an opportunity was created for continual interference in the university's affairs by the external authorities providing the salaries. The number of lectureships and the salaries paid varied from place to place and from year to year according to the prosperity of the university. At Freiburg in 1489 the university owed money to four doctors, one licenciate, four masters of arts and one "poet" for official lectures. The duke of Bavaria's foundation charter for the university of Ingolstadt established salaried lectureships in all faculties. There were to be one doctor in theology, two in canon law, one in civil law and one in medicine. For the Faculty of Arts six lectureships were endowed. The salaried lecturers also received free rooms in the university *collegium* or an allowance towards the rent of private rooms. In some universities the lecturers were also paid by the students in the usual manner; in others their lectures were given without charge. . . .

An interesting comment on the difficulties created by the establishment of a group of salaried lecturers within the regent body of the Faculty of Arts is recorded in the *Acta* of the rector at Freiburg. In 1490 the dean of the Faculty of Arts appeared before the university to present certain grievances. He stated that in the faculty were many masters "and they cannot obtain an income or sufficient exercises to pay for their own food and drink." The reason for this, he claimed, was that after the salaried lecturers of the faculty had given their statutory lectures and exercises, few subjects remained for the other masters to cover. The solution proposed by the dean was to reduce the number of subjects allotted to the salaried lecturers so that there would be sufficient remaining to be shared amongst the other masters. He also proposed that the lecturers should then all be hired by the university and the faculty so that the students need not make any payments to them. The university refused to accept this proposal, declaring that it was bound to carry out the royal ordinance which had established the salaried lectureships. The university, apparently, was not prepared to recognize that the co-existence of the traditional regency system and the practice of hiring lecturers was unfair to the non-salaried masters. This reluctance to break with the system that had been customary since the foundation of the older northern universities is perhaps understandable. Nevertheless, it is apparent from complaints such as these, that in Germany the abandonment of the traditional right of every regent master to lecture in return for fees paid by his students was being seriously considered by the Faculty of Arts.

The financial security enjoyed by the salaried lecturers set them apart from the poor masters so frequently mentioned in the records of the earlier northern universities. With the abandonment of the regent's traditional poverty, many earlier academic restrictions also disappeared. Lecturers grew ambitious for the comforts of a normal, respectable life. In some universities the habit of communal life amongst the salaried lecturers of the Faculty of Arts was abandoned or modified. Instead, the university made payments towards the renting of private houses for its lecturers. In contravention of the faculty statutes official exercises were frequently held in these private houses. Occasionally, usually after some disturbance, the authorities took steps to halt this development and to bring students under closer control. At Freiburg, for example, in 1498 after a quarrel between two students during a town fair, all masters teaching scholars outside the burses were ordered to carry out their future "resumptions"—revision lectures—and exercises only in the burses. This ruling was to apply in particular to the married lecturers. But despite these occasional attempts to reverse the development, there was a general movement away from the traditional academic practices evolved at a time when both masters and students lived communal lives.

The higher standard of living and the relative security brought by their position encouraged many salaried lecturers to venture on family life. One of the most interesting features of fifteenth-century university life in Germany is the general acceptance of the need to make provision for married lecturers. There were, of course, always traditionalists who wished to revert to earlier days and who poured scorn on their married colleagues. Such a person must have scribbled the often quoted words "becoming mad, he took a wife" in the matriculation rolls of the university of Vienna. Such phrases, however, give a wrong impression of the universities' general attitude to marriage and such exceptional outbursts of indignation should not be taken as typical of academic thinking on this subject. For those lecturers wishing for a future career in the Church or in the Faculty of Theology, marriage would be out of the question, but for lawyers, medical lecturers and artists married life proved very attractive now that financial security had been attained. For many of these lecturers, marriage with a wealthy widow or a well-endowed daughter brought additional income and an introduction to the middle-class society of the university towns. Unfortunately, these matrimonial adventures were in turn to involve the universities in disputes requiring constant attention. The married men are conspicuous by the frequency in which they appear in descriptions of the universities' legal difficulties and quarrels with the civic administration.

The traditional privileges sought by medieval universities were those thought necessary to protect students and lecturers from the judicial power of the local authorities and to prevent their exploitation by unscrupulous tradesmen. They were granted on the assumption that the university would be able to discipline its own members and prevent their illegitimate use of these privileges. In effect the university became independent of the judicial authority of the city and its members exempt from the taxes and such duties as watch service normally imposed on the burgesses. Purchases of basic necessities such as food and drink could also be made by members of the university without payment of the tolls levied by the city on the transactions made at its market. As we have noted above, in the fifteenth century amongst the salaried lecturers there was a movement away from university communal life towards a more normal manner of living, often involving marriage to a member of some local family. The wife of such a lecturer, her property and her children then fell under the jurisdiction and protection of the university. In such circumstances privileges possessed by a member of the university could be exploited to the benefit of his family and to the harm of the local municipality. It would clearly be impossible for a strong civic council to tolerate the abuse by rich lecturers of privileges originally granted to protect poor masters. On the other hand, the universities would be reluctant to withdraw protection from some of their most influential members. The stage was set, therefore, for a struggle in which both sides could appeal to strongly held prejudices and principles.

At Freiburg it is possible to trace in the university records the way in which the tension between the civic and academic authorities continually embittered relations between town and gown. In 1470 the citizens approached the university in an effort to obtain the adoption of a statute prohibiting all salaried lecturers from marrying "with the exception of medical teachers and lawyers." Nothing came of this proposal. In the following year the university was involved in a dispute with the town concerning the property of the married men. The question of whether such property could be exempt from civic jurisdiction and taxation was one that could not easily be resolved. The university preferred to remit the case to the royal council for a decision. In this dispute the university must have felt that its position was not very strong, for in the same year it refused to hire a master to lecture except on condition that he did not marry. The dispute dragged on with the town attempting to deprive the married members of the university of certain of their privileges and the rector insisting that the foundation charter must be maintained in its entirety. In April 1473 the quarrel flared up again. On this occasion the central figure was the important lecturer in the Faculty of Arts, John Knapp of Rutlingen. The citizens complained that Knapp had married a wealthy widow, had so deprived himself of the chance of future ecclesiastical promotion and should, therefore, now come under the jurisdiction of the Freiburg burghermaster. When Knapp sought refuge under the protection of the university's privileges, he was arrested. The town's claim was the not unreasonable one that the removal of individuals and property from its jurisdiction could not be tolerated. The loss of income and services previously rendered to the municipality was a severe blow to a relatively small town. Perhaps of more importance was the loss of prestige by the town council at every extension of the university's privileges. During the course of the inquiry an interesting addition to the charge against Knapp was made. He was accused of using his position to engage in trade, such trade, of course, being exempt from the normal duties paid to the town. It was even suggested that his journeys to Rome had been for commercial purposes. Whatever the truth of all these charges, the general situation is clear; a financially secure lecturer was taking advantage of the university's privileges to better his income and social position. As was usual, the case was remitted to the royal council for a decision.

Similar disputes appear frequently in the university records. In September 1480, however, the town council appears to have decided on stronger action to enforce its claims. Three doctors and one master were officially notified that they would be required to assist either in person or by proxy the town's attempt to re-establish a road damaged by flood water. This demand was made only to those "who possess their wives' property in Freiburg." The university's protestations were angrily rejected and a further claim was made that such doctors and masters were liable also to service with the watch. The university also stood firm, stating that its members "should not be instructed to undertake such menial tasks and duties as labouring, keeping watch or guard or any other undignified burdens." Appeal was once again made to the royal council for a settlement. On other occasions the citizens attempted to force the married men to take an oath to their burghermaster or to prohibit them from making purchases for their students in any place except the common market. These matters were settled amicably. Although in such cases the married men in general are attacked, it is apparent from the names of those involved in these disputes that the citizens were worried about the richer doctors and masters rather than the student body as a whole. It was the group of salaried lecturers who were seeking to expand their income and establish their social position by judicious marriages who aroused the citizens' anxieties. It is also a measure of the importance of this group that it was able to induce the university to defend the privileges of the married men with such vehemence.

The acceptance and defence of the married lecturers also involved the universities in their family affairs. There are frequent references in the Freiburg records to actions taken to protect the dependents of deceased lecturers. In 1478 the town council was warned against attempts to molest the widow and son of Matheus Hummel, the first rector of the university. The threat of an appeal to the royal authority "to safeguard our privileges" was intimated to the burgesses. Again, in June 1490, the university made payments to the widow of Dr. Menynger in settlement of the debt it owed to her dead husband. For Dr. Northofer's children the university provided guardians who were to ensure that they received possession of their father's goods and were allocated a suitable tutor. In its care for the children of its regents, the university appears to have been especially solicitous. All legitimate sons of regent masters and doctors by a statute of 1480 were allowed to be enrolled in the university Matricula without payment; one son succeeded in following his father as a salaried lecturer. It is clear that the university accepted its obligations to the married lecturer with family responsibilities. It was the town council, which saw itself indirectly being deprived of taxes, dues and services, that strongly opposed this extension of university authority to the property and families of the rich lecturers.

The Freiburg material also illustrates in an interesting manner the close co-operation between the salaried lecturers and the local secular overlord, in this case the house of Austria. In times of conflict with the town, an appeal from the university usually produced a favourable response from the royal council. In turn, the salaried lecturers, particularly in the legal and medical faculties, co-operated closely with the Austrian monarchy and gave professional advice when it was required. In fact, the salaried lecturers' concern for the affairs of the Austrian house was often over zealous. On many occasions the university found it necessary gently to rebuke the royal council for its too frequent employment of the lecturers, who were then distracted from their teaching programme. It is difficult to avoid the conclusion that with this increasing concern for social status and a secure income, the salaried lecturers were sacrificing that independence from secular control that had been the first demand of the masters at an earlier date. By the sixteenth century, most German universities were controlled by the local ruling houses through this dependable group of senior lecturers. It is interesting to note a similar development later in England. The Elizabethan Statutes which set up the Caput at Cambridge and the Laudian Statutes which established the Hebdomadal Council at Oxford gave the English monarchy systematic control of the universities by putting administrative power into the hands of a small group of compliant senior members. By these constitutional changes which are first seen in Germany at the close of the medieval period, the traditional democracy of the north European university system was destroyed. The universities, afterwards, became readily susceptible to governmental pressure.

In sharp contrast to the standard of living enjoyed by the nobility and the salaried lecturers was that of the poor students. The begging letters written by such students in which they describe their wretched condition, have already attracted the attention of historians. Some students suffered from cold; others had to beg from door to door through muddy streets; all complain of the expense of living in a university town and of the poor food that their poverty compels them to eat. Some pardonable exaggeration must be expected in such letters, but they do indicate that for some students life was always uncomfortable and occasionally unpleasant. It was Rashdall's opinion, however, that the poor students formed only a small minority amongst those attending the medieval universities. He speaks of the "vast majority of scholars" as being from an intermediate social group between the highest and the lowest classes. Nevertheless, the poor scholars were of sufficient importance to attract the attention of the German university authorities and to induce the Faculty of Arts in particular to make generous provision for them.

The first obstacle facing the poor scholar on his entry to the university was the necessity to pay the fee for enrolment in the Matricula. From this fee, a scholar who could satisfy the authorities as to his poverty was usually exempted. For example, at Wittenberg the normal matriculation fee was a quarter florin. Members of the mendicant orders were admitted at a reduced rate, and poor students paid what they could afford "or are to be enrolled without charge to show God's love." This *privilegium paupertatis* could be abused, and at Cologne the deceptions practised grew so notorious that the privilege was withdrawn in 1503. On the basis of these matriculation statistics at Cologne, Eulenburg was able to estimate that about 16 per cent of the students were classed as "poor," and from the records at Leipzig that 9 per cent of the students were so classified. These figures must be considered with scepticism in view of the unreliability of the matriculation tables as an adequate record of all students entering the university, but at least they do suggest a substantial minority of genuinely poor students at Cologne and Leipzig.

Within the university, the poor student was entitled to enjoy various privileges. He was generally exempted from the strict requirements concerning academic dress. The earliest Heidelberg statutes of the Faculty of Arts required from all candidates seeking permission to "determine"—that is, to complete their B.A. course—an oath that for the ceremony only new gowns should be worn. But the dean of the faculty was also given permission to dispense those students unable to afford a new gown from this requirement. Scholars seeking such a dispensation had first to swear that they were in fact poor, and were then allowed to determine in the gown they already possessed.

From such regulations it is clear that the university authorities had to have some criterion for judging whether or not a student should be classified as "poor." At Prague the criterion was simply financial. All students with an income of less than twelve florins per year were classed as "poor" provided that they could take an oath to this effect to their master or to the rector. At Tübingen the regulations were a little stricter. The statutes of 1488, revising early regulations for the Faculty of Arts, defined a poor student as someone not being able to raise sixteen florins from his own resources and those of his friends. An addition to this statute, however, prohibited the granting of relief to students who might overspend on food and drink either before or after they applied to the university for this privileged status. At Ingolstadt, enjoyment of the status of a poor student was conditional on the production of adequate testimonial letters sealed in the student's own native town certifying to his poverty. Even then, the student's manner of life at the university was to be noted, so that his privileges might be withdrawn if he showed himself to be undeserving of them.

One of the most important privileges granted to the poor scholars was that of living outside the communal life of the burses. This they shared with the noblemen, but for a very different reason. Poor students were not expected to be able to pay the low fees charged for food and lodging in the officially recognized burses. University statutes assume that rich doctors and masters would employ such poor scholars in their own households. The Freiburg definition of those scholars recognized by the university as *bona fide* students, for example, includes servants "who live with the said doctors and masters at their expense." At Basel the statutes of the Faculty of Arts forbid the regent masters to employ anyone except a poor scholar as a servant. So general was this employment of poor students as servants that the disciplinary ordinances of 1507 at Ingolstadt refused to recognize any scholar as "poor" unless he was employed as a servant living at someone's expense. Apart from serving rich masters and doctors, poor students also supported themselves by working in the burses. References to such scholars appear frequently in the university records. The revised Freiburg statutes of 1495, which exempt only the servants working in the burses from a new procedure for examining students claiming classification as "poor," would seem to indicate that these servants were regarded as the poorest of all students. There can, indeed, have been little financial reward obtained from work in a burse where the majority of students were themselves not from wealthy parents.

Certain universities also attempted to bring poor scholars under control by providing burses where the standard of living was not so high and the charges more suitable for the less well-endowed students. In the first years of its existence, the university of Freiburg took steps to establish three types of burses: "burses with different charges." One of these was to be a "house for poor scholars" charging a fee less than the two others. At Erfurt the *Bursa Pauperum* attempted to provide some security for poorer students reading for arts degrees. But the most interesting attempt to solve in this manner the problem presented by poor students was at Vienna. There, poor scholars were housed in special burses known as *codriae* where lower charges were made and fewer restrictions were imposed. This second characteristic of the *codriae* seems to have attracted the more unruly but not necessarily poorer members of the university. The Faculty of Arts attempted to control these undisciplined students by enacting in 1413 a series of statutes regulating behaviour, and by then adding a codicil that scholars living in the *codriae* who were found guilty of breaking the new rules would be more severely punished than other members of the university. This statute seems to have been only partially successful. At the beginning of the sixteenth century the faculty attempted to clear out of the *codriae* all those living there under false pretences. No student with an income above a certain yearly amount was to be allowed to live in the *codriae*. Those at present living there were to prove that their income was below this figure. At the same time the faculty took steps to regulate the distribution of money obtained by the members of the *codriae* from their legitimate begging activities. The dean of the faculty was also to ensure that specific masters were held responsible for the behaviour of specific scholars. It is apparent from these regulations that if the poverty of these students' lives was not pleasant, at least to some the absence of restrictions on their behaviour was a compensatory factor of some value.

Students who were hardly able to afford their accommodation, food and drink, could not be expected to pay the fees charged by the masters for their lectures and exercises, or offer to the university the statutory gifts required at graduation. Various forms of exemption from these payments were incorporated in the statutes of the German universities. The problem of the poor student was essentially one for the Faculty of Arts. In the higher faculties, although a student might have only a small regular income, at least he had the opportunity to earn money by lecturing in the Faculty of Arts where he had usually studied earlier. It is, therefore, the statutes of the faculties of arts which are the richest source of information concerning the dispensations from payment allowed to poor students.

Exemption from payment for official lectures and exercises usually followed automatically after a scholar had been examined by the faculty and classed as "poor." At Tübingen, for example, the statutes required the dean to announce once in every six months that any scholar unable to pay for his exercises should appear before a special panel for examination. The panel was composed of the dean, the *conventores* in charge of the burses who would be expected to give evidence of the candidate's manner of life, and representatives of the two philosophical sections, or *viae*, into which the faculty was divided. This committee would then impose on the candidate what proportion, if any, of the fees that it believed he could afford. With minor variations this procedure was in general use throughout Germany. It provided the means whereby a poor student could obtain the minimum amount of instruction necessary for his degree, and also included safeguards for the regents who might otherwise be deprived of their legitimate income. . . .

The cleavage between rich and poor in the German universities at the close of the Middle Ages was probably widening. While the group of secure, well-paid salaried lecturers was demanding and obtaining a better standard of living, with comforts previously known only to the middle classes of the towns, poorer students were generally unable to benefit fully even from those privileges granted to them. At an earlier date, university masters and students had been united by their relative poverty; the few noble students were exceptional by reason of their wealth. In the fifteenth century the division between rich and poor appears within the university itself, dividing masters from students and even salaried lecturers from those without salaries. The effect was to restrict that ability for corporate action which had been characteristic of the earlier universities, and to replace it by a mass of conflicting interests within the academic structure. The wretched student, working as a servant in a burse, could have felt little in common with the salaried lecturer, married, living in his private house and often enjoying the confidences of members of the local nobility. The resulting weakness of the German universities and their inability to oppose external pressures was already apparent in the fifteenth century.

Young Man Luther

ERIK H. ERIKSON

How are we to understand a leader who creates a revolution of incalculable effect on Western history? That question has been at the heart of biographies of Martin Luther since his contemporaries assessed his character. Aleander, who pronounced judgment against Luther in the Edict of Worms, claimed that the heretic had become so obsessed with obedience to God that he had renounced the authority of all earthly powers, even those that were ordained by God. Cochlaeus, another Catholic critic of Luther, sought an explanation of the rebellion in Luther's demonic possession and passed on the famous story of his raving in the monastery. The debate about whether great revolutions are caused by the course of history or the leadership of individual men has focused on Martin Luther perhaps more than any other heroic character in history. Did the man cause the revolution, or did the revolution bring forth the man? Erik Erikson answers this question by placing most of the responsibility for the revolution on Luther's shoulders, and this conclusion is implied in his method of studying the great reformer.

Erikson is a psychoanalyst fascinated by the psychological character of great men. He has written about Gandhi as well as Luther and has taken a broader look at the relationship between psychological development and social roles in his book *Childhood and Society* (New York, 1963). This approach rests on the assumption that it is in the man that we will find the wellsprings of historically significant change and that the individuals who lead revolutionary movements can be understood most profoundly if studied psychoanalytically. This approach to historical biography has engendered considerable debate among scholars. Nearly all recognize its general value, but there is disagreement over the nature of its contribution to historical knowledge.

Erikson focuses on specific expressions of Luther's (often statements largely ignored by other historians) to bring out the basic conflicts in his early personality development. His thesis is that Luther's inner personal development—his struggle for independence from his father, his dislike of his mother, his formation of an identity—explains his theology. The problem is that knowledge of the young Luther comes from the casual reminiscences of the old Luther and from sources even less reliable. Stories told by his enemy Cochlaeus, while perhaps true, are nevertheless a rather weak basis on which to build a complex psychological theory. In fact, concentration on particular statements considered revealing exposes the historiographical character not only of Erikson's work, but also of much work written on the history of the ancient and medieval world in general. The historian begins with the chance remains of his subject—be it a whole political movement or the life of an individual—and begins to build an interpretation. Each step of the analysis is a logical, or at least possible, result of the preceding one, but when the interpretive structure is complete, it becomes clear that the whole building stands on remarkably flimsy foundations. The ancient or medieval historian who has used all the available sources may shrug at this strange concoction and tiptoe away. Erikson's superstructure is based on only some of the available information and thus his work raises the question: Why focus on some things and not on others? The answer is that psychological theory predetermines the kinds of evidence that will be considered relevant and revealing. While all historians come to their sources with preconceived notions, they usually wince at so obvious a reliance on such preconceptions. And whatever their preconceptions are, they must be tested against all the evidence. Is the difference between Erikson and other historians one of degree? Or is Erikson doing something qualitatively different from the others?

Two statements of Luther's are frequently quoted: "My father once whipped me so that I ran away and felt ugly toward him until he was at pains to win me back." "My mother caned me for stealing a nut until the blood came. Such strict discipline drove me to a monastery although she meant it well." In spite of this last remark, Bainton, whose translation is quoted, does not think that these whippings aroused more than a "flash of resentment." Many authorities on Luther, making no attempt at psychological thinking, judge this matter of punishment either to be of no importance, or on the contrary, to have made an emotional cripple of Martin. It seems best, however, to outline a framework within which we may try to evaluate these data.

In my profession one learns to listen to exactly what people are saying; and Luther's utterances, even when they are reported secondhand, are often surprises in naïve clarification. The German text of Luther's reference to the whipping incidents of which I quoted Bainton's translation, adds, to the report of the whipping: "*dass ich ihn flohe und ward ihm gram, bis er mich wieder zu sich gewoehnte.*" These words are hard to render in another language, and Bainton, from his point of view, saw no reason to ponder them. He translated them into what an American boy might have said: "I ran away . . . I felt ugly." But a more literal translation would be, "I fled him and I became sadly resentful toward him, until he gradually got me accustomed (or habituated) to him again." Thus, "*ich ward ihm gram*" describes a less angry, sadder and more deeply felt hurt than "I felt ugly toward him." A child can feel ugly toward somebody for whom he does not specially care; but he feels sadly resentful toward somebody he loves. Similarly, a parent could be "at pains to win back" almost anybody, and for any number of reasons; but he would try to *reaccustom* somebody to himself only for the purpose of re-

Reprinted from pp. 64–67 and 254–60 of *Young Man Luther* by Erik H. Erikson. By permission of W. W. Norton & Company, Inc. Copyright © 1958, 1962 by Erik H. Erikson. Also reprinted by permission of Faber and Faber Ltd. from *Young Man Luther.*

storing an intimate daily association. The personal quality of that one sentence thus reveals two trends which (I believe) characterized Hans' and Martin's relationship. Martin, even when mortally afraid, *could not really hate his father*, he could only be sad; and Hans, while he could not let the boy come close, and was murderously angry at times, *could not let him go for long.* They had a mutual and deep investment in each other which neither of them could or would abandon, although neither of them was able to bring it to any kind of fruition. (The reader may feel this interpretation places too big a burden on one sentence; but we will find further support in the whole story as we proceed.)

I know this kind of parent-child relationship all too well from my young patients. In the America of today it is usually the mother whose all-pervasive presence and brutal decisiveness of judgment—although her means may be the sweetest—precipitate the child into a fatal struggle for his own identity: the child wants to be blessed by the one important parent, not for what he does and accomplishes, but for what he *is*, and he often puts the parent to mortal tests. The parent, on the other hand, has selected this one child, because of an inner affinity paired with an insurmountable outer distance, as the particular child who must *justify the parent.* Thus the parent asks only: What have you *accomplished?* and what have you done for *me?* It is my contention that Luther's father played this role in Martin's life, and so jealously that the mother was eclipsed far more than can be accounted for by the mere pattern of German housewifeliness.

I said that Luther could not hate his father openly. This statement presumes that he did hate him underneath. Do we have any proof of this? Only the proof which lies in action delayed, and delayed so long that the final explosion hits nonparticipants. In later life Luther displayed an extraordinary ability to hate quickly and persistently, justifiably and unjustifiably, with pungent dignity and with utter vulgarity. This ability to hate, as well as an inability to forgive those who in his weaker years had, to his mind, hindered him, he shares with other great men. However, as we follow his tortured obediences and erratic disobediences in later life, we cannot help asking what made it impossible for him to at least evade this father (as another brutalized son and later emancipator, Lincoln, did, sadly yet firmly), and even within the paternalistic system of those days eventually leave him aside, make compromises, and get his way. Erasmus, and Calvin, and many lesser people, met their crises in defying their father's wills, but settled them somehow without making their rebellion the very center of their self-justification.

I have so far mentioned two trends in the relationship between Hans and Martin: (1) the father's driving economic ambition, which was threatened by something (maybe even murder) done in the past, and by a feeling close to murder which he always carried inside; and (2) the concentration of the father's ambition on his oldest son, whom he treated with alternate periods of violent harshness and of habituating the son to himself in a manner which may well have been somewhat sentimental—a deadly combination.

I would add to these trends the father's display of righteousness. Hans seems to have considered himself the very conception, the *Inbegriff*, of justice. After all, he did not spare himself, and fought his own nature as ruthlessly as those of his children. But parents are dangerous who thus take revenge on their child for what circumstances and inner compulsion have done to them; who misuse one of the strongest forces in life—true indignation in the service of vital values—to justify their own small selves. Martin, however, seems to have sensed on more than one occasion that the father, behind his disciplined public identity, was possessed by an angry, and often alcoholic, impulsiveness which he loosed against his family (and would dare loose *only* against his family) under the pretense of being a hard taskmaster and righteous judge.

The fear of the father's anger, described as constant by some biographers, included the absolute injunction against any back-talk, any *Widerrede*. Here again the fact that only much later, and only after an attempt to screw down the lid with the rules of monastic silence, did Martin become one of the biggest and most effective back-talkers in history, forces us to ask what kept him silent for so long. But this was Martin: in Latin school he was caned for using the German language—and later he used that language with a vengeance! We can deduce from what burst forth later that which must have been forced to lie dormant in childhood; this may well have included some communality of experience with the mother, whose spontaneity and imagination are said to have suffered at the side of Hans Luder.

This much, I think, one can say about the paternal side of Martin's childhood dilemma. Faced with a father who made questionable use of his brute superiority; a father who had at his disposal the techniques of making others feel morally inferior without being quite able to justify his own moral superiority; a father to whom he could not get close and from whom he could not get away—faced with such a father, how was he going to submit without being emasculated, or rebel without emasculating the father?

Millions of boys face these problems and solve them in some way or another—they live, as Captain Ahab says, with half of their heart and with only one of their lungs, and the world is the worse for it. Now and again, however, an individual is called upon (called by *whom*, only the theologians claim to know, and by *what*, only bad psychologists) to lift his individual patienthood to the level of a universal one and to try to solve for all what he could not solve for himself alone. . . .

. . . At a given age, a human being, by dint of his physical, intellectual and emotional growth, becomes ready and eager to face a new life task, that is, a set of choices and tests which are in some traditional way prescribed and prepared for him by his society's structure. A new life task presents a *crisis* whose outcome can be a successful graduation, or alternatively, an impairment of the life cycle which will aggravate future crises. Each crisis prepares the next, as one step leads to another; and each crisis also lays one more corner-stone for the adult personality. I will enumerate all these crises (more thoroughly treated elsewhere) to remind us, in summary, of certain issues in Luther's life; and also to suggest a developmental root for the basic human values of faith, will, conscience, and reason—all necessary in rudimentary form for the identity which crowns childhood.

The first crisis is the one of early infancy. How this crisis is met decides whether a man's innermost mood will be determined more by basic trust or by basic mistrust. The outcome of this crisis—apart from accidents of heredity, gestation, and birth—depends largely on the quality of maternal care, that is, on the consistency and mutuality which guide the mother's ministrations and give a certain predictability and hopefulness to the baby's original cosmos of urgent and bewildering body feelings. The ratio and relation of basic trust to basic mistrust established during early infancy determines much of the individual's capacity for simple faith, and consequently also determines his future contribution to his society's store of faith—which, in turn, will feed into a future mother's ability to trust the world in which she teaches trust to newcomers. In this first stage we can assume that a historical process is already at work; history writing should therefore chart the influence of histori-cal events on growing generations to be able to judge the quality of their future contribution to history. As for little Martin, I have drawn conclusions about that earliest time when his mother could still claim the baby, and when he was still all hers, inferring that she must have provided him with a font of basic trust on which he was able to draw in his fight for a primary faith present before all will, conscience, and reason, a faith which is "the soul's virginity."

The first crisis corresponds roughly to what Freud has described as orality; the second corresponds to anality. An awareness of these correspon-dences is essential for a true understanding of the dynamics involved.

The second crisis, that of infancy, develops the infantile sources of what later becomes a human being's will, in its variations of willpower and wilfulness. The resolution of this crisis will determine whether an individual is apt to be dominated by a sense of autonomy, or by a sense of shame and doubt. The social limitations imposed on intensified wilfulness inevitably create doubt about the justice governing the relations of grown and growing people. The way this doubt is met by the grown-ups determines much of a man's future ability to combine an unimpaired will with ready self-discipline, rebellion with responsibility.

The interpretation is plausible that Martin was driven early out of the trust stage, out from "under his mother's skirts," by a jealously ambitious father who tried to make him precociously independent from women, and sober and reliable in his work. Hans succeeded, but not without storing in the boy violent doubts of the father's justification and sincerity; a lifelong shame over the persisting gap between his own precocious conscience and his actual inner state; and a deep nostalgia for a situation of infantile trust. His theological solution—spiritual return to a faith which is there before all doubt, combined with a political submission to those who by necessity must wield the sword of secular law—seems to fit perfectly his personal need for compromise. While this analysis does not explain either the ideological power or the theological consistency of his solution, it does illustrate that ontogenetic experience is an indispensable link and transformer between one stage of history and the next. This link is a psychological one, and the energy transformed and the process of transformation are both charted by the psychoanalytic method.

Freud formulated these matters in dynamic terms. Few men before him gave more genuine expression to those experiences which are on the borderline between the psychological and the theological than Luther, who gleaned from these experiences a religious gain formulated in theological terms. Luther described states of badness which in many forms pervade human existence from childhood. For instance, his description of shame, an emotion first experienced when the infant stands naked in space and feels belittled: "He is put to sin and shame before God . . . this shame is now a thousand times greater, that a man must blush in the presence of God. For this means that there is no corner or hole in the whole of creation into which a man might creep, not even in hell, but he must let himself be exposed to the gaze of the whole creation, and stand in the open with all his shame, as a bad conscience feels when it is really struck. . . ." Or his description of doubt, an emotion first experienced when the child feels singled out by demands whose rationale he does not comprehend: "When he is tormented in *Anfechtung* it seems to him that he is alone: God is angry only with him, and irreconcilably angry against him: then he alone is a sinner and all the others are in the right, and they work against him at God's orders. There is nothing left for him but this unspeakable sighing through which, without knowing it, he is supported by the Spirit and cries 'Why does God pick on me alone?' "

Luther was a man who would not settle for an easy appeasement of these feelings on any level, from childhood through youth to his manhood, or in any segment of life. His often impulsive and intuitive formulations transparently display the infantile struggle at the bottom of the lifelong emotional issue.

His basic contribution was a living reformulation of faith. This marks him as a theologian of the first order; it also indicates his struggle with the ontogenetically earliest and most basic problems of life. He saw as his life's work a new delineation of faith and will, of religion and the law: for it is clear that organized religiosity, in circumstances where faith in a world order is monopolized by religion, is the institution which tries to give dogmatic permanence to a reaffirmation of that basic trust—and a renewed victory over that basic mistrust—with which each human being emerges from early infancy. In this way organized religion cements the faith which will support future generations. Established law tries to formulate obligations and privileges, restraints and freedoms, in such a way that man can submit to law and order with a minimum of doubt and with little loss of face, and as an autonomous agent of order can teach the rudiments of discipline to his young. The relation of faith and law, of course, is an eternal human problem, whether it appears in questions of church and state, mysticism and daily morality, or existential aloneness and political commitment.

The third crisis, that of initiative versus guilt, is part of what Freud described as the central complex of the family, namely, the Oedipus complex. It involves a lasting unconscious association of sensual freedom with the body of the mother and the administrations received from her hand; a lasting association of cruel prohibition with the interference of the dangerous father; and the consequences of these associations for love and hate in reality and in phantasy. (I will not discuss here the cultural relativity of Freud's observations nor the dated origin of his term; but I assume that those who do wish to quibble about all this will feel the obligation to advance systematic propositions about family, childhood, and society which come closer to the core, rather than go back to the periphery, of the riddle which Freud was the first to penetrate.) We have reviewed the strong indications of an especially heavy interference by Hans Luder with Martin's attachment to his mother, who, it is suggested, secretly provided for him what Goethe openly acknowledged as his mother's gift—"*Die Frohnatur, die Lust zu fabulieren*": gaiety and the pleasure of confabulation. We have indicated how this gift, which later emerged in Luther's poetry, became guilt-laden and was broken to harness by an education designed to make a precocious student of the boy. We have also traced its relationship to Luther's lifelong burden of excessive guilt. Here is one of Luther's descriptions of that guilt: "And this is the worst of all these ills, that the conscience cannot run away from itself, but it is always present to itself and knows all the terrors of the creature which such things bring even in this present life, because the ungodly man is like a raging sea. The gird and greatest of all these horrors and the worst of all ills is to have a judge." He also said, "For this is the nature of a guilty conscience, to fly and to be terrified, even when all is safe and prosperous, to convert all into peril and death."

The stage of initiative, associated with Freud's phallic stage of psychosexuality, ties man's budding will to phantasy, play, games, and early work, and thus to the mutual delineation of unlimited imagination and aspiration and limiting, threatening conscience. As far as society is concerned, this is vitally related to the occupational and technological ideals perceived by the child; for the child can manage the fact that there is no return to the mother as a mother and no competition with the father as a father only to the degree

to which a future career outside of the narrower family can at least be envisaged in ideal future occupations: these he learns to imitate in play, and to
anticipate in school. We can surmise that for little Martin the father's own
occupation was early precluded from anticipatory phantasy, and that a life
of scholarly duty was obediently and sadly envisaged instead. This precocious
severity of obedience later made it impossible for young Martin to anticipate
any career but that of unlimited study for its own sake, as we have seen in
following his path of obedience—in disobedience.

In the fourth stage, the child becomes able and eager to learn systematically, and to collaborate with others. The resolution of this stage decides
much of the ratio between a sense of industry or work completion, and a
sense of tool-inferiority, and prepares a man for the essential ingredients of
the ethos as well as the rationale of his technology. He wants to know the
reason for things, and is provided, at least, with rationalizations. He learns to
use whatever simplest techniques and tools will prepare him most generally
for the tasks of his culture. In Martin's case, the tool was literacy, Latin
literacy, and we saw how he was molded by it—and how later he remolded,
with the help of printing, his nation's literary habits. With a vengeance he
could claim to have taught German even to his enemies.

But he achieved this only after a protracted identity crisis which is the
main subject of this book. Whoever is hard put to feel identical with one set
of people and ideas must that much more violently repudiate another set; and
whenever an identity, once established, meets further crises, the danger of
irrational repudiation of otherness and temporarily even of one's own identity
increases.

I have already briefly mentioned the three crises which follow the crisis
of identity; they concern problems of intimacy, generativity, and integrity.
The crisis of intimacy in a monk is naturally distorted in its heterosexual core.
What identity diffusion is to identity—its alternative and danger—isolation is
to intimacy. In a monk this too is subject to particular rules, since a monk
seeks intentional and organized isolation, and submits all intimacy to prayer
and confession.

Luther's intimacy crisis seems to have been fully experienced and resolved only on the Wartburg; that is, after his lectures had established him as
a lecturer, and his speech at Worms as an orator of universal stamp. On the
Wartburg he wrote *De Votis Monasticis*, obviously determined to take care
of his sexual needs as soon as a dignified solution could be found. But the
intimacy crisis is by no means only a sexual, or for that matter, a heterosexual,
one: Luther, once free, wrote to men friends about his emotional life, including his sexuality, with a frankness clearly denoting a need to share inti-
macies with them. The most famous example, perhaps, is a letter written at a
time when the tragicomedy of these priests' belated marriages to runaway
nuns was in full swing. Luther had made a match between Spalatin and an

ex-nun, a relative of Staupitz. In the letter, he wished Spalatin luck for the wedding night, and promised to think of him during a parallel performance to be arranged in his own marital bed.

Also on the Wartburg, Luther developed, with his translation of the Bible, a supreme ability to reach into the homes of his nation; as a preacher and a table talker he demonstrated his ability and his need to be intimate for the rest of his life. One could write a book about Luther on this theme alone; and perhaps in such a book all but the most wrathful utterances would be found to be communications exquisitely tuned to the recipient.

Owing to his prolonged identity crisis, and also to delayed sexual intimacy, intimacy and generativity were fused in Luther's life. We have given an account of the time when his generativity reached its crisis, namely, when within a short period he became both a father, and a leader of a wide following which began to disperse his teachings in any number of avaricious, rebellious, and mystical directions. Luther then tasted fully the danger of this stage, which paradoxically is felt by creative people more deeply than by others, namely, a sense of *stagnation*, experienced by him in manic-depressive form. As he recovered, he proceeded with the building of the edifice of his theology; yet he responded to the needs of his parishioners and students, including his princes, to the very end. Only his occasional outbursts expressed that fury of repudiation which was mental hygiene to him, but which set a lasting bad example to his people.

The Emergence
of a Concept of Family

PHILIPPE ARIÈS

It may seem strange to speak of the emergence of a concept of family in premodern society, since that society derived from a Germanic tribal culture wholly based on the family. In addition, ancient Roman society—the other element in the evolution of western European social institutions—was also family-oriented. But the growth of feudalism during the Middle Ages had a profound effect on the family. The family system of primitive Germanic society broke down as feudalism became the organizing principle of European society. Feudal lords could effectively control the position of the family by controlling the marriage of their vassals. Likewise, feudal law restricted the role of families in the system of power by insisting on primogeniture: while younger sons could receive fiefs from their fathers, and daughters could be given dowries, there were strict limitations on the size of these donations. A man could not disinherit his eldest son nor could he leave his heir so little land that he could not fulfill his obligations to his lord.

Families did, of course, occasionally gain a powerful position within the feudal hierarchy. The famous Clares of England used the favor of the English kings to spread through the baronage of the kingdom. Their success is indicated by their position within the party of rebellious barons that won the Magna Carta from King John in 1215. Of the twenty-four barons chosen to look after royal government on behalf of the rebels, sixteen were members of the Clare family. Yet it is significant that the power of the family consisted in its success in infiltrating the feudal structure. One Clare, for example, married the great William Marshal (see "The Training of a Knight" in Part 3). Feudal rank, not family connections, determined a man's place in the community.

Another indication of the declining importance of the family in medieval England is found in the common law of property. Progressively during the twelfth and thirteenth centuries, family rights of property—and the concomitant inability of the head of the family to alienate property—devolved on the paterfamilias. In 1225, the royal court decided that a man could alienate land and deprive his heirs of any right to it. Family rights of property had become individual rights.

Cases before the royal court did not much affect life in the peasant villages, which was in all likelihood much more traditional and thus more family-oriented than life among the upper classes. Yet the conclusions to be drawn from the documents of the upper classes are strikingly confirmed by another sort of evidence that was more popular, or at least more public, in character. The art of the cathedrals often protrayed aspects of everyday life, especially peasant life, but the family did not figure in these representations. That is the starting point of this selection from Philippe Ariès' book *Centuries of Childhood.*

Something should be said about Ariès' method before this selection is read. Art, particularly manuscript illuminations, has been used in some types of historical work. Lynn White, for example, used such material extensively to support his thesis about the technological revolution of the Middle Ages. But White's use of art is very different from Ariès'. For White, the art provides evidence for the dating and geographical extension of technology. For Ariès, it is evidence of a social attitude held by the artist and presumably by his public. White needs only to note the presence of a device in a picture that has been dated and localized; Ariès, however, must follow out the artistic themes over a long period. Furthermore, Ariès' conclusions depend on an assumption that the artist and his public are in agreement about the artist's theme. This assumption appears to be justifiable for the upper-class audience, since the medieval artists about whom there is information were members of the middle classes and presumably representative of the values of a wide spectrum of their society. Assessing the art of the cathedrals is more difficult because its audience was the illiterate masses; it was the scripture of the illiterate. With these comments in mind, Ariès' piece gains some significance as an approach to the problem he set himself.

It may seem debatable whether one can speak of a profane iconography in the Middle Ages before the fourteenth century, seeing that the distinction between sacred and profane was so slight. However, among the profane contributions is one theme whose frequency and popularity are highly significant: the theme of trades and crafts (*métiers*). The archaeologists have shown us that the Gauls in the Roman era were fond of depicting scenes of their working life on their mortuary bas-reliefs. This liking for the subject of trades and crafts is to be found nowhere else. The archaeologists have been struck by the rarity, if not the complete absence, of such scenes in the mortuary iconography of Roman Africa. The theme consequently dates back far into the past. It continued and even developed in the Middle Ages. To use an anachronistic expression, one may say, broadly speaking, but without deforming the truth, that the "profane" iconography of the Middle Ages consists above all of this subject of crafts. It is significant that it was their craft or trade which for a long time struck people as their foremost activity; this was a point of view that was linked with the mortuary cult of the Gallo-Roman epoch, and with the social and learned concept of the world in the Middle Ages, in the cathedral calendars. No doubt this seems perfectly natural to modern historians. But have they asked themselves how many people today would prefer to forget their trade and would choose to leave some other image of them-

From pp. 339–45 of *Centuries of Childhood* by Philippe Ariès translated by Robert Baldick. Copyright © 1962 by Jonathan Cape Limited. Reprinted by permission of Alfred A. Knopf, Inc. and Jonathan Cape Limited.

selves? People have tried in vain to inject a little lyricism into the functional aspects of contemporary life; the result is a sort of academic art without any roots in everyday life. The man of today would not choose his trade, even if he liked it, to propose as a subject for artists, even if the latter could accept it. The importance accorded to the trade or craft in medieval iconography is a sign of the sentimental value that was put on it. It is as if a man's private life were first of all and above all his trade.

One of the most popular representations of trades and crafts linked them with that other theme, the seasons, whose importance we have had occasion to recognize in connection with the "ages of life." We know that the Middle Ages in the West were fond of linking by means of symbols ideas whose secret connections, hidden behind external appearances, they wished to emphasize. They linked the various crafts to the seasons, as they did the ages of life or the elements. This is the significance of the calendars in stone and glass, the calendars of the cathedrals and the books of hours.

The traditional iconography of the twelve months of the year was established in the twelfth century, very much as we can find it at Saint-Denis, in Paris, at Senlis, at Chartres, at Amiens, at Reims, etc.—works and days. On the one hand, the great tasks of the countryman: hay, corn, wine and the vineyards, and pigs. On the other, the period of rest, that of the winter and the spring. It is the peasants who are shown working, but the pictures of leisure moments vary between peasant and noble. January (Twelfth Night) belongs to the noble, seen sitting at a groaning board. February belongs to the villein who is shown coming in from gathering wood and hurriedly sitting down by the fire. May is either a peasant resting in the midst of flowers or a young noble setting off for the chase and getting his falcon ready. In any case it is an evocation of youth taking part in the Maytime festivities. In these scenes the man is always alone, except that sometimes a young valet (as at Saint-Denis) is shown standing behind his master who is eating at table. The person depicted is always a man, never a woman . . .

We see this iconography evolving in the books of hours until the sixteenth century, revealing significant tendencies as it develops.

First of all we see woman appear, the lady of courtly love or the mistress of the house. In the Hours of the Duc de Berry, in the month of February, the peasant is no longer, as on the walls of Senlis, Paris or Amiens, the only person warming himself. Three women of the house are already sitting round the fire, while the peasant is still shivering outside in the snow-covered yard. Elsewhere the scene shows a winter evening at home: the man, sitting in front of the hearth, is warming his hands and feet, but beside him his wife is quietly working at her spinning-wheel (Charles d'Angoulême). In April appears the theme of the court of love: the lady and her lover in a walled garden (Charles d'Angoulême). She is also shown accompanying the knights in the chase. But even the noble lady does not remain the idle and somewhat imaginary heroine of the April gardens or the horsewoman of the Maytime festivities: she also superintends the work in the April garden (Turin). The peasant woman recurs more frequently. She works in the fields with the men (Berry, Angoulême). She takes drinks to the harvesters as they rest on a hot summer's day (Hennessy, Grimani). Her husband brings her back in a wheelbarrow with the wine-flask she has brought him. The knights and ladies are no longer isolated in the noble pleasures of April or May. Just as the lady of the Turin Book of Hours busied herself with her garden, the nobles mingle with the peasants and wine-harvesters (as in the cherry-picking scene in the Turin Hours). The further one goes in time, especially in the sixteenth century, the more often one finds the lord's family among the peasants, supervising their work and joining in their games. There are a great many sixteenth-century tapestries showing these rustic scenes in which the masters and their children are picking grapes or supervising the corn-harvest. The man is no longer alone, and the couple is no longer simply the imaginary couple of courtly love. Wife and family join in the man's work and live beside him, indoors or out in the fields. These are not, strictly speaking, family scenes: the children are still missing in the fifteenth century. But the artist feels the need to depict the collaboration of the married couple, of the men and women of the house, in the day's work, with a hitherto unknown attention to homely details.

At the same time the street appears in the calendars. The street was already a familiar theme in medieval iconography: it takes on a particularly expressive animation in the admirable views of the bridges of Paris in the thirteenth-century manuscript of the life of St. Denis. As in modern Arab towns, the street was the setting for commercial and professional activity, as also for gossiping, conversation, entertainments and games. Outside private life, which for a long time was ignored by artists, everything happened in the street. However, the calender scenes, being of rustic inspiration, neglected it for a long time. In the fifteenth century, the street took its place in the calendars. True, the months of November and December in the Turin Hours are illustrated by the traditional sacrifice of the pig. But here it is taking place in the street, and the neighbours have come to their doors to watch. Elsewhere (the calendar of the Hours of Adélaïde de Savoie) we are at the market: some little street-arabs are cutting the purse-strings of busy, absent-minded housewives: here we recognize the theme of the little pickpockets which was to recur all the way through picaresque genre-painting in the seventeenth century. Another scene in the same calendar shows the return from the market: a woman has stopped to talk to her neighbour who is looking out of the window; some men are sitting resting on a bench, protected by a screen, and watching the boys of the village wrestling and playing tennis. This medieval street, like the Arab street today, was not opposed to the intimacy of private life; it was an extension of that private life, the familiar setting of work and social relations. The artists, in their comparatively tardy attempts at depicting private life, would begin by capturing it in the street, before pursuing it into the house. It may well be that this private life took place as much in the street as in the house, if not more.

Together with the street, games invaded the calendar scenes: knightly games such as tournaments (Turin, Hennessy), games common to all, and festival pastimes such as dancing round the maypole. The calendar of the Hours of Adélaïde de Savoie consists chiefly of a description of a wide variety of games, parlour games, games of skill, traditional games: the bean-game on Twelfth Night, dancing on May Day, wrestling, hockey, football, water-jousting, snowballing. In other manuscripts we are shown a cross-bow contest (Hennessy), a musical boating party (Hennessy), and swimming (Grimani). We know that in those days games were not simply pastimes but a form of participation in the community or the group: games were played between members of a family, between neighbours, between age groups, between parishes.

Finally, as from the sixteenth century, a new character came on the scene in the calendars: the child. He was already frequently depicted in the iconography of the sixteenth century, especially in the *Miracles de Notre-Dame*. But he had remained absent from the calendars, as if that ancient form of iconography had been reluctant to accept this latecomer. In the fields, there no children to be seen with the women. Only a few are shown waiting at table during the January banquets. They can also be caught sight of at the market in the Hours of Adélaïde de Savoie; in the same manuscript they are depicted snowballing one another, heckling the preacher in church and being thrown out. In the last Flemish manuscripts of the sixteenth century, they are having their fling: one can sense the artist's liking for them. The calendars of Hennessy's and Grimani's Hours have imitated fairly closely the snow-covered village in the Très Riches Heurs du Duc de Berry, in the January scene which I have described above, with the peasant hurrying home to join his womenfolk by the fire. However, they have added another figure: the child. And the child is in the same position as the Manneken-Pis, which had become a common subject in the iconography of the time: the child piddling through the open door. This theme of the Manneken-Pis was to be found everywhere—witness the picture of St. John the Baptist in the Musée des Augustins at Toulouse (a picture which used to hang in the chapel of the High Court of the town), or a certain *putto* of Titian's.

In these Hours of Hennessy and Grimani, the children are shown skating and aping the grown-ups' tournaments (one of the children is supposed to be the young Charles the Fifth). In the Munich Hours they are having a snowball fight. In the *Hortulus animae*, they are playing at courts of love and also at tournaments—riding a barrel instead of a horse—and skating.

These successive pictures of the months of the year therefore introduced new characters: the woman, the neighbours and friends, and finally the child. And the child was associated with a hitherto unknown desire for homeliness, for familiar if not yet precisely "family" life.

In the course of the sixteenth century, this iconography of the months underwent a final transformation of great significance for our subject: it took on a family character. This it did by merging with the symbolism of another traditional allegory: the ages of life. There were several ways of representing the ages of life, but two of them took the lead: one, the more popular of the two, survived in the form of engravings and showed the ages on the steps of a pyramid rising from birth to maturity, and then going down to old age and death. The great painters scorned to copy this naive composition. On the other hand they frequently adopted the representation of the three ages of life in the form of a child, some adolescents—often a couple—and an old man. A Titian painting exemplifies this type: it shows two sleeping *putti*, and in the foreground a naked man and a fully-dressed peasant girl playing the flute, and in the background a bent old man who sits with a death's-head in his hands. The same subject would be treated by Van Dyck in the seventeenth century. In these compositions, the three or four ages of life are depicted separately, in accordance with the iconographic tradition. Nobody thought of bringing them together within a single family whose different generations would symbolize the ages of life. The artists, and the public opinion which they expressed, remained faithful to an individualistic concept of the ages: the same individual was depicted at the various stages of his destiny.

However, in the course of the sixteenth century, a new idea had appeared which symbolized the duration of life by the hierarchy of the family. We have already had occasion to quote *Le Grand Propriétaire de toutes choses*, the old medieval text translated into French and printed in 1556. The sixth book deals with the ages. It is illustrated by a woodcut depicting neither the steps of the ages nor the three or four ages shown separately, but simply a family gathering. The father is sitting with a little child on his knees. His wife is standing on his right; one of his sons is standing on his left, and another is kneeling to take something his father is giving to him. This is at once a family portrait, of a kind of which thousands were painted in this period in the Netherlands, Italy, England, France and Germany, and a family subject such as painters and engravers would produce in large numbers in the seventeenth century. This theme was destined to achieve the most extraordinary popularity.

It was not entirely unknown in the late Middle Ages. It is treated in a remarkable fashion on a capital, known as the marriage capital, in the loggias of the ducal palace in Venice. Venturi dates it about 1424; Toesca puts it at the end of the fourteenth century, which seems more probable in view of the style and dress, but more surprising in view of the precocity of the subject. The eight sides of this capital tell a story illustrating the fragility of life—a familiar theme in the fourteenth and fifteenth centuries, but here in the context of a family, which is something new. First we have the engagement. Then the young woman is dressed in a formal dress on which little metal discs have

been sewn: ornaments perhaps, or possibly coins, for coins played a part in
the marital and baptismal customs. The third face shows the wedding ceremony at the moment when one of the two holds a crown over the other's
head—a rite which has survived in the Oriental liturgy. Then the couple are
entitled to kiss. On the fourth face, they are lying naked in the marriage bed.
A child is born whom the father and mother hold between them, wrapped
in swaddling-clothes. Their own clothes look simpler than at the time of their
engagement and wedding: they have become serious people, who dress severely or in an old-fashioned style. The seventh face brings together the whole
family, who pose for their portrait. Each parent is holding the child by a
shoulder and a hand. This is already the family portrait such as that in *Le
Grand Propriétaire*. But with the eighth face, the story takes a dramatic turn:
the family is in mourning, for the child has died; he is stretched out on his
bed with his hands folded. The mother is wiping away her tears with one
hand and touching the child's arm with the other; the father is praying. Other
capitals near this one are adorned with naked *putti* playing with fruit, birds
and balls: more commonplace themes, but themes which enable us to place
the marriage capital in its iconographic context.

The story of the marriage begins as the story of a family but ends with
a different theme, that of premature death.

At the Musée Saint-Raimond at Toulouse, one can see the fragments of
a calendar which the costumes enable us to place in the second half of the
sixteenth century. In the picture for July we see the family gathered together
as in the contemporary engraving of *Le Grand Propriétaire*, with one additional detail which is not without importance: the presence of the servants
beside the parents. The father and mother are in the middle. The father is
holding his son by the hand and the mother her daughter. The valet is standing on the men's side, the maidservant on the women's, for the sexes are
separated as in the portraits of donors—the men, fathers and sons, on one
side, the women, mothers and daughters, on the other.

August remains the month of the harvest, but the painter has chosen
to depict not the actual harvesting but the delivery of the harvest to the
master, who has some money in his hand and is about to give it to the
peasants. This scene is connected with an iconography which was very common in the sixteenth century, especially in the tapestries of the period, where
country gentlemen are shown supervising their peasants or joining in their
games.

October: the family meal. The parents and their children are at table.
The smallest child is perched on a high chair which brings him up to the
level of the table: a chair specially made for children of his age, of a type still
to be found today. A boy with a napkin is serving the meal: possibly a valet,
possibly a relative given the task of waiting at table, a task which he would
not in any way consider humiliating.

November: the father is old and ill, so ill that the doctor has been called in. The doctor, with a commonplace gesture which belongs to a traditional iconography, is examining the urinal.

December: the whole family is gathered together in the bedroom around the bed in which the father is dying. The last sacraments have been brought to him. His wife is kneeling at the foot of the bed. Behind her, a young woman on her knees is weeping. A young man is standing with a taper in his hand. In the background we can see a little child: no doubt the grandson, the next generation which will continue the family.

Thus this calendar likens the succession of the months of the year to that of the ages of life, but it depicts the ages of life in the form of the story of a family: the youth of its founders, their maturity with their children, old age, sickness, and a death which is both the good death, the death of the good man, another traditional theme, and also that of the patriarch in the midst of his family.

The story on this calendar begins like that of the family on the marriage capital in the Palace of the Doges. But it is not the son, the beloved child, that death takes too soon. Things follow a more natural course: it is the father who dies at the end of a full life, surrounded by a united family and doubtless leaving them a well-managed estate. The calendar illustrates a new concept: the concept of the family.

A 3
B 4
C 5
D 6
E 7
F 8
G 9
H 0
I 1
J 2